Library of English Classics

DE QUINCEY

MACMILLAN AND CO., Limited
LONDON · BOMBAY · CALCUTTA · MADRAS
MELBOURNE

THE MACMILLAN COMPANY
NEW YORK · BOSTON · CHICAGO
DALLAS · SAN FRANCISCO

THE MACMILLAN CO. OF CANADA, Ltd.
TORONTO

The Confessions of an

English Opium - Eater

And other Essays

By Thomas de Quincey

MACMILLAN AND CO., LIMITED
ST. MARTIN'S STREET, LONDON
1924

COPYRIGHT

First printed in the Library of English Classics 1901
Reprinted 1906, 1915, 1924

PRINTED IN GREAT BRITAIN

BIBLIOGRAPHICAL NOTE

THE text followed throughout this volume has been that of the first collected edition of De Quincey's works, the issue of which was begun in 1853. For this collected edition De Quincey revised his essays with great care, and in the case of *The Confessions of an English Opium-Eater* re-wrote and expanded the articles which he had contributed to the *London Magazine* for October and November 1821, so as to form substantially a new work, the new version being about two and a half times the length of the original. Whether the result of this expansion was good or ill is open to debate. Had space permitted, it would have been pleasant to reprint here both versions, but in the necessity of choosing between the two, the general rule of this series to follow the author's latest text was reinforced by the consideration that the version of 1856 contains new passages with which all lovers of De Quincey are familiar, and that the substitution of an earlier version in which these do not occur might fairly be resented. For the original text, therefore, readers must be referred to the pretty reprint of it edited by Dr. Garnett in 1885. The preface to the 1821 edition, as well as to that of 1856, is printed at the end of this Note.

Of the two essays "On Murder considered as One of the Fine Arts," the first was one of De Quincey's earliest contributions to *Blackwood's Magazine*, in which it appeared in February 1827, the second, or "supplementary" paper, following, after an interval of twelve years, in November 1839, in the same magazine. After another fifteen years, in 1854, when preparing the collected edition of his works, De Quincey added a further supplement or postscript, in which he dropped the peculiar humour of the earlier essays, and told the story of certain murders without much reference to their "artistic" qualities. Like everything else De Quincey wrote, this postscript is abundantly interesting, but its difference in tone and marked inferiority to the first two papers are a sufficient justification for omitting it in order to find room for both "The Spanish Military Nun" and "The English Mail-Coach." Of these the first, under the clumsier title "The Nautico-Military Nun of Spain," appeared originally in *Tait's Magazine* in the months of May, June, and July 1847. In February of the same year an article on the same subject by the Vîcomte Alexis de Valon had appeared in the *Revue des Deux Mondes*, and this supplied De Quincey with the materials which he rehandled in his own inimitable way. Lastly, "The English Mail-Coach" originally appeared in the numbers of *Blackwood's Magazine* for October and December 1849, the second article, which contained "The Vision of Sudden Death," and "The Dream-Fugue," being plainly an afterthought. In 1854, in the collected edition, the two articles were brought together and very carefully revised.

A. W. POLLARD.

ORIGINAL PREFACE
TO 'THE CONFESSIONS OF AN ENGLISH
OPIUM-EATER' IN THE YEAR 1821

I HERE present you, courteous reader, with the record of a
remarkable period of my life ; and according to my application of it, I trust that it will prove, not merely an
interesting record, but, in a considerable degree, instructive.
In *that* hope it is that I have drawn it up ; and *that* must
be my apology for breaking through those restraints of
delicate reserve, which, for the most part, intercept the
public exposure of our own errors and infirmities.

Guilt and misery shrink, by a natural instinct, from
public notice : they court privacy and solitude ; and, even
in the choice of a grave, will sometimes voluntarily
sequester themselves from the general population of the
churchyard, as if declining to claim fellowship with the
great family of man ; thus, in a symbolic language universally understood, seeking (in the affecting language of
Wordsworth)

> Humbly to express
> A penitential loneliness.

It is well, upon the whole, and for the interest of us all,
that it should be so ; nor would I willingly, in my own
person, manifest a disregard of such salutary feelings.
But, on the one hand, as my self-accusation does not

b

amount to a confession of guilt, so, on the other, it is
possible that, if it did, the benefit resulting to others, from
the record of an experience purchased at so heavy a price
of suffering and of self-conquest, might compensate, by a
vast overbalance, any violence done to the feelings I have
noticed, and justify a breach of the general rule. Infirmity and misery do not, of necessity, imply guilt.
They approach, or recede from, the shades of that dark
alliance, in proportion to the probable motives and prospects of the offender, and to the palliations, known or
secret, of the offence ; in proportion as the temptations to
it were potent from the first, and the resistance to it, in
act or in effort, was earnest to the last. For my own
part, without breach of truth or modesty, I may affirm
that my life has been, on the whole, the life of a
philosopher : from my birth, I was made an intellectual
creature ; and intellectual in the highest sense my pursuits
and pleasures has been, even from my schoolboy days. If
opium-eating be a sensual pleasure, and if I am bound to
confess that I have indulged in it to an excess not yet
recorded of any other man, it is no less true that I have
struggled against this fascination with a fervent zeal, and
have at length accomplished what I never yet heard
attributed to any other man, have untwisted, almost to its
final links, the chain which fettered me. Such a self-
conquest may reasonably be set off in counterbalance to
any kind or degree of self-indulgence. Not to insist that,
in my case, the self-conquest was unquestionable, but the
self-indulgence open to doubts of casuistry, according as
that name shall be extended to acts aiming at the bare
relief of pain, or shall be restricted to such as aim at the
excitement of superfluous pleasure.

Guilt, therefore, I do not acknowledge ; and, if I did,
it is possible that I might still resolve on the present act
of confession, in consideration of the service which I may

thereby render to the whole class of opium-eaters. But who are they? Reader, I am bound to say, a very numerous class indeed. Of this I became convinced, some years ago, by computing, at that time, the number of those in one small class of English society (the class of men distinguished for talent and notoriety) who were known to me, directly or indirectly, as opium-eaters; such, for instance, as the eloquent and benevolent William Wilberforce; the late Dean of Carlisle, Dr. Isaac Milner;[1] the

---

[1] '*Isaac Milner*':—He was *nominally* known to the public as Dean of Carlisle, being colloquially always called *Dean* Milner; but virtually he was best known in his own circle as the head of Queen's College, Cambridge, where he usually resided. In common with his brother, Joseph of Hull, he was substantially a Wesleyan Methodist; and in that character, as regarded principles and the general direction of his sympathies, he pursued his deceased brother's History of the Christian Church down to the era of Luther. In these days, he would perhaps not be styled a Methodist, but simply a Low-Churchman. By whatever title described, it is meantime remarkable that a man confessedly so conscientious as Dean Milner could have reconciled to his moral views the holding of Church preferment so important as this deanery in combination with the headship of an important college. One or other must have been consciously neglected. Such a record, meantime, powerfully illustrates the advances made by the Church during the last generation in practical homage to self-denying religious scruples. A very lax man would not in these days allow himself to do that which thirty years ago a severe Church-Methodist (regarded by many even as a fanatic) persisted in doing, without feeling himself called on for apology. If I have not misapprehended its tenor, this case serves most vividly to illustrate the higher standard of moral responsibility which prevails in this current generation. We do injustice daily to our own age; which, by many a sign, palpable and secret, I feel to be more emphatically than any since the period of Queen Elizabeth and Charles I., an intellectual, a moving, and a self-conflicting age: and inevitably, where the intellect has been preternaturally awakened, the moral sensibility must soon be commensurately stirred. The very distinctions, psychologic or metaphysical, by which, as its hinges and articulations, our modern thinking moves, proclaim the subtler character of the questions which now occupy our thoughts. Not as pedantic only, but as suspiciously unintelligible such distinctions would, one hundred and thirty years ago, have been viewed as indictable; and perhaps (in company with Mandeville's *Political Economy*) would have been seriously presented as a nuisance to the Middlesex Quarter-Sessions. Recurring, however, to Dean Milner, and the re-

first Lord Erskine ; Mr. ——,[1] the philosopher ; a late Under-Secretary of State (viz., Mr. Addington, brother to the first Lord Sidmouth, who described to me the sensation which first drove him to the use of opium in the very same words as the Dean of Carlisle, viz., 'that he felt as though rats were gnawing at the coats of his stomach') ; Samuel Taylor Coleridge, and many others, hardly less celebrated.   Now, if one class, comparatively so limited, could furnish so many scores of cases (and those within the instant reach of one sudden and brief inquiry),

collections of his distinguished talents amongst the contemporary circles of the first generation in this nineteenth century, I wish to mention that these talents are most feebly measured by any of his occasional writings, all drawn from him apparently by mere pressure of casual convenience.   In conversation it was that he asserted *adequately* his pre-eminent place.   Wordsworth, who met him often at the late Lord Lonsdale's table, spoke of him uniformly as the chief potentate colloquially of his own generation, and as the man beyond all others (Burke being departed) who did not live upon his recollections, but met the demands of every question that engaged his sympathy by spontaneous and elastic movements of novel and original thought.   As an opium-eater, Dean Milner was understood to be a strenuous wrestler with the physical necessity that coerced him into this habit.   From several quarters I have heard that his daily *ration* was 34 grains (or about 850 drops of laudanum), divided into four portions, and administered to him at regular intervals of six hours by a confidential valet.

[1] Who is Mr. Dash, the philosopher ?   Really I have forgot.   Not through any fault of my own, but on the motion of some absurd coward having a voice potential at the press, all the names were struck out behind my back in the first edition of the book, thirty-five years ago. I was not consulted ; and did not discover the absurd blanks until months afterwards, when I was taunted with them very reasonably by a caustic reviewer.   Nothing could have a more ludicrous effect than this appeal to shadows—to my Lord Dash, to Dean Dash, and to Mr. Secretary Dash.   Very naturally it thus happened to Mr. Philosopher Dash that his burning light, alas ! was extinguished irrecoverably in the general *mêlée*.   Meantime, there was no excuse whatever for this absurd interference such as might have been alleged in any personality capable of causing pain to any one person concerned.   All the cases, except, perhaps, that of Wilberforce (about which I have at this moment some slight lingering doubts), were matters of notoriety to large circles of friends.   It is due to Mr. John Taylor, the accomplished publisher of the work, that I should acquit *him* of any share in this absurdity.

it was a natural inference that the entire population of England would furnish a number that, on first starting in such an inquiry, would have seemed incredible. The soundness of this inference, however, I doubted, until some facts became known to me, which satisfied me that it was not incorrect. I will mention two. First, three respectable London druggists, in widely remote quarters of London, from whom I happened to be purchasing small quantities of opium, assured me that the number of *amateur* opium-eaters (as I may term them) was at this time immense ; and that the difficulty of distinguishing these persons, to whom habit had rendered opium necessary, from such as were purchasing it with a view to suicide, occasioned them daily trouble and disputes. This evidence respected London only. But, secondly (which will possibly surprise the reader more), some years ago, on passing through Manchester, I was informed by several cotton manufacturers, that their work-people were rapidly getting into the practice of opium-eating ; so much so, that on a Saturday afternoon the counters of the druggists were strewed with pills of one, two, or three grains, in preparation for the known demand of the evening. The immediate occasion of this practice was the lowness of wages, which at that time would not allow them to indulge in ale or spirits ; and, wages rising, it may be thought that this practice would cease : but, as I do not readily believe that any man, having once tasted the divine luxuries of opium, will afterwards descend to the gross and mortal enjoyments of alcohol, I take it for granted

> That those eat now who never ate before ;
> And those who always ate, now eat the more.

Indeed, the fascinating powers of opium are admitted even by those medical writers who are its greatest enemies : thus, for instance, Awsiter, apothecary to Greenwich

Hospital, in his *Essay on the effects of Opium* (published in the year 1763), when attempting to explain why Mead had not been sufficiently explicit on the properties, counter-agents, etc., of this drug, expresses himself in the following mysterious terms (perfectly intelligible, however, to those who are in the secret) :—' Perhaps he thought the subject of too delicate a nature to be made common ; and, as many people might then indiscriminately use it, it would take from that necessary fear and caution which should prevent their experiencing the extensive power of this drug ; *for there are many properties in it, if universally known, that would habituate the use, and make it more in request with us than the Turks themselves ;* the result of which knowledge,' he adds, ' must prove a general misfortune.' In the necessity of this conclusion I do not at all concur ; but upon that point I shall have occasion to speak more freely in the body of the work itself. And at this point I shall say no more than that opium, as the one sole *catholic* anodyne which hitherto has been revealed to man ; secondly, as the one sole anodyne which in a vast majority of cases is *irresistible ;* thirdly, as by many degrees the most potent of all known counter-agents to nervous irritation, and to the formidable curse of *tædium vitæ ;* fourthly, as by possibility, under an argument undeniably plausible, alleged by myself, the sole known agent—not for curing *when* formed, but for intercepting whilst likely to be formed—the great English scourge of pulmonary consumption ;—I say that opium, as wearing these, or *any* of these, four beneficent characteristics—I say that any agent whatever making good such pretensions, no matter what its name, is entitled haughtily to refuse the ordinary classification and treatment which opium receives in books. I say that opium, or any agent of equal power, is entitled to assume that it was revealed to man for some higher object than that it should furnish a target for moral denunciations, ignorant where they are not hypocritical, childish where not dishonest ; that it should be set up as a theatrical scarecrow for superstitious terrors, of which the *result* is oftentimes to defraud human suffering of its readiest alleviation, and of which the *purpose* is, ' Ut pueris placeant et declamatio fiant.' [1]

In one sense, and remotely, all medicines and modes of medical treatment offer themselves as anodynes—that is, so far as they promise ultimately to relieve the suffering connected with physical maladies or infirmities. But we do not, in the special and ordinary sense, designate as ' anodynes' those remedies which obtain the relief from pain only as a secondary and distant effect following out from the *cure* of the ailment ; but those only we call anodynes which obtain this relief and pursue it as the *primary* and *immediate* object. If, by giving tonics to a child suffering periodic pains in the stomach, we were ultimately to banish those pains, this would not warrant us in calling such tonics by the name of anodynes : for the neutralisation of the pains would be a circuitous process of nature, and might probably require weeks for its evolution. But a true anodyne (as, for instance, half-a-dozen drops of laudanum, or a dessert-spoonful of some warm carminative mixed with brandy) will often banish the misery suffered by a child in five or six minutes. Amongst the most potent of anodynes, we may rank hemlock, henbane, chloroform, and opium. But unquestionably the three first have a most narrow field of action, by comparison with opium. This, beyond all other agents made known to man, is the mightiest for its command, and for the extent of its command, over pain ; and so much mightier than any other, that I should think,

[1] That they may win the applause of schoolboys, and furnish matter for a prize essay.

xiv AN ENGLISH OPIUM-EATER

in a Pagan land, supposing it to have been adequately made known[1] through experimental acquaintance with its revolutionary magic, opium would have had altars and priests consecrated to its benign and tutelary powers. But this is not my own object in the present little work. Very many people have thoroughly misconstrued this object ; and therefore I beg to say here, in closing my Original Preface, a little remodelled, that what I contemplated in these Confessions was to emblazon the power of opium—not over bodily disease and pain, but over the grander and more shadowy world of dreams.

---

[1] '*Adequately made known*' :—Precisely this, however, was impossible. No feature of ancient Pagan life has more entirely escaped notice than the extreme rarity, costliness, and circuitous accessibility of the more powerful drugs, especially of mineral drugs ; and of drugs requiring elaborate preparation, or requiring much manufacturing skill. When the process of obtaining any manufactured drug was slow and intricate, it could most rarely be called for. And rarely called for, why should it be produced? By looking into the history and times of Herod the Great, as reported by Josephus, the reader will gain some notion of the mystery and the suspicion surrounding all attempts at importing such drugs as could be applied to murderous purposes, consequently of the delay, the difficulty, and the peril in forming any familiar acquaintance with opium.

PREFATORY NOTICE
TO THE EDITION OF 1856 IN DE QUINCEY'S COLLECTED WORKS

WHEN it had been settled that, in the general series of these republications, the *Confessions of an English Opium-Eater* should occupy the Fifth Volume, I resolved to avail myself most carefully of the opening thus made for a revision of the entire work. By accident, a considerable part of the Confessions (all, in short, except the Dreams) had originally been written hastily; and, from various causes, had never received any strict revision, or, *virtually*, so much as an ordinary verbal correction. But a great deal more was wanted than this. The main narrative should naturally have moved through a succession of secondary incidents; and with leisure for recalling these, it might have been greatly inspirited. Wanting all opportunity for such advantages, this narrative had been needlessly impoverished. And thus it had happened, that not so properly correction and retrenchment were called for, as integration of what had been left imperfect, or amplification of what, from the first, had been insufficiently expanded.

With these views, it would not have been difficult (though toilsome) to re-cast the little work in a better mould; and the result might, in all reason, count upon the approbation at least of its own former readers. Compared with its own former self, the book must certainly tend, by its very principle of change, whatever should be the *execution* of that change, to become better : and in my own opinion, after all drawbacks and allowances for the faulty exemplification of a good principle, it *is* better. This should be a matter of mere logical or inferential necessity ; since, in pure addition to everything previously approved, there would now be a clear surplus of extra matter—all that might be good in the old work, and a great deal beside that was new. Meantime this improvement has been won at a price of labour and suffering that, if they could be truly stated, would seem incredible. A nervous malady, of very peculiar character, which has attacked me intermittingly for the last eleven years, came on in May last, almost concurrently with the commencement of this revision ; and so obstinately has this malady pursued its noiseless, and what I may call subterraneous, siege, since none of the symptoms are externally manifested, that, although pretty nearly dedicating myself to this one solitary labour, and not intermitting or relaxing it for a single day, I have yet spent, within a very few days, six calendar months upon the re-cast of this one small volume.

The consequences have been distressing to all concerned. The press has groaned under the chronic visitation ; the compositors shudder at the sight of my handwriting, though not objectionable on the score of legibility ; and I have much reason to fear that, on days when the pressure of my complaint has been heaviest, I may have so far given way to it, as to have suffered greatly in clearness of critical vision. Sometimes I may have overlooked blunders, mis-statements, or repetitions, implicit or even express. But more often I may have failed to appreciate the true effects from faulty management of style and its colourings.   Sometimes, for instance, a heavy or too intricate arrangement of sentences may have defeated the tendency of what, under its natural presentation, would have been affecting ; or it is possible enough that, by unseasonable levity at other times, I may have repelled the sympathy of my readers — all or some. Endless are the openings for such kinds of mistake— that is, of mistakes not fully seen *as* such.   But even in a case of unequivocal mistake, seen and acknowledged, yet when it is open to remedy only through a sudden and energetic act, then or never, the press being for twenty minutes, suppose, free to receive an alteration, but beyond that time closed and sealed inexorably : such being supposed the circumstances, the humane reader will allow for the infirmity which even wilfully and consciously surrenders itself to the error, acquiescing in it deliberately, rather than face the cruel exertion of correcting it most elaborately at a moment of sickening misery, and with the prevision that the main correction must draw after it half a dozen others for the sake of decent consistency. I am not speaking under any present consciousness of such a case existing against myself : I believe there *is* none such.   But I choose to suppose an extreme case of even conscious error, in order that venial cases of oversight may, under shelter of such an *outside* license, find toleration from a liberal critic.   To fight up against the wearing siege of an abiding sickness, imposes a fiery combat.   I attempt no description of this combat, knowing the unintelligibility and the repulsiveness of all attempts to communicate the Incommunicable.   But the generous reader will not, for that forbearance on my part, the less readily show his indulgence, if a case should (unexpectedly to myself) arise for claiming it.

I have thus made the reader acquainted with one out of two cross currents that tended to thwart my efforts for improving this little work. There was, meantime, another, less open to remedy from my own uttermost efforts. All along I had relied upon a crowning grace, which I had reserved for the final pages of this volume, in a succession of some twenty or twenty-five dreams and noon-day visions, which had arisen under the latter stages of opium influence. These have disappeared : some under circumstances which allow me a reasonable prospect of recovering them ; some unaccountably ; and some dishonourably. Five or six, I believe, were burned in a sudden conflagration which arose from the spark of a candle falling unobserved amongst a very large pile of papers in a bedroom, when I was alone and reading. Falling not *on*, but *amongst* and *within* the papers, the fire would soon have been ahead of conflict ; and, by communicating with the slight woodwork and draperies of a bed, it would have immediately enveloped the laths of a ceiling overhead, and thus the house, far from fire-engines, would have been burned down in half-an-hour. My attention was first drawn by a sudden light upon my book : and the whole difference between a total destruction of the premises and a trivial loss (from books charred) of five guineas, was due to a large Spanish cloak. This, thrown over, and then drawn down tightly, by the aid of one sole person, somewhat agitated, but retaining her presence of mind, effectually extinguished the fire. Amongst the papers burned partially, but not so burned as to be absolutely irretrievable, was the 'Daughter of Lebanon' ; and this I have printed, and have intentionally placed it at the end, as appropriately closing a record in which the case of poor Ann the Outcast formed not only the most memorable and the most suggestively pathetic incident, but also *that* which, more than any other, coloured—or (more truly I should say) shaped, moulded and remoulded, composed and decomposed — the great body of opium dreams. The search after the lost features of Ann, which I spoke of as pursued in the crowds of London, was in a more proper sense pursued through many a year in dreams. The general idea of a search and a chase reproduced itself in many shapes. The person, the rank, the age, the scenical position, all varied themselves for ever; but the same leading traits more or less faintly remained of a lost Pariah woman, and of some shadowy malice which withdrew her, or attempted to withdraw her, from restoration and from hope. Such is the explanation which I offer why that particular addition, which some of my friends had been authorised to look for, has not in the main been given, nor for the present *could* be given; and, secondly, why that part which *is* given has been placed in the conspicuous situation (as a closing passage) which it now occupies.

November 1856.

CONTENTS

CONFESSIONS OF
AN ENGLISH OPIUM-EATER

B

CONFESSIONS OF
AN ENGLISH OPIUM-EATER

I HAVE often been asked—how it was, and through what series of steps, that I became an opium-eater. Was it gradually, tentatively, mistrustingly, as one goes down a shelving beach into a deepening sea, and with a knowledge from the first of the dangers lying on that path ; half-courting those dangers, in fact, whilst seeming to defy them? Or was it, secondly, in pure ignorance of such dangers, under the misleadings of mercenary fraud? since oftentimes lozenges, for the relief of pulmonary affections, found their efficacy upon the opium which they contain, upon this, and this only, though clamorously disavowing so suspicious an alliance : and under such treacherous disguises multitudes are seduced into a dependency which they had not foreseen upon a drug which they had not known ; not known even by name or by sight : and thus the case is not rare—that the chain of abject slavery is first detected when it has inextricably wound itself about the constitutional system. Thirdly, and lastly, was it [*Yes*, by passionate anticipation, I answer, before the question is finished]—was it on a sudden, overmastering impulse derived from bodily anguish? Loudly I repeat, *Yes ;* loudly and indignantly—as in answer to a wilful calumny. Simply as an anodyne it was, under the mere coercion of pain the severest, that I first resorted to opium ; and precisely that same torment it is, or some variety of that torment, which drives most people to make acquaintance with that same insidious remedy. Such was the fact ; such by accident. Meantime, without blame it might have been otherwise. If in early days I had fully understood the subtle powers lodged in this mighty drug (when judiciously regulated), (1) to tranquillise all irritations of the nervous system ; (2) to stimulate the capacities of enjoyment ; and (3) under any call for extraordinary exertion (such as all men meet at times), to sustain through twenty-four consecutive hours the else drooping animal energies — most certainly, knowing or suspecting all this, I should have inaugurated my opium career in the character of one seeking *extra* power and enjoyment, rather than of one shrinking from *extra* torment. And why not? If *that* argued any fault, is it not a fault that most of us commit every day with regard to alcohol? Are we entitled to use *that* only as a medicine? Is wine unlawful, except as an anodyne? I hope not : else I shall be obliged to counterfeit and to plead some anomalous *tic* in my little finger ; and thus gradually, as in any Ovidian metamorphosis, I, that am at present a truth-loving man, shall change by daily inches into a dissembler. No : the whole race of man proclaim it lawful to drink wine without pleading a medical certificate as a qualification. That same license extends itself therefore to the use of opium ; what a man may lawfully seek in wine surely he may lawfully find in opium ; and much more so in those many cases (of which mine happens to be one) where opium deranges the animal economy less by a great deal than an equivalent quantity of alcohol. Coleridge, therefore, was doubly in error when he allowed himself to aim most unfriendly blows at my supposed voluptuousness in the use of opium ; in error as to a principle, and in error as to a fact. A letter of his, which I will hope that he did not design to have published, but which, however, *has* been published, points the attention of his correspondent to a broad distinction separating my case as an opium-eater from his own : he, it seems, had fallen excusably (because unavoidably) into

this habit of eating opium—as the one sole therapeutic
resource available against his particular malady; but
I, wretch that I am, being so notoriously charmed by
fairies against pain, must have resorted to opium in
the abominable character of an adventurous voluptuary,
angling in all streams for variety of pleasures. Coleridge
is wrong to the whole extent of what was possible; wrong
in his fact, wrong in his doctrine; in his little fact, and
his big doctrine. I did not do the thing which he charges
upon me; and if I *had* done it, this would not convict
me as a citizen of Sybaris or Daphne. There never was
a distinction more groundless and visionary than that
which it has pleased him to draw between my motives
and his own; nor could Coleridge have possibly owed
this mis-statement to any false information; since no man
surely, on a question of my own private experience, could
have pretended to be better informed than myself. Or,
if there really is such a person, perhaps he will not think
it too much trouble to re-write these Confessions from
first to last, correcting their innumerable faults; and, as
it happens that some parts of the unpublished sections for
the present are missing, would he kindly restore them—
brightening the colours that may have faded, rekindling
the inspiration that may have drooped; filling up all
those chasms which else are likely to remain as permanent
disfigurations of my little work? Meantime the reader,
who takes any interest in such a question, will find that
I myself (upon such a theme not simply the best, but
surely the sole authority) have, without a shadow of
variation, always given a different account of the matter.
Most truly I have told the reader, that not any search
after pleasure, but mere extremity of pain from rheumatic
toothache—this and nothing else it was that first drove
me into the use of opium. Coleridge's bodily affliction
was simple rheumatism. Mine, which intermittingly
raged for ten years, was rheumatism in the face combined
with toothache. This I had inherited from my father;
or inherited (I should rather say) from my own desperate
ignorance; since a trifling dose of colocynth, or of any

similar medicine, taken three times a-week, would more certainly than opium have delivered me from that terrific curse.[1] In this ignorance, however, which misled me into making war upon toothache when ripened and manifesting itself in effects of pain, rather than upon its germs and gathering causes, I did but follow the rest of the world. To intercept the evil whilst yet in elementary stages of formation, was the true policy; whereas I in my blindness sought only for some mitigation to the evil when already formed, and past all reach of interception. In this stage of the suffering, formed and perfect, I was thrown passively upon chance advice, and therefore, by a natural consequence, upon opium — that being the one sole anodyne that is almost notoriously such, and which in that great function is universally appreciated.

Coleridge, therefore, and myself, as regards our baptismal initiation into the use of that mighty drug, occupy the very same position. We are embarked in the self-same boat; nor is it within the compass even of angelic hair-splitting, to show that the dark shadow thrown

[1] '*That terrific curse*':—Two things blunt the general sense of horror, which would else connect itself with toothache—viz., first, its enormous diffusion; hardly a household in Europe being clear of it, each in turn having some one chamber intermittingly echoing the groans extorted by this cruel torture. There—viz., in its ubiquity—lies one cause of its slight valuation. A second cause is found in its immunity from danger. This latter ground of undervaluation is noticed in a saying ascribed (but on what authority I know not) to Sir Philip Sidney—viz., that supposing toothache liable in ever so small a proportion of its cases to a fatal issue, it would be generally ranked as the most dreadful amongst human maladies; whereas the certainty that it will in no extremity lead to death, and the knowledge that in the very midst of its storms sudden changes may be looked for, bringing long halcyon calms, have an unfair effect in lowering the appreciation of this malady considered as a trial of fortitude and patience. No stronger expression of its intensity and scorching fierceness can be imagined than this fact—that, within my private knowledge, two persons, who had suffered alike under toothache and cancer, have pronounced the former to be, on the scale of torture, by many degrees the worse. In both, there are *at times* what surgeons call 'lancinating' pangs—keen, glancing, arrowy radiations of anguish; and upon these the basis of comparison was rested—paroxysm against paroxysm—with the result that I have stated.

by our several trespasses in this field, mine and his, had
by so much as a pin's point any assignable difference.
Trespass against trespass (if any trespass there were)—
shadow against shadow (if any shadow were really thrown
by this trespass over the snowy disk of pure ascetic
morality), in any case, that act in either of us would read
into the same meaning, would count up as a debt into
the same value, would measure as a delinquency into the
same burden of responsibility.   And vainly, indeed, does
Coleridge attempt to differentiate two cases which ran
into absolute identity, differing only as rheumatism differs
from toothache.   Amongst the admirers of Coleridge,
I at all times stood in the foremost rank ; and the more
was my astonishment at being summoned so often to
witness his carelessness in the management of controversial
questions, and his demoniac inaccuracy in the statement
of facts.   The more also was my sense of Coleridge's
wanton injustice in relation to myself individually.   Coleridge's gross mis-statement of facts, in regard to our several
opium experiences, had its origin, sometimes in flighty
reading, sometimes in partial and incoherent reading,
sometimes in subsequent forgetfulness ; and any one of
these lax habits (it will occur to the reader) is a venial
infirmity.   Certainly it is ; but surely *not* venial, when it
is allowed to operate disadvantageously upon the character
for self-control of a brother, who had never spoken of
him but in the spirit of enthusiastic admiration ; of that
admiration which his exquisite works so amply challenge.
Imagine the case that I really *had* done something wrong,
still it would have been ungenerous—me it would have
saddened, I confess, to see Coleridge rushing forward with
a public denunciation of my fault :—'Know all men by
these presents, that I, S. T. C., *a noticeable man with
large grey eyes,*[1] am a licensed opium-eater, whereas this
other man is a buccaneer, a pirate, a flibustier,[2] and can

---

[1] See Wordsworth's exquisite picture of S. T. C. and himself as
occasional denizens in the *Castle of Indolence.*
[2] This word—in common use, and so spelled as I spell it, amongst
the grand old French and English buccaneers contemporary with our

have none but a forged licence in his disreputable pocket.
In the name of Virtue, arrest him!' But the truth is,
that inaccuracy as to facts and citations from books was in
Coleridge a mere necessity of nature. Not three days
ago, in reading a short comment of the late Archdeacon
Hare (*Guesses at Truth*) upon a bold speculation of
Coleridge's (utterly baseless) with respect to the machinery
of Etonian Latin verses, I found my old feelings upon this
subject refreshed by an instance that is irresistibly comic,
since everything that Coleridge had relied upon as a
citation from a book in support of his own hypothesis,
turns out to be a pure fabrication of his own dreams;
though, doubtless (which indeed it is that constitutes the
characteristic interest of the case), without a suspicion on his
part of his own furious romancing. The archdeacon's good-
natured smile upon that Etonian case naturally reminded
me of the case now before us, with regard to the history
of our separate careers as opium-eaters. Upon which
case I need say no more, as by this time the reader is
aware that Coleridge's entire statement upon that subject
is perfect moonshine, and, like the sculptured imagery of
the pendulous lamp in *Christabel*,

> All carvèd from the carver's brain.

This case, therefore, might now be counted on as disposed
of; and what sport it could yield might reasonably be
thought exhausted. Meantime, on consideration, another
and much deeper oversight of Coleridge's becomes apparent; and as this connects itself with an aspect of the
case that furnishes the foundation to the whole of these
ensuing Confessions, it cannot altogether be neglected.
Any attentive reader, after a few moments' reflection, will
perceive that, whatever may have been the casual *occasion*
of mine or Coleridge's opium-eating, this could not have

own admirable Dampier, at the close of the seventeenth century—has
recently been revived in the journals of the United States, with a view
to the special case of Cuba, but (for what reason I know not) is now
written always as *filli*busters. Meantime, written in whatsoever way,
it is understood to be a Franco-Spanish corruption of the English word
freebooter.

been the permanent *ground* of opium-eating; because neither rheumatism nor toothache is any *abiding* affection of the system. Both are intermitting maladies, and not at all capable of accounting for a *permanent* habit of opium-eating. Some months are requisite to found *that*. Making allowance for constitutional differences, I should say that *in less than* 120 *days* no habit of opium-eating could be formed strong enough to call for any extraordinary self-conquest in renouncing it, and even suddenly renouncing it. On Saturday you are an opium-eater, on Sunday no longer such. What then was it, after all, that made Coleridge a slave to opium, and a slave that could not break his chain? He fancies, in his headlong carelessness, that he has accounted for this habit and this slavery; and in the meantime he has accounted for nothing at all about which any question has arisen. Rheumatism, he says, drove him to opium. Very well; but with proper medical treatment the rheumatism would soon have ceased; or even, without medical treatment, under the ordinary oscillations of natural causes. And when the pain ceased, then the opium should have ceased. Why did it not? Because Coleridge had come to taste the genial pleasure of opium; and thus the very impeachment, which he fancied himself in some mysterious way to have evaded, recoils upon him in undiminished force. The rheumatic attack would have retired before the habit could have had time to form itself. Or suppose that I underrate the strength of the possible habit—this tells equally in *my* favour; and Coleridge was not entitled to forget in *my* case a plea remembered in his own. It is really memorable in the annals of human self-deceptions, that Coleridge could have held such language in the face of such facts. I, boasting not at all of my self-conquests, and owning no moral argument against the free use of opium, nevertheless on mere *prudential* motives break through the vassalage more than once, and by efforts which I have recorded as modes of transcendent suffering. Coleridge, professing to believe (without reason assigned) that opium-eating is criminal, and in some mysterious

sense more criminal than wine-drinking or porter-drinking,
having, therefore, the strongest *moral* motive for abstain-
ing from it, yet suffers himself to fall into a captivity to
this same wicked opium, deadlier than was ever heard of,
and under no coercion whatever that he has anywhere
explained to us.   A slave he was to this potent drug not
less abject than Caliban to Prospero—his detested and yet
despotic master.   Like Caliban, he frets his very heart-
strings against the rivets of his chain.   Still, at intervals
through the gloomy vigils of his prison, you hear muttered
growls of impotent mutineering swelling upon the breeze :

> Irasque leonum
> Vincla recusantum——

recusantum, it is true, still refusing yet still accepting,
protesting for ever against the fierce, overmastering curb-
chain, yet for ever submitting to receive it into the mouth.
It is notorious that in Bristol (to *that* I can speak myself,
but probably in many other places) he went so far as to
hire men — porters, hackney - coachmen, and others — to
oppose by force his entrance into any druggist's shop.   But,
as the authority for stopping him was derived simply from
himself, naturally these poor men found themselves in a
metaphysical fix, not provided for even by Thomas Aquinas
or by the prince of Jesuitical casuists.   And in this excruciating dilemma would occur such scenes as the following :—

'Oh, sir,' would plead the suppliant porter—suppliant,
yet semi-imperative (for equally if he *did*, and if he did
not, show fight, the poor man's daily 5s. seemed endangered)
—'really you must not ; consider, sir, your wife and——'

Transcendental Philosopher.—'Wife ! what wife ? I have
no wife.'[1]

Porter.—'But, really now, you must not, sir.   Didn't
you say no longer ago than yesterday——'

Transcend. Philos.—'Pooh, pooh ! yesterday is a long
time ago.   Are you aware, my man, that people are
known to have dropped down dead for timely want of
opium ?'

[1] Vide *Othello.*

Porter.—'Ay, but you tell't me not to hearken——'

Transcend. Philos.—'Oh, nonsense. An emergency, a shocking emergency, has arisen—quite unlooked for. No matter what I told you in times long past. That which I *now* tell you, is—that, if you don't remove that arm of yours from the doorway of this most respectable druggist, I shall have a good ground of action against you for assault and battery.'

Am I the man to reproach Coleridge with this vassalage to opium? Heaven forbid! Having groaned myself under that yoke, I pity, and blame him not. But undeniably, such a vassalage must have been created wilfully and consciously by his own craving after genial stimulation ; a thing which I do not blame, but Coleridge *did*. For my own part, duly as the torment relaxed in relief of which I had resorted to opium, I laid aside the opium, not under any meritorious effort of self-conquest ; nothing of that sort do I pretend to ; but simply on a prudential instinct warning me not to trifle with an engine so awful of consolation and support, nor to waste upon a momentary uneasiness what might eventually prove, in the midst of all-shattering hurricanes, the great elixir of resurrection. What was it that did in reality make me an opium-eater ? That affection which finally drove me into the *habitual* use of opium, what was it ? Pain was it ? No, but misery. Casual overcasting of sunshine was it ? No, but blank desolation. Gloom was it that might have departed ? No, but settled and abiding darkness—

> Total eclipse,
> Without all hope of day ! [1]

Yet whence derived ? Caused by what ? Caused, as I might truly plead, by youthful distresses in London ; were it not that these distresses were due, in their ultimate origin, to my own unpardonable folly ; and to that folly I trace many ruins. Oh, spirit of merciful interpretation, angel of forgiveness to youth and its aberrations, that

[1] *Samson Agonistes.*

hearkenest for ever as if to some sweet choir of far-off female intercessions! will ye, choir that intercede—wilt thou, angel that forgivest—join together, and charm away that mighty phantom, born amidst the gathering mists of remorse, which strides after me in pursuit from forgotten days—towering for ever into proportions more and more colossal, overhanging and overshadowing my head as if close behind, yet dating its nativity from hours that are fled by more than half-a-century? Oh heavens! that it should be possible for a child not seventeen years old, by a momentary blindness, by listening to a false, false whisper from his own bewildered heart, by one erring step, by a motion this way or that, to change the currents of his destiny, to poison the fountains of his peace, and in the twinkling of an eye to lay the foundations of a life-long repentance! Yet, alas! I must abide by the realities of the case. And one thing is clear, that amidst such bitter self-reproaches as are now extorted from me by the anguish of my recollections, it cannot be with any purpose of weaving plausible excuses, or of evading blame, that I trace the origin of my confirmed opium-eating to a necessity growing out of my early sufferings in the streets of London. Because, though true it is that the re-agency of these London sufferings did in after years *enforce* the use of opium, equally it is true that the sufferings themselves grew out of my own folly. What really calls for excuse, is not the recourse to opium, when opium had become the one sole remedy available for the malady, but those follies which had themselves produced that malady.

I, for my part, after I had become a regular opium-eater, and from mismanagement had fallen into miserable excesses in the use of opium, did nevertheless, four several times, contend successfully against the dominion of this drug; did four several times renounce it; renounced it for long intervals; and finally resumed it upon the warrant of my enlightened and deliberate judgment, as being of two evils by very much the least. In this I acknowledge nothing that calls for excuse. I repeat again and again, that not the application of opium, with its deep tranquillising powers to the mitigation of evils, bequeathed by my London hardships, is what reasonably calls for sorrow, but that extravagance of childish folly which precipitated me into scenes naturally producing such hardships.

These scenes I am now called upon to retrace. Possibly they are sufficiently interesting to merit, even on their own account, some short record ; but at present, and at this point, they have become indispensable as a key to the proper understanding of all which follows. For in these incidents of my early life is found the entire substratum, together with the secret and underlying motive [1] of those pompous dreams and dream-sceneries which were in reality the true objects—first and last—contemplated in these Confessions.

My father died when I was in my seventh year, leaving six children, including myself (viz., four sons and two daughters), to the care of four guardians and of our mother, who was invested with the legal authority of a guardian. This word '*guardian*' kindles a fiery thrilling in my nerves ; so much was that special power of guardianship, as wielded by one of the four, concerned in the sole capital error of my boyhood. To this error my own folly would hardly have been equal, unless by concurrence with the obstinacy of others. From the bitter remembrance of this error in myself—of this obstinacy in my hostile guardian, suffer me to draw the privilege of making a moment's pause upon this subject of legal guardianship.

There is not (I believe) in human society, under whatever form of civilisation, any trust or delegated duty which has more often been negligently or even perfidiously administered. In the days of classical Greece and Rome, my own private impression, founded on the collation of many incidental notices, is—that this, beyond all other

[1] *Motive:*—The word *motive* is here used in the sense attached by artists and connoisseurs to the technical word *motivo*, applied to pictures, or to the separate movements in a musical theme.

forms of domestic authority, furnished to wholesale rapine
and peculation their very amplest arena. The relation of
father and son, as was that of *patron* and *client*, was
generally, in the practice of life, cherished with religious
fidelity : whereas the solemn duties of the *tutor* (*i.e.* the
guardian) to his ward, which had their very root and
origin in the tenderest adjurations of a dying friend,
though subsequently refreshed by the hourly spectacle of
helpless orphanage playing round the margins of pitfalls
hidden by flowers, spoke but seldom to the sensibilities of
a Roman through any language of oracular power. Few
indeed, if any, were the obligations, in a proper sense
moral, which pressed upon the Roman. The main
fountains of moral obligation had in Rome, by law or by
custom, been thoroughly poisoned. Marriage had corrupted itself through the facility of divorce, and through
the consequences of that facility (viz., levity in choosing,
and fickleness in adhering to the choice), into so exquisite
a traffic of selfishness, that it could not yield so much as a
phantom model of sanctity. The relation of husband and
wife had, for all moral impressions, perished amongst the
Romans. The relation of father and child had all its
capacities of holy tenderness crushed out of it under the
fierce pressure of penal and vindictive enforcements.
The duties of the client to his patron stood upon no basis
of simple gratitude or simple fidelity (corresponding to
the feudal *fealty*), but upon a basis of prudential terror ;
terror from positive law, or from social opinion. From
the first intermeddling of law with the movement of the
higher moral affections, there is an end to freedom in the
act—to purity in the motive—to dignity in the personal
relation. Accordingly, in the France of the pre-revolu-
tionary period, and in the China of all periods, it has been
with baleful effects to the national morals that positive
law has come in aid of the paternal rights. And in the
Rome of ancient history it may be said that this one
original and rudimental wrong done to the holy freedom
of human affections, had the effect of extinguishing
thenceforward all *conscientious* movement in whatever

direction. And thus, amongst a people naturally more highly principled than the Greeks, if you except ebullitions of public spirit and patriotism (too often of mere ignoble nationality), no class of actions stood upon any higher basis of motive than (1) legal ordinance; (2) superstitious fear; or (3) servile compliance with the insolent exactions of popular usage. Strange, therefore, it would have been if the *tutor* of obscure orphans, with *extra* temptations and *extra* facilities for indulging them, should have shown himself more faithful to his trust than the governor of provinces—prætorian or proconsular. Yet who more treacherous and rapacious than he? Rarest of men was the upright governor that accepted no bribes from the criminal, and extorted no ransoms from the timid. He nevertheless, as a *public* trustee, was watched by the jealousy of political competitors, and had by possibility a solemn audit to face in the senate or in the forum; perhaps in both. But the tutor, who administered a private trust on behalf of orphans, might count on the certainty that no public attention could ever be attracted to concerns so obscure, and politically so uninteresting. Reasonably, therefore, and by all analogy, a Roman must have regarded the ordinary domestic *tutor* as almost inevitably a secret delinquent using the opportunities and privileges of his office as mere instruments for working spoliation and ruin upon the inheritance confided to his care. This deadly and besetting evil of Pagan days must have deepened a hundredfold the glooms overhanging the death-beds of parents. Too often the dying father could not fail to read in his own life-long experience, that, whilst seeking special protection for his children, he might himself be introducing amongst them a separate and imminent danger. Leaving behind him a little household of infants, a little fleet (as it might be represented) of fairy pinnaces, just raising their anchors in preparation for crossing the mighty deeps of life, he made signals for 'convoy.' Some one or two (at best imperfectly known to him), amongst those who traversed the same seas, he accepted in that character; but doubtfully, sorrowfully, fearfully; and at the very moment when the faces of his children were disappearing amongst the vapours of death, the miserable thought would cross his prophetic soul—that too probably this pretended 'convoy,' under the strong temptations of the case, might eventually become pirates; robbers, at the least; and by possibility wilful misleaders to the inexperience of his children.

From this dreadful aggravation of the anguish at any rate besetting the death-beds of parents summoned away from a group of infant children, there has been a mighty deliverance wrought in a course of centuries by the vast diffusion of Christianity. In these days, wheresoever an atmosphere is breathed that has been purified by Christian charities and Christian principles, this household pestilence has been continually dwindling: and in the England of this generation there is no class of peculation which we so seldom hear of: one proof of which is found in the indifference with which most of us regard the absolute security offered to children by the Court of Chancery. My father, therefore, as regarded the quiet of his dying hours, benefited by the felicity of his times and his country. He made the best selection for the future guardianship of his six children that his opportunities allowed; from his circle of intimate friends, he selected the four who stood highest in his estimation for honour and practical wisdom: which done, and relying for the redressing of any harsh tendencies in male guardians upon the discretional power lodged in my mother, thenceforth he rested from his anxieties. Not one of these guardians but justified his choice so far as honour and integrity were concerned. Yet, after all, there is a limit (and sooner reached perhaps in England than in other divisions of Christendom) to the good that can be achieved in such cases by prospective wisdom. For we, in England, more absolutely than can be asserted of any other nation, are not *fainéans*: rich and poor, all of us have something to do. To Italy it is that we must look for a peasantry idle through two-thirds of their time. To Spain it is that we must look for an aristocracy *physically*[1] degraded under the ignoble training of women and priests ; and for princes (such as Ferdinand VII.) that make it the glory of their lives to have embroidered a petticoat. Amongst ourselves of this current generation, whilst those functions of guardianship may be surely counted on which presume conscientious loyalty to the interests of their wards ; on the other hand, all which presume continued vigilance and provision from afar are, in simple truth, hardly compatible with our English state of society. The guardians chosen by my father, had they been the wisest and also the most energetic of men, could not in many conceivable emergencies have fulfilled his secret wishes. Of the four men, one was a merchant (not in the narrow sense of Scotland, derived originally from France, where no class of merchant princes has ever existed, but in the large noble sense of England—of Florence—of Venice) : consequently, his extensive relations with seaports and distant colonies continually drawing off his attention, and even his personal presence, from domestic affairs, made it hopeless that he should even attempt more on behalf of his wards than slightly to watch the administration of their pecuniary interests. A second of our guardians was a rural magistrate, but in a populous district close upon Manchester, which even at that time was belted with a growing body of turbulent aliens—Welsh and Irish. He therefore, overwhelmed by the distractions of his official station, rightly perhaps conceived himself to have fulfilled his engagements as a guardian, if he stood ready to come forward upon any difficulty arising, but else in ordinary cases devolved his functions upon those who enjoyed more leisure. In that category stood, beyond a doubt, a third of our guardians, the Rev. Samuel H., who

---

[1] It is asserted by travellers—English, French, and German alike —that the ducal order in Spain (as that order of the Spanish peerage most carefully withdrawn from what Kentucky would call the *rough-and-tumble* discipline of a popular education) exhibit in their very persons and bodily development undisguised evidences of effeminate habits operating through many generations. It would be satisfactory to know the unexaggerated truth on this point ; the truth unbiassed alike by national and by democratic prejudices.

was at the time of my father's death a curate at some
church (I believe) in Manchester or in Salford.[1]   This
gentleman represented a class—large enough at all times
by necessity of human nature, but in those days far larger
than at present—that class, I mean, who sympathise with
no spiritual sense or spiritual capacities in man ; who
understand by religion simply a respectable code of ethics
—leaning for support upon some great mysteries dimly
traced in the background, and commemorated in certain
great church festivals by the *elder* churches of Christendom ; as, *e.g.*, by the English, which does not stand as to
age on the Reformation epoch, by the Romish, and by the
Greek.   He had composed a body of about 330 sermons,
which thus, at the rate of two every Sunday, revolved
through a cycle of three years ; that period being modestly
assumed as sufficient for insuring to their eloquence total
oblivion.   Possibly to a cynic, some shorter cycle might
have seemed equal to that effect, since their topics rose
but rarely above the level of prudential ethics ; and the
style, though scholarly, was not impressive.   As a preacher,
Mr. H. was sincere, but not earnest.   He was a good
and conscientious man ; and he made a high valuation of
the pulpit as an organ of civilisation for co-operating
with books ; but it was impossible for any man, starting
from the low ground of themes so unimpassioned and so
desultory as the benefits of industry, the danger from bad
companions, the importance of setting a good example, or
the value of perseverance—to pump up any persistent
stream of earnestness either in himself or in his auditors.
These auditors, again, were not of a class to desire much

---

[1] Salford is a large town legally distinguished from Manchester for
parliamentary purposes, and divided from it physically by a river, but
else virtually, as regards intercourse and reciprocal influence, is a
quarter of Manchester ; in fact, holding the same relation to Manchester that Southwark does to London ; or, if the reader insists upon
having a classical illustration of the case, the same relation that in
ancient days Argos did to Mycenæ.   An invitation to dinner given by
the public herald of Argos could be heard to the centre of Mycenæ,
and by a gourmand, if the dinner promised to be specially good, in the
remoter suburb.

earnestness. There were no naughty people among them :
most of them were rich, and came to church in carriages :
and, as a natural result of their esteem for my reverend
guardian, a number of them combined to build a church
for him—viz., St. Peter's, at the point of confluence
between Moseley Street and the newly projected Oxford
Street—then existing only as a sketch in the portfolio of
a surveyor. But what connected myself individually with
Mr. H. was, that two or three years previously I, together
with one of my brothers (five years my senior), had been
placed under his care for classical instruction. This was
done, I believe, in obedience to a dying injunction of my
father, who had a just esteem for Mr. S. H. as an upright
man, but apparently too exalted an opinion of his scholarship : for he was but an indifferent Grecian. In whatever
way the appointment arose, so it was that this gentleman,
previously *tutor* in the Roman sense to all of us, now
became to my brother and myself tutor also in the common
English sense. From the age of eight, up to eleven and
a-half, the character and intellectual attainments of Mr.
H. were therefore influentially important to myself in the
development of my powers, such as they were. Even his
330 sermons, which rolled overhead with such slender
effect upon his general congregation, to me became a real
instrument of improvement. One-half of these, indeed,
were all that I heard ; for, as my father's house (Greenhay)
stood at this time in the country, Manchester not having
yet overtaken it, the distance obliged us to go in a carriage,
and only to the morning service ; but every sermon in this
morning course was propounded to me as a textual basis
upon which I was to raise a mimic duplicate—sometimes
a pure miniature abstract—sometimes a rhetorical expansion—but preserving as much as possible of the original
language, and also (which puzzled me painfully) preserving the exact succession of the thoughts ; which might
be easy where they stood in some dependency upon each
other, as, for instance, in the development of an argument,
but in arbitrary or chance arrangements was often as trying
to my powers as any feat of rope-dancing. I, therefore,

amongst that whole congregation,[1] was the one sole care-
worn auditor—agitated about that which, over all other
heads, flowed away like water over marble slabs—viz., the
somewhat torpid sermon of my somewhat torpid guardian.
But this annoyance was not wholly lost : and those same
$\frac{330}{2}$ sermons, which (lasting only through sixteen minutes
each) were approved and forgotten by everybody else, for
me became a perfect palæstra of intellectual gymnastics
far better suited to my childish weakness than could have
been the sermons of Isaac Barrow or Jeremy Taylor. In
these last, the gorgeous imagery would have dazzled my
feeble vision, and in both the gigantic thinking would have
crushed my efforts at apprehension. I drew, in fact, the
deepest benefits from this weekly exercise. Perhaps,
also, in the end it ripened into a great advantage for me,
though long and bitterly I complained of it, that I was
not allowed to use a pencil in taking notes : all was to be
charged upon the memory. But it is notorious that the
memory strengthens as you lay burdens upon it, and

1 ' *That whole congregation* ' :—Originally at churches which I do
not remember, where, however, in consideration of my tender age, the
demands levied upon my memory were much lighter. Two or three
years later, when I must have been nearing my tenth year, and when
St. Peter's had been finished, occurred the opening, and consequently
(as an indispensable pre-condition) the consecration of that edifice by
the bishop of the diocese (viz., Chester). I, as a ward of the incum-
bent, was naturally amongst those specially invited to the festival ; and
I remember a little incident which exposed broadly the conflict of
feelings inherited by the Church of England from the Puritans of the
seventeenth century. The architecture of the church was Grecian ;
and certainly the enrichments, inside or outside, were few enough,
neither florid nor obtrusive. But in the centre of the ceiling, for the
sake of breaking the monotony of so large a blank white surface, there
was moulded, in plaster-of-Paris, a large tablet or shield, charged with
a cornucopia of fruits and flowers. And yet, when we were all
assembled in the vestry waiting—rector, churchwardens, architect, and
trains of dependants—there arose a deep buzz of anxiety, which soon
ripened into an articulate expression of fear, that the bishop would
think himself bound, like the horrid eikonoclasts of 1645, to issue his
decree of utter *averruncation* to the simple decoration overhead. Fearfully did we all tread the little aisles in the procession of the prelate.
Earnestly my lord looked upwards ; but finally—were it courtesy, or
doubtfulness as to his ground, or approbation—he passed on.

becomes trustworthy as you trust it.   So that, in my third
year of practice, I found my abstracting and condensing
powers sensibly enlarged.   My guardian was gradually
better satisfied : for unfortunately (and in the beginning
it *was* unfortunate) always one witness could be summoned
against me upon any impeachment of my fidelity—viz.,
the sermon itself ; since, though lurking amongst the 330,
the wretch was easily forked out.   But these appeals grew
fewer ; and my guardian, as I have said, was continually
better satisfied.   Meantime, might not I be continually
less satisfied with *him* and his 330 sermons ? Not at all :
loving and trusting, without doubt or reserve, and with
the deepest principles of veneration rooted in my nature,
I never, upon meeting something more impressive than
the average complexion of my guardian's discourses, for
one moment thought of him as worse or feebler than
others, but simply as different ; and no more quarrelled
with him for his characteristic languor, than with a green
riband for not being blue.   By mere accident, I one day
heard quoted a couplet which seemed to me sublime.   It
described a preacher such as sometimes arises in difficult
times, or in fermenting times, a son of thunder, that looks
all enemies in the face, and volunteers a defiance even when
it would have been easy to evade it.   The lines were
written by Richard Baxter—who baffled often with self-
created storms from the first dawn of the Parliamentary
War in 1642, through the period of Cromwell (to whom
he was personally odious), and, finally, through the trying
reigns of the second Charles and of the second James.   As
a pulpit orator, he was perhaps the Whitfield of the seventeenth century—the *Leuconomos* of Cowper.   And thus it
is that he describes the impassioned character of his own
preaching—

> I preach'd, as never sure to preach again ;

[Even *that* was telling ; but then followed this thunder-
peal]

> And as a dying man to dying men.

This couplet, which seemed to me equally for weight and

for splendour like molten gold, laid bare another aspect
of the Catholic church ; revealed it as a Church militant
and crusading.

Not even thus, however, did I descry any positive
imperfection in my guardian. He and Baxter had fallen
upon different generations. Baxter's century, from first
to last, was revolutionary. Along the entire course of
that seventeenth century, the great principles of representative government and the rights of conscience [1] were
passing through the anguish of conflict and fiery trial.
Now again in my own day, at the close of the eighteenth
century, it is true that all the elements of social life were
thrown into the crucible—but on behalf of our neighbours,
no longer of ourselves. No longer, therefore, was invoked
the heroic pleader, ready for martyrdom, preaching, therefore, 'as never sure to preach again' ; and I no more
made it a defect in my guardian that he wanted energies
for combating evils now forgotten, than that he had not
in patriotic fervour leaped into a gulf, like the fabulous
Roman martyr Curtius, or in zeal for liberty had not
mounted a scaffold, like the real English martyr Algernon
Sidney. Every Sunday, duly as it revolved, brought with
it this cruel anxiety. On Saturday night under sad anticipation, on Sunday night under sadder experimental knowledge, of my trying task, I slept ill: my pillow was stuffed
with thorns ; and until Monday morning's inspection and
armilustrium had dismissed me from parade to 'stand at
ease,' verily I felt like a false steward summoned to some
killing audit. Then suppose Monday to be invaded by
some horrible intruder, visitor perhaps from a band of my
guardian's poor relations, that in some undiscovered nook
of Lancashire seemed in fancy to blacken all the fields,
and suddenly at a single note of '*caw, caw,*' rose in one

---

[1] '*The rights of conscience*' :—With which it is painful to know
that Baxter did not sympathise. Religious toleration he called 'Soul-
murder.' And, if you reminded him that the want of this toleration
had been his own capital grievance, he replied, 'Ah, but the cases
were very different : I was in the right ; whereas the vast majority of
those who will benefit by this newfangled toleration are shockingly in
the wrong.'

vast cloud like crows, and settled down for weeks at the
table of my guardian and his wife, whose noble hospitality
would never allow the humblest among them to be saddened by a faint welcome. In such cases, very possibly
the whole week did not see the end of my troubles.

On these terms, for upwards of three-and-a-half years
—that is, from my eighth to beyond my eleventh birthday
—my guardian and I went on cordially ; he never once
angry, as indeed he never had any reason for anger ; I
never once treating my task either as odious (which in the
most abominable excess it was), or, on the other hand, as
costing but a trivial effort, which practice might have
taught me to hurry through with contemptuous ease. To
the very last I found no ease at all in this weekly task,
which never ceased to be ' a thorn in the flesh ' : and I
believe that my guardian, like many of the grim Pagan
divinities, inhaled a flavour of fragrant incense, from the
fretting and stinging of anxiety which, as it were some holy
vestal fire, he kept alive by this periodic exaction. It
gave him pleasure that he could reach me in the very
recesses of my dreams, where even a Pariah might look
for rest ; so that the Sunday, which to man, and even to
the brutes within his gates, offered an interval of rest, for
me was signalised as a day of martyrdom. Yet in this,
after all, it is possible that he did me a service : for my
constitutional infirmity of mind ran but too determinately
towards the sleep of endless reverie, and of dreamy
abstraction from life and its realities.

Whether serviceable or not, however, the connexion
between my guardian and myself was now drawing to its
close. Some months after my eleventh birthday, Greenhay[1]
was sold, and my mother's establishment—both children
and servants—was translated to Bath : only that for a few
months I and one brother were still left under the care of

[1] ' Greenhay ' :—A country-house built by my father ; and at the
time of its foundation (say in 1791 or 1792) separated from the last
outskirts of Manchester by an entire mile ; but now, and for many a
year, overtaken by the hasty strides of this great city, and long since
(I presume) absorbed into its mighty uproar.

Mr. Samuel H. ; so far, that is, as regarded our education.
Else, as regarded the luxurious comforts of a thoroughly
English home, we became the guests, by special invitation,
of a young married couple in Manchester—viz., Mr. and
Mrs. K——l. This incident, though otherwise without
results, I look back upon with feelings inexpressibly profound, as a jewelly parenthesis of pathetic happiness—such
as emerges but once in any man's life. Mr. K. was a
young and rising American merchant ; by which I mean,
that he was an Englishman who exported to the United
States. He had married about three years previously a
pretty and amiable young woman — well educated, and
endowed with singular compass of intellect. But the
distinguishing feature in this household was the spirit of
love which, under the benign superintendence of the mistress, diffused itself through all its members.

The late Dr. Arnold of Rugby, amongst many novel
ideas, which found no welcome even with his friends,
insisted earnestly and often upon this—viz., that a great
danger was threatening our social system in Great Britain,
from the austere separation existing between our educated
and our working classes, and that a more conciliatory style
of intercourse between these two bisections of our social
body must be established, or else—a tremendous revolution. This is not the place to discuss so large a question ;
and I shall content myself with making two remarks.
The first is this—that, although a change of the sort
contemplated by Dr. Arnold might, if considered as an
operative *cause*, point forward to some advantages, on the
other hand, if considered as an *effect*, it points backward
to a less noble constitution of society by much than we
already enjoy. Those nations whose upper classes speak
paternally and caressingly to the working classes, and to
servants in particular, do so because they speak from the
lofty stations of persons having civil rights to those who
have none. Two centuries back, when a military chieftain
addressed his soldiers as '*my children*,' he did so because
he was an irresponsible despot exercising uncontrolled
powers of life and death. From the moment when legal

rights have been won for the poorest classes, inevitable respect on the part of the higher classes extinguishes for ever the affectionate style which belongs naturally to the state of pupilage or infantine bondage.

That is my first remark : my second is this—that the change advocated by Dr. Arnold, whether promising or not, is practically impossible ; or possible, I should say, through one sole channel—viz., that of domestic servitude. There only do the two classes concerned come hourly into contact. On that stage only they meet without intrusion upon each other. There only is an opening for change. And a wise mistress, who possesses tact enough to combine a gracious affability with a self-respect that never slumbers nor permits her to descend into gossip, will secure the attachment of all young and impressible women. Such a mistress was Mrs. K———. She had won the gratitude of her servants from the first, by making the amplest provision for their comfort ; their confidence, by listening with patience, and counselling with prudence ; and their respect, by refusing to intermeddle with gossiping personalities always tending to slander. To this extent, perhaps, most mistresses might follow her example. But the happiness which reigned in Mrs. K———'s house at this time depended very much upon special causes. All the eight persons had the advantage of youth ; and the three young female servants were under the spell of fascination, such as could rarely be counted on, from a spectacle held up hourly before their eyes, that spectacle which of all others is the most touching to womanly sensibilities, and which any one of these servants might hope, without presumption, to realise for herself—the spectacle, I mean, of a happy marriage union between two persons, who lived in harmony so absolute with each other, as to be independent of the world outside. How tender and self-sufficing such a union might be, they saw with their own eyes. The season was then mid-winter, which of itself draws closer all household ties. Their own labours, as generally in respectable English services, were finished for the most part by two o'clock ; and as the hours of evening drew nearer, when the master's return might be looked for without fail, beautiful was the smile of anticipation upon the gentle features of the mistress : even more beautiful the reflex of that smile, half-unconscious, and half-repressed, upon the features of the sympathising hand-maidens. One child, a little girl of two years old, had then crowned the happiness of the K——s. She naturally lent her person at all times, and apparently in all places at once, to the improvement of the family groups. My brother and myself, who had been trained from infancy to the courteous treatment of servants, filled up a vacancy in the graduated scale of ascending ages, and felt in varying degrees the depths of a peace which we could not adequately understand or appreciate. Bad tempers there were none amongst us ; nor any opening for personal jealousies ; nor, through the privilege of our common youth, either angry recollections breathing from the past, or fretting anxieties gathering from the future. The spirit of hope and the spirit of peace (so it seemed to me, when looking back upon this profound calm) had, for their own enjoyment, united in a sisterly league to blow a solitary bubble of visionary happiness—and to sequester from the unresting hurricanes of life one solitary household of eight persons within a four months' lull, as if within some Arabian tent on some untrodden wilderness, withdrawn from human intrusion, or even from knowledge, by worlds of mist and vapour.

How deep was that lull ! and yet, as in a human atmosphere, how frail ! Did the visionary bubble burst at once ? Not so : but silently and by measured steps, like a dissolving palace of snow, it collapsed. In the superb expression of Shakspere, minted by himself, and drawn from his own aerial fancy, like a cloud it '*dis-limned*' ; lost its lineaments by stealthy steps. Already the word '*parting*' (for myself and my brother were under summons for Bath) hoisted the first signal for breaking up. Next, and not very long afterwards, came a mixed signal : alternate words of joy and grief—marriage and death severed the sisterly union amongst the young female servants. Then, thirdly, but many years later, vanished from earth, and from peace the deepest that can support itself on earth, summoned to a far deeper peace, the mistress of the household herself, together with her first-born child. Some years later, perhaps twenty from this time, as I stood sheltering myself from rain in a shop within the most public street of Manchester, the master of the establishment drew my attention to a gentleman on the opposite side of the street—roaming along in a reck-less style of movement, and apparently insensible to the notice which he attracted. 'That,' said the master of the shop, 'was once a leading merchant in our town ; but he met with great commercial embarrassments. There was no impeachment of his integrity, or (as I believe) of his discretion. But what with these commercial calamities, and deaths in his family, he lost all hope ; and you see what sort of consolation it is that he seeks '—meaning to say that his style of walking argued intoxication. I did not think so. There was a settled misery in his eye, but complicated with *that* an expression of nervous distraction, that, if it should increase, would make life an intolerable burden. I never saw him again, and thought with horror of his being called in old age to face the fierce tragedies of life. For many reasons, I recoiled from forcing myself upon his notice : but I had ascertained, some time previously to this casual rencontre, that he and myself were, at that date, all that remained of the once joyous household. At present, and for many a year, I am myself the sole relic from that household sanctuary—sweet, solemn, profound—that concealed, as in some ark float-ing on solitary seas, eight persons, since called away, all except myself, one after one, to that rest which only could be deeper than ours was then.

When I left the K——s, I left Manchester ; and dur-ing the next three years I was sent to two very different schools ; first, to a public one—viz., the Bath Grammar School, then and since famous for its excellence—secondly, to a private school in Wiltshire. At the end of the three years, I found myself once again in Manchester. I was then fifteen years old, and a trifle more ; and as it had come to the knowledge of Mr. G., a banker in Lincoln- shire (whom hitherto I have omitted to notice amongst my guardians, as the one too generally prevented from interfering by his remoteness from the spot, but whom otherwise I should have recorded with honour, as by much the ablest amongst them), that some pecuniary advantages were attached to a residence at the Manchester Grammar School, whilst in other respects that school seemed as eligible as any other, he had counselled my mother to send me thither. In fact, a three years' residence at this school obtained an annual allowance for seven years of nearly (if not quite) £50 ; which sum, added to my own patrimonial income of £150, would have made up the annual £200 ordinarily considered the proper allowance for an Oxford under-graduate. No objection arising from any quarter, this plan was adopted, and soon after- wards carried into effect.

On a day, therefore, it was in the closing autumn (or rather in the opening winter) of 1800 that my first intro- duction took place to the Manchester Grammar School. The school-room showed already in its ample proportions some hint of its pretensions as an endowed school, or school of that class which I believe peculiar to England. To this limited extent had the architectural sense of power been timidly and parsimoniously invoked. Beyond that, nothing had been attempted ; and the dreary expanse of whitewashed walls, that at so small a cost might have been embellished by plaster-of-Paris friezes and large medallions, illustrating to the eye of the youthful student the most memorable glorifications of literature—these were bare as the walls of a poor-house or a lazaretto ; buildings whose functions, as thoroughly sad and gloomy, the mind recoils from drawing into relief by sculpture or painting. But this building was dedicated to purposes that were noble. The naked walls clamoured for decora- tion : and how easily might tablets have been moulded— exhibiting (as a first homage to literature) Athens, with the wisdom of Athens, in the person of Pisistratus, concentrating the general energies upon the revisal and the re-casting of the *Iliad*.   Or (second) the Athenian captives in Sicily, within the fifth century B.C., as winning noble mercy for themselves by some

> Repeated air
> Of sad Electra's poet.

Such, and so sudden, had been the oblivion of earthly passions wrought by the contemporary poet of Athens that in a moment the wrath of Sicily, with all its billows, ran down into a heavenly calm ; and he that could plead for his redemption no closer relation to Euripides than the accident of recalling some scatterings from his divine verses, suddenly found his chains dropping to the ground ; and himself, that in the morning had risen a despairing slave in a stone-quarry, translated at once as a favoured brother into a palace of Syracuse.   Or, again, how easy to represent (third) ' the great Emathian conqueror,' that in the very opening of his career, whilst visiting Thebes with vengeance, nevertheless relented at the thought of literature, and

> Bade spare
> The house of Pindarus, when Temple and tower
> Went to the ground.

Alexander might have been represented amongst the colonnades of some Persian capital—Ecbatana or Babylon, Susa or Persepolis—in the act of receiving from Greece, as a *nuzzur* more awful than anything within the gift of the ' barbaric East,' a jewelled casket containing the *Iliad* and the *Odyssey ;* creations that already have lived almost as long as the Pyramids.

Puritanically bald and odious therefore, in my eyes, was the hall up which my guardian and myself paced solemnly—though not Miltonically ' riding up to the Soldan's chair,' yet in fact, within a more limited kingdom, advancing to the chair of a more absolute despot.   This potentate was the head-master, or *archididascalus*, of the Manchester Grammar School ; and that school was variously distinguished.   It was (1) ancient, having in

fact been founded by a bishop of Exeter in an early part
of the sixteenth century, so as to be now, in 1856, more
than 330 years old ; (2) it was rich, and was annually
growing richer ; and (3) it was dignified by a beneficial
relation to the magnificent University of Oxford.

The head-master at that time was Mr. Charles
Lawson. In former editions of this work, I created him
a doctor ; my object being to evade too close an approach
to the realities of the case, and consequently to personalities, which (though indifferent to myself) would have
been in some cases displeasing to others. A doctor, however, Mr. Lawson was not ; nor in the account of law a
clergyman. Yet most people, governed unconsciously by
the associations surrounding their composite idea of a
dignified schoolmaster, invested him with the clerical
character. And in reality he *had* taken deacon's orders
in the Church of England. But not the less he held
himself to be a layman, and was addressed as such by all
his correspondents of rank, who might be supposed best
to understand the technical rules of English etiquette.
Etiquette in such cases cannot entirely detach itself from
law. Now, in English law, as was shown in Horne
Tooke's case, the rule is, *once a clergyman, and always a
clergyman.* The sacred character with which ordination
clothes a man is indelible. But, on the other hand, who
is a clergyman ? Not he that has taken simply the initial
orders of a deacon, so at least I have heard, but he that
has taken the second and full orders of a priest. If otherwise, then there was a great mistake current amongst
Mr. Lawson's friends in addressing him as an esquire.

Squire or not a squire, however, parson or not a
parson—whether sacred or profane—Mr. Lawson was in
some degree interesting by his position and his recluse
habits. Life was over with him, for its hopes and for its
trials. Or at most one trial yet awaited him, which was
—to fight with a painful malady, and fighting to die.
He still had his dying to do : he was in arrear as to *that :*
else all was finished. It struck me (but, with such limited
means for judging, I might easily be wrong) that his

understanding was of a narrow order. But that did not
disturb the interest which surrounded him now in his old
age (probably seventy-five, or more), nor make any drawback from the desire I had to spell backwards and re-
compose the text of his life. What had been his fortunes
in this world ? Had they travelled upwards or downwards? What triumphs had he enjoyed in the sweet and
solemn cloisters of Oxford? What mortifications in the
harsh world outside? Two only had survived in the
malicious traditions of 'his friends.' He was a Jacobite
(as were so many amongst my dear Lancastrian compatriots); had drunk the Pretender's health, and had
drunk it in company with that Dr. Byrom who had graced
the *symposium* by the famous equivocating *impromptu* [1] to
the health of that prince. Mr. Lawson had therefore
been obliged to witness the final prostration of his political
party. That was his earliest mortification. His second,
about seven years later, was, that he had been jilted ; and
with circumstances (at least so I heard) of cruel scorn.
Was it that *he* had interpreted in a sense too flattering for
himself ambiguous expressions of favour in the lady? or
that she in cruel caprice had disowned the hopes which
she had authorised? However this might be, half-a-
century of soothing and reconciling years had cicatrised
the wounds of Mr. Lawson's heart. The lady of 1752,

[1] '*Equivocating impromptu*' :—The party had gathered in a
tumultuary way; so that some Capulets had mingled with the
Montagues, one of whom called upon Dr. Byrom to drink *The King,
God bless him! and Confusion to the Pretender!* Upon which the
doctor sang out—

> God bless the king, of church and state defender ;
> God bless (no harm in *blessing*) the Pretender !
> But who Pretender is, and who the King—
> God bless us all ! that's quite another thing.

Dr. Byrom was otherwise famous than as a Jacobite—viz., as the
author of a very elaborate shorthand, which (according to some who
have examined it) rises even to a philosophic dignity. David Hartley
in particular said of it that, 'if ever a philosophic language (as projected by Bishop Wilkins, by Leibnitz, etc.) should be brought to
bear, in that case Dr. Byrom's work would furnish the proper character
for its notation.'

if living in 1800, must be furiously wrinkled. And a
strange metaphysical question arises : Whether, when the
object of an impassioned love has herself faded into a
shadow, the fiery passion itself can still survive as an
abstraction, still mourn over its wrongs, still clamour for
redress. I have heard of such cases. In Wordsworth's
poem of *Ruth* (which was founded, as I happen to know,
upon facts), it is recorded as an affecting incident, that,
some months after the first frenzy of her disturbed mind
had given way to medical treatment, and had lapsed into
a gentler form of lunacy, she was dismissed from confinement ; and upon finding herself uncontrolled among the
pastoral scenes where she played away her childhood,
she gradually fell back to the original habits of her life
whilst yet undisturbed by sorrow. Something similar had
happened to Mr. Lawson ; and some time after his first
shock, amongst other means for effacing that deep-grooved
impression, he had laboured to replace himself, as much
as was possible, in the situation of a college student. In
this effort he was assisted considerably by the singular
arrangement of the house attached to his official station.
For an English house it was altogether an oddity, being,
in fact, built upon a Roman plan. All the rooms on
both storeys had their windows looking down upon a
little central court. This court was quadrangular, but so
limited in its dimensions, that by a Roman it would have
been regarded as the *impluvium :* for Mr. Lawson, however, with a little exertion of fancy, it transmuted itself
into a college quadrangle. Here, therefore, were held
the daily 'callings-over,' at which every student was
obliged to answer upon being named. And thus the
unhappy man, renewing continually the fancy that he was
still standing in an Oxford quadrangle, perhaps cheated
himself into the belief that all had been a dream which
concerned the caprices of the lady, and the lady herself a
phantom. College usages also, which served to strengthen
this fanciful *alibi*—such, for instance, as the having two
plates arranged before him at dinner (one for the animal,
the other for the vegetable, food)—were reproduced in

Millgate. One sole luxury also, somewhat costly, which, like most young men of easy income, he had allowed himself at Oxford, was now retained long after it had become practically useless. This was a hunter for himself, and another for his groom, which he continued to keep, in spite of the increasing war-taxes, many a year after he had almost ceased to ride. Once in three or four months he would have the horses saddled and brought out. Then, with considerable effort, he swung himself into the saddle, moved off at a quiet amble, and, in about fifteen or twenty minutes, might be seen returning from an excursion of two miles, under the imagination that he had laid in a stock of exercise sufficient for another period of a hundred days. Meantime Mr. Lawson had sought his main consolation in the great classics of elder days. His senior *alumni* were always working their way through some great scenic poet that had shaken the stage of Athens; and more than one of his classes, never ending, still beginning, were daily solacing him with the gaieties of Horace, in his Epistles or in his Satires. The Horatian jests indeed to *him* never grew old. On coming to the *plagosus Orbilius*, or any other sally of pleasantry, he still threw himself back in his arm-chair, as he *had* done through fifty years, with what seemed heart-shaking bursts of sympathetic merriment. Mr. Lawson, indeed, could afford to be sincerely mirthful over the word *plagosus*. There are gloomy tyrants, exulting in the discipline of fear, to whom and to whose pupils this word must call up remembrances too degrading for any but affected mirth. Allusions that are too fearfully personal cease to be subjects of playfulness. Sycophancy only it is that laughs; and the artificial merriment is but the language of shrinking and grovelling deprecation. Different, indeed, was the condition of the Manchester Grammar School. It was honourable both to the masters and the upper boys, through whom only such a result was possible, that in that school, during my knowledge of it (viz., during the closing year of the eighteenth century, and the two opening years of the nineteenth), all punishments, that appealed to the sense of bodily pain, had fallen into disuse ; and this at a period long before any public agitation had begun to stir in that direction. How then was discipline maintained ? It was maintained through the self-discipline of the senior boys, and through the efficacy of their example, combined with their system of rules. Noble are the impulses of opening manhood, where they are not utterly ignoble : at that period, I mean, when the poetic sense begins to blossom, and when boys are first made sensible of the paradise that lurks in female smiles. Had the school been entirely a day-school, too probable it is that the vulgar brawling tendencies of boys left to themselves would have prevailed. But it happened that the elder section of the school—those on the brink of manhood, and by incalculable degrees the more scholar-like section, all who read, meditated, or began to kindle into the love of literature—were boarders in Mr. Lawson's house. The students, therefore, of the house carried an overwhelming influence into the school. They were bound together by links of brotherhood ; whereas the day-scholars were disconnected. Over and above this, it happened luckily that there was no playground, not the smallest, attached to the school ; that is, none was attached to the *upper* or *grammar* school. But there was also, and resting on the same liberal endowment, a *lower* school, where the whole machinery of teaching was applied to the lowest mechanical accomplishments of reading and writing. The hall in which this servile business was conducted ran under the upper school ; it was, therefore, I presume, a subterraneous duplicate of the upper hall. And, since the upper rose only by two or three feet above the level of the neighbouring streets, the lower school should naturally have been at a great depth *below* these streets. In that case it would be a dark crypt, such as we see under some cathedrals ; and it would have argued a singular want of thoughtfulness in the founder to have laid one part of his establishment under an original curse of darkness. As the access to this plebeian school lay downwards through long flights of steps, I never found surplus energy enough for investigating the problem. But, as the ground broke away precipitously at that point into lower levels, I presume, upon consideration, that the subterranean crypt will be found open on one side to visitations from sun and moon. So that, for this base mechanic school there may, after all, have been a playground. But for ours in the upper air, I repeat, there was none ; not so much as would have bleached a lady's pocket-handkerchief ; and this one defect carried along with it unforeseen advantages.

Lord Bacon it is who notices the subtle policy which may lurk in the mere external figure of a table. A square table, having an undeniable head and foot, two polar extremities of what is highest and lowest, a perihelion and an aphelion, together with equatorial sides, opens at a glance a large career to ambition ; whilst a circular table sternly represses all such aspiring dreams, and so does a triangular table. Yet, if the triangle should be right-angled, then the Lucifer seated at the right angle might argue that he *subtended* all the tenants of the hypothenuse ; being, therefore, as much nobler than they as Atlas was nobler than the globe which he carried. It was, by the way, some arrangement of this nature which constituted the original feature of distinction in John o' Groat's house, and not at all (as most people suppose) the high northern latitude of this house. John, it seems, finished the feuds for precedency, not by legislating this way or that, but by cutting away the possibility of such feuds through the assistance of a round table. The same principle must have guided King Arthur amongst his knights, Charlemagne amongst his paladins, and sailors in their effectual distribution of the peril attached to a mutinous remonstrance by the admirable device of a 'round-robin.' Even two little girls, as Harrington remarks in his *Oceana*, have oftentimes hit upon an expedient, through pure mother-wit, more effectual than all the schools of philosophy could have suggested, for insuring the impartial division of an orange ; which expedient is that either of the two shall divide, but then that the other shall have the right of choice. You divide and I choose. Such is the formula ; and an angel could not devise a more absolute guarantee for the equity of the division than by thus forcing the divider to become the inheritor of any possible disadvantages that he may have succeeded in creating by his own act of division. In all these cases one seemingly trivial precaution opens, in the next stage, into a world of irresistible consequences. And, in our case, an effect not less disproportionate followed out of that one accident, apparently so slight, that we had no playground. We of the seniority, who, by thoughtfulness, and the conscious dignity of dealing largely with literature, were already indisposed to boyish sports, found through the defect of a playground, that our choice and our pride were also our necessity. Even the proudest of us benefited by that coercion ; for many would else have sold their privilege of pride for an hour's amusement, and have become, at least, occasional conformists. A day more than usually fine, a trial of skill more than usually irritating to the sense of special superiority, would have seduced most of us in the end into the surrender of our exclusiveness. Indiscriminate familiarity would have followed as an uncontrollable result ; since to mingle with others in common acts of business may leave the sense of reserve undisturbed : but all reserve gives way before a common intercourse in pleasure. As it was, what with our confederation through house-membership, what with our reciprocal sympathies in the problems suggested by books, we had become a club of boys (amongst whom might be four or five that were even young men, counting eighteen or nineteen years) altogether as thoughtful and as self-respecting as can often exist even amongst adults. Even the subterraneous school contributed something to our self-esteem. It formed a subordinate section of our own establishment, that kept before our eyes, by force of contrast, the dignity inherent in our own constitution. Its object was to master humble accomplishments that were within the reach of *mechanic* efforts : everything mechanic is limited ; whereas we felt that *our* object,

even if our name of *grammar* school presented that object
in what seemed too limited a shape, was substantially
noble, and tended towards the infinite. But in no long
time I came to see that, as to the *name*, we were all of
us under a mistake. Being asked what a *grammar* school
indicates, what it professes to teach, there is scarcely any
man who would not reply, 'Teach? why, it teaches
grammar, what else?' But this is a mistake : as I have
elsewhere explained, *grammatica* in this combination does
not mean grammar (though grammar also obeys the
movements of a most subtle philosophy), but *literature*.
Look into Suetonius. Those '*grammatici*' whom he
memorialises as an order of men flocking to Rome in the
days of the Flavian family, were not *grammarians* at all,
but what the French by a comprehensive name style
littérateurs—that is, they were men who (1) studied
literature, (2) who taught literature, (3) who practically
produced literature. And, upon the whole, *grammatica*
is perhaps the least objectionable Latin equivalent for
our word *literature*.

Having thus sketched the characteristic points distinguishing the school and the presiding master (for of
masters, senior and junior, there were four in this upper
school), I return to my own inaugural examination.
On this day, memorable to myself, as furnishing the
starting-point for so long a series of days, saddened by
haughty obstinacy on one side, made effective by folly
on the other, no sooner had my guardian retired than
Mr. Lawson produced from his desk a volume of the
Spectator, and instructed me to throw into as good Latin
as I could some paper of Steele's—not the whole, but
perhaps a third part. No better exercise could have
been devised for testing the extent of my skill as a
Latinist. And here I ought to make an explanation. In
the previous edition of these *Confessions*, writing sometimes too rapidly, and with little precision in cases of
little importance, I conveyed an impression which I had
not designed with regard to the true nature of my
pretensions as a Grecian ; and something of the same

correction will apply to that narrower accomplishment
which was the subject of my present examination.
Neither in Greek nor in Latin was my *knowledge* very
extensive ; my age made *that* impossible ; and especially
because in those days there were no decent guides through
the thorny jungles of the Latin language, far less of the
Greek. When I mention that the *Port Royal* Greek
Grammar translated by Dr. Nugent was about the best
key extant in English to the innumerable perplexities of
Greek diction, and that, for the *res metrica*, Morell's
valuable *Thesaurus*, having then never been reprinted,
was rarely to be seen, the reader will conclude that a
schoolboy's *knowledge* of Greek could not be other than
slender. Slender indeed was mine. Yet stop ? *what*
was slender ? Simply my *knowledge* of Greek ; for that
knowledge stretches by tendency to the infinite ; but not
therefore my *command* of Greek. The *knowledge* of
Greek must always hold some gross proportion to the
time spent upon it,—probably, therefore, to the age of
the student ; but the *command* over a language, the power
of adapting it plastically to the expression of your own
thoughts, is almost exclusively a gift of nature, and has
very little connection with time. Take the supreme
trinity of Greek scholars that flourished between the
English Revolution of 1688 and the beginning of the
nineteenth century — which trinity I suppose to be,
confessedly, Bentley, Valckenaer, and Porson : such are
the men, it will be generally fancied, whose aid should
be invoked, in the event of our needing some eloquent
Greek inscription on a public monument. I am of a
different opinion. The greatest scholars have usually
proved to be the poorest composers in either of the classic
languages. Sixty years ago, we had, from four separate
doctors, four separate Greek versions of Gray's *Elegy*, all
unworthy of the national scholarship. Yet one of these
doctors was actually Porson's predecessor in the Greek
chair at Cambridge. But, as he (Dr. Cooke) was an
obscure man, take an undeniable Grecian, of punctilious
precision—viz., Richard Dawes, the well-known author

of the *Miscellanea Critica*. This man, a very *martinet* in the delicacies of Greek composition—and who *should* have been a Greek scholar of some mark, since often enough he flew at the throat of Richard Bentley—wrote and published a specimen of a Greek *Paradise Lost*, and also two most sycophantic idyls addressed to George II. on the death of his 'august' papa. It is difficult to imagine anything meaner in conception or more childish in expression than these attempts. Now, against *them* I will stake in competition a copy of iambic verses by a boy, who died, I believe, at sixteen—viz., a son of Mr. Pitt's tutor, Tomline, Bishop of Winchester.[1] Universally I contend that the faculty of clothing the thoughts in a Greek dress is a function of natural sensibility, in a great degree disconnected from the extent or the accuracy of the writer's grammatical skill in Greek.

These explanations are too long. The reader will understand, as their sum, that what I needed in such a case was, not so much a critical familiarity with the syntax of the language, or a *copia verborum*, as great agility in reviewing the relations of one idea to another, so as to present modern and unclassical objects under such aspects as might suggest periphrases in substitution for direct names, where names could not be had, and everywhere to colour my translation with as rich a display of idiomatic forms as the circumstances of the case would allow. I succeeded, and beyond my expectation. For once—being the first time that he had been known to do

---

[1] '*A copy of iambic verses*':—They will be found in the work on the Greek article by Middleton, Bishop of Calcutta, who was the boy's tutor. On this occasion I would wish to observe that verses like Dawes's, meant to mimic Homer or Theocritus, or more generally dactylic hexameters, are perfectly useless as tests of power to think freely in Greek. If such verses are examined, it will be found that the orchestral magnificence of the metre, and the sonorous cadence of each separate line, absolutely *force* upon the thoughts a mere necessity of being discontinuous. From this signal defect only iambic senarii are free; this metre possessing a power of plastic interfusion similar in kind, though inferior in degree, to the English blank verse when Miltonically written.

such a thing, but also the very last—Mr. Lawson did absolutely pay me a compliment. And with another compliment more than verbal he crowned his gracious condescensions—viz., with my provisional instalment in his highest class ; not the highest at that moment, since there was one other class above us ; but this other was on the wing for Oxford within some few weeks ; which change being accomplished, we (viz., I and two others) immediately moved up into the supreme place.

Two or three days after this examination—viz., on the Sunday following—I transferred myself to headquarters at Mr. Lawson's house. About nine o'clock in the evening, I was conducted by a servant up a short flight of stairs, through a series of gloomy and unfurnished little rooms, having small windows but no doors, to the common room (as in Oxford it would technically be called) of the senior boys. Everything had combined to depress me. To leave the society of accomplished women—*that* was already a signal privation. The season besides was rainy, which in itself is a sure source of depression ; and the forlorn aspect of the rooms completed my dejection. But the scene changed as the door was thrown open : faces kindling with animation became visible ; and from a company of boys, numbering sixteen or eighteen, scattered about the room, two or three, whose age entitled them to the rank of leaders, came forward to receive me with a courtesy which I had not looked for. The grave kindness and the absolute sincerity of their manner impressed me most favourably. I had lived familiarly with boys gathered from all quarters of the island at the Bath Grammar School : and for some time (when visiting Lord Altamont at Eton) with boys of the highest aristocratic pretensions. At Bath and at Eton, though not equally, there prevailed a tone of higher polish ; and in the air, speech, deportment of the majority could be traced at once a premature knowledge of the world. They had indeed the advantage over my new friends in graceful self-possession ; but, on the other hand, the best of them suffered by comparison with these Manchester boys in the qualities of visible self-restraint and of self-respect. At Eton high rank was distributed pretty liberally; but in the Manchester school the parents of many boys were artisans, or of that rank; some even had sisters that were menial servants; and those who stood higher by pretensions of birth and gentle blood were, at the most, the sons of rural gentry or of clergymen. And I believe that, with the exception of three or four brothers, belonging to a clergyman's family at York, all were, like myself, natives of Lancashire. At that time my experience was too limited to warrant me in expressing any opinion, one way or the other, upon the relative pretensions—moral and intellectual—of the several provinces in our island. But since then I have seen reason to agree with the late Dr. Cooke Taylor in awarding the pre-eminence, as regards energy, power to face suffering, and other high qualities, to the natives of Lancashire. Even a century back, they were distinguished for the culture of refined tastes. In musical skill and sensibility, no part of Europe, with the exception of a few places in Germany, could pretend to rival them: and, accordingly, even in Handel's days, but for the chorus-singers from Lancashire, his oratorios must have remained a treasure, if not absolutely sealed, at any rate most imperfectly revealed.

One of the young men, noticing my state of dejection, brought out some brandy—a form of alcohol which I, for my part, tasted now for the first time, having previously taken only wine, and never once in quantities to affect my spirits. So much the greater was my astonishment at the rapid change worked in my state of feeling—a change which at once reinstalled me in my natural advantages for conversation. Towards this nothing was wanting but a question of sufficient interest. And a question arose naturally out of a remark addressed by one of the boys to myself, implying that perhaps I had intentionally timed my arrival so as to escape the Sunday evening exercise. No, I replied; not at all; what *was* that exercise? Simply an off-hand translation from the little work of Grotius[1] on the Evidences of Christianity.

[1] Entitled *De Veritate Christianæ Religionis.*

Did I know the book? No, I did not; all the direct knowledge which I had of Grotius was built upon his metrical translations into Latin of various fragments surviving from the Greek scenical poets, and these translations had struck me as exceedingly beautiful. On the other hand, his work of highest pretension, *De Jure Belli et Pacis*, so signally praised by Lord Bacon, I had not read at all; but I had heard such an account of it from a very thoughtful person as made it probable that Grotius was stronger, and felt himself stronger, on literary than on philosophic ground. Then, with regard to his little work on the Mosaic and Christian revelations, I had heard very disparaging opinions about it; two especially. One amounted to no more than this—that the question was argued with a logic far inferior, in point of cogency, to that of Lardner and Paley. Here several boys interposed their loud assent, as regarded Paley in particular. Paley's *Evidences*, at that time just seven years old, had already become a subject of study amongst them. But the other objection impeached not so much the dialectic acuteness as the learning of Grotius—at least, the appropriate learning. According to the anecdote current upon this subject, Dr. Edward Pococke, the great oriental scholar of England in the seventeenth century, when called upon to translate the little work of Grotius into Arabic or Turkish, had replied by pointing to the idle legend of Mahomet's pigeon or dove, as a reciprocal messenger between the prophet and heaven—which legend had been accredited and adopted by Grotius in the blindest spirit of credulity. Such a baseless fable, Pococke alleged, would work a double mischief: not only it would ruin the authority of that particular book in the East, but would damage Christianity for generations, by making known to the followers of the Prophet that their master was undervalued amongst the Franks on the authority of nursery tales, and that these tales were accredited by the leading Frankish scholars.

A twofold result of evil would follow: not only would our Christian erudition and our Christian scholars be scandalously disparaged; a consequence that in some

cases might not be incompatible with a sense amongst
Mahometans that the strength of Christianity itself was
left unaffected by the errors and blunders of its champions;
but, secondly, there would be in this case a strong reaction
against Christianity itself. Plausibly enough it would be
inferred that a vast religious philosophy could have no
powerful battery of arguments in reserve, when it placed
its main anti-Mahometan reliance upon so childish a fable:
since, allowing even for a blameless assent to this fable
amongst nations having no direct intercourse with Mussulmans, still it would argue a shocking frailty in Christianity
that its main pleadings rested, not upon any strength of
its own, but simply upon a weakness in its antagonist.

At this point, when the cause of Grotius seemed
utterly desperate, G—— (a boy whom subsequently I had
reason to admire as equally courageous, truthful, and far-
seeing) suddenly changed the whole field of view. He
offered no defence for the ridiculous fable of the pigeon ;
which pigeon, on the contrary, he represented as drawing in
harness with that Christian goose which at one time was
universally believed by Mahometans to lead the vanguard
of the earliest Crusaders, and which, in a limited extent,
really had been a true historical personage. So far he gave
up Grotius as indefensible. But on the main question, and
the very extensive question, of his apparent imbecility
when collated with Paley, etc., suddenly and in one
sentence he revolutionised the whole logic of that comparison. Paley and Lardner, he said, what was it that
they sought ! *Their* object was avowedly to benefit by
any argument, evidence, or presumption whatsoever, no
matter whence drawn, so long as it was true or probable,
and fitted to sustain the credibility of any element in the
Christian creed. Well, was not *that* object common to
them and to Grotius ? Not at all. Too often had he
(the boy G——) secretly noticed the abstinence of Grotius
(apparently unaccountable) from certain obvious advantages
of argument, not to suspect that, in narrowing his own
field of disputation, he had a deliberate purpose, and was
moving upon the line of some very different policy. Clear

it was to *him* that Grotius, for some reason, declined to receive evidence except from one special and limited class of witnesses. Upon this, some of us laughed at such a self-limitation as a wild bravado, recalling that rope-dancing feat of some verse-writers who, through each several stanza in its turn, had gloried in dispensing with some one separate consonant, some vowel, or some diphthong, and thus achieving a triumph such as crowns with laurel that pedestrian athlete who wins a race by hopping on one leg, or wins it under the inhuman condition of confining both legs within a sack. ' *No, no*,' impatiently interrupted G———. ' All such fantastic conflicts with self-created difficulties terminate in pure ostentation, and profit nobody. But the self-imposed limitations of Grotius had a special purpose, and realise a value not otherwise attainable.' If Grotius accepts no arguments or presumptions except from Mussulmans, from Infidels, or from those who rank as Neutrals, then has he adapted his book to a separate and peculiar audience. The Neutral man will hearken to authorities notoriously Neutral ; Mussulmans will show deference to the statements of Mussulmans ; the Sceptic will bow to the reasonings of Scepticism. All these persons, that would have been repelled on the very threshold from such testimonies as begin in a spirit of hostility to themselves, will listen thoughtfully to suggestions offered in a spirit of conciliation ; much more so if offered by people occupying the same ground at starting as themselves.

At the cost of some disproportion, I have ventured to rehearse this inaugural conversation amongst the leaders of the school. Whether G——— were entirely correct in this application of a secret key to the little work of Grotius, I do not know. I take blame to myself that I do not ; for I also must have been called upon for my quota to the Sunday evening studies on the *De Veritate*, and must therefore have held in my hands the ready means for solving the question.[1]

[1] Some excuse, however, for my own want of energy is suggested by the fact that very soon after my matriculation Mr. Lawson sub-

Meantime, as a solitary act of silent observation in a boy not fifteen, this deciphering idea of G——'s, in direct resistance to the received idea, extorted my admiration ; and equally, whether true or false as regarded the immediate fact. That any person, in the very middle storm of chase, when a headlong movement carries all impulses into one current, should in the twinkling of an eye recall himself to the unexpected 'doubles' of the game, wheel as *that* wheels, and sternly resist the instincts of the one preoccupying assumption, argues a sagacity not often heard of in boyhood. Was G—— right? In that case he picked a lock which others had failed to pick. Was he wrong? In that case he sketched the idea and outline of a better work (better, as more original and more special in its service) than any which Grotius has himself accomplished.

Not, however, the particular boy, but the particular school, it was my purpose, in this place, to signalise for praise and gratitude. In after years, when an undergraduate at Oxford, I had an opportunity of reading as it were in a mirror the characteristic pretensions and the average success of many celebrated schools. Such a mirror I found in the ordinary conversation and in the favourite reading of young gownsmen belonging to the many different colleges of Oxford. Generally speaking, each college had a filial connexion (strict [1] or not strict) with some one or more of our great public schools. These, fortunately for England, are diffused through all her counties : and, as the main appointments to the capital offices in such *public* schools are often vested by law in Oxford or Cambridge, this arrangement guarantees a sound

stituted for Grotius, as the Sunday evening lecture-book, Dr. Clarke's Commentary on the New Testament. 'Out of sight, out of mind'; and in that way only can I account for my own neglect to clear up the question. Or perhaps, after all, I *did* clear it up, and in a long life-march subsequently may have dropped it by the wayside.

[1] '*Strict or not strict*' :—In some colleges the claims of *alumni* from certain schools were absolute ; in some, I believe, conditional ; in others, again, concurrent with rival claims from favoured schools or favoured counties.

system of teaching ; so that any failures in the result must presumably be due to the individual student. Failures, on the whole, I do not suppose that there were. Classical attainments that might be styled even splendid were not then, nor are now, uncommon. And yet in one great feature many of those schools, even the very best, when thus tried by their fruits, left a painful memento of failure ; or rather not of failure as in relation to any purpose that they steadily recognised, but of *wilful* and *intentional* disregard, as towards a purpose alien from any duty of theirs, or any task which they had ever undertaken—a failure, namely, in relation to *modern* literature—a neglect to unroll its mighty charts : and amongst this modern literature a special neglect (such as seems almost brutal) of our own English literature, though pleading its patent of precedency in a voice so trumpet-tongued. To myself, whose homage ascended night and day towards the great altars of English Poetry or Eloquence, it was shocking and revolting to find in high-minded young countrymen, burning with sensibility that sought vainly for a correspond-ing object, deep unconsciousness of an all-sufficient object —namely, in that great inheritance of our literature which sometimes kindled enthusiasm in our public enemies. How painful to see or to know that vast revelations of grandeur and beauty are wasting themselves for ever— forests teeming with gorgeous life, floral wildernesses hidden inaccessibly ; whilst, at the same time, in contra-position to that evil, behold a corresponding evil—viz., that with equal prodigality the great capacities of enjoyment are running also to waste, and are everywhere burning out unexercised—waste, in short, in the world of things *enjoyable*, balanced by an equal waste in the organs and the machineries of enjoyment ! This picture—would it not fret the heart of an Englishman? Some years (say twenty) after the era of my own entrance at that Oxford which then furnished me with records so painful of slight regard to our national literature, behold at the court of London a French ambassador, a man of genius blazing (as some people thought) with nationality, but, in fact, with something inexpressibly nobler and deeper—viz., patriotism. For true and unaffected patriotism will show its love in a noble form by sincerity and truth. But nationality, as I have always found, is mean ; is dishonest ; is ungenerous ; is incapable of candour ; and, being continually besieged with temptations to falsehood, too often ends by becoming habitually mendacious. This Frenchman above all things valued literature : his own trophies of distinction were all won upon that field : and yet, when called upon to review the literature of Europe, he found himself conscientiously coerced into making his work a mere monument to the glory of one man, and that man the son of a hostile land. The name of Milton, in *his* estimate, swallowed up all others. This Frenchman was Chateaubriand. The personal splendour which surrounded him gave a corresponding splendour to his act. And, because he, as an ambassador, was a representative man, this act might be interpreted as a representative act. The tutelary genius of France in this instance might be regarded as bending before that of England. But homage so free, homage so noble, must be interpreted and received in a corresponding spirit of generosity. It was not, like the testimony of Balaam on behalf of Israel, an unwilling submission to a hateful truth : it was a concession, in the spirit of saintly magnanimity, to an interest of human nature that *as* such, transcended by many degrees all considerations merely national.

Now, then, with this unlimited devotion to one great luminary of our literary system emblazoned so conspicuously in the testimony of a Frenchman—that is, of one trained, and privileged to be a public enemy—contrast the humiliating spectacle of young Englishmen suffered (so far as their training is concerned) to ignore the very existence of this mighty poet. Do I mean, then, that it would have been advisable to place the *Paradise Lost*, and the *Paradise Regained*, and the *Samson*, in the library of schoolboys? By no means. That mode of sensibility which deals with the Miltonic sublimity is rarely developed in boyhood. And these divine works should in prudence be reserved to the period of mature manhood. But then it should be made known that they *are* so reserved, and upon what principle of reverential regard for the poet himself. In the meantime, selections from Milton, from Dryden, from Pope, and many other writers, though not everywhere appreciable by those who have but small experience of life, would not generally transcend the intellect or sensibility of a boy sixteen or seventeen years old. And, beyond all other sections of literature, the two which I am going to mention are fitted (or might be fitted by skilful management) to engage the interest of those who are no longer boys, but have reached the age which is presumable in English university matriculation—viz., the close of the eighteenth year. Search through all languages, from Benares the mystical, and the banks of the Ganges, travelling westwards to the fountains of the Hudson, I deny that any two such *bibliothecæ* for engaging youthful interest could be brought together as these two which follow :—

First, In contradiction to M. Cousin's recent audacious assertion (redeemed from the suspicion of mendacity simply by the extremity of ignorance on which it reposes) that we English have no tolerable writer of prose subsequent to Lord Bacon, it so happens that the seventeenth century, and specially that part of it concerned in this case—viz., the latter seventy years (A.D. 1628-1700)—produced the highest efforts of eloquence (philosophic, but at the same time rhetorical and impassioned, in a degree unknown to the prose literature of France) which our literature possesses, and not a line of it but is posterior to the death of Lord Bacon. Donne, Chillingworth, Sir Thomas Browne, Jeremy Taylor, Milton, South, Barrow, form a *plëiad*, a constellation of seven golden stars, such as no literature can match in their own class. From these seven writers, taken apart from all their contemporaries, I would undertake to build up an entire body of philosophy[1] upon the

---

[1] '*Philosophy*':—At this point it is that the main misconception would arise. Theology, and not philosophy, most people will fancy, is likely to form the staple of these writers. But I have elsewhere

supreme interests of humanity.   One error of M. Cousin's doubtless lay in overlooking the fact that all conceivable problems of philosophy can reproduce themselves under a theological mask : and thus he had absolved himself from reading many English books, as presumably mere professional pleadings of Protestant polemics, which are in fact mines inexhaustible of eloquence and philosophic speculation.

Secondly, A full abstract of the English Drama from about the year 1580 to the period (say 1635) at which it was killed by the frost of the Puritanical spirit seasoning all flesh for the Parliamentary War.   No literature, not excepting even that of Athens, has ever presented such a multiform theatre, such a carnival display, mask and anti-mask, of impassioned life—breathing, moving, acting, suffering, laughing.

> Quicquid agunt homines—votum, timor, ira, voluptas,
> Gaudia, discursus ; [1]

—all this, but far more truly and adequately than was or could be effected in that field of composition which the gloomy satirist contemplated,—whatsoever in fact our mediæval ancestors exhibited in their 'Dance of Death,' drunk with tears and laughter,—may here be reviewed, scenically grouped, draped, and gorgeously coloured. What other national drama can pretend to any competition with this ?   The Athenian has in a great proportion perished ; the Roman was killed prematurely by the bloody realities of the amphitheatre, as candle-light by day-light ; the Spanish, even in the hands of Calderon, offers only undeveloped sketchings ; and the French,

---

maintained that the main bulk of English philosophy has always hidden itself in the English divinity. In Jeremy Taylor, for instance, are exhibited all the *practical* aspects of philosophy ; of philosophy as it bears upon Life, upon Ethics, and upon Transcendent Prudence—*i.e.* briefly upon the Greek *summum bonum.*

[1] 'All that is done by men—movements of prayer, panic, wrath, revels of the voluptuous, festivals of triumph, or gladiatorship of the intellect '—*Juvenal,* in the prefatory lines which rehearse the prevailing themes of his own Satires gathered in the great harvests of Rome.

E

besides other and profounder objections, to which no
justice had yet been done, lies under the signal disadvantage
of not having reached its meridian until sixty years (or
two generations) after the English. In reality, the great
period of the English Drama was exactly closing as the
French opened[1] : consequently the French lost the
prodigious advantage for scenical effects of a romantic and
picturesque age. This had vanished when the French
theatre culminated ; and the natural result was that the
fastidiousness of French taste, by this time too powerfully
developed, stifled or distorted the free movements of
French genius.

I beg the reader's pardon for this disproportioned
digression, into which I was hurried by my love for our
great national literature, my anxiety to see it amongst
educational resources invested with a ministerial agency
of far ampler character, but at all events to lodge a
protest against that wholesale neglect of our supreme
authors which leaves us open to the stinging reproach of
' treading daily with our clouted shoon ' (to borrow the
words of Comus) upon that which high-minded foreigners
regard as the one paramount jewel in our national diadem.

---

[1] It is remarkable that in the period immediately anterior to that
of Corneille, a stronger and more *living* nature was struggling for
utterance in French tragedy. Guizot has cited from an early drama (I
forget whether of Rotrou or of Hardy) one scene most thoroughly
impassioned. The situation is that of a prince who has fixed his love
upon a girl of low birth. She is faithful and constant : but the
courtiers about the prince, for malicious purposes of their own,
calumniate her : the prince is deluded by the plausible air of the
slanders which they disperse : he believes them ; but not with the
result (anticipated by the courtiers) of dismissing the girl from his
thoughts. On the contrary, he is haunted all the more morbidly by
her image ; and, in a scene which brings before us one of the vilest
amongst these slanderers exerting himself to the uttermost in drawing
off the prince's thoughts to alien objects, we find the prince vainly
attempting any self-control, vainly striving to attend, till he is overruled
by the tenderness of his sorrowing love into finding new occasions for
awakening thoughts of the lost girl in the very words chiefly relied on
for calling off his feelings from her image. The scene (as Guizot
himself remarks) is thoroughly Shaksperian ; and I venture to think
that this judgment would have been countersigned by Charles Lamb.

That reproach fell heavily, as my own limited experience inclined me to fear, upon most of our great public schools, otherwise so admirably conducted.[1] But from the Manchester Grammar School any such reproach altogether rebounded. My very first conversation with the boys had arisen naturally upon a casual topic, and had shown them to be tolerably familiar with the outline of the Christian polemics in the warfare with Jew, Mahometan, Infidel, and Sceptic. But this was an exceptional case ; and naturally it happened that most of us sought for the ordinary subjects of our conversational discussions in literature—viz., in our own native literature. Here it was that I learned to feel a deep respect for my new school-fellows : deep it was, then; and a larger experience has made it deeper. I have since known many literary men ; men whose profession was literature ; who were understood to have dedicated themselves to literature ; and who sometimes had with some one special section or little nook of literature an acquaintance critically minute. But amongst such men I have found but three or four who had a knowledge which came as near to what I should consider a comprehensive knowledge as really existed amongst those boys collectively. What one boy had not, another had ; and thus, by continual intercourse, the fragmentary contribution of one being integrated by the fragmentary contributions of others, gradually the attainments of each separate individual became, in some degree, the collective attainments of the whole senior common room. It is true, undoubtedly, that some parts of literature were inaccessible, simply because the books were inaccessible to boys at school—for instance, Froissart in the old translation by Lord Berners, now more than three centuries old ; and some parts were, to the young, essentially repulsive.

[1] It will strike everybody that such works as the *Microcosm*, conducted notoriously by Eton boys, and therefore, in part, by Canning as one of their leaders at that period, must have had an admirable effect, since not only it must have made it the interest of each contributor, but must even have made it his necessity, to cultivate some acquaintance with his native literature.

But, measuring the general qualifications by that standard which I have since found to prevail amongst professional *littérateurs*, I felt more respectfully towards the majority of my senior school-fellows than ever I had fancied it possible that I should find occasion to feel towards any boys whatever.   My intercourse with those amongst them who had any conversational talents greatly stimulated my intellect.

This intercourse, however, fell within narrower limits soon after the time of my entrance.   I acknowledge, with deep self-reproach, that every possible indulgence was allowed to me which the circumstances of the establishment made possible.   I had, for example, a private room allowed, in which I not only studied, but also slept at night.   The room being airy and cheerful, I found nothing disagreeable in this double use of it.   Naturally, however, this means of retirement tended to sequester me from my companions : for, whilst liking the society of some amongst them, I also had a deadly liking (perhaps a morbid liking) for solitude.   To make my present solitude the more fascinating, my mother sent me five guineas *extra*, for the purchase of an admission to the Manchester Library; a library which I should not at present think *very* extensive, but which, however, benefited in its composition, as also in its administration, by the good sense and intelligence of some amongst its original committees.   These two luxuries were truly and indeed such : but a third, from which I had anticipated even greater pleasure, turned out a total failure; and for a reason which it may be useful to mention, by way of caution to others.   This was a pianoforte, together with the sum required for regular lessons from a music-master. But the first discovery I made was that practice through eight or even ten hours a day was indispensable towards any great proficiency on this instrument.   Another discovery finished my disenchantment : it was this.   For the particular purpose which I had in view, it became clear that no mastery of the instrument, not even that of Thalberg, would be available.   Too soon I became aware

that to the deep voluptuous enjoyment of music absolute
passiveness in the hearer is indispensable.   Gain what
skill you please, nevertheless activity, vigilance, anxiety
must always accompany an elaborate effort of musical
execution : and so far is that from being reconcilable
with the entrancement and lull essential to the true
fruition of music, that, even if you should suppose a
vast piece of mechanism capable of executing a whole
oratorio, but requiring, at intervals, a co-operating
impulse from the foot of the auditor, even *that*, even so
much as an occasional touch of the foot, would utterly
undermine all your pleasure.   A single psychological
discovery, therefore, caused my musical anticipations to
evanesce.   Consequently, one of my luxuries burst like
a bubble at an early stage.   In this state of things,
when the instrument had turned out a bubble, it followed
naturally that the music-master should find himself to be
a bubble.   But he was so thoroughly good-natured and
agreeable that I could not reconcile myself to such a
catastrophe.   Meantime, though accommodating within
certain limits, this music-master was yet a conscientious
man, and a man of honourable pride.   On finding, therefore, that I was not seriously making any effort to
improve, he shook hands with me one fine day, and
took his leave for ever.   Unless it were to point a
moral and adorn a tale, the piano had then become
useless.   It was too big to hang upon willows, and
willows there were none in that neighbourhood.   But
it remained for months as a lumbering monument of
labour misapplied, of bubbles that had burst, and of
musical visions that, under psychological tests, had
foundered for ever.

Yes, certainly, this particular luxury—one out of three
—had proved a bubble; too surely this had foundered;
but not, therefore, the other two.   The quiet study,
lifted by two storeys above the vapours of earth, and
liable to no unseasonable intrusion; the Manchester
Library, so judiciously and symmetrically mounted in
all its most attractive departments—no class dispro-

portioned to the rest: these were no bubbles; these had
not foundered. Oh, wherefore, then, was it—through
what inexplicable growth of evil in myself or in others—
that now in the summer of 1802, when peace was
brooding over all the land, peace succeeding to a bloody
seven years' war, but peace which already gave signs of
breaking into a far bloodier war, some dark sympathising
movement within my own heart, as if echoing and repeating in mimicry the political menaces of the earth, swept
with storm-clouds across that otherwise serene and radiant
dawn which should have heralded my approaching entrance
into life? *Inexplicable* I have allowed myself to call
this fatal error in my life, because such it *must* appear
to others; since, even to myself, so often as I fail to
realise the case by reproducing a reflex impression in
kind, and in degree, of the suffering before which my
better angel gave way—yes, even to myself this collapse
of my resisting energies seems inexplicable. Yet again,
in simple truth, now that it becomes possible, through
changes worked by time, to tell the *whole* truth (and not,
as in former editions, only a part of it), there really was
no absolute mystery at all. But this case, in common
with many others, exemplifies to my mind the mere
impossibility of making full and frank 'Confessions,'
whilst many of the persons concerned in the incidents
are themselves surviving, or (which is worse still) if
themselves dead and buried, are yet vicariously surviving
in the persons of near and loving kinsmen. Rather
than inflict mortifications upon people so circumstanced,
any kind-hearted man will choose to mutilate his narrative; will suppress facts, and will mystify explanations.
For instance, at this point in my record, it has become
my right, perhaps I might say my duty, to call a
particular medical man of the penultimate generation a
blockhead; nay, doubtfully, to call him a criminal blockhead. But could I do this without deep compunction,
so long as sons and daughters of his were still living,
from whom I, when a boy, had received most hospitable
attentions? Often, on the very same day which brought

home to my suffering convictions the atrocious ignorance
of papa, I was benefiting by the courtesies of the
daughters, and by the scientific accomplishments of the
son. Not the less this man, at that particular moment
when a crisis of gloom was gathering over my path,
became effectually my evil genius. Not that singly
perhaps he could have worked any durable amount of
mischief: but he, as a co-operator unconsciously with
others, sealed and ratified that sentence of stormy sorrow
then hanging over my head. Three separate persons, in
fact, made themselves unintentional accomplices in that
ruin (a ruin reaching me even at this day by its shadows)
which threw me out a homeless vagrant upon the earth
before I had accomplished my seventeenth year. Of
these three persons, foremost came myself, through my
wilful despair and resolute abjuration of all *secondary*
hope : since, after all, some mitigation was possible,
supposing that perfect relief might *not* be possible.
Secondly, came that medical ruffian through whose brutal
ignorance it happened that my malady had not been
arrested before reaching an advanced stage. Thirdly,
came Mr. Lawson, through whose growing infirmities it
had arisen that this malady ever reached its very earliest
stage. Strange it was, but not the less a fact, that Mr.
Lawson was gradually becoming a curse to all who fell
under his influence, through pure zealotry of conscientiousness. Being a worse man, he would have carried
far deeper blessings into his circle. If he could have
reconciled himself to an imperfect discharge of his duties,
he would not have betrayed his insufficiency for those
duties. But this he would not hear of. He persisted
in travelling over the appointed course to the last inch :
and the consequences told most painfully upon the comfort of all around him. By the old traditionary usages
of the school, going in at seven A.M., we ought to have
been dismissed for breakfast and a full hour's repose at
nine. This hour of rest was in strict justice a *debt* to the
students—liable to no discount either through the caprice
or the tardiness of the supreme master. Yet such were

the gradual encroachments upon this hour that at length
the bells of the collegiate church,—which, by an ancient
usage, rang every morning from half-past nine to ten,
and through varying modifications of musical key and
rhythmus that marked the advancing stages of the half-
hour,—regularly announced to us, on issuing from the
school-room, that the bread and milk which composed
our simple breakfast must be despatched at a pace fitter
for the fowls of the air than students of Grecian
philosophy. But was no compensatory encroachment
for our benefit allowed upon the next hour from ten to
eleven? Not for so much as the fraction of a second.
Inexorably as the bells, by stopping, announced the hour
of ten, was Mr. Lawson to be seen ascending the steps
of the school; and he that suffered most by this rigorous
exaction of duties could not allege that Mr. Lawson
suffered less. If he required others to pay, he also paid
up to the last farthing. The same derangement took
place, with the same refusal to benefit by any indemnification, at what *should* have been the two-hours' pause
for dinner. Only for some mysterious reason, resting
possibly upon the family arrangements of the day-
scholars,—which, if once violated, might have provoked
a rebellion of fathers and mothers,—he still adhered
faithfully to five o'clock P.M. as the closing hour of the
day's labours.

Here then stood arrayed the whole machinery of
mischief in good working order ; and through six months
or more, allowing for one short respite of four weeks, this
machinery had been operating with effect. Mr. Lawson,
to begin, had (without meaning it, or so much as perceiving
it) barred up all avenues from morning to night through
which any bodily exercise could be obtained. Two or
three chance intervals of five minutes each, and even these
not consecutively arranged, composed the whole available
fund of leisure out of which any stroll into the country
could have been attempted. But in a great city like
Manchester the very suburbs had hardly been reached
before that little fraction of time was exhausted. Very

soon after Mr. Lawson's increasing infirmities had begun
to tell severely in the contraction of our spare time, the
change showed itself powerfully in my drooping health.
Gradually the liver became affected : and connected with
that affection arose, what often accompanies such ailments,
profound melancholy. In such circumstances, indeed under
any the slightest disturbance of my health, I had authority
from my guardians to call for medical advice : but I was
not left to my own discretion in selecting the adviser.
This person was not a physician, who would of course have
expected the ordinary fee of a guinea for every visit ; nor
a surgeon ; but simply an apothecary. In any case of
serious illness a physician would have been called in. But
a less costly style of advice was reasonably held to be
sufficient in any illness which left the patient strength
sufficient to walk about. Certainly it ought to have been
sufficient here : for no case could possibly be simpler.
Three doses of calomel or blue pill, which unhappily I did
not then know, would no doubt have re-established me in
a week. But far better, as acting always upon me with a
magical celerity and a magical certainty, would have been
the authoritative prescription (privately notified to Mr.
Lawson) of seventy miles' walking in each week. Unhappily my professional adviser was a comatose old gentleman, rich beyond all his needs, careless of his own practice,
and standing under that painful necessity (according to the
custom then regulating medical practice, which prohibited
fees to apothecaries) of seeking his remuneration in excessive deluges of medicine. Me, however, out of pure
idleness, he forbore to plague with any *variety* of medicines.
With sublime simplicity he confined himself to one horrid
mixture, that must have suggested itself to him when
prescribing for a tiger. In ordinary circumstances, and
with plenty of exercise, no creature could be healthier than
myself. But my organisation was perilously frail. And
to fight simultaneously with such a malady and such
a medicine seemed really too much. The proverb
tells us that three 'flittings' are as bad as a fire.
Very possibly. And I should think that, in the same

spirit of reasonable equation, three such tiger-drenches must be equal to one apoplectic fit, or even to the tiger himself.   Having taken two of them, which struck me as quite enough for one life, I declined to comply with the injunction of the label pasted upon each several phial— viz., *Repetatur haustus*;[1] and, instead of doing any such dangerous thing, called upon Mr. ——— (the apothecary), begging to know if his art had not amongst its reputed infinity of resources any less abominable, and less shatter- ing to a delicate system than this.   'None whatever,' he replied.   Exceedingly kind he was ; insisted on my drinking tea with his really amiable daughters ; but continued at intervals to repeat 'None whatever — none whatever' ; then, as if rousing himself to an effort, he sang out loudly 'None whatever,' which in this final utterance he toned down syllabically into 'what*ever—ever—ver— er.*'   The whole wit of man, it seems, had exhausted itself upon the preparation of that one infernal mixture.

Now then we three — Mr. Lawson, the somnolent apothecary, and myself—had amongst us accomplished a climax of perplexity.   Mr. Lawson, by mere dint of conscientiousness, had made health for me impossible. The apothecary had subscribed *his* little contribution, by ratifying and trebling the ruinous effects of this sedentari- ness.   And for myself, as last in the series, it now remained to clench the operation by my own little con- tribution, all that I really had to offer — viz., absolute despair.   Those who have ever suffered from a profound derangement of the liver may happen to know that of human despondencies through all their infinite gamut none is more deadly.   Hope died within me.   I could not look for medical relief, so deep being my own ignorance, so equally deep being that of my official counsellor.   I could not expect that Mr. Lawson would modify his system— his instincts of duty being so strong, his incapacity to face that duty so steadily increasing.   'It comes then to this,' thought I, 'that in myself only there lurks any arrear of help' : as always for every man the ultimate reliance

[1] 'Let the draught be repeated.'

should be on himself. But this *self* of mine seemed absolutely bankrupt ; bankrupt of counsel or device—of effort in the way of action, or of suggestion in the way of plan. I had for two months been pursuing with one of my guardians what I meant for a negotiation upon this subject ; the main object being to obtain some considerable abbreviation of my school residence. But *negotiation* was a self-flattering name for such a correspondence, since there never had been from the beginning any the slightest leaning on my guardian's part towards the shadow or pretence of a compromise. What compromise, indeed, was possible where neither party could concede a *part*, however small : the *whole* must be conceded, or nothing : since no *mezzo termine* was conceivable. In reality, when my eyes first glanced upon that disagreeable truth—that no opening offered for *reciprocal* concession, that the concession must all be on one side— naturally it struck me that no guardian could be expected to do *that*. At the same moment it also struck me that my guardian had all along never for a moment been arguing with a view to any *practical* result, but simply in the hope that he might win over my assent to the reasonableness of what, reasonable or not, was settled immovably. These sudden discoveries, flashing upon me simultaneously, were quite sufficient to put a summary close to the correspondence. And I saw also, which strangely had escaped me till this general revelation of disappointments, that any individual guardian—even if he *had* been disposed to concession—was but one after all amongst five. Well : this amongst the general blackness really brought a gleam of comfort. If the whole object on which I had spent so much excellent paper and midnight tallow (I am ashamed to use so vile a word, and yet truth forbids me to say *oil*), if this would have been so nearly worthless when gained, then it became a kind of pleasure to have lost it. All considerations united now in urging me to waste no more of either rhetoric, tallow, or logic, upon my impassive granite block of a guardian. Indeed, I suspected, on reviewing his last communication, that he had just reached

the last inch of his patience, or (in nautical diction) had
'paid out' the entire cable by which he swung; so that,
if I, acting on the apothecary's precedent of '*repetatur
haustus*,' had endeavoured to administer another bolus or
draught of expostulation, he would have followed my
course as to the tiger-drench, in applying his potential *No*
to any such audacious attempt.   To my guardian, meantime, I owe this justice—that, over and above the absence
on my side of any arguments wearing even a colourable
strength (for to him the suffering from biliousness must
have been a mere word), he had the following weighty
consideration to offer, 'which even this foolish boy' (to
himself he would say) 'will think material some three years
ahead.'   My patrimonial income, at the moment of my
father's death, like that of all my brothers (then three),
was exactly £150 per annum.[1]   Now, according to the
current belief, or boldly, one might say, according to the
avowed traditional maxim throughout England, such an
income was too little for an under-graduate, keeping his
four terms annually at Oxford or Cambridge.   Too little
—by how much?   By £50: the adequate income being
set down at just £200.   Consequently the precise sum by
which my income was supposed (falsely supposed, as subsequently my own experience convinced me) to fall short
of the income needed for Oxford, was that very sum which
the funds of the Manchester Grammar School allocated to
every student resident for a period of three years; and
allocated not merely through a corresponding period of
three years, but of seven years.   Strong should have been
the reasons that could neutralise such overwhelming
pleadings of just and honourable prudence for submitting
to the further residence required.   O reader, urge not the
crying arguments that spoke so tumultuously against me.
Too sorrowfully I feel them.   Out of thirty-six months'

[1] '£150 *per annum*':—Why in a long minority of more than
fourteen years this was not improved, I never could learn. Nobody
was open to any suspicion of positive embezzlement: and yet this case
must be added to the other cases of passive neglects and negative
injuries which so extensively disfigure the representative picture of
guardianship all over Christendom.

residence required, I had actually completed nineteen—*i.e.* the better half. Still, on the other hand, it is true that my sufferings were almost insupportable ; and, but for the blind unconscious conspiracy of two persons, these sufferings would either (1) never have existed, or (2) would have been instantly relieved. In a great city like Manchester lay, probably, a ship-load of that same mercury which, by one fragment, not so large as an acorn, would have changed the colour of a human life, or would have intercepted the heavy funeral knell—heavy, though it may be partially muffled—of his own fierce self-reproaches.

But now, at last, came over me, from the mere excess of bodily suffering and mental disappointments, a frantic and rapturous re-agency. In the United States the case is well known, and many times has been described by travellers, of that furious instinct which, under a secret call for saline variations of diet, drives all the tribes of buffaloes for thousands of miles to the common centre of the ' Salt-licks.' Under such a compulsion does the locust, under such a compulsion does the leeming, traverse its mysterious path. They are deaf to danger, deaf to the cry of battle, deaf to the trumpets of death. Let the sea cross their path, let armies with artillery bar the road, even these terrific powers can arrest only by destroying ; and the most frightful abysses, up to the very last menace of engulfment, up to the very instant of absorption, have no power to alter or retard the line of their inexorable advance.

Such an instinct it was, such a rapturous command—even so potent, and alas ! even so blind—that, under the whirl of tumultuous indignation and of new-born hope, suddenly transfigured my whole being. In the twinkling of an eye, I came to an adamantine resolution—not as if issuing from any act or any choice of my own, but as if passively received from some dark oracular legislation external to myself. That I would elope from Manchester —this was the resolution. *Abscond* would have been the word, if I had meditated anything criminal. But whence came the indignation, and the hope ? The indignation arose naturally against my three tormentors (guardian, Archididascalus, and the professor of tigrology) for those who *do* substantially co-operate to one result, however little designing it, unavoidably the mind unifies as a hostile confederacy. But the hope—how shall I explain *that?* Was it the first-born of the resolution, or was the resolution the first-born of the hope? Indivisibly they went together, like thunder and lightning; or each interchangeably ran before and after the other. Under that transcendent rapture which the prospect of sudden liberation let loose, all that natural anxiety which should otherwise have interlinked itself with my anticipations was actually drowned in the blaze of joy, as the light of the planet Mercury is lost and confounded on sinking too far within the blaze of the solar beams. Practically I felt no care at all stretching beyond two or three weeks. Not as being heedless and improvident; my tendencies lay generally in the other direction. No; the cause lurked in what Wordsworth, when describing the festal state of France during the happy morning-tide of her First Revolution (1788-1790), calls '*the senselessness of joy*': this it was, joy—headlong—frantic—irreflective—and (as Wordsworth truly calls it), for that very reason, *sublime* [1] —which swallowed up all capacities of rankling care or heart-corroding doubt. I was, I had been long, a captive: I was in a house of bondage: one fulminating word—*Let there be freedom*—spoken from some hidden recess in my own will, had as by an earthquake rent asunder my prison gates. At any minute I could walk out. Already I trod by anticipation the sweet pastoral hills, already I breathed gales of the everlasting mountains, that to my feelings blew from the garden of Paradise; and in that vestibule of an earthly heaven it was no more possible for me to see vividly or in any lingering detail the thorny cares which might hereafter multiply around me than amongst the

---

[1] '*The senselessness of joy was then sublime.*'—Wordsworth at Calais in 1802 (see his sonnets), looking back through thirteen years to the great era of social resurrection, in 1788-89, from a sleep of ten centuries.

roses of June, and on the loveliest of June mornings, I could gather depression from the glooms of the last December.

. To go was settled. But *when* and *whither?* *When* could have but one answer ; for on more reasons than one I needed summer weather, and as much of it as possible. Besides that, when August came, it would bring along with it my own birth-day : now, one codicil in my general vow of freedom had been that my seventeenth birth-day should not find me at school. Still I needed some trifle of preparation. Especially I needed a little money. I wrote, therefore, to the only confidential friend that I had—viz., Lady Carbery. Originally, as early friends of my mother's, both she and Lord Carbery had distinguished me at Bath and elsewhere, for some years, by flattering attentions ; and, for the last three years in particular, Lady Carbery, a young woman some ten years older than myself, and who was as remarkable for her intellectual pretensions as she was for her beauty and her benevolence, had maintained a correspondence with me upon questions of literature. She thought too highly of my powers and attainments, and everywhere spoke of me with an enthusiasm that, if I had been five or six years older, and had possessed any personal advantages, might have raised smiles at her expense. To her I now wrote, requesting the loan of five guineas. A whole week passed without any answer. This perplexed and made me uneasy : for her ladyship was rich by a vast fortune removed entirely from her husband's control ; and, as I felt assured, would have cheerfully sent me twenty times the sum asked, unless her sagacity had suggested some suspicion (which seemed impossible) of the real purposes which I contemplated in the employment of the five guineas. Could I incautiously have said anything in my own letter tending that way ? Certainly not ; then why—— But at that moment my speculations were cut short by a letter bearing a coroneted seal. It was from Lady Carbery, of course, and enclosed ten guineas instead of five. Slow in those days were the mails ; besides which, Lady Carbery happened to be down at the seaside, whither my letter had been sent after her. Now, then, including my own pocket-money, I possessed a dozen guineas; which seemed sufficient for my immediate purpose; and all ulterior emergencies, as the reader understands, I trampled under foot. This sum, however, spent at inns on the most economic footing, could not have held out for much above a calendar month; and, as to the plan of selecting secondary inns, these are not always cheaper; but the main objection is that in the solitary stations amongst the mountains (Cambrian no less than Cumbrian) there is often no choice to be found : the high-priced inn is the only one. Even this dozen of guineas it became necessary to diminish by three. The age of 'vails' and perquisites to three or four servants at any gentleman's house where you dined—this age, it is true, had passed away by thirty years perhaps. But that flagrant abuse had no connexion at all with the English custom of distributing money amongst that part of the domestics whose daily labours may have been increased by a visitor's residence in the family for some considerable space of time. This custom (almost peculiar, I believe, to the English gentry) is honourable and just. I personally had been trained by my mother, who detested sordid habits, to look upon it as ignominious in a gentleman to leave a household without acknowledging the obliging services of those who cannot openly remind him of their claims. On this occasion, mere necessity compelled me to overlook the housekeeper : for to her I could not have offered less than two or three guineas; and, as she was a fixture, I reflected that I might send it at some future period. To three inferior servants I found that I ought not to give less than one guinea each : so much, therefore, I left in the hands of G——, the most honourable and upright of boys; since to have given it myself would have been prematurely to publish my purpose. These three guineas deducted, I still had nine, or thereabouts. And now all things were settled, except one : the *when* was settled, and the *how;* but not the *whither.* That was still *sub judice.*

My plan originally had been to travel northwards—

viz., to the region of the English Lakes. That little mountainous district, lying stretched like a pavilion between four well-known points—viz., the small towns of Ulverstone and Penrith as its two poles, south and north ; between Kendal, again, on the east, and Egremont on the west—measuring on the one diameter about forty miles, and on the other perhaps thirty-five—had for me a secret fascination, subtle, sweet, fantastic, and even from my seventh or eighth year spiritually strong. The southern section of that district, about eighteen or twenty miles long, which bears the name of Furness, figures in the eccentric geography of English law as a section of Lancashire, though separated from that county by the estuary of Morecambe Bay : and therefore, as Lancashire happened to be my own native county, I had from childhood, on the strength of this mere legal fiction, cherished as a mystic privilege, slender as a filament of air, some fraction of denizenship in the fairy little domain of the English Lakes. The major part of these lakes lies in Westmoreland and Cumberland : but the sweet reposing little water of Esthwaite, with its few emerald fields, and the grander one of Coniston, with the sublime cluster of mountain groups, and the little network of quiet dells lurking about its head [1] all the way back to Grasmere, lie in or near the upper chamber of Furness ; and all these, together with

---

[1] ' *Its head* ' :—That end of a lake which receives the rivulets and brooks feeding its waters is locally called its *head;* and, in continuation of the same constructive image, the counter terminus, which discharges its surplus water, is called its *foot*. By the way, as a suggestion from this obvious distinction, I may remark that in all cases the very existence of a head and foot to any sheet of water defeats the malice of Lord Byron's sneer against the Lake Poets, in calling them by the contemptuous designation of ' *pond* poets ' ; a variation which some part of the public readily caught up as a natural reverberation of that spitefulness, so petty and apparently so groundless, which notoriously Lord Byron cherished against Wordsworth steadily, and more fitfully against Southey. The effect of transforming a living image—an image of restless motion — into an image of foul stagnation was tangibly apprehensible. But was it that contradistinguished the ' *vivi lacus* ' of Virgil from rotting ponds mantled with verdant slime ? To have, or *not* to have, a head and a foot (*i.e.* a principle of perpetual change) is at the very heart of this distinction ; and to substitute for *lake* a term which

the ruins of the once glorious abbey, had been brought
out not many years before into sunny splendour by the
great enchantress of that generation—Anne Radcliffe. But
more even than Anne Radcliffe had the landscape painters,
so many and so various, contributed to the glorification of
the English lake district; drawing out and impressing
upon the heart the sanctity of repose in its shy recesses—
its alpine grandeurs in such passes as those of Wastdale-
head, Langdale-head, Borrowdale, Kirkstone, Hawsdale,
etc., together with the monastic peace which seems to
brood over its peculiar form of pastoral life, so much
nobler (as Wordsworth notices) in its stern simplicity and
continual conflict with danger hidden in the vast draperies
of mist overshadowing the hills, and amongst the armies
of snow and hail arrayed by fierce northern winters, than
the effeminate shepherd's life in the classical Arcadia, or
in the flowery pastures of Sicily.

Amongst these attractions that drew me so strongly to
the Lakes, there had also by that time arisen in this lovely
region the deep deep magnet (as to me *only* in all this
world it then was) of William Wordsworth. Inevitably
this close connexion of the poetry which most of all had
moved me with the particular region and scenery that
most of all had fastened upon my affections, and led captive
my imagination, was calculated, under ordinary circumstances, to impress upon my fluctuating deliberations a
summary and decisive bias. But the very depth of the impressions which had been made upon me, either as regarded
the poetry or the scenery, was too solemn and (unaffectedly
I may say it) too spiritual, to clothe itself in any hasty
or chance movement as at all adequately expressing its
strength, or reflecting its hallowed character. If you,
reader, were a devout Mahometan, throwing gazes of
mystical awe daily towards Mecca, or were a Christian
devotee looking with the same rapt adoration to St. Peter's
at Rome, or to El Kodah, the Holy City of Jerusalem (so
called even amongst the Arabs, who hate both Christian

ignores and negatives the very differential principle that constitutes a
lake—viz., its current and its eternal mobility—is to offer an insult in
which the insulted party has no interest or concern.

and Jew)—how painfully would it jar upon your sensibilities if some friend, sweeping past you upon a high road, with a train (according to the circumstances) of dromedaries or of wheel carriages, should suddenly pull up, and say, 'Come, old fellow, jump up alongside of me ; I'm off for the Red Sea, and here's a spare dromedary,' or 'Off for Rome, and here's a well-cushioned barouche.' Seasonable and convenient it might happen that the invitation were ; but still it would shock you that a journey which, with or without your consent, could not *but* assume the character eventually of a saintly pilgrimage, should arise and take its initial movement upon a casual summons, or upon a vulgar opening of momentary convenience. In the present case, under no circumstances should I have dreamed of presenting myself to Wordsworth. The principle of 'veneration' (to speak phrenologically) was by many degrees too strong in me for any such overture on my part. Hardly could I have found the courage to meet and to answer such an overture coming from *him*. I could not even tolerate the prospect (as a bare possibility) of Wordsworth's hearing my name first of all associated with some case of pecuniary embarrassment. And, apart from all *that*, it vulgarised the whole 'interest' (no other term can I find to express the case collectively)—the whole 'interest' of poetry and the enchanted land—equally it vulgarised person and thing, the vineyard and the vintage, the gardens and the ladies, of the Hesperides, together with all their golden fruitage, if I should rush upon them in a hurried and thoughtless state of excitement. I remembered the fine caution on this subject involved in a tradition preserved by Pausanias. Those (he tells us) who visited by night the great field of Marathon (where at certain times phantom cavalry careered, flying and pursuing) in a temper of vulgar sight-seeking, and under no higher impulse than the degrading one of curiosity, were met and punished severely in the dark, by the same sort of people, I presume, as those who handled Falstaff so roughly in the venerable shades of Windsor : whilst loyal visitors, who came bringing a true and filial sympathy with the grand deeds of their Athenian ancestors, who came as children of the same hearth, met with the most gracious acceptance, and fulfilled all the purposes of a pilgrimage or sacred mission. Under my present circumstances, I saw that the very motives of love and honour, which would have inclined the scale so powerfully in favour of the northern lakes, were exactly those which drew most heavily in the other direction—the circumstances being what they were as to hurry and perplexity. And just at that moment suddenly unveiled itself another powerful motive against taking the northern direction—viz., consideration for my mother—which made my heart recoil from giving her too great a shock; and in what other way could it be mitigated than by my personal presence in a case of emergency? For such a purpose North Wales would be the best haven to make for, since the road thither from my present home lay through Chester—where at that time my mother had fixed her residence.

If I had hesitated (and hesitate I did very sincerely) about such a mode of expressing the consideration due to my mother, it was not from any want of decision in my feeling, but really because I feared to be taunted with this act of tenderness, as arguing an exaggerated estimate of my own importance in my mother's eyes. To be capable of causing any alarming shock, must I not suppose myself an object of special interest? No: I did not agree to that inference. But no matter. Better to stand ten thousand sneers than one abiding pang, such as time could not abolish, of bitter self-reproach. So I resolved to face this taunt without flinching, and to steer a course for St. John's Priory,—my mother's residence near Chester. At the very instant of coming to this resolution, a singular accident occurred to confirm it. On the very day before my rash journey commenced, I received through the post-office a letter bearing this address in a foreign handwriting —*A Monsieur Monsieur de Quincy, Chester*. This iteration of the *Monsieur*, as a courteous French fashion[1] for

---

1 '*As a courteous French fashion*' :—And not at all a modern fashion. That famous Countess of Derby (Charlotte de Tremouille) who pre-

effecting something equivalent to our own *Esquire*, was to me at that time an unintelligible novelty. The best way to explain it was to read the letter; which, to the extent of *mon possible*, I did, but vainly attempted to decipher. So much, however, I spelled out as satisfied me that the letter could not have been meant for myself. The post-mark was, I think, *Hamburgh:* but the date within was from some place in Normandy; and eventually it came out that the person addressed was a poor emigrant, some relative of Quatremère de Quincy,[1] who had come to Chester, probably as a teacher of French, and now in 1802 found his return to France made easy by the brief and hollow peace of Amiens. Such an obscure person was naturally unknown to any English post-office; and the letter had been forwarded to myself, as the oldest male member of a family at that time necessarily well known in Chester.

I was astonished to find myself translated by a touch of the pen not only into a *Monsieur*, but even into a self-multiplied *Monsieur;* or, speaking algebraically, into the square of Monsieur; having a chance at some future day of being perhaps cubed into Monsieur. From the letter, as I had hastily torn it open, out dropped a draft upon Smith, Payne & Smith for somewhere about forty guineas. At this stage of the revelations opening upon me, it might be fancied that the interest of the case thickened: since

---

sided in the defence of Lathom House (which, and not Knowsley, was then the capital domicile of the Stanleys), when addressing Prince Rupert, sometimes superscribes her envelope *A Monseigneur le Prince Rupert*, but sometimes *A Monsieur Monsieur le Prince Rupert*. This was in 1644, the year of Marston Moor, and the penultimate year of the Parliamentary War.

[1] '*De Quincy*':—The family of De Quincey, or Quincy, or Quincie (spelt of course, like all proper names, under the anarchy prevailing as to orthography until the last one hundred and fifty years, in every possible form open to human caprice), was originally Norwegian. Early in the eleventh century this family emigrated from Norway to the South; and since then it has thrown off three separate swarms—French, English, and Anglo-American—each of which writes the name with its own slight variations. A brief outline of their migrations will be found in the Appendix.

undoubtedly, if this windfall could be seriously meant for myself, *and no mistake*, never descended upon the head of man, in the outset of a perilous adventure, aid more season-able, nay, more melodramatically critical.   But alas! my eye is quick to value the logic of evil chances.   Prophet of evil I ever am to myself : forced for ever into sorrowful auguries that I have no power to hide from my own heart, no, not through one night's solitary dreams.   In a moment I saw too plainly that I was not Monsieur. I might be *Monsieur*, but not *Monsieur to the second power.* Who indeed could be *my* debtor to the amount of forty guineas ?   If there really *was* such a person, why had he been so many years in liquidating his debt ?   How shameful to suffer me to enter upon my seventeenth year before he made known his debt, or even his amiable existence!   Doubtless, in strict morals, this dreadful pro-crastination could not be justified.   Still, as the man was apparently testifying his penitence, and in the most prac-tical form (viz., payment), I felt perfectly willing to grant him absolution for past sins, and a general release from all arrears, if any should remain, through all coming genera-tions.   But alas! the mere seasonableness of the remittance floored my hopes.   A five-guinea debtor might have been a conceivable being : such a debtor might exist in the flesh : *him* I could believe in ; but further my faith would not go ; and, if the money were, after all, *bonâ fide* meant for myself, clearly it must come from the Fiend : in which case it became an open question whether I ought to take it.   At this stage the case had become a Sphinx's riddle ; and the solution, if any, must be sought in the letter. But, as to the letter, O heaven and earth! if the Sphinx of old conducted her intercourse with Œdipus by way of letter, and propounded her wicked questions through the post-office of Thebes, it strikes me that she needed only to have used French penmanship in order to baffle that fatal decipherer of riddles for ever and ever.   At Bath, where the French emigrants mustered in great strength (six thousand, I have heard) during the three closing years of the last century, I, through my mother's acquaintance with several leading families amongst them, had gained a large experience of French caligraphy. From this experience I had learned that the French aristocracy still persisted (*did* persist at that period, 1797-1800) in a traditional contempt for all accomplishments of that class as clerkly and plebeian, fitted only (as Shakspere says, when recording similar prejudices amongst his own countrymen) to do 'yeoman's service.' One and all, they delegated the care of their spelling to *valets* and *femmes-de-chambre*; sometimes even those persons who scoured their blankets and counterpanes scoured their spelling—that is to say, their week-day spelling; but, as to their Sunday spelling, that superfine spelling which they reserved for their efforts in literature, this was consigned to the care of compositors. Letters written by the royal family of France in 1792-93 still survive, in the memoirs of Cléry and others amongst their most faithful servants, which display the utmost excess of ignorance as to grammar and orthography. Then, as to the penmanship, all seemed to write the same hand, and with the same piece of most ancient wood, or venerable skewer; all alike scratching out stiff perpendicular letters, as if executed (I should say) with a pair of snuffers. I do not speak thus in any spirit of derision. Such accomplishments were *wilfully* neglected, and even ambitiously, as if in open proclamation of scorn for the arts by which humbler people oftentimes got their bread. And a man of rank would no more conceive himself dishonoured by any deficiencies in the snobbish accomplishments of penmanship, grammar, or correct orthography, than a gentleman amongst ourselves by inexpertness in the mystery of cleaning shoes, or of polishing furniture. The result, however, from this systematic and ostentatious neglect of caligraphy is oftentimes most perplexing to all who are called upon to decipher their MSS. It happens, indeed, that the product of this carelessness thus far differs: always it is coarse and inelegant, but sometimes (say in 1-20th of the cases) it becomes specially legible. Far otherwise was the case before me. Being greatly hurried on this my farewell day, I could not make out two consecutive sentences.

Unfortunately, one-half of a sentence sufficed to show that the enclosure belonged to some needy Frenchman living in a country not his own, and struggling probably with the ordinary evils of such a condition—friendlessness and exile. Before the letter came into my hands, it had already suffered some days' delay. When I noticed this, I found my sympathy with the poor stranger naturally quickened. Already, and unavoidably, he had been suffering from the vexation of a letter delayed; but henceforth, and continually more so, he must be suffering from the anxieties of a letter gone astray. Throughout this farewell day I was unable to carve out any opportunity for going up to the Manchester Post-office; and, without a distinct explanation in my own person, exonerating myself, on the written acknowledgment of the post-office, from all farther responsibility, I was most reluctant to give up the letter. It is true that the necessity of committing a forgery (which crime in those days was punished inexorably with death) before the money could have been fraudulently appropriated would, *if made known to the public*, have acquitted any casual holder of the letter from all suspicion of dishonest intentions. But the danger was that, during the suspense and progress of the case whilst awaiting its final settlement, ugly rumours should arise and cling to one's name amongst the many that would hear only a fragmentary version of the whole affair.

At length all was ready. Midsummer, like an army with banners, was moving through the heavens; already the longest day had passed; those arrangements, few and imperfect, through which I attempted some partial evasion of disagreeable contingencies likely to arise, had been finished: what more remained for me to do of things that I was able to do? None; and yet, though now at last free to move off, I lingered; lingered as under some sense of dim perplexity, or even of relenting love for the very captivity itself which I was making so violent an effort to abjure, but more intelligibly for all the external objects, living or inanimate, by which that captivity had been surrounded and gladdened. What I was hastening to desert, nevertheless I grieved to desert; and, but for the foreign letter, I might have long continued to loiter and procrastinate. That, however, through various and urgent motives which it suggested, quickened my movements; and the same hour which brought this letter into my hands witnessed my resolution (uttered *audibly* to myself in my study) that early on the next day I would take my departure. A day, therefore, had at length arrived, had somewhat suddenly arrived, which would be the last, the very last, on which I should make my appearance in the school.

It is a just and a feeling remark of Dr. Johnson's that we never do anything consciously for the last time (of things, that is to say, which we have been long in the habit of doing) without sadness of heart. The secret sense of a farewell or testamentary act I carried along with me into every word or deed of this memorable day. Agent or patient, singly or one of a crowd, I heard for ever some sullen echo of valediction in every change, casual or periodic, that varied the revolving hours from morning to night. Most of all, I felt this valedictory sound as a pathetic appeal when the closing hour of five P.M. brought with it the solemn evening service of the English Church —read by Mr. Lawson; read now, as always, under a reverential stillness of the entire school. Already in itself, without the solemnity of prayers, the decaying light of the dying day suggests a mood of pensive and sympathetic sadness. And, if the changes in the light are less impressively made known so early as five o'clock in the depth of summer-tide, not the less we are sensible of being as near to the hours of repose, and to the secret dangers of the night, as if the season were mid-winter. Even thus far there was something that oftentimes had profoundly impressed me in this evening liturgy, and its special prayer against the perils of darkness. But greatly was that effect deepened by the symbolic treatment which this liturgy gives to this darkness and to these perils. Naturally, when contemplating that treatment, I had been led vividly to

feel the memorable *rhabdomancy*[1] or magical power of
evocation which Christianity has put forth here and in
parallel cases. The ordinary physical rhabdomantist, who
undertakes to evoke from the dark chambers of our earth
wells of water lying far below its surface, and more rarely
to evoke minerals, or hidden deposits of jewels and gold,
by some magnetic sympathy between his rod and the
occult object of his divination, is able to indicate the spot
at which this object can be hopefully sought for. Not
otherwise has the marvellous magnetism of Christianity
called up from darkness sentiments the most august,
previously inconceivable, formless, and without life; for
previously there had been no religious philosophy equal to

[1] ' *Rhabdomancy* ':—The Greek word *manteia* (μαντεία), represented
by the English form *mancy*, constitutes the stationary element in a large
family of compounds : it means *divination*, or the art of magically de-
ducing some weighty inference (generally prophetic) from any one of the
many dark sources sanctioned by Pagan superstition. And universally
the particular source relied on is expressed in the prior half of the
compound. For instance, *oneiros* is the Greek word for a dream ; and
therefore *oneiromancy* indicates that mode of prophecy which is founded
upon the interpretation of dreams. *Ornis*, again (in the genitive case
ornithos), is the common Greek word for a bird; accordingly, *ornitho-
mancy* means prophecy founded on the particular mode of flight noticed
amongst any casual gathering of birds. *Cheir* (χείρ) is Greek for the
hand ; whence *cheiromancy* expresses the art of predicting a man's
fortune by the lines in his hand, or (under its Latin form from *palma*)
palmistry : *Nekros*, a dead man, and consequently *necromancy*, prophecy
founded on the answer extorted either from phantoms, as by the Witch
of Endor, or from the corpse itself, as by Lucan's witch Erichtho. I
have allowed myself to wander into this ample illustration of the case,
having for many years been taxed by ingenuous readers (confessing their
own classical ignorance) with too scanty explanations of my meaning.
I go on to say that the Greek word *rhabdos* (ῥάβδος), a rod—not that
sort of rod which the Roman lictors carried, viz., a bundle of twigs, but
a wand about as thick as a common cedar pencil, or at most, as the
ordinary brass rod of stair-carpets—this, when made from a willow-tree,
furnished of old, and furnishes to this day in a southern county of
England, a potent instrument of divination. But let it be understood
that *divination* expresses an idea ampler by much than the word *prophecy :*
whilst even this word *prophecy*, already more limited than divination,
is most injuriously narrowed in our received translation of the Bible.
To unveil or decipher what is hidden—that is, in effect, the meaning
of divination. And, accordingly, in the writings of St. Paul the phrase

the task of ripening such sentiments; but also, at the same time, by incarnating these sentiments in images of corresponding grandeur, it has so exalted their character as to lodge them eternally in human hearts.

Flowers, for example, that are so pathetic in their beauty, frail as the clouds, and in their colouring as gorgeous as the heavens, had through thousands of years been the heritage of children—honoured as the jewellery of God only by *them*—when suddenly the voice of Christianity, countersigning the voice of infancy, raised them to a grandeur transcending the Hebrew throne, although founded by God himself, and pronounced Solomon in all his glory not to be arrayed like one of these.

gifts of prophecy never once indicates what the English reader supposes, but *exegetic* gifts, gifts of interpretation applied to what is dark, of analysis applied to what is logically perplexed, of expansion applied to what is condensed, of practical improvement applied to what might else be overlooked as purely speculative. In Somersetshire, which is a county the most ill-watered of all in England, upon building a house, there arises uniformly a difficulty in selecting a proper spot for sinking a well. The remedy is to call in a set of local rhabdomantists. These men traverse the adjacent ground, holding the willow rod horizontally: wherever that dips, or inclines itself spontaneously to the ground, *there* will be found water. I have myself not only seen the process tried with success, but have witnessed the enormous trouble, delay, and expense, accruing to those of the opposite faction who refused to benefit by this art. To pursue the tentative plan (*i.e.* the plan of trying for water by boring at haphazard) ended, so far as I was aware, in multiplied vexation. In reality, these poor men are, after all, more philosophic than those who scornfully reject their services. For the artists obey unconsciously the logic of Lord Bacon: *they* build upon a long chain of induction, upon the uniform results of their life-long experience. But the counter faction do not deny this experience: all they have to allege is that agreeably to any laws known to themselves *a priori*, there ought not to be any such experience. Now, a sufficient course of facts overthrows all antecedent plausibilities. Whatever science or scepticism may say, most of the tea-kettles in the vale of Wrington are filled by *rhabdomancy*. And, after all, the supposed *a priori* scruples against this rhabdomancy are only such scruples as would, antecedently to a trial, have pronounced the mariner's compass impossible. There is in both cases alike a blind sympathy of some unknown force, which no man can explain, with a passive index that practically guides you aright—even if Mephistopheles should be at the bottom of the affair.

Winds again, hurricanes, the eternal breathings, soft or loud, of Æolian power, wherefore had they, raving or sleeping, escaped all moral arrest and detention? Simply because vain it were to offer a nest for the reception of some new moral birth whilst no religion is yet moving amongst men that can furnish such a birth. Vain is the image that should illustrate a heavenly sentiment, if the sentiment is yet unborn. Then, first, when it had become necessary to the purposes of a spiritual religion that the spirit of man, as the fountain of all religion, should in some commensurate reflex image have its grandeur and its mysteriousness emblazoned, suddenly the pomp and mysterious path of winds and tempests, blowing whither they list, and from what fountains no man knows, are cited from darkness and neglect, to give and to receive reciprocally an impassioned glorification, where the lower mystery enshrines and illustrates the higher. Call for the grandest of all earthly spectacles, what is *that*? It is the sun going to his rest. Call for the grandest of all human sentiments, what is *that*? It is that man should forget his anger before he lies down to sleep. And these two grandeurs, the mighty sentiment and the mighty spectacle, are by Christianity married together.

Here again, in his prayer 'Lighten our darkness, we beseech thee, O Lord!' were the darkness and the great shadows of night made symbolically significant: these great powers, Night and Darkness, that belong to aboriginal Chaos, were made representative of the perils that continually menace poor afflicted human nature. With deepest sympathy I accompanied the prayer against the perils of darkness—perils that I seemed to see, in the ambush of midnight solitude, brooding around the beds of sleeping nations; perils from even worse forms of darkness shrouded within the recesses of blind human hearts; perils from temptations weaving unseen snares for our footing; perils from the limitations of our own misleading knowledge.

Prayers had finished. The school had dissolved itself. Six o'clock came, seven, eight. By three hours nearer stood the dying day to its departure. By three hours nearer, therefore, stood we to that darkness which our English liturgy calls into such symbolic grandeur, as hiding beneath its shadowy mantle all perils that besiege our human infirmity. But in summer, in the immediate suburbs of mid-summer, the vast scale of the heavenly movements is read in their slowness. Time becomes the expounder of Space. And now, though eight o'clock has struck, the sun was still lingering above the horizon: the light, broad and gaudy, having still two hours of travel to face before it would assume that tender fading hue pre-lusive to the twilight.[1] Now came the last official cere-mony of the day : the students were all mustered ; and the names of all were challenged according to the order of precedency. My name, as usual, came first.[2] Stepping

[1] ‘ *To the twilight*’:—*i.e.* to the second twilight : for I remember to have read in some German work upon Hebrew antiquities, and also in a great English divine of 1630 (namely, Isaac Ambrose), that the Jews in elder times made two twilights, first and second ; the first they called the dove's twilight, or crepusculum of the day ; the second they called the raven's twilight, or crepusculum of the night.

[2] ‘ *First*’:—Within the school I should *not* have been first: for in the trinity which composed the head class there was no absolute or meritorious precedency, but simply a precedency of chance. Our dignity, as leaders of the school, raised us above all petty competitions ; yet, as it was unavoidable to stand in some order, this was regulated by seniority. I, therefore, as junior amongst the three, was *tertius inter pares*. But my two seniors happened to be day-scholars : so that, in Mr. Lawson's house, I rose into the supreme place. *There*, I was *princeps senatûs*. Such trivial circumstantialities I notice, as checks upon all openings to inaccuracy, great or small. It would vitiate the interest which any reader might otherwise take in this narrative, if for one moment it were supposed that any feature of the case were var-nished or distorted. From the very first, I had been faithful to the most rigorous law of accuracy—even in absolute trifles. But I became even more jealous over myself, after an Irish critic, specially brilliant as a wit and as a scholar, but also specially malicious, had attempted to impeach the accuracy of my narrative, in its London section, upon alleged internal grounds.

I wish it could have been said with truth, that we of the leading form were, not a triad, but a duad. The facts, however, of the case will not allow me to say this. Facts, as people generally remark, are stubborn things. Yes, and too often very spiteful things; as in this case, where, if it were not for *them*, I might describe myself as having

forward, I passed Mr. Lawson, and bowed to him, looking
earnestly in his face, and saying to myself, 'He is old and
infirm, and in this world I shall not see him again.'   I
was right; I never *did* see him again, nor ever shall.   He
looked at me complacently; smiled placidly; returned my
salutation (not knowing it to be my valediction); and we
parted for ever.   Intellectually, I might not have seen
cause to reverence him in any emphatic sense.   But very
sincerely I respected him as a conscientious man, faithful
to his duties, and as, even in his latter ineffectual struggle
with these duties, inflicting more suffering upon himself
than upon others; finally, I respected him as a sound and
accurate (though not brilliant) scholar.   Personally I
owed him much gratitude; for he had been uniformly
kind to me, and had allowed me such indulgences as lay
in his power; and I grieved at the thought of the mortification I should inflict upon him.

The morning came which was to launch me into the
world ; that morning from which, and from its consequences, my whole succeeding life has, in many important
points, taken its colouring.   At half after three I rose, and
gazed with deep emotion at the ancient collegiate church,
'dressed in earliest light,' and beginning to crimson with
the deep lustre of a cloudless July morning.   I was firm and
immovable in my purpose, but yet agitated by anticipation
of uncertain danger and troubles.   To this agitation the
deep peace of the morning presented an affecting contrast,
and in some degree a medicine.   The silence was more
profound than that of midnight : and to me the silence of
a summer morning is more touching than all other silence,
because, the light being broad and strong as that of noon-
day at other seasons of the year, it seems to differ from
perfect day chiefly because man is not yet abroad, and
thus the peace of nature, and of the innocent creatures of
God, seems to be secure and deep only so long as the

one sole assessor in the class, and in that case he and I might have been
likened to Castor and Pollux, who went up and down like alternate
buckets—one rising with the dawn (or Phosphorus), and the other
(viz., myself) rising with Hesperus, and reigning all night long.

presence of man, and his unquiet spirit, are not there to trouble its sanctity. I dressed myself, took my hat and gloves, and lingered a little in the room. For nearly a year and a half this room had been my 'pensive citadel': here I had read and studied through all the hours of night; and, though true it was that, for the latter part of this time, I had lost my gaiety and peace of mind during the strife and fever of contention with my guardian, yet, on the other hand, as a boy passionately fond of books, and dedicated to intellectual pursuits, I could not fail to have enjoyed many happy hours in the midst of general dejection.

Happy hours? Yes; and was it certain that ever again I should enjoy hours *as* happy? At this point it is not impossible that, left to my own final impressions, I might have receded from my plan. But it seemed to me, as too often happens in such cases, that no retreat was now open. The confidence which unavoidably I had reposed in a groom of Mr. Lawson's made it dangerous. The effect of this distracted view was, not to alter my plan, but to throw despondency for one sad half hour over the whole prospect before me. In that condition, with my eyes open, I dreamed. Suddenly a sort of trance, a frost as of some death-like revelation, wrapped round me; and I found renewed within me a hateful remembrance derived from a moment that I had long left behind. Two years before, when I wanted about as much of my fifteenth birthday as now of my seventeenth, I happened to be in London for part of a single day, with a friend of my own age. Naturally, amongst some eight or ten great spectacles which challenged our earnest attention, St. Paul's Cathedral had been one. This we had visited, and consequently the Whispering Gallery.[1] More than by all beside I had been impressed by this:

[1] To those who have never visited the Whispering Gallery, nor have read any account of it amongst other acoustic phenomena described in scientific treatises, it may be proper to mention, as the distinguishing feature of the case, that a word or a question, uttered at one end of the gallery in the gentlest of whispers, is reverberated at the other end in peals of thunder.

and some half-hour later, as we were standing beneath the
dome, and I should imagine pretty nearly on the very
spot where rather more than five years subsequently Lord
Nelson was buried,—a spot from which we saw, pompously
floating to and fro in the upper spaces of a great aisle
running westwards from ourselves, many flags captured
from France, Spain, and Holland,—I, having my previous
impressions of awe deepened by these solemn trophies of
chance and change amongst mighty nations, had suddenly
been surprised by a dream, as profound as at present, in
which a thought that often had persecuted me figured
triumphantly. This thought turned upon the fatality
that must often attend an evil choice. As an oracle of
fear I remembered that great Roman warning, *Nescit vox
missa reverti* (that a word once uttered is irrevocable),
a freezing arrest upon the motions of hope too sanguine
that haunted me in many shapes. Long before that
fifteenth year of mine, I had noticed, as a worm lying at
the heart of life and fretting its security, the fact that
innumerable acts of choice change countenance and are
variously appraised at varying stages of life—shift with
the shifting hours. Already, at fifteen, I had become
deeply ashamed of judgments which I had once pronounced, of idle hopes that I had once encouraged,
false admirations or contempts with which once I had
sympathised. And, as to acts which I surveyed with any
doubts at all, I never felt sure that after some succession
of years I might not feel withering doubts about them,
both as to principle and as to inevitable results.

This sentiment of nervous recoil from any word or
deed that could not be recalled had been suddenly re-
awakened on that London morning by the impressive
experience of the Whispering Gallery. At the earlier end
of the gallery had stood my friend, breathing in the softest
of whispers a solemn but not acceptable truth. At the
further end, after running along the walls of the gallery,
that solemn truth reached me as a deafening menace in
tempestuous uproars. And now in these last lingering
moments, when I dreamed ominously with open eyes in

my Manchester study, once again that London menace broke angrily upon me as out of a thick cloud with redoubled strength ; a voice, too late for warning, seemed audibly to say, 'Once leave this house, and a Rubicon is placed between thee and all possibility of return. Thou wilt not say that what thou doest is altogether approved in thy secret heart. Even now thy conscience speaks against it in sullen whispers ; but at the other end of thy long life-gallery that same conscience will speak to thee in volleying thunders.'

A sudden step upon the stairs broke up my dream, and recalled me to myself. Dangerous hours were now drawing near, and I prepared for a hasty farewell.

I shed tears as I looked round on the chair, hearth, writing-table, and other familiar objects, knowing too certainly that I looked upon them for the last time. Whilst I write this, it is nineteen[1] years ago ; and yet, at this moment, I see, as if it were but yesterday, the lineaments and expressions of the object on which I fixed my parting gaze. It was the picture of a lovely lady, which hung over the mantelpiece ; the eyes and mouth of which were so beautiful, and the whole countenance so radiant with divine tranquillity, that I had a thousand times laid down my pen, or my book, to gather consolation from it, as a devotee from his patron saint.[2]

[1] Written in the August of 1821.

[2] The housekeeper was in the habit of telling me that the lady had *lived* (meaning, perhaps, had been *born*) two centuries ago ; that date would better agree with the tradition that the portrait was a copy from Vandyke. All that she knew further about the lady was that either to the grammar school, or to that particular college at Oxford with which the school was connected, or else to that particular college at Oxford with which Mr. Lawson personally was connected, or else, fourthly, to Mr. Lawson himself as a private individual, the unknown lady has been a special benefactress. She was also a special benefactress to me, through eighteen months, by means of her sweet Madonna countenance. And in some degree it serves to spiritualise and to hallow this service that of her who unconsciously rendered it I know neither the name, nor the exact rank or age, nor the place where she lived and died. She was parted from me by perhaps two centuries ; I from her by the gulf of eternity.

G

Whilst I was yet gazing upon it, the deep tones of the old church clock proclaimed that it was six o'clock. I went up to the picture, kissed it, then gently walked out, and closed the door for ever.

.   .   .   .   .

So blended and intertwisted in this life are occasions of laughter and of tears that I cannot yet recall without smiling an incident which occurred at that time, and which had nearly put a stop to the immediate execution of my plan. I had a trunk of immense weight; for, besides my clothes, it contained nearly all my library. The difficulty was to get this removed to a carrier's, my room being at an aerial elevation in the house; and (what was worse) the staircase which communicated with this angle of the building was accessible only by a gallery, which passed the head-master's chamber-door. I was a favourite with all the servants; and, knowing that any of them would screen me, and act confidentially, I communicated my embarrassment to a groom of the head-master's. The groom declared his readiness to do anything I wished; and, when the time arrived, went upstairs to bring the trunk down. This I feared was beyond the strength of any one man: however, the groom was a man 'of Atlantean shoulders' and had a back as spacious as Salisbury Plain. Accordingly he persisted in bringing down the trunk alone, whilst I stood waiting at the foot of the last flight, in great anxiety for the event. For some time I heard him descending with steps slow and steady; but, unfortunately, from his trepidation, as he drew near the dangerous quarter, within a few steps of the gallery, his foot slipped; and the mighty burden, falling from his shoulders, gained such increase of impetus at each step of the descent, that on reaching the bottom, it trundled, or rather leaped, right across, with the noise of twenty devils, against the very bedroom-door of the Archididascalus. My first thought suggested that all was lost, and that my sole chance for effecting a retreat was to sacrifice my baggage. However, on reflection, I determined to abide the issue. The groom, meantime, was in the utmost alarm, both on his own account and mine : but, in spite of this, so irresistibly had the sense of the ludicrous, in this unhappy *contretemps*, taken possession of his fancy that he sang out a long, loud, and canorous peal of laughter, that might have wakened the 'Seven Sleepers.' At the sound of this resonant merriment, within the very ears of insulted authority, I could not forbear joining in it ; subdued to this, not so much by the comic wilfulness of the trunk, trundling down from step to step with accelerated pace and multiplying uproar, like the λᾶας ἀναιδής[1] (the contumacious stone) of Sisyphus, as by the effect it had upon the groom. We both expected, as a matter of course, that Mr. Lawson would sally out of his room ; for, in general, if but a mouse stirred, he sprang out like a mastiff from his kennel. Strange to say, however, on this occasion, when the noise of laughter had subsided, no sound, or rustling even, was to be heard in the bedroom. Mr. Lawson had a painful complaint, which, oftentimes keeping him awake, made his sleep, when it *did* come, peculiarly deep. Gathering courage from the silence, the groom hoisted his burden again, and accomplished the remainder of his descent without accident. I waited until I saw the trunk placed on a wheelbarrow, and on its road to the carrier's : then, 'with Providence my guide,' or more truly it might be said, with my own headstrong folly for law and impulse, I set off on foot ; carrying a small parcel with some articles of dress under my arm, a favourite English poet in one pocket, and an old volume, containing about one-half of Canter's *Euripides*, in the other.

On leaving Manchester, by a south-western route, towards Chester and Wales, the first town that I reached (to the best of my remembrance) was Altrincham— colloquially called *Awtrigem*. When a child of three years old, and suffering from the hooping-cough, I had been carried for change of air to different places on the Lancashire coast ; and in order to benefit by as large a

---

[1] 'Αὖτις ἔπειτα πεδόνδε κυλίνδετο λᾶας ἀναιδής.'—Hom. *Odyss.*

compass as possible of varying atmospheres, I and my
nurse had been made to rest for the first night of our
tour at this cheerful little town of Altrincham.   On the
next morning, which ushered in a most dazzling day of
July, I rose earlier than my nurse fully approved : but in
no long time she found it advisable to follow my example ;
and after putting me through my morning's drill of
ablutions and the Lord's-prayer, no sooner had she fully
arranged my petticoats than she lifted me up in her arms,
threw open the window, and let me suddenly look down
upon the gayest scene I had ever beheld—viz., the little
market-place of Altrincham at eight o'clock in the
morning.   It happened to be the market-day ; and I, who
till then had never consciously been in any town whatever,
was equally astonished and delighted with the novel gaiety
of the scene.   Fruits, such as can be had in July, and
flowers were scattered about in profusion : even the stalls
of the butchers, from their brilliant cleanliness, appeared
attractive : and the bonny young women of Altrincham
were all tripping about in caps and aprons coquettishly
disposed.   The general hilarity of the scene at this early
hour, with the low murmurings of pleasurable conversation
and laughter, that rose up like a fountain to the open
window, left so profound an impression upon me that I
never lost it.   All this occurred, as I have said, about
eight o'clock on a superb July morning.   Exactly at that
time of the morning, on exactly such another heavenly
day of July, did I, leaving Manchester at six A.M.,
naturally enough find myself in the centre of the
Altrincham market-place.   Nothing had altered.   There
were the very same fruits and flowers ; the same bonny
young women tripping up and down in the same (no, *not*
the same) coquettish bonnets ; everything was apparently
the same : perhaps the window of my bedroom was still
open, only my nurse and I were not looking out ; for
alas ! on recollection, fourteen years precisely had passed
since then.   Breakfast-time, however, is always a cheerful
stage of the day ; if a man can forget his cares at any
season, it is then ; and after a walk of seven miles it is

doubly so. I felt it at the time, and have stopped, therefore, to notice it, as a singular coincidence, that twice, and by the merest accident, I should find myself, precisely as the clocks on a July morning were all striking eight, drawing inspiration of pleasurable feelings from the genial sights and sounds in the little market-place of Altrincham. There I breakfasted; and already by the two hours' exercise I felt myself half restored to health. After an hour's rest, I started again upon my journey: all my gloom and despondency were already retiring to the rear; and, as I left Altrincham, I said to myself, 'All places, it seems, are not Whispering Galleries.'

The distance between Manchester and Chester *was* about forty miles. What it *is* under railway changes I know not. This I planned to walk in two days: for, though the whole might have been performed in one, I saw no use in exhausting myself; and my walking powers were rusty from long disuse. I wished to bisect the journey; and, as nearly as I could expect—*i.e.* within two or three miles—such a bisection was attained in a clean roadside inn, of the class so commonly found in England. A kind, motherly landlady, easy in her circumstances, having no motive for rapacity, and looking for her livelihood much less to her inn than to her farm, guaranteed to me a safe and profound night's rest. On the following morning there remained not quite eighteen miles between myself and venerable Chester. Before I reached it, so mighty now (as ever before and since) had become the benefit from the air and the exercise that oftentimes I felt inebriated and crazy with ebullient spirits. But for the accursed letter, which sometimes

> Came over me,
> As doth the raven o'er the infected house,

I should have too much forgot my gravity under this newborn health. For two hours before reaching Chester, from the accident of the south-west course which the road itself pursued, I saw held up aloft before my eyes that matchless spectacle,

> New, and yet as old
> As the foundations of the heavens and earth,

an elaborate and pompous sunset hanging over the
mountains of North Wales. The clouds passed slowly
through several arrangements, and in the last of these I
read the very scene which six months before I had read
in a most exquisite poem of Wordsworth's, extracted
entire into a London newspaper (I think the *St. James's
Chronicle*). It was a Canadian lake,

> With all its fairy crowds
> Of islands that together lie
> As quietly as spots of sky
> Amongst the evening clouds.

The scene in the poem ('Ruth'), that had been originally
mimicked by the poet from the sky, was here re-mimicked
and rehearsed to the life, as it seemed, by the sky from
the poet. Was I then, in July 1802, really quoting from
Wordsworth? Yes, reader; and I only in all Europe. In
1799 I had become acquainted with 'We are Seven' at Bath.
In the winter of 1801-2 I had read the whole of 'Ruth';
early in 1803 I had written to Wordsworth. In May 1803
I had received a very long answer from Wordsworth.

The next morning after reaching Chester, my first
thought on rising was directed to the vexatious letter in
my custody. The odious responsibility, thrust upon me
in connexion with this letter, was now becoming every
hour more irritating, because every hour more embarrassing to the freedom of my own movements, since it must
by this time have drawn the post-office into the ranks of
my pursuers. Indignant I was that this letter should
have the power of making myself an accomplice in causing anxiety, perhaps even calamity, to the poor emigrant
—a man doubly liable to unjust suspicion; first, as by
his profession presumably poor, and, secondly, as an alien.
Indignant I was that this most filthy of letters should also
have the power of forcing me into all sorts of indirect
and cowardly movements at inns; for beyond all things it
seemed to me important that I should not be arrested, or

even for a moment challenged, as the wrongful holder of
an important letter, before I had testified, by my own
spontaneous transfer of it, that I had not dallied with any
idea of converting it to my own benefit. In some way I
must contrive to restore the letter. But was it not then the
simplest of all courses to take my hat before sitting down
to breakfast, present myself at the post-office, tender my
explanation, and then (like Christian in Bunyan's allegory)
to lay down my soul-wearying burden at the feet of those
who could sign my certificate of absolution ? Was not
that simple ? Was not *that* easy ? Oh yes, beyond a
doubt. And, if a favourite fawn should be carried off by
a lion, would it not be a very simple and easy course to
walk after the robber, follow him into his den, and reason
with the wretch on the indelicacy of his conduct ? In my
particular circumstances, the post-office was in relation to
myself simply a lion's den. Two separate parties, I felt
satisfied, must by this time be in chase of me ; and the
two chasers would be confluent at the post-office. Beyond
all other objects which I had to keep in view, paramount
was that of fencing against my own re-capture. Anxious
I was on behalf of the poor foreigner ; but it did not
strike me that to this anxiety I was bound to sacrifice
myself. Now, if I went to the post-office, I felt sure that
nothing else would be the result ; and afterwards it turned
out that in this anticipation I had been right. For it
struck me that the nature of the enclosure in the French
letter—viz., the fact that without a forgery it was not
negotiable—could not be known certainly to anybody but
myself. Doubts upon that point must have quickened
the anxieties of all connected with myself, or connected
with the case. More urgent consequently would have
been the applications of 'Monsieur Monsieur' to the
post-office ; and consequently of the post-office to the
Priory ; and consequently more easily suggested and
concerted between the post-office and the Priory would
be all the arrangements for stopping me, in the event of
my taking the route of Chester—in which case it was
natural to suppose that I might *personally* return the

letter to the official authorities. Of course, none of these
measures was certainly known to myself; but I guessed
at them as reasonable probabilities; and it was evident
that the fifty and odd hours since my elopement from
Manchester had allowed ample time for concerting all the
requisite preparations. As a last resource, in default of
any better occurring, it is likely enough that my anxiety
would have tempted me into this mode of surrendering
my abominable trust, which by this time I regarded with
such eyes of burning malice as Sinbad must have directed
at intervals towards the venerable ruffian that sat astride
upon his shoulders. But things had not yet come to
Sinbad's state of desperation; so, immediately after breakfast, I took my hat, determining to review the case and
adopt some final decision in the open air. For I have
always found it easier to think over a matter of perplexity
whilst walking in wide open spaces, under the broad eye
of the natural heavens, than whilst shut up in a room.
But at the very door of the inn I was suddenly brought
to a pause by the recollection that some of the servants
from the Priory were sure on every forenoon to be at
times in the streets. The streets, however, could be
evaded by shaping a course along the city walls; which
I did, and descended into some obscure lane that brought
me gradually to the banks of the river Dee. In the infancy of its course amongst the Denbighshire mountains,
this river (famous in our pre-Norman history for the
earliest parade[1] of English monarchy) is wild and picturesque; and even below my mother's Priory it wears a
character of interest. But, a mile or so nearer to its
mouth, when leaving Chester for Parkgate, it becomes
miserably tame; and the several reaches of the river
take the appearance of formal canals. On the right
bank[2] of the river runs an artificial mound, called the

[1] '*Earliest Parade*':—It was a very scenical parade, for somewhere
along this reach of the Dee—viz. immediately below St. John's Priory—
Edgar, the first sovereign of all England, was rowed by nine vassal *reguli*.

[2] '*Right bank*':—But which bank *is* right, and which left, under
circumstances of position varying by possibility without end? This is
a reasonable demur; but yet it argues an inexperienced reader. For

Cop. It was, I believe, originally a Danish work; and certainly its name is Danish (*i.e.* Icelandic, or old Danish), and the same from which is derived our architectural word *coping*. Upon this bank I was walking, and throwing my gaze along the formal vista presented by the river. Some trifle of anxiety might mingle with this gaze at the first, lest perhaps Philistines might be abroad; for it was just possible that I had been watched. But I have generally found that, if you are in quest of some certain escape from Philistines of whatsoever class — sheriff - officers, bores, no matter what—the surest refuge is to be found amongst hedgerows and fields, amongst cows and sheep: in fact, cows are amongst the gentlest of breathing creatures; none show more passionate tenderness to their young when deprived of them; and, in short, I am not ashamed to profess a deep love for these quiet creatures. On the present occasion there were many cows grazing in the fields below the Cop: but all along the Cop itself I could descry no person whatever answering to the idea of a Philistine: in fact, there was nobody at all, except one woman, apparently middle-aged (meaning by *that* from thirty-five to forty-five), neatly dressed, though perhaps in rustic fashion, and by no possibility belonging to any class of my enemies; for already I was near enough to see so much. This woman might be a quarter of a mile distant, and was steadily advancing towards me — face to face. Soon, therefore, I was beginning to read the character of her features pretty distinctly; and her countenance naturally served as a mirror to echo and reverberate my own feelings, consequently my own horror (horror without

always the position of the spectator is conventionally fixed. In military tactics, in philosophic geography, in history, etc., the uniform assumption is that you are standing with your back to the source of the river, and your eyes travelling along with its current. That bank of the river which under these circumstances lies upon your right is the right bank *absolutely*, and not *relatively* only (as would be the case if a room, and not a river, were concerned). Hence it follows that the Middlesex side of the Thames is always the left bank, and the Surrey side always the right bank, no matter whether you are moving from London to Oxford, or reversely from Oxford to London.

exaggeration it was), at a sudden uproar of tumultuous sounds rising clamorously ahead. *Ahead* I mean in relation to myself, but to *her* the sound was from the rear. Our situation was briefly this. Nearly half-a-mile behind the station of the woman, that reach of the river along which we two were moving came to an abrupt close; so that the next reach, making nearly a right-angled turn, lay entirely out of view. From this unseen reach it was that the angry clamour, so passionate and so mysterious, arose: and I, for *my* part, having never heard such a fierce battling outcry, nor even heard *of* such a cry, either in books or on the stage, in prose or verse, could not so much as whisper a guess to myself upon its probable cause. Only this I felt, that blind, unorganised nature it must be—and nothing in human or in brutal wrath—that could utter itself by such an anarchy of sea-like uproars. What was it? Where was it? Whence was it? Earthquake was it? convulsion of the steadfast earth? or was it the breaking loose from ancient chains of some deep morass like that of Solway? More probable it seemed that the ἄνω ποτάμων of Euripides (the flowing backwards of rivers to their fountains) now, at last, after ages of expectation, had been suddenly realised. Not long I needed to speculate; for within half a minute, perhaps, from the first arrest of our attention, the proximate cause of this mystery declared itself to our eyes, although the remote cause (the hidden cause of that visible cause) was still as dark as before. Round that right-angled turn which I have mentioned as wheeling into the next succeeding reach of the river, suddenly as with the trampling of cavalry—but all dressing accurately —and the water at the outer angle sweeping so much faster than that at the inner angle, as to keep the front of advance rigorously in line, violently careered round into our own placid watery vista a huge charging block of waters, filling the whole channel of the river, and coming down upon us at the rate of forty miles an hour. Well was it for us, myself and that respectable rustic woman, us the Deucalion and Pyrrha of this perilous moment, sole survivors apparently of the deluge (since by accident there was at that particular moment on that particular Cop nothing else to survive), that by means of this Cop, and of ancient Danish hands (possibly not yet paid for their work), we *could* survive. In fact, this watery breastwork, a perpendicular wall of water carrying itself as true as if controlled by a mason's plumb-line, rode forward at such a pace, that obviously the fleetest horse or dromedary would have had no chance of escape. Many a decent railway even, among railways since born its rivals, would not have had above the third of a chance. Naturally, I had too short a time for observing much or accurately ; and universally I am a poor hand at observing ; else I should say, that this riding block of crystal waters did not gallop, but went at a long trot ; yes, long trot—that most frightful of paces in a tiger, in a buffalo, or in a rebellion of waters. Even a ghost, I feel convinced, would appal me more if coming up at a long diabolical trot, than at a canter or gallop. The first impulse to both of us was derived from cowardice ; cowardice the most abject and selfish. Such is man, though a Deucalion elect ; such is woman, though a decent Pyrrha. Both of us ran like hares ; neither did I, Deucalion, think of poor Pyrrha at all for the first sixty seconds. Yet, on the other hand, why *should* I ? It struck me seriously that St. George's Channel (and, if so, beyond a doubt, the Atlantic Ocean) had broke loose, and was, doubtless, playing the same insufferable gambols upon all rivers along a seaboard of six to seven thousand miles ; in which case, as all the race of woman must be doomed, how romantic a speculation it was for me, sole relic of literature, to think specially of one poor Pyrrha, probably very illiterate, whom I had never yet spoken to. That idea pulled me up. *Not spoken to her?* Then I *would* speak to her ; and the more so, because the sound of the pursuing river told me that flight was useless. And, besides, if any reporter or sub-editor of some Chester chronicle should, at this moment, with his glass be sweeping the Cop, and discover me flying under these

unchivalrous circumstances, he might gibbet me to all
eternity. Halting, therefore (and really I had not run
above eighty or a hundred steps), I waited for my
solitary co-tenant of the Cop. She was a little blown
by running, and could not easily speak ; besides which,
at the very moment of her coming up, the preternatural
column of waters, running in the very opposite direction
to the natural current of the river, came up with us, ran
by with the ferocious uproar of a hurricane, sent up the
sides of the Cop a salute of waters, as if hypocritically
pretending to kiss our feet, but secretly understood by all
parties as a vain treachery for pulling us down into the
flying deluge ; whilst all along both banks the mighty
refluent wash was heard as it rode along, leaving
memorials, by sight and by sound, of its victorious
power. But my female associate in this terrific drama,
what said she, on coming up with me ? Or what said
I ? For, by accident, I it was that spoke first ; notwithstanding the fact, notorious and undeniable, that *I had
never been introduced to her*. Here, however, be it
understood, as a case now solemnly adjudicated and set
at rest, that, in the midst of any great natural convulsion
—earthquake, suppose, waterspout, tornado, or eruption
of Vesuvius—it shall and may be lawful in all time
coming (any usage or tradition to the contrary notwithstanding), for two English people to communicate
with each other, although, by affidavit made before two
justices of the peace, it shall have been proved that no
previous introduction had been possible ; in all other
cases the old statute of non-intercourse holds good.
Meantime, the present case, in default of more circumstantial evidence, might be regarded, if not as an earthquake, yet as ranking amongst the first-fruits or blossoms
of an earthquake. So I spoke without scruple. All
my freezing English reserve gave way under this boiling
sense of having been so recently running for life : and
then, again, suppose the water column should come back
—riding *along with* the current, and no longer riding
against it—in that case, we and all the County Palatine

might soon have to run for our lives. Under such threatenings of common peril, surely the παρρησία, or unlimited license of speech, ought spontaneously to proclaim itself without waiting for sanction.

So I asked her the meaning of this horrible tumult in the waters : how did she read the mystery ? Her answer was, that though she had never before seen such a thing, yet from her grandmother she had often heard of it ; and, if she had run before it, *that* was because *I* ran ; and a little, perhaps, because the noise frightened her. What was it, then ? I asked. ' It was,' she said, ' the *Bore ;* and it was an affection to which only some few rivers here and there were liable ; and the Dee was one of these.' So ignorant was I, that, until that moment, I had never heard of such a nervous affection in rivers. Subsequently I found that, amongst English rivers, the neighbouring river Severn, a far more important stream, suffered at spring-tides the same kind of hysterics, and, perhaps, some few other rivers in this British Island ; but amongst Indian rivers, only the Ganges.

At last, when the *Bore* had been discussed to the full extent of our united ignorance, I went off to the subject of that other curse, far more afflicting than any conceivable bore—viz., the foreign letter in my pocket. The *Bore* had certainly alarmed us for ninety or a hundred seconds, but the letter would poison my very existence, like the bottle-imp, until I could transfer it to some person truly qualified to receive it. Might not my fair friend on the Cop be marked out by Fate as ' the coming woman ' born to deliver me from this pocket curse ? It is true that she displayed a rustic simplicity somewhat resembling that of Audrey in *As you like it.* *Her*, in fact, not at all more than Audrey, had the gods been pleased to make ' poetical.' But, for my particular mission, *that* might be amongst her best qualifications. At any rate, I was wearied in spirit under my load of responsibility : personally to liberate myself by visiting the post-office, too surely I felt as the ruin of my enterprise in its very outset. Some agent *must* be employed ; and where could one be found promising by looks, words, manners, more trustworthiness than this agent, sent by accident ? The case almost explained itself. She readily understood how the resemblance of a name had thrown the letter into my possession ; and that the simply remedy was—to restore it to the right owner through the right channel, which channel was the never-enough-to-be-esteemed General Post-office, at that time pitching its tents and bivouacking nightly in Lombard Street, but for this special case legally represented by the Chester head-office : a service of no risk to *her*, for which, on the contrary, all parties would thank her. I, to begin, begged to put *my* thanks into the shape of half-a-crown : but, as some natural doubts arose with respect to her precise station in life (for she might be a farmer's wife, and not a servant), I thought it advisable to postulate the existence of some youthful daughter : to which mytho-logical person I begged to address my offering, when incarnated in the shape of a doll.

I therefore, Deucalion that was or had been provision-ally through a brief interval of panic, took leave of my Pyrrha, sole partner in the perils and anxieties of that astounding Bore, dismissing her—Thessalian Pyrrha—not to any Thessalian vales of Tempe, but—O ye powers of moral anachronism ! — to the Chester Post-office ; and warning her on no account to be prematurely wheedled out of her secret. Her position, diplomatically speaking, was better (as I made her understand) than that of the post-office : she having something in her gift—viz., an appointment to forty guineas ; whereas in the counter-gift of the proud post-office was nothing ; neither for instant fruition nor in far-off reversion. Her, in fact, one might regard as a Pandora, carrying a box with something better than hope at the bottom ; for hope too often betrays ; but a draft upon Smith, Payne, & Smith, which never betrays, and for a sum which, on the authority of Goldsmith, makes an English clergyman 'passing rich' through a whole twelvemonth, entitled her to look scornfully upon every second person that she met.

In about two hours the partner of my solitary kingdom

upon the Cop re-appeared, with the welcome assurance that Chester had survived the Bore, that all was right, and that anything which ever *had* been looking crooked was now made straight as the path of an arrow. She had given 'my love' (so she said) to the post-office; had been thanked by more than either one or two amongst the men of letters who figured in the equipage of that establishment; and had been assured that, long before daylight departed, one large cornucopia of justice and felicity would be emptied out upon the heads of all parties in the drama. I myself, not the least afflicted person on the roll, was already released—suddenly released, and fully—from the iniquitous load of responsibility thrust upon me; the poor emigrant was released from his conflict with fears that were uncertain, and creditors too certain; the post-office was released from the scandal and embarrassment of a gross irregularity, that might eventually have brought the post-master-general down upon their haunches; and the household at the Priory were released from all anxieties, great and small, sound and visionary, on the question of my fancied felony.

In those anxieties, one person there was that never had condescended to participate. This was my eldest sister Mary—just eleven months senior to myself. She was among the gentlest of girls, and yet from the very first she had testified the most incredulous disdain of all who fancied *her* brother capable of any thought so base as that of meditating a wrong to a needy exile. At present, after exchanging a few parting words, and a few final or farewell farewells with my faithful female [1] agent, further business I had none to detain me in Chester, except what concerned this particular sister. My business with *her* was not to thank her for the resolute justice which she had done me,

[1] Some people are irritated, or even fancy themselves insulted, by overt acts of alliteration, as many people are by puns. On their account let me say, that, although there are here eight separate f's in less than half a sentence, this is to be held as pure accident. In fact, at one time there were nine f's in the original cast of the sentence, until I, in pity of the affronted people, substituted *female agent* for *female friend.*

since as yet I could not know of that service, but simply
to see her, to learn the domestic news of the Priory, and,
according to the possibilities of the case, to concert with
her some plan of regular correspondence. Meantime it
happened that a maternal uncle, a military man on the
Bengal establishment, who had come to England on a
three-years' leave of absence (according to the custom in
those days), was at this time a visitor at the Priory. My
mother's establishment of servants was usually limited to
five persons—all, except one, elderly and torpid. But my
uncle, who had brought to England some beautiful Arab
and Persian horses, found it necessary to gather about his
stables an extra body of men and boys. These were all
alert and active; so that, when I reconnoitred the windows
of the Priory in the dusk, hoping in some way to attract
my sister's attention, I not only failed in that object,
seeing no lights in any room which could naturally have
been occupied by her, but I also found myself growing
into an object of special attention to certain unknown
servants, who, having no doubt received instructions to
look out for me, easily inferred from my anxious movements that I must be the person 'wanted.' Uneasy at
all the novel appearances of things, I went away, and
returned, after an hour's interval, armed with a note to
my sister, requesting her to watch for an opportunity
of coming out for a few minutes under the shadows of
the little ruins in the Priory garden,[1] where I meantime

1 '*The little ruins in the Priory garden*':—St. John's Priory had
been part of the monastic foundation attached to the very ancient
church of St. John, standing beyond the walls of Chester. Early in
the seventeenth century, this Priory, or so much of it as remained, was
occupied as a dwelling-house by Sir Robert Cotton the antiquary.
And there, according to tradition, he had been visited by Ben Jonson.
All that remained of the Priory when used as a domestic residence by
Cotton was upon a miniature scale, except only the kitchen—a noble
room, with a groined roof of stone, exactly as it had been fitted to the
uses of the monastic establishment. The little hall of entrance, the
dining-room, and principal bedroom, were in a modest style of
elegance, fitted by the scale of accommodation for the abode of a
literary bachelor, and pretty nearly as Cotton had left them two
centuries before. But the miniature character of the Priory, which

would be waiting.   This note I gave to a stranger, whose
costume showed him to be a groom, begging him to give
it to the young lady whose address it bore.   He answered,
in a respectful tone, that he would do so ; but he could
not sincerely have meant it, since (as I soon learned) it
was impossible.   In fact, not one minute had I waited,
when in glided amongst the ruins—not my fair sister, but
my bronzed Bengal uncle !   A Bengal tiger would not
more have startled me.   Now, to a dead certainty, I said,
here comes a fatal barrier to the prosecution of my scheme.
I was mistaken.   Between my mother and my uncle there
existed the very deepest affection ; for they regarded each
other as sole reliques of a household once living together
in memorable harmony.   But in many features of character no human beings could stand off from each other in
more lively repulsion.   And this was seen on the present
occasion.   My dear excellent mother, from the eternal

had dwindled by successive abridgments from a royal quarto into a
pretty duodecimo, was seen chiefly in the beautiful ruins which
adorned the little lawn, across which access was gained to the house
through the hall.   These ruins amounted at the most to three arches
—which, because round and not pointed, were then usually called
Saxon, as contradistinguished from Gothic.   What might be the exact
classification of the architecture I do not know.   Certainly the very
ancient church of St. John, to which at one time the Priory must have
been an appendage, wore a character of harsh and naked simplicity
that was repulsive.   But the little ruins were really beautiful, and
drew continual visits from artists and sketchers through every successive summer.   Whether they had any architectural enrichments, I
do not remember.   But they interested all people—first by their
miniature scale, which would have qualified them (if portable) for a
direct introduction amongst the 'properties' and *dramatis personæ* on
our London opera boards ; and, secondly, by the exquisite beauty of
the shrubs, wild-flowers, and ferns, that surmounted the arches with
natural coronets of the richest composition.   In this condition of
attractiveness my mother saw this little Priory, which was then on
sale.   As a residence, it had the great advantage of standing somewhat
aloof from the city of Chester, which, however (like all cathedral
cities), was quiet and respectable in the composition of its population.
My mother bought it, added a drawing-room, eight or nine bedrooms,
dressing-rooms, etc., all on the miniature scale corresponding to the
original plan ; and thus formed a very pretty residence, with the grace
of monastic antiquity hanging over the whole little retreat.

quiet of her decorous household, looked upon every
violent or irregular movement, and therefore upon mine
at present, much as she would have done upon the
opening of the seventh seal in the Revelations. But
my uncle was thoroughly a man of the world, and
what told even more powerfully on my behalf in this
instance, he was a man of even morbid activity. It
was so exquisitely natural in his eyes that any rational
person should prefer moving about amongst the breezy
mountains of Wales, to a slavish routine of study amongst
books grim with dust and masters too probably still
more dusty, that he seemed disposed to regard my conduct as an extraordinary act of virtue. On his advice,
it was decided that there could be no hope in any contest
with my main wishes, and that I should be left to pursue
my original purpose of walking amongst the Welsh
mountains ; provided I chose to do so upon the slender
allowance of a guinea a-week. My uncle, whose Indian
munificence ran riot upon all occasions, would gladly have
had a far larger allowance made to me, and would himself
have clandestinely given me anything I asked. But I
myself, from general ignorance (in which accomplishment
I excelled), judged this to be sufficient ; and at this point
my mother, hitherto passively acquiescent in my uncle's
proposals, interfered with a decisive rigour that in my own
heart I could not disapprove. Any larger allowance, most
reasonably she urged, what was it but to ' make proclamation to my two younger brothers that rebellion bore a
premium, and that mutiny was the ready road to ease and
comfort ? ' My conscience smote me at these words : I
felt something like an electric shock on this sudden
reference, so utterly unexpected, to my brothers ; for,
to say the truth, I never once admitted them to my
thoughts in forecasting the eventual consequences that
might possibly unroll themselves from my own headstrong act. Here now, within three days, rang like a
solemn knell, reverberating from the sounding - board
within my awakened conscience, one of those many
self-reproaches so dimly masked, but not circumstantially

prefigured, by the secret thought under the dome of
St. Paul's Cathedral about its dread Whispering Gallery.
In this particular instance, I know that the evil consequences from my own example never did take effect.
But at the moment of my mother's sorrowful suggestion,
the fear that they *might* take effect thrilled me with
remorse. My next brother, a boy of generous and
heroic temper, was at a school governed by a brutal
and savage master. This brother, I well know, had
justifying reasons, ten times weightier than any which
I could plead, for copying my precedent. Most probable it was that he would do so; but I learned many
years subsequently from himself that in fact he did not.
The man's diabolical malice at last made further toleration
impossible. Without thinking of my example, under very
different circumstances my brother won his own emancipa-
tion in ways suggested by his own views and limited by
his own resources: he got afloat upon the wide, wide
world of ocean; ran along a perilous seven-years' career
of nautical romance; had his name almost blotted out
from all memories in England; became of necessity a
pirate amongst pirates; was liable to the death of a pirate
wherever taken; then suddenly, on a morning of battle,
having effected his escape from the bloody flag, he joined
the English storming party at Monte Video, fought under
the eye of Sir Home Popham, the commodore, and within
twenty-four hours after the victory was rated as a midship-
man on board the *Diadem* (a 64-gun ship), which bore
Sir Home's flag. All this I have more circumstantially
narrated elsewhere. I repeat the sum of it here, as showing that his elopement from a brutal tyrant was not due
to any misleading of mine. I happen to know this now
—but then I could not know it. And if I had so entirely
overlooked one such possible result, full of calamity to my
youthful brothers, why might I not have overlooked many
hundreds beside, equally probable—equally full of peril?
That consideration saddened me, and deepened more and
more the ominous suggestion—the oracle full of woe—
that spoke from those Belshazzar thunderings upon the

wall of the Whispering Gallery. In fact, every intricate and untried path in life, where it was from the first a matter of arbitrary choice to enter upon it or avoid it, is effectually a path through a vast Hercynian forest, unexplored and unmapped, where each several turn in your advance leaves you open to new anticipations of what is next to be expected, and consequently open to altered valuations of all that has been already traversed. Even the character of your own absolute experience, past and gone, which (if anything in this world) you might surely answer for as sealed and settled for ever—even this you must submit to hold in suspense, as a thing conditional and contingent upon what is yet to come—liable to have its provisional character affirmed or reversed, according to the new combinations into which it may enter with elements only yet perhaps in the earliest stages of development.

Saddened by these reflections, I was still more saddened by the chilling manner of my mother. If I could presume to descry a fault in my mother, it was—that she turned the chilling aspects of her high-toned character too exclusively upon those whom, in any degree, she knew or supposed to be promoters of evil. Sometimes her austerity might seem even unjust. But at present the whole artillery of her displeasure seemed to be unmasked, and *justly* unmasked, against a moral aberration, that offered for itself no excuse that was obvious in one moment, that was legible at one glance, that could utter itself in one word. My mother was predisposed to think ill of all causes that required many words : I, predisposed to subtleties of all sorts and degrees, had naturally become acquainted with cases that could not unrobe their apparellings down to that degree of simplicity. If in this world there is one misery having no relief, it is the pressure on the heart from the *Incommunicable*. And if another Sphinx should arise to propose another enigma to man— saying, What burden is that which only is insupportable by human fortitude? I should answer at once—*It is the burden of the Incommunicable*. At this moment, sitting in

the same room of the Priory with my mother, knowing
how reasonable she was—how patient of explanations—
how candid—how open to pity—not the less I sank away
in a hopelessness that was immeasurable from all effort at
explanation.   She and I were contemplating the very same
act ; but she from one centre, I from another.   Certain I
was, that if through one half minute she could realise in
one deadly experience the suffering with which I had
fought through more than three months, the amount of
physical anguish, the desolation of all genial life, she
would have uttered a rapturous absolution of that which
else must always seem to her a mere explosion of wilful
insubordination.   'In this brief experience,' she would
exclaim, 'I read the record of your acquittal ; in this
fiery torment I acknowledge the gladiatorial resistance.'
Such in the case supposed would have been her revised
verdict.   But this case was exquisitely impossible.   Nothing which offered itself to my rhetoric gave any but the
feeblest and most childish reflection of my past sufferings.
Just so helpless did I feel, disarmed into just the same
languishing impotence to face (or make an effort at facing)
the difficulty before me, as most of us have felt in the
dreams of our childhood when lying down without a
struggle before some all-conquering lion.   I felt that the
situation was one without hope ; a solitary word, which I
attempted to mould upon my lips, died away into a sigh ;
and passively I acquiesced in the apparent confession
spread through all the appearances—that in reality I had
no palliation to produce.

One alternative, in the offer made to me, was, that I
had permission to stay at the Priory.   The Priory, or the
mountainous region of Wales, was offered freely to my
choice.   Either of the two offered an attractive abode.
The Priory, it may be fancied, was clogged with the
liability to fresh and intermitting reproaches.   But this
was not so.   I knew my mother sufficiently to be assured
that, once having expressed her sorrowful condemnation
of my act, having made it impossible for me to misunderstand her views, she was ready to extend her wonted

hospitality to me, and (as regarded all practical matters) her wonted kindness; but not that sort of kindness which could make me forget that I stood under the deepest shadows of her displeasure, or could leave me for a moment free to converse at my ease upon any and every subject. A man that is talking on simple toleration, and, as it were, under permanent protest, cannot feel himself morally at his ease, unless very obtuse and coarse in his sensibilities.

Mine, under any situation approaching to the present, were so far from being obtuse that they were morbidly and extravagantly acute. I had erred: that I knew, and did not disguise from myself. Indeed, the rapture of anguish with which I had recurred involuntarily to my experience of the Whispering Gallery, and the symbolic meaning which I had given to that experience, manifested indirectly my deep sense of error through the dim misgiving which attended it—that in some mysterious way the sense and the consequences of this error would magnify themselves at every stage of life, in proportion as they were viewed retrospectively from greater and greater distances. I had, besides, through the casual allusion to my brothers, suddenly become painfully aware of another and separate failure in the filial obligations resting on myself. Any mother, who is a widow, has especial claims on the co-operation of her eldest son in all means of giving a beneficial bias to the thoughts and purposes of the younger children: and, if *any* mother, then by a title how special could my own mother invoke such co-operation, who had on *her* part satisfied all the claims made upon her maternal character, by self-sacrifices as varied, as privately I knew them to be exemplary. Whilst yet comparatively young, not more than thirty-six, she had sternly refused all countenance, on at least two separate occasions, to distinguished proposals of marriage, out of pure regard to the memory of my father, and to the interests of his children. Could I fail to read, in such unostentatious exemplifications of maternal goodness, a summons to a corresponding earnestness on my part in lightening, as much as possible, the burden of her responsibilities? Alas! too certainly, as regarded *that* duty, I felt my own failure : one opportunity had been signally lost, and yet, on the other hand, I also felt that more might be pleaded on my behalf than could by possibility be apparent to a neutral bystander. But this, to be pleaded effectually, needed to be said—not by myself, but by a disinterested advocate : and no such advocate was at hand. In blind distress of mind, conscience-stricken and heart-stricken, I stretched out my arms, seeking for my one sole auxiliary ; that was my eldest sister Mary ; for my younger sister Jane was a mere infant. Blindly and mechanically, I stretched out my arms as if to arrest her attention ; and giving utterance to my labouring thoughts, I was beginning to speak, when all at once I became sensible that Mary was not there. I had heard a step behind me, and supposed it hers : since the groom's ready acceptance of my letter to her had pre-occupied me with the belief that I should see her in a few moments. But she was far away, on a mission of anxious, sisterly love. Immediately after my elopement, an express had been sent off to the Priory from Manchester ; this express, well mounted, had not spent more than four hours on the road. He must have passed me on my first day's walk ; and, within an hour after *his* arrival, came a communication from the post-office, explaining the nature and value of the letter that had been so vexatiously thrust into my hands. Alarm spread through the Priory : for it must be confessed that the coincidence of my elopement with this certified delivery of the letter to myself, gave but too reasonable grounds for connecting the two incidents. I was grateful to dear Mary for resisting such strong plausibilities against me ; and yet I could not feel entitled to complain of those who had *not* resisted. The probability seemed that I must have violated the laws to some extent, either by forgery or by fraudulent appropriation. In either case, the most eligible course seemed to be my instant expatriation. France (this being the year of peace) or Holland would offer the best asylum until the affair should be settled ;

and, as there could be no anxieties in any quarter as to
the main thing concerned in the issue—viz., the money—
in any case there was no reason to fear a vindictive pursuit,
even on the worst assumption as regarded the offence.
An elderly gentleman, long connected with the family,
and in many cases an agent for the guardians, at this
moment offered his services as counsellor and protector to
my sister Mary.   Two hours therefore from the arrival
of the Manchester express (who, starting about 11 A.M.,
had reached Chester at 3 P.M.), all the requisite steps
having been concerted with one of the Chester banks for
getting letters of credit, etc., a carriage-and-four was at
the Priory gate, into which stepped my sister Mary, with
one female attendant and her friendly escort.   And thus,
the same day, on which I had made my exit from Mr.
Lawson's, saw the chase after me commencing.   Sunset
saw the pursuers crossing the Mersey, and trotting into
Liverpool.   Thence to Ormskirk, thirteen miles, and
thence to *proud Preston*, about twenty more.   Within a
trifle, these three stages make fifty miles ; and so much
did my chasers, that pursued when no man fled, accomplish
before sleeping.   On the next day, long and long before
the time when I, in my humble pedestrian character,
reached Chester, my sister's party had reached Ambleside
—distant about ninety-two miles from Liverpool, consequently somewhere about a hundred and seven miles
from the Priory.   This chasing party, with good reason,
supposed themselves to be on my traces ever after reaching
'proud Preston,' which is the point of confluence for
the Liverpool and Manchester roads northwards.   For
I myself, having originally planned my route for the
English Lakes, purposely suffered some indications of
that plan to remain behind me, in the hope of thus giving
a false direction to any pursuit that might be attempted.

The further course of this chase was disagreeably
made known to me about four years later, on attaining
my majority, by a 'little account' of about £150 against
my little patrimonial fortune.   Of all the letters from the
Priory (which, however, from natural oversight were not

thought of until the day after my own arrival at the
Priory—*i.e.*, the third day after my sister's departure),
not one caught them : which was unfortunate. For the
journey to and from the Lakes, together with a circuit of
more than one hundred and fifty miles amongst the Lakes,
would at any rate have run up to nearly four hundred
miles. But it happened that my pursuers, not having
time to sift such intelligence as they received, were misled
into an excursus of full two hundred miles more, by
chasing an imaginary ' *me* ' to the Caves, thence to Bolton
Abbey, thence nearly to York. Altogether, the journey
amounted to above six hundred miles, all performed with
four horses. Now at that time the cost of four horses—
which in the cheapest hay and corn seasons was three
shillings a-mile, and in dear seasons four—was three-and-
sixpence a-mile ; to which it was usual to compute an
average addition of one shilling a-mile for gates, postilions,
ostlers ; so that the total amount, with the natural expenses of the three travellers at the inns, ran up to five
shillings a-mile. Consequently, five shillings being the
quarter of a pound, six hundred miles cost the quarter of
£600. The only item in this long account which consoled
me to the amount of a solitary smile for all this money
thrown away, was an item in a bill at Patterdale (head of
Ulleswater)—

To an echo, first quality .	.	.	.	£0 10	0
To do., second quality	.	.	.	0 5	0

It seems the price of echoes varied, reasonably enough,
with the amount of gunpowder consumed. But at Low-
wood, on Windermere, half-crown echoes might be had
by those base snobs who would put up with a vile
Brummagem substitute for ' the genuine article.'

Trivial, meantime, as regarded any permanent consequences, would have been this casual inroad upon my
patrimony. Had I waited until my sister returned home,
which I might have been sure could only have been
delayed through the imperfectly concerted system of correspondence, all would have prospered. From her I should

have received the cordiality and the genial sympathy
which I needed; I could have quietly pursued my studies;
and my Oxford matriculation would have followed
as a matter of course.   But, unhappily, having for so
long a time been seriously shaken in health, any interruption of my wild open-air system of life instantly threw
me back into nervous derangements.   Past all doubt it
had now become that the *al fresco* life, to which I had
looked with so much hopefulness for a sure and rapid
restoration to health, was even more potent than I had
supposed it.   Literally irresistible it seemed in re-organis-
ing the system of my languishing powers.   Impatient,
therefore, under the absence of my sister, and agitated
every hour so long as my home wanted its central charm
in some household countenance, some σύντροφον ὄμμα,
beaming with perfect sympathy, I resolved to avail myself
of those wild mountainous and sylvan attractions which at
present lay nearest to me.   Those parts, indeed, of Flintshire, or even of Denbighshire, which lay near to Chester,
were not in any very eminent sense attractive.   The vale
of Gressford, for instance, within the Flintshire border,
and yet not more than seven miles distant, offered a lovely
little seclusion; and to this I had a privileged access; and
at first I tried it; but it was a dressed and ornamented
pleasure-ground: and two ladies of some distinction,
nearly related to each other, and old friends of my mother,
were in a manner the ladies paramount within the ring
fence of this Arcadian vale.   But this did not offer what
I wanted.   Everything was elegant, polished, quiet,
throughout the lawns and groves of this verdant retreat:
no rudeness was allowed here; even the little brooks were
trained to 'behave themselves'; and the two villas of the
reigning ladies (Mrs. Warrington and Mrs. Parry) showed
the perfection of good taste.   For both ladies had culti-
vated a taste for painting, and [had] I believe some
executive power.   Here my introductions were rather too
favourable; since they forced me into society.   From
Gressford, however, the character of the scene, considered
as a daily residence, very soon repelled me, however

otherwise fascinating by the accomplishments of its two possessors. Just two-and-twenty miles from Chester, meantime, lay a far grander scene, the fine vale of Llangollen in the centre of Denbighshire. Here, also, the presiding residents were two ladies, whose romantic retirement from the world at an early age had attracted for many years a general interest to their persons, habits, and opinions. These ladies were Irish—Miss Ponsonby, and Lady Eleanor Butler, a sister of Lord Ormond. I had twice been formally presented to them by persons of a rank to stamp a value upon this introduction. But, naturally, though high-bred courtesy concealed any such open expressions of feeling, they must have felt a very slight interest in myself or my opinions.[1] I grieve to say that my own feelings were not more ardent towards *them*. Nevertheless, I presented myself at their cottage as often as I passed through Llangollen ; and was always courteously received when they happened to be in the country. However, as it was not ladies that I was seeking in Wales, I now pushed on to Carnarvonshire ; and for some weeks took a very miniature suite of rooms—viz., one room and a closet—at Bangor.

My landlady had been a lady's-maid, or a nurse, or something of that sort, in the Bishop of Bangor's family ; and had but lately married away from that family, or (to use her own expression) had 'settled.' In a little town like Bangor, barely to have lived in the bishop's family

---

[1] It is worthy of notice that, when I, in this year 1802, and again in after years, endeavoured to impress them favourably with regard to Wordsworth as a poet (that subject having not been introduced by myself, but by one of the ladies, who happened to have a Cambridge friend intimate with the man, and perhaps with his works), neither of them was disposed to look with any interest or hopefulness upon his pretensions. But, at a period long subsequent to this, when the House of Commons had rung with applause on Sergeant Talfourd's mention of his name, and when all American tourists of any distinction flocked annually to Rydal Mount, Wordsworth's own poems bear witness that a great revolution had been worked at Llangollen. I mention this anecdote, because I have good reason to think that a large proportion of the 'conversions' in the case of Wordsworth took place under the same influence.

conferred some distinction; and my good landlady had
rather more than her share of the pride natural to that
glorious advantage. What 'my lord' said, and what 'my
lord' did, how useful he was in Parliament, and how indispensable at Oxford, formed the daily burden of her talk.
All this I bore very well; for it cost no great effort to
make allowance for the garrulity of an old servant; and
luckily nothing in our daily routine of life brought us
often into each other's company. Sometimes, however,
we met; and of necessity, on such occasions, I must have
appeared in her eyes very inadequately impressed with the
bishop's importance, and with the grandeur of having lived
in a palace; and, perhaps, to punish me for my indifference,
or it might, after all, be mere accident, she one day repeated to me a conversation in which I was indirectly a
party concerned. She had been to the palace; and, dinner
being over, she had been summoned into the dining-room.
In giving an account of her household economy, she happened to mention that she had let what she styled somewhat magnificently her 'apartments.' The good bishop
(it seemed) had thence taken occasion to caution her as to
her selection of inmates; 'for,' said he, 'you must recollect, Betty, that Bangor is in the high road to the Head'
(*the Head* was the common colloquial expression for Holyhead); 'so that multitudes of Irish swindlers, running
away from their debts into England, and of English
swindlers, running away from their debts to the Isle of
Man, are likely to take this place in their route.' Such
advice was certainly not without reasonable grounds, but
rather fitted to be stored up for Mrs. Betty's private
meditations, than specially reported to me. What followed was worse :—'O my lord,' answered my landlady
(according to her own representation of the matter), 'I
really don't think that this young gentleman is a swindler;
because——'—'You don't *think* me a swindler?' said I,
interrupting her, in a tumult of indignation; 'for the
future I shall spare you the trouble of thinking about it.'
And without delay I prepared for my departure. Some
concessions the good woman seemed disposed to make;

but a harsh and contemptuous expression, which I fear that I applied to the learned dignitary himself, roused *her* indignation in turn ; and reconciliation then became impossible : I was, indeed, greatly irritated at the bishop's having suggested any grounds of suspicion, however remotely, against a person whom he had never seen ; and I thought of letting him know my mind in Greek ; which, at the same time that it would furnish some presumption in behalf of my respectability, might also (I hoped) compel the bishop to answer in the same language ; and in that case I doubted not to make good my superiority as a versatile wielder of arms, rarely managed with effect, against all the terrors of his lordship's wig.

I was wrong if I said anything in my anger that was disparaging or sceptical as to the bishop's intellectual pretensions ; which were not only very sound, but very appropriate to the particular stations which he filled. For the Bishop of Bangor (at that time Dr. Cleaver) was also the head of Brasenose, Oxford—which college was indebted to him for its leadership [1] at that era in scholarship and

---

[1] The rank to which Brasenose had suddenly risen in the estimation of the world was put to the test in the following year. The leading family in the house (the *gens*) of Grenville was, at this time, that of the Marquis of Buckingham, not long after elevated to the ducal rank. The second son of this nobleman—viz., Lord George Grenville (subsequently succeeding to the peerage of Nugent, and known in his literary character only as Lord Nugent)—happened, in this or the following year, to be ripe for college ; which means, in England, that he was a young man, and not a boy ; generally, at the very least, eighteen years old. According to all known precedent, he should have gone to Christ Church. But, on such a question arising, naturally his uncle, Lord Grenville, under whose patronage the Grenville *Homer* had been published, and who was reputed an accomplished scholar, assisted at the family council ; and by *his* advice, to the astonishment of Oxford, Brasenose was selected in preference to Christ Church ; and, I believe, on the one sole ground of deference for the administrative talents (combined with singular erudition) of Dr. Cleaver. This casual precedency, however, of Brasenose, resting (as it did) on a mere *personal* basis, ran down as suddenly as it had run up, and has long since been forgotten. The fact is, that rustic families, at a distance from Oxford, naturally presume some superior dignity in any college that should happen to have a bishop for its ruler ; not knowing that, in Oxford and Cambridge, all heads of con-

discipline. In this academic character I learned afterwards
that he might be called almost a reformer : a wise, temperate, and successful reformer ; and, as a scholar, I saw
many years later that he had received the laudatory notice
of Porson. But, on the other hand, the bishop was not
altogether without blame in unchaining his local influence,
were it only by hint or insinuation, against a defenceless
stranger. For so great a man, in so small a town as
Bangor, was really as much of an autocrat as a post-captain
on the quarterdeck of his own vessel. A 'sea-lawyer'
in such a case must contrive to pocket his wrongs, until
he finds himself and the captain on shore. Yet, after all,
my scheme was not altogether so absurd ; and the anger,
in which perhaps it might begin, all melted away in the
fun which would have accompanied its execution. It will
strike the reader that my plan of retaliation must have
failed by arming against me the official pride of the bishop.
Any man, it will be thought, occupying so dignified a place
in public life—a lord of Parliament, holder of a prize in
the episcopal lottery (for Bangor was worth six thousand
a-year), a leading Don at Oxford—in short, a splendid
pluralist, armed with diocesan thunder and lightning—
would never stoop from his Jovian altitude to notice any
communication whatever from a boy. But it would make
all the difference in the world that this communication by
the supposition was to be in Greek. Mere curiosity in

siderable colleges hold themselves (and *are* held) equals in rank and
dignity to the bench of bishops. In Oxford more especially, this doctrine
receives a standing illustration ; for *there* the dean of the diocese is
necessarily and *ex officio* the head of Christ Church, which (by the
number and the rank of its population) is beyond all competition the
supreme college in the whole university. In that character, therefore
(of college head), Mr. Dean is a very much greater man than my lord
the Bishop. This virtual inferiority in the face of an ostensible
superiority was, until the new regulations for somewhat equalising the
bishoprics, further reinforced by the poverty of Oxford as an episcopal
see. It ought to be added, that to hold the headship of a college in
combination with a bishopric, considering the burdensomeness of irreconcilable functions attached to each of the offices, is a scandalous
violation of public duty, such as ought never to have won an hour's
toleration.

such a case would compel the Bishop to read it.   And
then, shockingly irregular as such a course would be, a
fatal temptation would arise to the hazardous experiment
of answering it in Greek.   It would not be pleasant to
shrink from the sort of silent challenge thrown out by
such an eccentric form of epistle, when worded in the
tone of respect due to the bishop's age and spiritual office.
And certainly the degradation would be conspicuously
less in replying even to a boy, if armed with that sort of
accomplishment.   But was not the bishop a learned man,
well qualified to answer, whose reading must naturally be
greater by a score of times than mine ?   I had heard so ;
and I was told also, but long after, that he had written
well and learnedly (*but not in Greek*) on the Arundel
marbles ; even to attempt which, in our days, when the
forestalling labours of two centuries have so much narrowed
the field open to original sagacity, argues an erudition
far from common.   But I have already given it as my
opinion, that there is no proportion held between a man's
general knowledge of Greek, and the special art of writing
Greek ; that is, using it as a vehicle for ordinary and
familiar intercourse.   This advantage, not necessarily or
usually belonging to the most exquisite Greek scholarship,
I myself wielded with a preternatural address for varying
the forms of expression, and for bringing the most refractory ideas within the harness of Grecian phraseology.
Had the bishop yielded to the temptation of replying,
then I figured to myself the inevitable result—the episcopal hulk lying motionless on the water like a huge three-
decker, not able to return a gun, whilst I, as a light agile
frigate, should have sailed round and round him, and
raked him at pleasure, as opportunity offered.   He could
have had no opening for his erudition (as, for instance,
upon the Arundel marbles), without too flagrantly recalling the cosmogony man in the *Vicar of Wakefield*, with his
ἄναρχον ἄρα καὶ ἀτελεύταιον τὸ πᾶν.   Once falling into the
snare of replying at all, his lordship would not be at liberty
either to break off the correspondence abruptly, or to
continue it without damage to his episcopal pomp.   My

anger, meantime, sudden and fiery, as under a sense of real
injury, had not been malicious; and it was already pro-
pitiated beforehand by the mere fun and comic effect
of the picture which I thus prefigured as arising between
us. In no case could I have found pleasure in causing
any mortifications to the bishop—mortifications which
the Methodists (by this time swarming in Carnarvonshire)
would exultingly have diffused. In the end I should
probably have confined myself to a grave and temperate
remonstrance, simply stating the distressing consequences
which were likely to result to me from the too unguarded
insinuations of his lordship.

But these consequences travelled fast upon the traces
of those insinuations; and already upon the very day
when my foolish landlady (more, perhaps, in thoughtlessness than with any purpose of mischief) had repeated the
bishop's words in what seemed to me so insulting a tone,
and so entirely without provocation (since there never had
been the smallest irregularity in our little weekly settle-
ments), one of those consequences was, that I became
houseless. For I disdained to profit by the shelter of a
house from which truth and courtesy seemed alike
banished. And from that one consequence naturally
enough flowed others; for, having, at any rate, to
seek a new home, I left Bangor[1] at once, and rambled
away to Carnarvon—distant about two-and-a-half hours'
smart walking. At Carnarvon I found no lodging that
altogether suited my purposes; hired lodgings being then

---

[1] In this, except for what concerned the cheapness and the
brilliant cleanliness of the lodgings, under the management of an
English housemaid approved by an English bishop's housekeeper, there
was little to regret. Bangor, indeed, had few attractions, fewer than
any other spot in Carnarvonshire. And yet, was there not the
cathedral? Certainly there was; and that might have been a great
resource to me, had there been the regular choir services, but there
were none. Indeed, there could be none; for, so far as I ever heard,
there was no choir. The cathedral cemetery was at that time famous
as the most beautiful in the whole kingdom. But the beauty was
scarcely appropriate: it was the beauty of a well-kept shrubbery, and
not of a cemetery. It contrived to look smiling and attractive by the
entire dissembling of its real purposes.

thinly sown in North Wales; and for some time, therefore, having a small reserve of guineas, I lived very much
at inns.

This change of abode naturally drew my thoughts
away from the bishop. And thus gradually all my
thoughts of expostulation faded away. This I am
disposed to regard as an unfortunate solution of the
affair, which otherwise would probably have taken the
following course. The bishop, as I afterwards heard
when resident myself at Oxford and personally acquainted
with men of Brasenose (to which college, indeed, subsequently, my own youngest brother belonged), was a
reasonable and even amiable man. On receiving, therefore, my Greek remonstrance, he was sure as a scholar to
have taken some interest in the writer; and he was too
equitable to have neglected any statement, Greek or not
Greek, which reflected, with some apparent justice, upon
his own conduct as not sufficiently considerate. He
would, therefore, almost certainly have replied to me in
courteous terms; regretting the accident which had made
me houseless; but reminding me that all communications
made to a dependant within a man's own gates, and never
meant as grounds of action, but simply as cautions—
general and not special—are in law and usage held to be
privileged communications, and equally whether written
or spoken. The insulting use made of this caution, he
would have treated as due simply to the woman's coarse-
ness, but in part, perhaps, as due to a cause which has
much to do with the harsh and uncivil expressions of
uneducated people—viz., their very limited command of
language. They use phrases much stronger than naturally
belong to their thoughts and meaning, simply because the
narrowness of their vocabulary oftentimes suggests to their
embarrassed choice no variation of expression wearing a
character less offensive. To such a letter I should have
made a suitable reply; and, thenceforward, it is probable
that, until the Michaelmas term drew the bishop's family
away to Oxford, I should have found my abode in Bangor,
or its neighbourhood, much improved as regards the

I

command of books. That advantage would have been
fugitive. But other and remoter advantages might have
been more serious. It happened that the college to which
the Manchester Grammar School would have consigned
me as a privileged *alumnus*, was that very college over
which the bishop presided. I have no reason to think
that the bishop would have had power to retrieve for me
any part of the privileges which by my elopement I had
wilfully forfeited : but he would have had it abundantly
in his power to place the ordinary college advantages of
Fellowships, etc., within my reach : whereas afterwards,
going under erroneous counsel to a college disconnected
from my own country and my own schools, I never
enjoyed those ordinary opportunities of advancement, and
consequently of literary leisure, which the English universities open to almost every man who qualifies himself duly
to obtain them. All this, however, was thrown into the
world of dreams and fable by my hasty movement to
Carnarvon, and that region which Pennant first distinguished by the name of Snowdonia.

There were already, even in those days of 1802,
numerous inns, erected at reasonable distances from each
other, for the accommodation of tourists : and no sort of
disgrace attached in Wales, as too generally upon the
great roads of England, to the pedestrian style of
travelling. Indeed, the majority of those whom I met as
fellow-tourists in the quiet little cottage-parlours of the
Welsh posting-houses were pedestrian travellers. All the
way from Shrewsbury through Llangollen, Llanrwst,[1] Con-
way, Bangor, then turning to the left at right angles through
Carnarvon, and so on to Dolgelly (the chief town of
Merionethshire), Tan-y-Bwlch, Harlech, Barmouth, and
through the sweet solitudes of Cardiganshire, or turning
back sharply towards the English border through the
gorgeous wood scenery of Montgomeryshire—everywhere
at intermitting distances of twelve to sixteen miles, I

[1] '*Llanrwst*' :—This is an alarming word for the eye ; one vowel
to what the English eye counts as seven consonants : but it is easily
pronounced as *Tlanroost*.

found the most comfortable inns.   One feature indeed of
repose in all this chain of solitary resting-houses—viz.,
the fact that none of them rose above two storeys in
height — was due to the modest scale on which the
travelling system of the Principality had moulded itself
in correspondence to the calls of England, which then
(but be it remembered this *then* was in 1802, a year of
peace) threw a very small proportion of her vast migratory
population annually into this sequestered channel.   No
huge Babylonian centres of commerce towered into the
clouds on these sweet sylvan routes : no hurricanes of
haste, or fever-stricken armies of horses and flying
chariots, tormented the echoes in these mountain recesses.   And it has often struck me that a world-wearied
man, who sought for the peace of monasteries separated
from their gloomy captivity—peace and silence such as
theirs combined with the large liberty of nature—could
not do better than revolve amongst these modest inns in
the five northern Welsh counties of Denbigh, Mont-
gomery, Carnarvon, Merioneth, and Cardigan.   Sleeping,
for instance, and breakfasting at Carnarvon ; then, by an
easy nine-mile walk, going forwards to dinner at Bangor,
thence to Aber—nine miles ; or to Llanberris ; and so on
for ever, accomplishing seventy to ninety or one hundred
miles in a week.   This, upon actual experiment, and for
week after week, I found the most delightful of lives.
Here was the eternal motion of winds and rivers, or of
the Wandering Jew liberated from the persecution which
compelled him to move, and turned his breezy freedom
into a killing captivity.   Happier life I cannot imagine
than this vagrancy, if the weather were but tolerable,
through endless successions of changing beauty, and
towards evening a courteous welcome in a pretty rustic
home—that having all the luxuries of a fine hotel (in
particular some luxuries [1] that are almost sacred to Alpine
regions), was at the same time liberated from the inevi-

[1] But a luxury of another class, and quite peculiar to Wales, was
in those days (I hope in these) the Welsh harp, in attendance at every
inn.

table accompaniments of such hotels in great cities or at great travelling stations—viz., the tumult and uproar.

Life on this model was but too delightful; and to myself especially, that am never thoroughly in health unless when having pedestrian exercise to the extent of fifteen miles at the most, and eight to ten miles at the least. Living thus, a man earned his daily enjoyment. But what did it cost? About half a guinea a day : whilst my boyish allowance was not a third of this. The flagrant health, health boiling over in fiery rapture, which ran along, side by side, with exercise on this scale, whilst all the while from morning to night I was inhaling mountain air, soon passed into a hateful scourge. Perquisites to servants and a bed would have absorbed the whole of my weekly guinea. My policy therefore was, if the autumnal air were warm enough, to save this expense of a bed and the chambermaid by sleeping amongst ferns or furze upon a hillside ; and perhaps with a cloak of sufficient *weight* as well as compass, or an Arab's burnoose, this would have been no great hardship. But then in the daytime what an oppressive burden to carry ! So perhaps it was as well that I had no cloak at all. I did, however, for some weeks try the plan of carrying a canvas tent manufactured by myself, and not larger than an ordinary umbrella : but to pitch this securely I found difficult ; and on windy nights it became a troublesome companion. As winter drew near, this bivouacking system became too dangerous to attempt. Still one may bivouack decently, barring rain and wind, up to the end of October. And I counted, on the whole, that in a fortnight I spent nine nights abroad. There are, as perhaps the reader knows by experience, no jaguars in Wales—nor pumas—nor anacondas—nor (generally speaking) any Thugs. What I feared most, but perhaps only through ignorance of zoology, was, lest, whilst my sleeping face was upturned to the stars, some one of the many little Brahminical-looking cows on the Cambrian hills, one or other, might poach her foot into the centre of my face. I do not suppose any fixed hostility of that nature to English faces in Welsh cows : but everywhere I observe in the feminine mind something of beautiful caprice, a floral exuberance of that charming wilfulness which characterises our dear human sisters I fear through all worlds. Against Thugs I had Juvenal's license to be careless in the emptiness of my pockets (*cantabit vacuus*[1] *coram latrone viator*). But I fear that Juvenal's license will not always hold water. There are people bent upon cudgelling one who will persist in excusing one's having nothing but a bad shilling in one's purse, without reading in that Juvenalian *vacuitas* any privilege or license of exemption from the general fate of travellers that intrude upon the solitude of robbers.

Dr. Johnson, upon some occasion, which I have forgotten, is represented by his biographers as accounting for an undeserving person's success in these terms : ' Why, I suppose that *his* nonsense suited *their* nonsense.' Can *that* be the humiliating solution of my own colloquial success at this time in Carnarvonshire inns ? Do not suggest such a thought, most courteous reader. No matter : won in whatsoever way, success *is* success ; and even nonsense, if it is to be victorious nonsense—victorious over the fatal habit of yawning in those who listen, and in some cases over the habit of disputing—must involve a deeper art or more effective secret of power than is easily attained. Nonsense, in fact, is a very difficult thing. Not every seventh son of a seventh son (to use Milton's words) is equal to the task of keeping and maintaining a company of decent men in orthodox nonsense for a matter of two hours. Come from what fountain it may, all talk that succeeds to the extent of raising a wish to meet the talker again, must contain *salt;* must be seasoned with some flavouring element pungent enough to neutralise the

[1] '*Vacuus*' :—I am afraid, though many a year has passed since last I read Juvenal, that the true classical sense of *vacuus* is, *careless, clear from all burden of anxiety*, so that *vacuitas* will be the *result* of immunity from robbery. But suffer me to understand it in the sense of *free from the burden of property*, in which sense *vacuitas* would be the *cause* of such an immunity.

natural tendencies of all mixed conversation, not vigilantly
tended, to lose itself in insipidities and platitudes. Above
all things, I shunned, as I would shun a pestilence, Coleridge's capital error, which through life he practised, of
keeping the audience in a state of passiveness. Unjust
this was to others, but most of all to himself. This
eternal stream of talk which never for one instant inter-
mitted, and allowed no momentary opportunity of reaction
to the persecuted and baited auditor, was absolute ruin to
the interests of the talker himself. Always passive—
always acted upon, never allowed to react, into what state
did the poor afflicted listener—he that played the *rôle* of
listener—collapse? He returned home in the exhausted
condition of one that has been drawn up just before death
from the bottom of a well occupied by foul gases ; and,
of course, hours before he had reached that perilous point
of depression, he had lost all power of distinguishing,
understanding, or connecting. I, for my part, without
needing to think of the unamiable arrogance involved in
such a habit, simply on principles of deadliest selfishness,
should have avoided thus incapacitating my hearer from
doing any justice to the rhetoric or the argument with
which I might address him.

Some great advantages I had for colloquial purposes,
and for engaging the attention of people wiser than myself.
Ignorant I was in a degree past all imagination of daily
life—even as it exists in England. But, on the other
hand, having the advantage of a prodigious memory, and
the far greater advantage of a logical instinct for feeling
in a moment the secret analogies or parallelisms that connected things else apparently remote, I enjoyed these two
peculiar gifts for conversation : first, an inexhaustible
fertility of topics, and therefore of resources for illustrating
or for varying any subject that chance or purpose suggested ; secondly, a prematurely awakened sense of *art*
applied to conversation. I had learned the use of vigilance
in evading with civility the approach of wearisome discussions, and in impressing, quietly and oftentimes imperceptibly, a new movement upon dialogues that loitered

painfully, or see-sawed unprofitably. That it was one
function of art to hide and mask itself (*artis est artem
celare*), this I well knew. Neither was there much art
required. The chief demand was for new facts, or new
views, or for views newly-coloured impressing novelty
upon old facts. To throw in a little of the mysterious
every now and then was useful, even with those that by
temperament were averse to the mysterious; pointed
epigrammatic sayings and jests—even somewhat worn—
were useful; a seasonable quotation in verse was always
effective; and illustrative anecdotes diffused a grace over
the whole movement of the dialogue. It would have
been coxcombry to practise any elaborate or any conspicuous art : few and simple were any artifices that I
ever employed; but, being hidden and seasonable, they
were often effective. And the whole result was, that I
became exceedingly popular within my narrow circle of
friends. This circle was necessarily a fluctuating one,
since it was mainly composed of tourists that happened to
linger for a few weeks in or near Snowdonia, making their
headquarters at Bethgellert or Carnarvon, or at the utmost
roaming no farther than the foot of Cader Idris. Amongst
these fugitive members of our society, I recollect with
especial pleasure Mr. De Haren, an accomplished young
German, who held, or *had* held, the commission of lieutenant in our British navy, but now, in an interval of
peace, was seeking to extend his knowledge of England,
and also of the English language; though in *that*, as
regarded the fullest command of it colloquially, he had
little, indeed, to learn. From him it was that I obtained
my first lessons in German, and my first acquaintance with
German literature. Paul Richter I then first heard of,
together with Hippel, a humorist admired by Kant, and
Hamann, also classed as a humorist, but a nondescript
writer, singularly obscure, whom I have never since seen
in the hands of any Englishman, except once of Sir
William Hamilton. With all these writers Mr. De
Haren had the means of making me usefully acquainted
in the small portable library which filled one of his trunks.

But the most stationary members of this semi-literary circle were Welshmen ; two of them lawyers, one a clergyman. This last had been regularly educated at Oxford—as a member of Jesus (the Welsh college)—and was a man of extensive information. The lawyers had not enjoyed the same advantages, but they had read diligently, and were interesting companions. Wales, as is pretty well known, breeds a population somewhat litigious. I do not think the worse of them for *that*. The martial Butlers and the heroic Talbots of the fifteenth century, having no regular opening for their warlike fury in the seventeenth century, took to quarrelling with each other ; and no letters are more bitter than those which to this day survive from the hostile correspondence of the brother Talbots contemporary with the last days of Shakspere.[1] One channel being closed against their martial propensities, naturally they opened such others as circumstances made available. This temper, widely spread amongst the lower classes of the Welsh, made it a necessity that the lawyers should itinerate on market-days through all the principal towns in their districts. In those towns continually I met them ; and continually we renewed our literary friendship.

Meantime alternately I sailed upon the high-priced and the low-priced tack. So exceedingly cheap were provisions at that period, when the war taxation of Mr. Pitt was partially intermitting, that it was easy beyond measure upon any three weeks' expenditure, by living with cottagers, to save two guineas out of the three. Mr. De Haren assured me that even in an inn, and not in a poor man's cottage (but an unpretending rustic inn, where the mistress of the house took upon herself the functions of every possible servant in turn—cook, waiter, chambermaid, boots, ostler), he had passed a day or two ; and for what he considered a really elegant dinner, as regarded everything except the table equipage (that being rude and coarse), he had paid only sixpence. This very inn, about ten or twelve miles south of Dolgelly, I myself visited

[1] See especially a book written by Sir Egerton Brydges (I forget the title) on the Peerage in the reign of James I.

some time later; and I found Mr. De Haren's account
in all points confirmed: the sole drawback upon the
comfort of the visitor being that the fuel was chiefly of
green wood, and with a chimney that smoked. I suffered
so much under this kind of smoke, which irritates and
inflames the eyes more than any other, that on the following day reluctantly I took leave of that obliging pluralist
the landlady, and really felt myself blushing on settling
the bill, until I bethought me of the green wood, which,
upon the whole, seemed to balance the account. I could
not then, nor can I now, account for these preposterously
low prices; which same prices, strange to say, ruled (as
Wordsworth and his sister often assured me) among the
same kind of scenery—*i.e.*, amongst the English Lakes—
at the very same time. To account for it, as people often
do, by alleging the want of markets for agricultural produce, is crazy political economy; since the remedy for
paucity of markets, and consequent failure of competition,
is, certainly not to sell at losing rates, but to forbear producing, and consequently not to sell at all.[1]

[1] Thirteen years later—viz., in the year of Waterloo—happening
to walk through the whole Principality from south to north, beginning
at Cardiff, and ending at Bangor, I turned aside about twenty-five
miles to inquire after the health of my excellent hostess, that determined pluralist and intense antipole of all possible sinecurists. I found
her cleaning a pair of boots and spurs, and purposing (I rather think)
to enter next upon the elegant office of greasing a horse's heels. In
that design, however, she was thwarted for the present by myself and
another tourist, who claimed her services in three or four other characters previously. I inquired after the chimney—was it still smoking?
She seemed surprised that it had ever been suspected of anything
criminal; so, as it was not a season for fires, I said no more. But I
saw plenty of green wood, and but a small proportion of peats. I fear,
therefore, that this, the state-room of the whole concern, still poisons
the peace of the unhappy tourists. One personal indemnification,
meantime, I must mention which this little guilty room made to me
on that same night for all the tears it had caused me to shed. It
happened that there was a public dance held at this inn on this very
night. I therefore retired early to my bedroom, having had so long a
walk, and not wishing to annoy the company, or the excellent landlady, who had, I daresay, to play the fiddle to the dancers. The noise
and uproar were almost insupportable; so that I could not sleep at all.
At three o'clock all became silent, the company having departed in a

So cheap in fact were all provisions, which one had
any chance of meeting with in a labouring man's house,
that I found it difficult under such a roof to spend sixpence a-day. Tea or coffee there was none: and I did
not at that period very much care for either. Milk, with
bread (coarse, but more agreeable by much than the insipid
whity-grey bread of towns), potatoes if one wished, and
also a little goat's, or kid's, flesh — these composed the
cottager's choice of viands ; not luxurious, but palatable
enough to a person who took much exercise. And, if
one wished, fresh-water fish could be had cheap enough ;
especially trout of the very finest quality. In these
circumstances, I never found it easy to spend even five
shillings (no, not three shillings, unless whortleberries or
fish had been bought) in one week. And thus it was
easy enough to create funds for my periodical transmigra-
tions back into the character of gentleman-tourist. Even
the half of five shillings I could not always find means
to spend: for in some families, raised above dependence
upon daily wages, when I performed any services in the
way of letter-writing, I found it impossible at times to
force any money at all upon them. Once, in particular,
near the small lake of Talyllyn (so written, I believe, but
pronounced Taltlyn), in a sequestered part of Merionethshire, I was entertained for upwards of three days by a
family of young people, with an affectionate and fraternal
kindness that left an impression upon my heart not yet
impaired. The family consisted, at that time, of four
sisters and three brothers, all grown up, and remarkable
for elegance and delicacy of manners. So much beauty,

body. Suddenly from the little parlour, separated from my bedroom
overhead by the slightest and most pervious of ceilings, arose with the
rising dawn the very sweetest of female voices perhaps that ever I had
heard, although for many years an *habitué* of the opera. She was a
stranger ; a visitor from some distance ; and (I was told in the morning)
a Methodist. What she sang, or at least sang last, were the beautiful
verses of Shirley, ending—

> Only the actions of the just
> Smell sweet, and blossom in the dust.

This incident caused me to forget and forgive the wicked little
chimney.

or so much native good breeding and refinement, I do not remember to have seen before or since in any cottage, except once or twice in Westmoreland and Devonshire. They spoke English ; an accomplishment not often met with in so many members of one Welsh family, especially in villages remote from the high road. Here I wrote, on my first introduction, a letter about prize-money for one of the brothers, who had served on board an English man-of-war ; and, more privately, two letters to sweethearts for two of the sisters. They were both interesting in appearance ; and one of uncommon loveliness. In the midst of their confusion and blushes, whilst dictating, or rather giving me general instructions, it did not require any great penetration to discover that they wished their letters to be as kind as was consistent with proper maidenly reserve. I contrived so to temper my expressions as to reconcile the gratification of both feelings ; and they were as much pleased with the way in which I had given expression to their thoughts, as (in their simplicity) they were astonished at my having so readily discovered them. The reception one meets with from the women of a family generally determines the tenor of one's whole entertainment. In this case I had discharged my confidential duties as secretary so much to the general satisfaction, perhaps also amusing them with my conversation, that I was pressed to stay ; and pressed with a cordiality which I had little inclination to resist. I slept unavoidably with the brothers, the only unoccupied bed standing in the chamber of the young women : but in all other points they treated me with a respect not usually paid to purses as light as mine ; making it evident that my scholarship and courteous demeanour were considered sufficient arguments of gentle blood. Thus I lived with them for three days, and great part of a fourth ; and, from the undiminished kindness which they continued to show me, I believe that I might have stayed with them up to this time, if their power had corresponded with their wishes. On the last morning, however, I perceived upon their countenances, as they sat at breakfast, the approach of some unpleasant communication ; and soon after, one of the brothers explained to me that, on the day before my arrival, their parents had gone to an annual meeting of Methodists, held at Carnarvon,[1] and in the course of that day were expected to return ; 'and if they should not be so civil as they ought to be,' he begged, on the part of all the young people, that I would not take it amiss. The parents returned with churlish faces, and ' *Dym Sassenach* ' (*no English*) in answer to all my addresses. I saw how matters stood ; and so, taking an affectionate leave of my kind and interesting young hosts, I went my way. For, though they spoke warmly to their parents on my behalf, and often excused the manner of the old people by saying that it was 'only their way,' yet I easily understood that my talent for writing love-letters would do as little to recommend me with two sexagenarian Welsh Methodists as my Greek Sapphics or Alcaics ; and what had been hospitality, when offered with the gracious courtesy of my young friends, would become charity, when connected with the harsh demeanour of their parents.

About this time—just when it was becoming daily more difficult to eke out the weekly funds for high-priced inns by the bivouacking system—as if some overmastering fiend, some instinct of migration, sorrowful but irresistible, were driving me forth to wander like the unhappy Io of the Grecian mythus, some oestrum of hidden persecution that bade me fly when no man pursued ; not in false hope —for my hopes whispered but a doubtful chance, not in reasonable fear — for all was sweet pastoral quiet and autumnal beauty around me, suddenly I took a fierce resolution to sacrifice my weekly allowance, to slip my anchor, and to throw myself in desperation upon London.

---

[1] ' *At Carnarvon* ' :—It was on this occasion that I learned how vague are the ideas of *number* in unpractised minds. ' What number of people, do you think,' said I to an elderly person, ' will be assembled this day at Carnarvon ? '—' What number ? ' rejoined the person addressed—' what number ? Well, really now, I should reckon— perhaps a matter of four millions.' Four millions of *extra* people in little Carnarvon, that could barely find accommodation (I should calculate) for an extra four hundred.

Not to make the case more frantic than it really was, let the reader remember what it was that I found grievous in my present position, and upon what possibilities it was that I relied for bettering it.   With a more extended know-ledge of life than I at that time had, it would not have been so hopeless a speculation for a boy, having my accomplishments, to launch himself on the boundless ocean of London.   I possessed attainments that bore a money value.   For instance, as a ' *Reader* ' to the Press in the field of Greek re-publications, I might perhaps have earned a livelihood.   But these chances, which I really had, never occurred to me in the light of useful resources ; or, to speak the truth, they were unknown to me : and those, which I chiefly relied on, were most unlikely to prove available.   But what, meantime, was it that I complained of in the life that I was at present living ?   It was this : the dilemma proposed to my choice was—that if I *would* —positively *would*—have society, I must live at inns. But if I reconciled myself to a quiet stationary abode in some village or hamlet, in that case for *me*, so transcend-ently careless about diet, my weekly guinea would have procured all that I wanted : and in some houses the advantage, quite indispensable to my comfort, of a private sitting-room.   Yet even here the expense was most need-lessly enhanced by the aristocratic luxuriousness of our English system, which presumes it impossible for a gentle-man to sleep in his sitting-room.   On this footing, however, I might perhaps have commanded clean and comfortable accommodations in some respectable families, to whom my noiseless habits, and my respectful courtesy to women, would have recommended me as a desirable inmate.   But the deadly drawback on this scheme was—the utter want of access to books, or (generally speaking) to any intel-lectual intercourse.   I languished all the day through, and all the week through—with nothing whatever, not so much as the county newspaper once in seven days to relieve my mortal ennui.

I have told the reader how inexplicably cheap was the life in poor men's cottages.   But this did not affect the

prices at the first-class hotels, where only I had any chance
of meeting society. Those, and chiefly on the plea that
the season was so brief, charged London prices. To meet
such prices, it would no longer be possible, as winter came
on, to raise one-half the funds by passing half the time in
a less costly mode. There was an end of any feasible plan
for interleaving days of hardship with days of ease and
intellectual luxury. Meantime, whilst this perplexity was
resounding in one ear, in the other were continually echoing
the kind offers of my Welsh friends, especially the two
lawyers, to furnish me with any money which I might
think necessary for my visit to London. Twelve guineas,
at length, I mentioned as probably enough. This they
lent me on the spot. And now, all at once, I was—ready
for London.

My farewell to the Principality was in the same unas-
suming character of pedestrian tourist as that in which I
had entered it. *Impedimenta* of any kind—that is, the
encumbrances of horse or baggage—I had none even to
the last. Where I pleased, and *when* I pleased, I could
call a halt. My last halt of any duration was at Oswestry ;
mere accident carried me thither, and accident very naturally in so small a town threw me across the path of the
very warmest amongst my Welsh friends, who, as it turned
out, resided there. He, by mere coercion of kindness,
detained me for several days ; for denial he would not
take. Being as yet unmarried, he could not vivify the
other attractions of his most hospitable abode by the rein-
forcement of female society. His own, however, coming
recommended as it did by the graces of a youthful frankness and a kindling intellect, was all-sufficient for the
beguiling of the longest day. This Welsh friend was one
of many whom I have crossed in life, chained by early
accident or by domestic necessity to the calls of a professional service, whilst all the while his whole nature, wild
and refractory, ran headlong into intellectual channels that
could not be trained into reconciliation with his hourly
duties. His library was already large, and as select as
under the ordinary chances of provincial book-collection

could be reasonably expected. For generally one-half, at
the least, of a young man's library in a provincial town
may be characterised as a mere dropping or deposition
from local accidents, a casual windfall of fruits stripped
and strewed by the rough storms of bankruptcy. In many
cases, again, such a provincial library will represent simply
that part of the heavy baggage which many a family, on
removing to some distant quarter, has shrunk from the
cost of transporting, books being amongst the heaviest of
household goods. Sometimes also, though more rarely, it
happens that an ancient family dying out, having unavoidably left to executors the duty of selling every chattel
attached to its ancient habits of life, suddenly with meteoric
glare there emerges from its hiding-place of centuries
some great jewel of literature, a First Folio of the 1623
Shakspere, an uncastrated *Decamerone*, or other dazzling
κειμήλιον. And thus it is that a large provincial library,
though naturally and peacefully accumulated, yet sometimes shows mute evidence of convulsions and household
tragedies ; speaks as if by records of storms, and through
dim mementoes of half-forgotten shipwrecks. Real shipwrecks present often such incoherent libraries on the floors
of the hungry sea. Magnificent is the library that sleeps
unvexed by criticism at the bottom of the ocean, Indian or
Atlantic, from the mere annual contributions and keep-
sakes, the never-ending *Forget-me-nots*, of mighty English
Indiamen. The Halsewell, with its sad parting between
the captain and his daughters, the Grosvenor, the Winter-
ton, the Abergavenny, and scores of vessels on the same
scale, with populations varying by births, deaths, and
marriages, populations large as cities, and rich as gold
mines, capable of factions and rebellions, all and each have
liberally patronised, by the gift of many *Large-Paper*
copies, that vast submarine Bodleian, which stands in far
less risk from fire than the insolent Bodleian of the upper
world. This private Oswestry library wore something of
the same wild tumultuary aspect, fantastic and disordinate,
but was not for that reason the less attractive ; everything
was there that you never expected to meet anywhere, but

certainly not to meet in company ; so that, what between the library and the mercurial conversation of its proprietor, elated by the rare advantage of fraternal sympathy, I was in danger of finding attractions strong enough to lay me asleep over the proprieties of the case, or even to set me a-dreaming over imaginary cases. In fact, I had some excuse for doing so ; since I knew very imperfectly the common routine of my friend's life ; and from *his* lofty Castilian sense of the obligations imposed by the great goddess Hospitality, I never should have been suffered to guess at the extent in which I was now gradually and unconsciously coming daily into collision with the regular calls upon his time. To ride off, under mask of ' business,' upon a circuit of a week, would, in *his* eyes, have been *virtually*, as regards the result, meanly and evasively, as regards the mode, to turn me out of his house. He would sooner have died. But in the meantime an accident, which revealed to me the true state of things, or at least revealed a suspicion of it, all at once armed my sense of delicacy against any further lingering. Suddenly and peremptorily I announced my departure—*that* and the mode of it. For a long time he fought with unaffected zeal against my purpose, as nowise essential to his own free action. But at last, seeing that I was in earnest, he forbore to oppose my plan, contenting himself with guiding and improving its details. My plan had been, to walk over the border into England, as far as Shrewsbury (distant from Oswestry, I think, about eighteen miles), and there to ascend any of the heavy stages which would convey me cheaply to Birmingham—the grand focus to which all the routes of England in its main central area converge. Any such plan moved on the assumption that rain would be falling steadily and heavily—a reasonable assumption at the close of November. But, in the possible event of fair weather lasting over four or five days, what should prevent me from traversing the whole distance on foot ? It is true, that the aristocratic scowl of the landlord might be looked for as a customary salutation at the close of each day's journey ; but, unless at solitary posting-houses, this criminal fact of having advanced by base pedestrian methods, known only to patriarchs of older days and to modern '*tramps*' (so they are called in solemn acts of Parliament), is easily expiated and cleansed, by distributing your dust, should you fortunately have any to show, amongst the streets that you have invaded as a stranger. Happily the scandal of pedestrianism is in one respect more hopefully situated than that of scrofula or leprosy ; it is not in any case written in your face. The man who is guilty of pedestrianism, on entering any town whatever, by the simple artifice of diving into the crowds of those untainted by that guilt, will emerge, for all practical purposes, washed and re-baptised. The landlord, indeed, of any one inn knows that you did not reach *him* on horse-back, or in a carriage ; but you may have been visiting for weeks at the house of some distinguished citizen, whom it might be dangerous to offend ; and you may even be favourably known at some other inn. Else, as a general imputation, undoubtedly pedestrianism, in the estimate of English landlords, carries with it the most awful shadow and shibboleth of the pariah. My Welsh friend knew this, and strongly urged me to take advantage of the public carriages, both on that motive and others. A journey of a hundred and eighty miles, as a pedestrian, would cost me nine or ten days ; for which extent the mere amount of expenses at inns would more than defray the fare of the dearest carriage. To this there was no sound reply, except that corresponding expenses would arise, at any rate, on these nine or ten days, wherever I might be—in London, or on the road. However, as it seemed ungracious to offer too obstinate a resistance to suggestions prompted so entirely by consideration for my own comfort, I submitted to my friend's plan in all its details ; one being that I should go by the Holyhead Mail, and not by any of the heavy coaches. This stipulation pointed to a novel feature in the machinery of travelling just then emerging. The light coaches charged almost mail prices. But the heavy coaches were at that time beginning to assume a new and dreadful form. Locomo-

K

tion was so prodigiously on the increase, that, in order to meet its demands, the old form of coach (carrying at most six insides) was exchanging itself, on all great roads, for a long, boatlike vehicle, very much resembling our modern detestable *omnibus*, but without our modern improvements. This carriage was called a ' *long coach*,' and the passengers, twelve or fourteen insides, sat along the sides ; and, as ventilation was little regarded in those days—the very existence of an atmosphere being usually ignored — it followed that the horrors of Governor Holwell's black cage at Calcutta were every night repeated, in smaller proportions, upon every great English road. It was finally agreed that I should leave Oswestry on foot, simply with a view to the best enjoyment of the lovely weather ; but that, as the mail passed through Oswestry, my friend should secure a place for me the whole way to London, so as to shut out competitors.

The day on which I left Oswestry (convoyed for nearly five miles by my warm-hearted friend) was a day of golden sunshine amongst the closing days of November. As truly as Jessica's moonlight (*Merchant of Venice*), this golden sunshine might be said to *sleep* upon the woods and the fields ; so awful was the universal silence, so profound the death-like stillness. It was a day belonging to a brief and pathetic season of farewell summer resurrection, which, under one name or other, is known almost everywhere. In North America it is called the ' Indian Summer.' In North Germany and Midland Germany it is called the ' Old Wives' Summer,' and more rarely the ' Girls' Summer.' It is that last brief resurrection of summer in its most brilliant memorials, a resurrection that has no root in the past, nor steady hold upon the future, like the lambent and fitful gleams from an expiring lamp, mimicking what is called the ' lightning before death ' in sick patients, when close upon their end. There is the feeling of a conflict that has been going on between the lingering powers of summer and the strengthening powers of winter, not unlike that which moves by antagonist forces in some deadly inflammation hurrying forwards through fierce struggles into the final repose of mortification.   For a time the equilibrium has been maintained between the hostile forces ; but at last the antagonism is overthrown ; the victory is accomplished for the powers that fight on the side of death ; simultaneously with the conflict, the pain of conflict has departed : and thenceforward the gentle process of collapsing life, no longer fretted by counter-movements, slips away with holy peace into the noiseless deeps of the Infinite.   So sweet, so ghostly, in its soft, golden smiles, silent as a dream, and quiet as the dying trance of a saint, faded through all its stages this departing day, along the whole length of which I bade farewell for many a year to Wales, and farewell to summer.   In the very aspect and the sepulchral stillness of the motionless day, as solemnly it wore away through morning, noontide, afternoon, to meet the darkness that was hurrying to swallow up its beauty, I had a fantastic feeling as though I read the very language of resignation when bending before some irresistible agency.   And at intervals I heard—in how different a key !—the raving, the everlasting uproar of that dreadful metropolis, which at every step was coming nearer, and beckoning (as it seemed) to myself for purposes as dim, for issues as incalculable, as the path of cannon-shots fired at random and in darkness.

It was not late, but it was at least two hours after nightfall, when I reached Shrewsbury.   Was I not liable to the suspicion of pedestrianism ?   Certainly I was : but, even if my criminality had been more unequivocally attested than it could be under the circumstances, still there is a *locus penitentiæ* in such a case.   Surely a man may repent of *any* crime ; and therefore of pedestrianism. I might have erred ; and a court of *pié poudré* (dusty foot) might have found the evidences of my crime on my shoes.   Yet secretly I might be forming good resolutions to do so no more.   Certainly it looked like this, when I announced myself as a passenger 'booked' for that night's mail.   This character at once installed me as rightfully a guest of the inn, however profligate a life I might have

previously led as a pedestrian.   Accordingly I was received
with special courtesy; and it so happened that I was
received with something even like pomp.   Four wax-
lights carried before me by obedient mutes, these were but
ordinary honours, meant (as old experience had instructed
me) for the first engineering step towards effecting a
lodgment upon the stranger's purse.   In fact the wax-
lights are used by innkeepers, both abroad and at home,
to 'try the range of their guns.'   If the stranger submits
quietly, as a good anti-pedestrian ought surely to do, and
fires no counter gun by way of protest, then he is recognised
at once as passively within range, and amenable to orders.
I have always looked upon this fine of five or seven
shillings (for wax that you do not absolutely need) as a
sort of inaugural *honorarium* entrance-money, what in
jails used to be known as *smart* money, proclaiming me to
be a man *comme il faut;* and no toll in this world of tolls
do I pay so cheerfully.   This, meantime, as I have said,
was too customary a form to confer much distinction.
The wax-lights, to use the magnificent Grecian phrase
ἐπόμπευε, moved pompously before me, as the holy—holy
fire, the inextinguishable fire and its golden hearth, moved
before Cæsar *semper* Augustus, when he made his official
or ceremonial *avatars.*   Yet still this moved along the
ordinary channels of glorification : it rolled along ancient
grooves : I might say, indeed, like one of the twelve
Cæsars when dying, *Ut puto, Deus fio* (It's my private
opinion that at this very moment I am turning into a
god), but still the metamorphosis was not complete.   *That*
was accomplished when I stepped into the sumptuous room
allotted to me.   It was a ball-room [1] of noble proportions
—lighted, if I chose to issue orders, by three gorgeous
chandeliers, not basely wrapped up in paper, but sparkling
through all their thickets of crystal branches, and flashing

---

[1] '*It was a ball-room*' :—The explanation of the case was simply,
that the hotel was under some extensive process of purification,
adornment, and, I believe, extension : and, under the accident of
being myself on that particular night the sole visitor of the house, I
slipped unavoidably into the honours of a semi-regal reception.

back the soft rays of my tall waxen lights. There were, moreover, two orchestras, which money would have filled within thirty minutes. And, upon the whole, one thing only was wanting—viz., a throne—for the completion of my *apotheosis*.

It might be seven P.M. when first I entered upon my kingdom. About three hours later I rose from my chair, and with considerable interest looked out into the night. For nearly two hours I had heard fierce winds arising ; and the whole atmosphere had, by this time, become one vast laboratory of hostile movements in all directions. Such a chaos, such a distracting wilderness of dim sights, and of those awful ' sounds that live in darkness ' (Wordsworth's *Excursion*), never had I consciously witnessed. Rightly, and by a true instinct, had I made my farewell adieus to summer. All through the day, Wales and her grand mountain ranges—Penmaenmawr, Snowdon, Cader Idris—had divided my thoughts with London. But now rose London—sole, dark, infinite—brooding over the whole capacities of my heart. Other object—other thought —I could not admit. Long before midnight, the whole household (with the exception of a solitary waiter) had retired to rest. Two hours, at least, were left to me, after twelve o'clock had struck, for heart-shaking reflections. More than ever I stood upon the brink of a precipice ; and the local circumstances around me deepened and intensified these reflections, impressed upon them solemnity and terror, sometimes even horror. It is all but inconceivable to men of unyielding and callous sensibilities, how profoundly others find their reveries modified and overruled by the external characters of the immediate scene around them. Many a suicide that hung dubiously in the balances has been ratified, and carried into summary effect, through the forlorn, soul-revolting aspect of a crazy, dilapidated home. Oftentimes, without extravagance, the whole difference between a mind that spurns life and the same mind reconciled to life, turns upon the outside features of that particular domestic scenery which hourly besieges the eyes. I, in this Shrewsbury hotel, naturally contemplated a group of objects tending to far different results. And yet in some respects they agreed.

The unusual dimensions of the rooms, especially their towering height, brought up continually and obstinately, through natural links of associated feelings or images, the mighty vision of London waiting for me afar off. An altitude of nineteen or twenty feet showed itself unavoidably upon an exaggerated scale in some of the smaller side-rooms—meant probably for cards or for refreshments. This single feature of the rooms—their unusual altitude, and the echoing hollowness which had become the exponent of that altitude—this one terrific feature (for terrific it was in the effect), together with crowding and evanescent images of the flying feet that so often had spread gladness through these halls on the wings of youth and hope at seasons when every room rang with music—all this, rising in tumultuous vision, whilst the dead hours of night were stealing along, all around me— household and town—sleeping, and whilst against the windows more and more the storm outside was raving, and to all appearance endlessly growing, threw me into the deadliest condition of nervous emotion under contradictory forces, high over which predominated horror recoiling from that unfathomed abyss in London into which I was now so wilfully precipitating myself. Often I looked out and examined the night. Wild it was beyond all description, and dark as 'the inside of a wolf's throat.' But at intervals, when the wind, shifting continually, swept in such a direction as to clear away the vast curtain of vapour, the stars shone out, though with a light unusually dim and distant. Still, as I turned inwards to the echoing chambers, or outwards to the wild, wild night, I saw London expanding her visionary gates to receive me, like some dreadful mouth of Acheron (*Acherontis avari*). Thou also, Whispering Gallery! once again in those moments of conscious and wilful desolation didst to my ear utter monitorial sighs. For once again I was preparing to utter an irrevocable word, to enter upon one of those fatally tortuous paths of which the windings can never be unlinked.

Such thoughts, and visions without number corresponding to them, were moving across the *camera obscura* of my fermenting fancy, when suddenly I heard a sound of wheels ; which, however, soon died off into some remote quarter. I guessed at the truth—viz., that it was the Holyhead Mail [1] wheeling off on its primary duty of delivering its bags at the post-office. In a few minutes it was announced as having changed horses ; and off I was to London.

All the mails in the kingdom, with one solitary exception (that of Liverpool), in those days, were so arranged as to reach London early in the morning. Between the hours of four and six A.M., one after the other, according to their station upon the roll, all the mails from the N[orth]—the E[ast]—the W[est]—the S[outh]— whence, according to some curious etymologists, comes the magical word *NEWS*—drove up successively to the post-office, and rendered up their heart-shaking budgets ; none earlier than four o'clock, none later than six. I am speaking of days when all things moved slowly. The condition of the roads was then such, that, in order to face it, a corresponding build of coaches hyperbolically massive was rendered necessary : the mails were upon principle made so strong as to be the heaviest of all

---

[1] The Holyhead Mail, depending in its earliest stages upon winds and waters (though not upon tides), could not realise the same exquisite accuracy as mails that moved exclusively upon land. Sixty miles of watery transit between Dublin and Holyhead were performed with miraculous precision. The packets were intrusted by the General Post-office to none but post-captains, who had commanded frigates. And the salaries were so high as to make these commands confessedly prizes in nautical life, and objects of keen competition. No evil, therefore, which care, foresight, and professional skill could remedy, was suffered to exist. Yet, after all, baffling winds would now and then (especially in three or four weeks *after* the equinox) make it impossible for the very ablest man, under the total defect of steam resources, to keep his time. Six hours, I believe, were allowed by the Post-office for the sixty miles ; but at times this must have proved a very inadequate allowance.

carriages known to the wit or the experience of man; and from these joint evils of ponderous coaches and roads that were quagmires, it was impossible for even the picked breed of English-coach-horses, all bone and blood, to carry forward their huge tonnage at a greater rate than six-and-a-half miles an hour. Consequently, it cost eight-and-twenty massy hours for us, leaving Shrewsbury at two o'clock in the dead of night, to reach the General Post-office, and faithfully to deposit upon the threshing-floors of Lombard Street, all that weight of love and hatred which Ireland had found herself able to muster through twenty-four hours in the great depot of Dublin, by way of donation to England.

On reflection, I have done myself some injustice. Not altogether without a plan had I been from the first; and in coming along I had matured it. My success in such a plan would turn upon my chance of borrowing on personal security. £200, without counting any interest upon it, would sub-divide into four sums of £50. Now, what interval was it that divided me from my majority? Simply an interval of four years. London, I knew or believed, was the dearest of all cities for three items of expenditure: (1) servants' wages; (2) lodgings;[1] (3) dairy produce. In other things, London was often cheaper than most towns. Now, in a London street, having no pretensions beyond those of decent respectability, it has always been possible for the last half century to obtain two furnished rooms at a weekly cost of half a guinea. This sum (or say £25) deducted would leave me annually about the same sum for my other expenses. Too certainly I knew that this would suffice. If, therefore, I could obtain the £200, my plan was to withdraw from

[1] Not universally. Glasgow, if you travel from Hammerfest southwards (that is, from the northernmost point of Norway, or Swedish Lapland, traversing all latitudes of Europe to Gibraltar on the west, or Naples on the east), is the one dearest place for lodgings known to man. A decent lodging for a single person, in Edinburgh, which could be had readily for half-a-guinea a-week, will in Glasgow cost a guinea. Glasgow, except as to servants, is a dearer abode than London.

the knowledge of all my connexions until I should become *mei juris* by course of law.   In such a case, it is true that I must have waived all the advantages, fancied or real, small or great, from residence at a university.   But, as in fact I never drew the slightest advantage or emolument from any university, my scheme when realised would have landed me in the same point which finally I attained by its failure.   The plan was simple enough, but it rested on the assumption that I could melt the obduracy of money-lenders.   On this point I had both hopes and fears.   But more irritating than either was the *delay*, which eventually I came to recognise as an essential element in the policy of all money-lenders : in that way only can they raise up such claims on behalf of their law-agents as may be fitted for sustaining their zeal.

.   .   .   .   .   .

I lost no time in opening the business which had brought me to London.   By ten A.M., an hour when all men of business are presumed to be at their posts, personally or by proxy, I presented myself at the money-lender's office.   My name was already known there : for I had, by letters from Wales, containing very plain and very accurate statements of my position in life and my pecuniary expectations (some of which statements it afterwards appeared that he had personally investigated and verified), endeavoured to win his favourable attention. The money-lender, as it turned out, had one fixed rule of action.   He never granted a personal interview to any man ; no, not to the most beloved of his clients.   One and all—myself, therefore, among the crowd—he referred for information, and for the means of prosecuting any kind of negotiation, to an attorney, who called himself, on most days of the week, by the name of Brunell, but occasionally (might it perhaps be on *red-letter* days ?) by the more common name of Brown.   Mr. Brunell-Brown, or Brown-Brunell, had located his hearth (if ever he had possessed one), and his household gods (when they were not in the custody of the sheriff), in Greek Street, Soho. The house was not in itself, supposing that its face had

been washed now and then, at all disrespectable. But it
wore an unhappy countenance of gloom and unsocial fret-
fulness, due in reality to the long neglect of painting,
cleansing, and in some instances of repairing.   There were,
however, no fractured panes of glass in the windows ; and
the deep silence which invested the house, not only from
the absence of all visitors, but also of those common
household functionaries, bakers, butchers, beer-carriers,
sufficiently accounted for the desolation, by suggesting an
excuse not strictly true—viz., that it might be tenantless.
The house already had tenants through the day, though
of a noiseless order, and was destined soon to increase
them.   Mr. Brown-Brunell, after reconnoitring me
through a narrow side-window (such as is often attached
to front-doors in London), admitted me cheerfully, and
conducted me, as an honoured guest, to his private *officina
diplomatum* at the back of the house.   From the expression
of his face, but much more from the contradictory and
self-counteracting play of his features, you gathered in a
moment that he was a man who had much to conceal,
and much, perhaps, that he would gladly forget.   His
eye expressed wariness against surprise, and passed in a
moment into irrepressible glances of suspicion and alarm.
No smile that ever his face naturally assumed, but was
pulled short up by some freezing counteraction, or was
chased by some close-following expression of sadness.
One feature there was of relenting goodness and nobleness
in Mr. Brunell's character, to which it was that subsequently I myself was most profoundly indebted for an
asylum that saved my life.   He had the deepest, the
most liberal, and unaffected love of knowledge, but, above
all, of that specific knowledge which we call literature.
His own stormy (and no doubt oftentimes disgraceful)
career in life, that had entangled him in perpetual feuds
with his fellow-men, he ascribed, with bitter imprecations,
to the sudden interruption of his studies consequent upon
his father's violent death, and to the necessity which threw
him, at a boyish age, upon a professional life in the lower
branches of law—threw him, therefore, upon daily tempt-

ations, by surrounding him with opportunities for taking
advantages not strictly honourable, before he had formed
any fixed principles at all.   From the very first, Mr.
Brunell had entered zealously into such conversations with
myself as either gave openings for reviving his own delightful remembrances of classic authors, or brought up
sometimes doubts for solution, sometimes perplexities and
cases of intricate construction for illustration and disen-
tanglement.   Hunger-bitten as the house and the household
genius seemed, wearing the legend of *Famine* upon every
mantelpiece or 'coigne of vantage,' and vehemently protesting, as it must have done through all its echoes, against
the introduction of supernumerary mouths, nevertheless
there was (and, I suppose, of necessity) a clerk, who bore
the name of Pyment, or Pyemont, then first of all, then
last of all, made known to me as a possible surname.
Mr. Pyment had no *alias*—or not to my knowledge—
except, indeed, in the vituperative vocabulary of Mr.
Brunell, in which most variegated nomenclature he bore
many scores of opprobrious names, having no reference
whatever to any real habits of the man, good or bad.   At
two rooms' distance, Mr. Brunell always assumed a minute
and circumstantial knowledge of what Pyment was doing
then, and what he was going to do next.   All which
Pyment gave himself little trouble to answer, unless it
happened (as now and then it did) that he could do so
with ludicrous effect.   What made the necessity for
Pyment was the continual call for 'an appearance' to be
put in at some of the subordinate courts in Westminster
—courts of conscience, sheriff courts, etc.   But it happens
often that he who is most indispensable, and gets through
most work at one hour, becomes a useless burden at
another ; as the hardest working reaper seems, in the eyes
of an ignoramus, on a wet, wintry day, to be a luxurious
idler.   Of these ups and downs in Pyment's working life,
Mr. Brunell made a most cynical use ; making out that
Pyment not only did nothing, but also that he created
much work for the afflicted Brunell.   However, it
happened occasionally that the truth vindicated itself, by

making a call upon Pyment's physics—aggressive or defensive—that needed an instant attention. 'Pyment, I say ; this way, Pyment—you're wanted, Pyment.' In fact, both were big, hulking men, and had need to be so ; for sometimes, whether with good reason or none, clients at the end of a losing suit, or of a suit nominally gained, but unexpectedly laden with heavy expenses, became re-fractory, showed fight, and gave Pyment reason for saying that at least on this day he had earned his salary by serv-ing an ejectment on a client whom on any other plan it might have been hard to settle with.

But I am anticipating. I go back, therefore, for a few explanatory words, to the day of my arrival in London. How beneficial to me would a little candour have been at that early period ! If (which was the simple truth, known to all parties but myself) I had been told that nothing would be brought to a close in less than six months, even assuming the ultimate adoption of my pro-posals, I should from the first have dismissed all hopes of this nature, as being unsuited to the practicabilities of my situation. It will be seen further on, that there was a real and sincere intention of advancing the money wanted. But it was then too late. And universally I believe my-self entitled to say, that even honourable lawyers will not in a case of this nature move at a faster pace : they will all alike loiter upon varied allegations through six months ; and for this reason, that any shorter period, they fancy, will hardly seem to justify, in the eyes of their client, the sum which they find themselves entitled to charge for their trouble and their preliminary correspondence. How much better for both sides, and more honourable, as more frank and free from disguises, that the client should say, 'Raise this sum' (of, suppose, £400) 'in three weeks, which can be done, if it can be done in three years, and here is a *bonus* of £100. Delay for two months, and I decline the whole transaction.' Treated with that sort of openness, how much bodily suffering of an extreme order, and how much of the sickness from hope deferred, should I have escaped ! Whereas, under the system (pursued

with me as with all clients) of continually refreshing my
hopes with new delusions, whiling me on with pretended
preparation of deeds, and extorting from me, out of every
little remittance I received from old family friends casually
met in London, as much as possible for the purchase of
imaginary stamps, the result was, that I myself was brought
to the brink of destruction through pure inanition ; whilst,
on the other hand, those concerned in these deceptions
gained nothing that might not have been gained honourably and rightfully under a system of plain dealing.   As
it was, subject to these eternal deceptions, I continued
for seven or eight weeks to live most parsimoniously in
lodgings.   These lodgings, though barely decent in my
eyes, ran away with at the least two-thirds of my remaining
guineas.   At length, whilst it was yet possible to reserve
a solitary half-guinea towards the more urgent interest of
finding daily food, I gave up my rooms ; and, stating
exactly the circumstances in which I stood, requested permission of Mr. Brunell to make use of his large house as
a nightly asylum from the open air.   Parliament had not
then made it a crime, next door to a felony, for a man to
sleep out-of-doors (as some twenty years later was done
by our benign legislators) ; as yet *that* was no crime.   By
the law I came to know sin ; and looking back to the
Cambrian hills from distant years, discovered to my surprise what a parliamentary wretch I had been in elder
days, when I slept amongst cows on the open hill-sides.
Lawful as yet this was ; but not, therefore, less full of
misery.   Naturally, then, I was delighted when Mr.
Brunell not only most readily assented to my request, but
begged of me to come that very night, and turn the house
to account as fully as I possibly could.   The cheerfulness
of such a concession brought with it one drawback.   I
now regretted that I had not, at a much earlier period,
applied for this liberty ; since I might thus have saved a
considerable fund of guineas, applicable, of course, to all
urgent necessities, but at this particular moment to one of
clamorous urgency—viz., the purchase of blankets.   O
ancient women, daughters of toil and suffering, amongst

all the hardships and bitter inheritances of flesh that ye
are called upon to face, not one—not even hunger—seems
in my eyes comparable to that of nightly cold.   To seek
a refuge from cold in bed, and then, from the thin, gauzy
texture of the miserable, worn-out blankets, 'not to sleep
a wink,' as Wordsworth records of poor old women in
Dorsetshire, where coals, from local causes, were at the
very dearest—what a terrific enemy was *that* for poor old
grandmothers to face in fight!   How feelingly I learned
at this time, as heretofore I had learned on the wild hill-
sides in Wales, what an unspeakable blessing is that of
warmth!   A more killing curse there does not exist for
man or woman, than that bitter combat between the weariness that prompts sleep, and the keen, searching cold that
forces you from the first access of sleep to start up horror-
stricken, and to seek warmth vainly in renewed exercise,
though long since fainting under fatigue.   However, even
without blankets, it was a fine thing to have an asylum
from the open air ; and to be assured of this asylum as
long as I was likely to want it.

Towards nightfall I went down to Greek Street ; and
found, on taking possession of my new quarters, that the
house already contained one single inmate, a poor, friendless child, apparently ten years old ; but she seemed
hunger-bitten ; and sufferings of that sort often make
children look older than they are.   From this forlorn
child I learned that she had slept and lived there alone for
some time before I came ; and great joy the poor creature
expressed, when she found that I was in future to be her
companion through the hours of darkness.   The house
could hardly be called large—that is, it was not large on
each separate storey ; but, having four storeys in all, it was
large enough to impress vividly the sense of its echoing
loneliness ; and, from the want of furniture, the noise of
the rats made a prodigious uproar on the staircase and
hall ; so that, amidst the real fleshly ills of cold and
hunger, the forsaken child had found leisure to suffer still
more from the self-created one of ghosts.   Against these
enemies I could promise her protection ; human com-

panionship was in itself protection ; but of other and more needful aid I had, alas ! little to offer. We lay upon the floor, with a bundle of law-papers for a pillow, but with no other covering than a large horseman's cloak ; afterwards, however, we discovered in a garret an old sofa-cover, a small piece of rug, and some fragments of other articles, which added a little to our comfort. The poor child crept close to me for warmth, and for security against her ghostly enemies. When I was not more than usually ill, I took her into my arms, so that, in general, she was tolerably warm, and often slept when I could not ; for, during the last two months of my sufferings, I slept much in the daytime, and was apt to fall into transient dozings at all hours. But my sleep distressed me more than my watching ; for, besides the tumultuousness of my dreams (which were only not so awful as those which I shall have hereafter to describe as produced by opium), my sleep was never more than what is called *dog-sleep ;* so that I could hear myself moaning ; and very often I was awakened suddenly by my own voice. About this time, a hideous sensation began to haunt me as soon as I fell into a slumber, which has since returned upon me, at different periods of my life—viz., a sort of twitching (I knew not where, but apparently about the region of the stomach), which com-pelled me violently to throw out my feet for the sake of relieving it. This sensation coming on as soon as I began to sleep, and the effort to relieve it constantly awaking me, at length I slept only from exhaustion ; and through increasing weakness (as I said before), I was constantly fall-ing asleep, and constantly awaking. Too generally the very attainment of any deep repose seemed as if mechanically linked to some fatal necessity of self-interruption. It was as though a cup were gradually filled by the sleepy overflow of some natural fountain, the fulness of the cup expressing symbolically the completeness of the rest : but then, in the next stage of the process, it seemed as though the rush and torrent-like babbling of the redundant waters, when running over from every part of the cup, inter-rupted the slumber which in their earlier stage of silent gathering they had so naturally produced. Such and so regular in its swell and its collapse—in its tardy growth and its violent dispersion—did this endless alternation of stealthy sleep and stormy awaking travel through stages as natural as the increments of twilight, or the kindlings of the dawn : no rest that was not a prologue to terror ; no sweet tremulous pulses of restoration that did not suddenly explode through rolling clamours of fiery disruption. Meantime, the master of the house sometimes came in upon us suddenly, and very early ; sometimes not till ten o'clock ; sometimes not at all. He was in constant fear of arrest. Improving on the plan of Cromwell, every night he slept in a different quarter of London ; and I observed that he never failed to examine, through a private window, the appearance of those who knocked at the door, before he would allow it to be opened. He breakfasted alone ; indeed, his tea equipage would hardly have admitted of his hazarding an invitation to a second person, any more than the quantity of esculent *material*, which, for the most part, was little more than a roll, or a few biscuits, purchased on his road from the place where he had slept. Or, if he *had* asked a party, as I once learnedly observed to him, the several members of it must have *stood* in the relation to each other (not *sat* in any relation whatever) of succession, and not of co-existence ; in the relation of parts of time, and not of the parts of space. During his breakfast, I generally contrived a reason for lounging in ; and, with an air of as much indifference as I could assume, took up such fragments as might chance to remain ; sometimes, indeed, none at all remained. In doing this, I committed no robbery, except upon Mr. Brunell himself, who was thus obliged, now and then, to send out at noon for an extra biscuit ; but he, through channels subsequently explained, was repaid a thousand-fold ; and, as to the poor child, *she* was never admitted into his study (if I may give that name to his chief depository of parchments, law-writings, etc.) ; that room was to her the Bluebeard room of the house, being regularly locked on his departure to dinner, about six o'clock,

which usually was his final departure for the day. Whether
this child were an illegitimate daughter of Mr. Brunell, or
only a servant, I could not ascertain ; she did not herself
know ; but certainly she was treated altogether as a menial
servant. No sooner did Mr. Brunell make his appearance
than she went below-stairs, brushed his shoes, coat, etc. ;
and, except when she was summoned to run upon some
errand, she never emerged from the dismal Tartarus of
the kitchens to the upper air, until my welcome knock
towards nightfall called up her little trembling footsteps
to the front-door. Of her life during the daytime, however, I knew little but what I gathered from her own
account at night ; for, as soon as the hours of business
commenced, I saw that my absence would be acceptable ;
and, in general, therefore, I went off and sat in the parks
or elsewhere until the approach of twilight.

But who, and what, meantime, was the master of the
house himself? Reader, he was one of those anomalous
practitioners in lower departments of the law who, on
prudential reasons, or from necessity, deny themselves all
indulgence in the luxury of too delicate a conscience.
In many walks of life, a conscience is a more expensive
encumbrance than a wife or a carriage ; and, as people
talk of 'laying down' their carriages, so I suppose my
friend Mr. Brunell had 'laid down' his conscience for a
time ; meaning, doubtless, to resume it as soon as he
could afford it. He was an advertising attorney, who
continually notified to the public, through the morning
papers, that he undertook to raise loans for approved
parties in what would generally be regarded as desperate
cases—viz., where there was nothing better than *personal*
security to offer. But, as he took good care to ascertain
that there were ample funds in reversion to be counted
on, or near connections that would not suffer the family
name to be dishonoured, and as he insured the borrower's
life over a sufficient period, the risk was not great ; and
even of this the whole rested upon the actual money-
lender, who stood aloof in the background, and never
revealed himself to clients in his proper person, transacting

L

all affairs through his proxies learned in the law—Mr. Brunell or others. The inner economy of such a man's daily life would present a monstrous picture. Even with my limited opportunities for observing what went on, I saw scenes of intrigue and complex chicanery, at which I sometimes smile to this day, and at which I smiled then, in spite of my misery. My situation, however, at that time, gave me little experience, in my own person, of any qualities in Mr. Brunell's character but such as did him honour ; and of his whole strange composition I ought to forget everything, but that towards me he was obliging, and, to the extent of his power, generous.

That power was not, indeed, very extensive. However, in common with the rats, I sat rent free ; and as Dr. Johnson has recorded that he never but once in his life had as much wall-fruit as he wished, so let me be grateful that, on that single occasion, I had as large a choice of rooms, or even of apartments, in a London mansion—viz., as I am now at liberty to add, at the north-west corner of Greek Street, being the house on that side the street nearest to Soho Square—as I could possibly desire. Except the Bluebeard room, which the poor child believed to be permanently haunted, and which, besides, was locked, all others, from the attics to the cellars, were at our service. 'The world was all before us,' and we pitched our tent for the night in any spot we might fancy. This house I have described as roomy and respectable. It stands in a conspicuous situation, and in a well-known part of London. Many of my readers will have passed it, I doubt not, within a few hours of reading this. For myself, I never fail to visit it when accident draws me to London. About ten o'clock this very night (August 15, 1821, being my birthday), I turned aside from my evening walk along Oxford Street, in order to take a glance at it. It is now in the occupation of some family, apparently respectable. The windows are no longer coated by a paste, composed of ancient soot and superannuated rain ; and the whole exterior no longer wears an aspect of gloom. By the lights

in the front drawing-room, I observed a domestic party,
assembled, perhaps, at tea, and apparently cheerful and gay
—marvellous contrast, in my eyes, to the darkness, cold,
silence, and desolation, of that same house nineteen years
ago, when its nightly occupants were one famishing
scholar and a poor, neglected child. Her, by the bye,
in after years, I vainly endeavoured to trace. Apart
from her situation, she was not what would be called
an interesting child. She was neither pretty, nor quick
in understanding, nor remarkably pleasing in manners.
But, thank God! even in those years I needed not the
embellishments of elegant accessories to conciliate my
affections. Plain human nature, in its humblest and most
homely apparel, was enough for me ; and I loved the
child because she was my partner in wretchedness. If she
is now living, she is probably a mother, with children of
her own ; but, as I have said, I could never trace her.

This I regret ; but another person there was, at that
time, whom I have since sought to trace with far deeper
earnestness, and with far deeper sorrow at my failure.
This person was a young woman, and one of that
unhappy class who belong to the outcasts and pariahs of
our female population. I feel no shame, nor have any
reason to feel it, in avowing that I was then on familiar
and friendly terms with many women in that unfortunate condition. Smile not, reader too carelessly facile !
Frown not, reader too unseasonably austere ! Little call
was there here either for smiles or frowns. A penniless
schoolboy could not be supposed to stand within the
range of such temptations ; besides that, according to the
ancient Latin proverb, ' *sine Cerere et Baccho*,' etc. These
unhappy women, to me, were simply sisters in calamity ;
and sisters amongst whom, in as large measure as amongst
any other equal number of persons, commanding more
of the world's respect, were to be found humanity, disinterested generosity, courage that would not falter in
defence of the helpless, and fidelity that would have
scorned to take bribes for betraying. But the truth is,
that at no time of my life have I been a person to hold

myself polluted by the touch or approach of any creature
that wore a human shape. I cannot suppose, I will not
believe, that any creatures wearing the form of man or
woman are so absolutely rejected and reprobate outcasts,
that merely to talk with them inflicts pollution. On the
contrary, from my very earliest youth, it has been my pride
to converse familiarly, *more Socratico*, with all human
beings—man, woman, and child—that chance might fling
in my way; for a philosopher should not see with the
eyes of the poor limitary creature calling himself a man
of the world, filled with narrow and self-regarding
prejudices of birth and education, but should look upon
himself as a catholic creature, and as standing in an equal
relation to high and low, to educated and uneducated, to
the guilty and the innocent. Being myself, at that time,
of necessity a peripatetic, or a walker of the streets, I
naturally fell in more frequently with those female
peripatetics who are technically called street-walkers.
Some of these women had occasionally taken my part
against watchmen who wished to drive me off the steps
of houses where I was sitting; others had protected
me against more serious aggressions. But one amongst
them—the one on whose account I have at all introduced
this subject—yet no! let me not class thee, O noble-
minded Ann ——, with that order of women; let me
find, if it be possible, some gentler name to designate the
condition of her to whose bounty and compassion—
ministering to my necessities when all the world stood
aloof from me—I owe it that I am at this time alive.
For many weeks I had walked, at nights, with this
poor friendless girl up and down Oxford Street, or had
rested with her on steps and under the shelter of
porticos. She could not be so old as myself: she told
me, indeed, that she had not completed her sixteenth
year. By such questions as my interest about her
prompted, I had gradually drawn forth her simple history.
Hers was a case of ordinary occurrence (as I have since
had reason to think), and one in which, if London
beneficence had better adapted its arrangements to meet

it, the power of the law might oftener be interposed to protect and to avenge. But the stream of London charity flows in a channel which, though deep and mighty, is yet noiseless and underground;—not obvious or readily accessible to poor, houseless wanderers; and it cannot be denied that the outside air and framework of society in London, as in all vast capitals, is unavoidably harsh, cruel, and repulsive. In any case, however, I saw that part of her injuries might have been redressed; and I urged her often and earnestly to lay her complaint before a magistrate. Friendless as she was, I assured her that she would meet with immediate attention; and that English justice, which was no respecter of persons, would speedily and amply avenge her on the brutal ruffian who had plundered her little property. She promised me often that she would; but she delayed taking the steps I pointed out, from time to time; for she was timid and dejected to a degree which showed how deeply sorrow had taken hold of her young heart; and perhaps she thought justly that the most upright judge and the most righteous tribunals could do nothing to repair her heaviest wrongs. Something, however, would perhaps have been done; for it had been settled between us at length (but, unhappily, on the very last time but one that I was ever to see her), that in a day or two I, accompanied by her, should state her case to a magistrate. This little service it was destined, however, that I should never realise. Meantime, that which she rendered to me, and which was greater than I could ever have repaid her, was this. One night, when we were pacing slowly along Oxford Street, and after a day when I had felt unusually ill and faint, I requested her to turn off with me into Soho Square. Thither we went; and we sat down on the steps of a house, which to this hour I never pass without a pang of grief, and an inner act of homage to the spirit of that unhappy girl, in memory of the noble act which she there performed. Suddenly, as we sat, I grew much worse. I had been leaning my head against her bosom, and all at once I sank from her arms, and fell backwards on the steps. From the sensations I then had, I felt an inner conviction of the liveliest kind, that, without some powerful and reviving stimulus, I should either have died on the spot, or should, at least, have sunk to a point of exhaustion from which all re-ascent, under my friendless circumstances, would soon have become hopeless. Then it was, at this crisis of my fate, that my poor orphan companion, who had herself met with little but injuries in this world, stretched out a saving hand to me. Uttering a cry of terror, but without a moment's delay, she ran off into Oxford Street, and, in less time than could be imagined, returned to me with a glass of port-wine and spices, that acted upon my empty stomach (which at that time would have rejected all solid food) with an instantaneous power of restoration; and for this glass the generous girl, without a murmur, paid out of her own humble purse, at a time, be it remembered, when she had scarcely wherewithal to purchase the bare necessaries of life, and when she could have no reason to expect that I should ever be able to reimburse her. O youthful benefactress! how often in succeeding years, standing in solitary places, and thinking of thee with grief of heart and perfect love—how often have I wished that, as in ancient times the curse of a father was believed to have a supernatural power, and to pursue its object with a fatal necessity of self-fulfilment, even so the benediction of a heart oppressed with gratitude might have a like prerogative; might have power given it from above to chase, to haunt, to waylay, to pursue thee into the central darkness of a London brothel, or (if it were possible) even into the darkness of the grave, there to awaken thee with an authentic message of peace and forgiveness, and of final reconciliation!

Some feelings, though not deeper or more passionate, are more tender than others; and often when I walk, at this time, in Oxford Street by dreamy lamp-light, and hear those airs played on a common street-organ which years ago solaced me and my dear youthful companion, I shed tears, and muse with myself at the mysterious dispensation which so suddenly and so critically separated us for ever. How it happened, the reader will understand from what remains of this introductory narration.

Soon after the period of the last incident I have recorded, I met in Albemarle Street a gentleman of his late Majesty's household. This gentleman had received hospitalities, on different occasions, from my family; and he challenged me upon the strength of my family likeness. I did not attempt any disguise, but answered his questions ingenuously; and, on his pledging his word of honour that he would not betray me to my guardians, I gave him my real address in Greek Street. The next day I received from him a ten-pound banknote. The letter enclosing it was delivered, with other letters of business, to the attorney; but, though his look and manner informed me that he suspected its contents, he gave it up to me honourably, and without demur.

This present, from the particular service to which much of it was applied, leads me naturally to speak again of the original purpose which had allured me up to London, and which I had been without intermission prosecuting through Mr. Brunell from the first day of my arrival in London.

In so mighty a world as London, it will surprise my readers that I should not have found some means of staving off the last extremities of penury; and it will strike them that two resources, at least, must have been open to me: viz., either to seek assistance from the friends of my family, or to turn my youthful accomplishments, such as they were, into some channel of pecuniary emolument. As to the first course, I may observe, generally, that what I dreaded beyond all other evils was the chance of being reclaimed by my guardians; not doubting that whatever power the law gave them would have been enforced against me to the utmost; that is, to the extremity of forcibly restoring me to the school which I had quitted; a restoration which, as it would, in my eyes, have been a dishonour, even if submitted to voluntarily, could not fail, when extorted from me in contempt and

defiance of my own known wishes and earnest resistance,
to have proved a humiliation worse to me than death, and
which would, indeed, have terminated in death. I was,
therefore, shy enough of applying for assistance even in
those quarters where I was sure of receiving it, if at any
risk of furnishing my guardians with a clue for tracing me.
My father's friends, no doubt, had been many, and were
scattered all over the kingdom ; but, as to London in
particular, though a large section of these friends would
certainly be found there, yet (as full ten years had passed
since his death) I knew very few of them even by name ;
and never having seen London before—except once, in
my fifteenth year, for a few hours—I knew not the
address of even those few. To this mode of gaining help,
therefore, in part the difficulty, but much more the danger
which I have mentioned, habitually indisposed me. In
regard to the other mode—that of turning any talents or
knowledge that I might possess to a lucrative use—I now
feel half inclined to join my reader in wondering that I
should have overlooked it. As a corrector of Greek
proofs (if in no other way), I might surely have gained
enough for my slender wants. Such an office as this
I could have discharged with an exemplary and punctual
accuracy that would soon have gained me the confidence
of my employers. And there was this great preliminary
advantage in giving such a direction to my efforts, that
the intellectual dignity and elegance associated with all
ministerial services about the press would have saved my
pride and self-respect from mortification. In an extreme
case, such as mine had now become, I should not have
absolutely disdained the humble station of 'devil.' A
subaltern situation in a service inherently honourable is
better than a much higher situation in a service pointing
to ultimate objects that are mean or ignoble. I am,
indeed, not sure that I could adequately have discharged the
functions of this office. To the perfection of the diabolic
character I fear that patience is one of the indispensable
graces ; more, perhaps, than I should be found on trial to
possess for dancing attendance upon crotchety authors,

superstitiously fastidious in matters of punctuation. But why talk of my qualifications? Qualified or not, where could I obtain such an office? For it must not be forgotten that even a diabolic appointment requires interest. Towards *that*, I must first of all have an introduction to some respectable publisher; and this I had no means of obtaining. To say the truth, however, it had never once occurred to me to think of literary labours as a source of profit. No mode sufficiently speedy of obtaining money had ever suggested itself, but that of borrowing it on the strength of my future claims and expectations. This mode I sought by every avenue to compass; and amongst other persons I applied to a Jew named D———.[1]

---

[1] At this period (autumn of 1856), when thirty-five years have elapsed since the first publication of these memoirs, reasons of delicacy can no longer claim respect for concealing the Jew's name, or at least the name which he adopted in his dealings with the Gentiles. I say, therefore, without scruple, that the name was Dell: and some years later it was one of the names that came before the House of Commons in connection with something or other (I have long since forgotten *what*) growing out of the parliamentary movement against the Duke of York, in reference to Mrs. Clark, etc. Like all the other Jews with whom I have had negotiations, he was frank and honourable in his mode of conducting business. What he promised he performed; and, if his terms were high, as naturally they could not *but* be, to cover his risks, he avowed them from the first.

To this same Mr. Dell, by the way, some eighteen months afterwards, I applied again on the same business; and, dating at that time from a respectable college, I was fortunate enough to win his serious attention to my proposals. My necessities had not arisen from any extravagance or youthful levities (these my habits forbade), but simply from the vindictive malice of my guardian, who, when he found himself no longer able to prevent me from going to the university, had, as a parting token of his regard, refused to sign an order for granting me a shilling beyond the allowance made to me at school— viz., £100 per annum. Upon this sum it was, in my time (*i.e.*, in the first decennium of this century), barely possible to have lived at college; and not possible to a man who, though above the affectation of ostentatious disregard for money, and without any expensive tastes, confided, nevertheless, rather too much in servants, and did not delight in the petty details of minute economy. I soon, therefore, became embarrassed: in a movement of impatience, instead of candidly avowing my condition to my mother, or to some one of the guardians,

To this Jew, and to other advertising moneylenders, I had introduced myself, with an account of my expectations ; which account they had little difficulty in ascertaining to be correct. The person there mentioned as the second son of ——, was found to have all the claims (or more than all) that I had stated : but one question still remained, which the faces of the Jews pretty significantly suggested,—was I that person ? This doubt had never occurred to me as a possible one ; I had rather feared, whenever my Jewish friends scrutinised me keenly, that I might be too well known to be that person, and that some scheme might be passing in their minds for entrapping me and selling me to my guardians. It was strange to me to find my own self, *materialiter* considered (so I expressed it, for I doted on logical accuracy of distinctions), suspected of counterfeiting my own self, *formaliter* considered. However, to satisfy their scruples, I took the only course in my power. Whilst I was in Wales, I had received various letters from young friends ; these I produced, for I carried them constantly in my pocket. Most of these letters were from the Earl of Altamont, who was at that time, and had been for some years back, amongst my confidential friends. These were dated from Eton. I had also some from the Marquis of Sligo, his father ; who, though absorbed in agricultural pursuits, yet having been an Etonian himself, and as good a scholar as a nobleman needs to be, still retained an affection for classical studies and for youthful scholars. He had, accordingly, from the time that I was fifteen, corresponded

more than one or whom would have advanced me the £250 wanted (not in his legal character of guardian, but as a private friend), I was so foolish as to engage in a voluminous negotiation with the Jew, and was put in possession of the sum I asked for, on the 'regular' terms of paying seventeen and a-half per cent by way of annuity on all the money furnished ; Israel, on his part, graciously resuming no more than about ninety guineas of the said money, on account of an attorney's bill (for what services, to whom rendered, and when— whether at the siege of Jerusalem, or at the building of the Second Temple—I have not yet discovered). How many perches this bill measured I really forget ; but I still keep it in a cabinet of natural curiosities.

with me—sometimes upon the great improvements which
he had made, or was meditating, in the counties of Mayo
and Sligo, since I had been there ; sometimes upon the
merits of a Latin poet ; at other times, suggesting subjects
on which he fancied that I could write verses myself,
or breathe poetic inspiration into the mind of my once
familiar companion, his son.

On reading the letters, one of my Jewish friends
agreed to furnish two or three hundred pounds on my
personal security, provided I could persuade the young
earl—who was, by the way, not older than myself—to
guarantee the payment on our joint coming of age ; the
Jew's final object being, as I now suppose, not the trifling
profit he could expect to make by me, but the prospect
of establishing a connection with my noble friend, whose
great expectations were well known to him.   In pursuance
of this proposal on the part of the Jew, about eight or
nine days after I had received the £10, I prepared to visit
Eton.   Nearly three guineas of the money I had given to
my money-lending friend in the background ; or, more
accurately, I had given that sum to Mr. Brunell, *alias*
Brown, as representing Mr. Dell, the Jew ; and a smaller
sum I had given directly to himself, on his own separate
account.   What he alleged in excuse for thus draining
my purse at so critical a moment was, that stamps must
be bought, in order that the writings might be prepared
whilst I was away from London.   I thought in my heart
that he was lying, but I did not wish to give him any
excuse for charging his own delays upon me.   About
fifteen shillings I had employed in re-establishing (though
in a very humble way) my dress.   Of the remainder,
I gave one-quarter (something more than a guinea) to
Ann, meaning, on my return, to have divided with her
whatever might remain.   These arrangements made, soon
after six o'clock, on a dark winter evening, I set off,
accompanied by Ann, towards Piccadilly ; for it was my
intention to go down as far as the turn to Salt Hill and
Slough on the Bath or Bristol mail.   Our course lay
through a part of the town which has now totally dis-

appeared, so that I can no longer retrace its ancient boundaries—having been replaced by Regent Street and its adjacencies. *Swallow Street* is all that I remember of the names superseded by this large revolutionary usurpation. Having time enough before us, however, we bore away to the left, until we came into Golden Square. There, near the corner of Sherrard Street, we sat down, not wishing to part in the tumult and blaze of Piccadilly. I had told Ann of my plans some time before, and now I assured her again that she should share in my good fortune, if I met with any, and that I would never forsake her, as soon as I had power to protect her. This I fully intended, as much from inclination as from a sense of duty; for, setting aside gratitude (which in any case must have made me her debtor for life), I loved her as affectionately as if she had been my sister; and at this moment with sevenfold tenderness, from pity at witnessing her extreme dejection. I had apparently most reason for dejection, because I was leaving the saviour of my life; yet I, considering the shock my health had received, was cheerful and full of hope. She, on the contrary, who was parting with one who had had little means of serving her, except by kindness and brotherly treatment, was overcome by sorrow, so that, when I kissed her at our final farewell, she put her arms about my neck, and wept, without speaking a word. I hoped to return in a week, at furthest, and I agreed with her, that on the fifth night from that, and every night afterwards, she should wait for me, at six o'clock, near the bottom of Great Titchfield Street; which had formerly been our customary haven of rendezvous, to prevent our missing each other in the great Mediterranean of Oxford Street. This, and other measures of precaution, I took; one, only, I forgot. She had either never told me, or (as a matter of no great interest) I had forgotten, her surname. It is a general practice, indeed, with girls of humble rank in her unhappy condition, not (as novel-reading women of higher pretensions) to style themselves *Miss Douglas*, *Miss Montague*, etc., but simply by their Christian names,

Mary, *Jane*, *Frances*, etc. Her surname, as the surest
means of tracing her, I ought now to have inquired ; but
the truth is, having no reason to think that our meeting
again could, in consequence of a short interruption, be
more difficult or uncertain than it had been for so many
weeks, I scarcely for a moment adverted to it as necessary,
or placed it amongst my memoranda against this parting
interview ; and my final anxieties being spent in com-
forting her with hopes, and in pressing upon her the
necessity of getting some medicine for a violent cough
with which she was troubled, I wholly forgot this precaution until it was too late to recall her.

When I reached the Gloucester Coffee-house in
Piccadilly, at which, in those days, all the western mails
stopped for a few minutes in going out of London, it was
already a quarter of an hour past eight o'clock ; the Bristol
Mail was on the point of going off, and I mounted on the
outside. The fine fluent motion [1] of this mail soon laid
me asleep. It is somewhat remarkable, that the first
easy or refreshing sleep which I had enjoyed for some
months was on the outside of a mail-coach—a bed which,
at this day, I find rather an uneasy one. Connected with
this sleep was a little incident which served, as hundreds of
others did at that time, to convince me how easily a man,
who has never been in any great distress, may pass through
life without knowing in his own person, and experimentally testing, the possible goodness of the human heart, or,
as unwillingly I add, its possible churlishness. So thick a
curtain of *manners* is drawn over the features and expression of men's natures, that, to the ordinary observer, the
two extremities, and the infinite field of varieties which
lie between them, are all confounded under one neutral
disguise. The case was this. For the first four or five
miles out of London, I annoyed my fellow-passenger on

[1] The Bristol Mail was at that time the best appointed in the
kingdom—owing that advantage, first of all, to an unusually good road,
—and this advantage it shared with the Bath Mail (their route being
exactly the same for a hundred and five miles) ; but, secondly, it had
the separate advantage of an *extra* sum for expenses subscribed by the
Bristol merchants.

the roof by occasionally falling against him when the coach
gave a lurch; and, indeed, if the road had been less
smooth and level than it was, I should have fallen off from
weakness. Of this annoyance he complained heavily; as,
perhaps, in the same circumstances, most people would.
He expressed his complaint, however, more morosely than
the occasion seemed to warrant; and if I had parted with
him at that moment, I should have thought of him as a
surly and almost brutal fellow. Still I was conscious that
I had given him some cause for complaint; and therefore
I apologised, assuring him that I would do what I could
to avoid falling asleep for the future; and, at the same
time, in as few words as possible, I explained to him that I
was ill, and in a weak state from long suffering, and that
I could not afford to take an inside place. The man's
manner changed upon hearing this explanation in an
instant: and when I next woke for a minute, from the
noise and lights of Hounslow (for, in spite of my efforts,
I had again fallen asleep within two minutes), I found
that he had put his arm round me to protect me from
falling off; and for the rest of my journey he behaved to
me with the gentleness of a woman. And this was the
more kind, as he could not have known that I was not
going the whole way to Bath or Bristol. Unfortunately,
indeed, I *did* go further than I intended; for so genial
and refreshing was my sleep, being in the open air, that,
upon the sudden pulling up of the mail (possibly at a post-
office), I found that we had reached some place six or
seven miles to the west of Salt Hill. Here I alighted;
and, during the half-minute that the mail stopped, I was entreated by my friendly companion (who, from the transient
glimpse I had of him under the glaring lights of Piccadilly,
might be a respectable upper servant) to go to bed without delay. This, under the feeling that some consideration was due to one who had done me so seasonable a
service, I promised, though with no intention of doing so;
and, in fact, I immediately moved forward on foot. It
must then have been nearly eleven; but so slowly did I
creep along that I heard a clock in a cottage strike four as

I was on the point of turning down the road from Slough
to Eton.   The air and the sleep had both refreshed me ;
but I was weary, nevertheless.   I remember a thought
(obvious enough, and pointedly expressed by a Roman
poet) which gave me some consolation, at that moment,
under my poverty.   There had been, some weeks before,
a murder committed on Hounslow Heath, which at that
time was really a heath, entirely unenclosed, and exhibiting
a sea-like expanse in all directions, except one.   I cannot
be mistaken when I say that the name of the murdered
person was *Steele*, and that he was the owner of a lavender
plantation in that neighbourhood.[1]   Every step of my
regress (for I now walked with my face towards London)
was bringing me nearer to the heath ; and it naturally
occurred to me, that I and the accursed murderer, if
he were that night abroad, might, at every instant, be
unconsciously approaching each other through the darkness ; in which case, said I, supposing myself—instead of
being little better than an outcast,

> Lord of my learning, and no land beside—

like my friend Lord Altamont, heir, by general repute, to
£30,000 per annum, what a panic should I be under at
this moment about my throat !   Indeed, it was not likely
that Lord Altamont should ever be in my situation ; but,
nevertheless, the spirit of the remark remains true, that

---

[1] Two men, Holloway and Haggerty, were long afterwards con-
victed, upon very questionable evidence, as the perpetrators of this
murder.   The main testimony against them was that of a Newgate
turnkey, who had imperfectly overheard a conversation between the
two men.   The current impression was that of great dissatisfaction with
the evidence ; and this impression was strengthened by the pamphlet
of an acute lawyer, exposing the unsoundness and incoherency of the
statements relied upon by the court.   They were executed, however,
in the teeth of all opposition.   And as it happened that an enormous
wreck of life occurred at the execution (not fewer, I believe, than
sixty persons having been trampled under foot by the unusual pressure
of some brewers' draymen forcing their way with linked arms to the
space below the drop), this tragedy was regarded for many years by a
section of the London mob as a providential judgment upon the passive
metropolis.

vast power and possessions make a man shamefully afraid of dying ; and I am convinced that many of the most intrepid adventurers, who, being poor, enjoy the full use of their natural energies, would, if at the very instant of going into action news were brought to them that they had unexpectedly succeeded to an estate in England of £50,000 a-year, feel their dislike to bullets furiously sharpened,[1] and their efforts at self-possession proportionably difficult.   So true it is, in the language of a wise man, whose own experience had made him acquainted equally with good and evil fortune, that riches are better fitted

> To slacken virtue, and abate her edge,
> Than tempt her to do aught may merit praise.
> *Paradise Regained.*

I dally with my subject, because, to myself, the remembrance of these times is profoundly interesting.   But my reader shall not have any further cause to complain ; for now I hasten to its close.   In the road between Slough and Eton I fell asleep ; and, just as the morning began to dawn, I was awakened by the voice of a man standing over me, and apparently studying my *physics*, whilst to me— upon so sudden an introduction to him in so suspicious a situation—his *morals* naturally suggested a more interesting subject of inquiry.   I know not what he was.   He was an ill-looking fellow, but not, therefore, of necessity, an ill-meaning fellow ; or, if he were, I suppose he thought that no person sleeping out-of-doors in winter could be worth robbing.   In which conclusion, however, as it regarded myself, I have the honour to assure him, supposing him ever to find himself amongst my readers, that he was entirely mistaken.   I was not sorry at his disturbance, as it roused me to pass through Eton before people were generally astir.   The night had been heavy and misty, but

[1] It will be objected that many men, of the highest rank and wealth, have, notwithstanding, in our own day, as well as throughout our history, been amongst the foremost in courting danger on the field of battle.   True ; but this is not the case supposed.   Long familiarity with power and with wealth has, to them, deadened their effect and attractions.

towards the morning it had changed to a slight frost, and
the trees were now covered with rime.   I slipped through
Eton unobserved ; washed myself, and as far as possible
adjusted my dress, at a little public-house in Windsor ;
and, about eight o'clock, went down towards the precincts
of the college, near which were congregated the houses of
the 'Dames.'   On my road I met some junior boys, of
whom I made inquiries.   An Etonian is always a gentleman ; and, in spite of my shabby habiliments, they
answered me civilly.   My friend Lord Altamont was gone
to Jesus College, Cambridge.   ' Ibi omnis effusus labor ! '
I had, however, other friends at Eton ; but it is not to all
who wear that name in prosperity that a man is willing to
present himself in distress.   On recollecting myself, however, I asked for the Earl of Desart,[1] to whom (though
my acquaintance with him was not so intimate as with
some others) I should not have shrunk from presenting
myself under any circumstances.   He was still at Eton,
though, I believe, on the wing for Cambridge.   I called,
was received kindly, and asked to breakfast.

Lord Desart placed before me a magnificent breakfast.
It was really such ; but in my eyes it seemed trebly
magnificent from being the first regular meal, the first
' good man's table,' that I had sat down to for months.
Strange to say, I could scarcely eat anything.   On the day
when I first received my ten-pound bank-note, I had gone
to a baker's shop and bought a couple of rolls ; this very
shop I had some weeks before surveyed with an eagerness
of desire which it was humiliating to recollect.   I remembered the story (which, however, I now believed to be a
falsehood) about Otway ; and feared that there might be
danger in eating too rapidly.   But there was no cause for
alarm ; my appetite was utterly gone, and I nauseated food
of every kind.   This effect, from eating what approached

---

[1] I had known Lord Desart, the eldest son of a very large family,
some years earlier, when bearing the title of Lord Castlecuffe. Cuffe
was the family name ; and I believe that they traced their descent
from a person of some historic interest—viz., that Cuffe who was
secretary to the unhappy Earl of Essex during his treasonable *émeute*
against the government of Queen Elizabeth.

M

to a meal, I continued to feel for weeks.   On the present occasion, at Lord Desart's table, I found myself not at all better than usual ; and, in the midst of luxuries, appetite I had none.   I had, however, unfortunately, at all times a craving for wine : I explained my situation, therefore, to Lord Desart, and gave him a short account of my late sufferings ; with which he expressed deep sympathy, and called for wine.   This gave me instantaneous relief and immoderate pleasure ; and on all occasions, when I had an opportunity, I never failed to drink wine.   Obvious it is, however, that this indulgence in wine would continue to strengthen my malady, for the tone of my stomach was apparently quite sunk ; but, by a better regimen, it might sooner, and, perhaps, effectually, have been restored.   I hope that it was not from this love of wine that I lingered in the neighbourhood of my Eton friends ; I persuaded myself *then*, that it was from reluctance to ask Lord Desart, on whom I was conscious of having no sufficient claims, the particular service in quest of which I had come to Eton.   I was, however, unwilling to lose my journey, and —I asked it.   Lord Desart, whose good-nature was un-bounded, and which, in regard to myself, had been measured rather by his compassion, perhaps, for my condi-tion, and his knowledge of my intimacy with several of his relatives, than by an over-rigorous inquiry into the extent of my own direct claims, faltered, nevertheless, at this request.   He acknowledged that he did not like to have any dealings with money-lenders, and feared lest such a transaction might come to the ears of his connexions. Moreover, he doubted whether *his* signature, whose ex-pectations were so much more bounded than those of his cousin, would avail with my unchristian friends.   Still he did not wish, apparently, to mortify me by a refusal peremptory and absolute ; for, after a little consideration, he promised, under certain conditions, which he pointed out, to give his security.   Lord Desart was at this time not above eighteen years of age ; but I have often doubted, on recollecting, since, the good sense and prudence which on this occasion he mingled with so much urbanity of

manner (which in him wore the grace of youthful sincerity),
whether any statesman—the oldest and the most accomplished in diplomacy—could have acquitted himself better
under the same circumstances.

Re-comforted by this promise, which was not quite
equal to the best, but far above the worst that I had
anticipated, I returned in a Windsor coach to London
three days after I had quitted it. And now I come to
the end of my story. The Jews did not approve of Lord
Desart's conditions, or so they said ; whether they would
in the end have acceded to them, and were only seeking
time for making further inquiries, I know not ; but many
delays were made—time passed on—the small fragment
of my bank-note had just melted away, and before any
conclusion could have been put to the business, I must
have relapsed into my former state of wretchedness.
Suddenly, at this crisis, an opening was made, almost by
accident, for reconciliation with my guardians. I quitted
London in haste, and returned to the Priory ; after some
time, I proceeded to Oxford ; and it was not until many
months had passed away that I had it in my power again
to revisit the ground which had become so interesting to
me, and to this day remains so, as the chief scene of my
youthful sufferings.

Meantime, what had become of Ann ? Where was
she ? Whether had she gone ? According to our agree-
ment, I sought her daily, and waited for her every night,
so long as I staid in London, at the corner of Titchfield
Street ; and during the last days of my stay in London I
put into activity every means of tracing her that my
knowledge of London suggested, and the limited extent
of my power made possible. The street where she had
lodged I knew, but not the house ; and I remembered, at
last, some account which she had given of ill-treatment
from her landlord, which made it probable that she had
quitted those lodgings before we parted. She had few
acquaintance ; most people, besides, thought that the
earnestness of my inquiries arose from motives which
moved their laughter or their slight regard ; and others,

thinking that I was in chase of a girl who had robbed me of some trifles, were naturally and excusably indisposed to give me any clue to her, if indeed they had any to give. Finally, as my despairing resource, on the day I left London I put into the hands of the only person who (I was sure) must know Ann by sight, from having been in company with us once or twice, an address to the Priory. All was in vain. To this hour I have never heard a syllable about her. This, amongst such troubles as most men meet with in this life, has been my heaviest affliction. If she lived, doubtless we must have been sometimes in search of each other, at the very same moment, through the mighty labyrinths of London ; perhaps even within a few feet of each other—a barrier no wider, in a London street, often amounting in the end to a separation for eternity ! During some years I hoped that she *did* live ; and I suppose that, in the literal and unrhetorical use of the word *myriad*, I must, on my different visits to London, have looked into many myriads of female faces, in the hope of meeting Ann. I should know her again amongst a thousand, and if seen but for a moment. Handsome she was not ; but she had a sweet expression of countenance, and a peculiarly grace- ful carriage of the head. I sought her, I have said, in hope. So it was for years ; but now I should fear to see her ; and her cough, which grieved me when I parted with her, is now my consolation. Now I wish to see her no longer, but think of her, more gladly, as one long since laid in the grave—in the grave, I would hope, of a Magdalen ; taken away before injuries and cruelty had blotted out and transfigured her ingenuous nature, or the brutalities of ruffians had completed the ruin they had begun.

.   .   .   .   .   .

So then, Oxford Street, stony-hearted stepmother, thou that listenest to the sighs of orphans, and drinkest the tears of children, at length I was dismissed from thee ! The time was come that I no more should pace in anguish thy never-ending terraces ; no more should wake and dream in captivity to the pangs of hunger. Successors too many to myself and Ann have, doubtless, since then trodden in our footsteps, inheritors of our calamities. Other orphans than Ann have sighed ; tears have been shed by other children ; and thou, Oxford Street, hast since those days echoed to the groans of innumerable hearts. For myself, however, the storm which I had outlived seemed to have been the pledge of a long fair weather ; the premature sufferings which I had paid down, to have been accepted as a ransom for many years to come, as a price of long immunity from sorrow ; and if again I walked in London, a solitary and contemplative man (as oftentimes I did), I walked for the most part in serenity and peace of mind. And, although it is true that the calamities of my novitiate in London had struck root so deeply in my bodily constitution, that afterwards they shot up and flourished afresh, and grew into a noxious umbrage that has overshadowed and darkened my latter years, yet these second assaults of suffering were met with a fortitude more confirmed, with the resources of a maturer intellect, and with alleviations, how deep ! from sympathising affection.

Thus, however, with whatsoever alleviations, years far asunder were bound together by subtle links of suffering derived from a common root. And herein I notice the short-sightedness of human desires—that oftentimes, on moonlight nights, during my first mournful abode in London, my consolation was (if such it could be thought) to gaze from Oxford Street up every avenue in succession which pierces northwards through the heart of Marylebone to the fields and the woods ; for *that*, said I, travelling with my eyes up the long vistas which lay part in light and part in shade—' *that* is the road to the north, and, therefore, to Grasmere ' (upon which, though as yet unknown to me, I had a presentiment that I should fix my choice for a residence) ; ' and if I had the wings of a dove, *that* way I would fly for rest.' Thus I said, and thus I wished in my blindness ; yet, even in that very northern region it was, in that very valley to which my erroneous wishes pointed, that this second birth of my sufferings began, and that they again threatened to besiege the citadel of life and hope.

There it was that for years I was persecuted by visions as ugly, and by phantoms as ghastly, as ever haunted the couch of Orestes; and in this unhappier than he—that sleep, which comes to all as a respite and a restoration, and to him especially as a blessed balm for his wounded heart and his haunted brain, visited me as my bitterest scourge. Thus blind was I in my desires. And yet, if a veil interposes between the dim-sightedness of man and his future calamities, the same veil hides from him their alleviations; and a grief which had not been feared, is met by consolations which had not been hoped. I, therefore, who participated, as it were, in the troubles of Orestes (excepting only in his agitated conscience), participated no less in all his supports; my Eumenides, like his, were at my bed-feet, and stared in upon me through the curtains; but, watching by my pillow, or defrauding herself of sleep to bear me company through the heavy watches of the night, sat my Electra; for thou, beloved M——, dear companion of my later years, thou wast my Electra! and neither in nobility of mind nor in long-suffering affection wouldst permit that a Grecian sister should excel an English wife. For thou thoughtest not much to stoop to humble offices of kindness, and to servile ministrations of tenderest affection; to wipe away for years the unwholesome dews upon the forehead, or to refresh the lips when parched and baked with fever; nor even when thy own peaceful slumbers had by long sympathy become infected with the spectacle of my dread contest with phantoms and shadowy enemies, that often-times bade me 'sleep no more!'—not even then didst thou utter a complaint or any murmur, nor withdraw thy angelic smiles, nor shrink from thy service of love, more than Electra did of old. For she, too, though she was a Grecian woman, and the daughter of the king of men,[1] yet wept sometimes, and hid her face[2] in her robe.

---

[1] Agamemnon—ἄναξ ἀνδρῶν.

[2] Ὄμμα θεῖσ' εἰς πέπλον. The scholar will know that throughout this passage I refer to the early scenes of the *Orestes*—one of the most beautiful exhibitions of the domestic affections which even the dramas

But these troubles are past, and thou wilt read these records of a period so dolorous to us both as the legend of some hideous dream that can return no more.   Meantime I am again in London ; and again I pace the terraces of Oxford Street by night; and oftentimes—when I am oppressed by anxieties that demand all my philosophy and the comfort of thy presence to support, and yet remember that I am separated from thee by three hundred miles and the length of three dreary months—I look up the streets that run northward from Oxford Street, upon moonlight nights, and recollect my youthful ejaculation of anguish ; but then, remembering that thou art sitting alone in that same valley, and mistress of that very house to which my heart turned in its blindness nineteen years ago, I think that, though blind indeed, and scattered to the winds of late, the promptings of my heart may yet have had reference to a remoter time, and may be justified if read in another meaning ; and if I could allow myself to descend again to the impotent wishes of childhood, I should again say to myself, as I look to the north, ' Oh, that I had the wings of a dove ! ' and with how just a confidence in thy good and gracious nature might I add the other half of my early ejaculation—' and *that* way I would fly for comfort ! '

THE PLEASURES OF OPIUM

It is very long since I first took opium ; *so* long, that if it had been a trifling incident in my life, I might have forgotten its date : but cardinal events are not to be forgotten ; and, from circumstances connected with it, I remember that this inauguration into the use of opium must be referred to the spring or to the autumn of 1804 ; during which seasons I was in London, having come

of Euripides can furnish.   To the unlearned reader, it may be necessary to say that the situation at the opening of the drama is that of a brother attended only by his sister during the demoniacal possession of a suffering conscience (or, in the mythology of the play, haunted by the Furies), under circumstances of immediate danger from enemies, and of desertion or cold regard from nominal friends.

thither for the first time since my entrance at Oxford.
And this event arose in the following way : from an early
age I had been accustomed to wash my head in cold water
at least once a day ; being suddenly seized with toothache,
I attributed it to some relaxation caused by a casual intermission of that practice ; jumped out of bed, plunged my
head into a basin of cold water, and with hair thus wetted
went to sleep. The next morning, as I need hardly say,
I awoke with excruciating rheumatic pains of the head
and face, from which I had hardly any respite for about
twenty days. On the twenty-first day I think it was, and
on a Sunday, that I went out into the streets ; rather to
run away, if possible, from my torments, than with any
distinct purpose of relief. By accident, I met a college
acquaintance, who recommended opium. Opium ! dread
agent of unimaginable pleasure and pain ! I had heard of
it as I had heard of manna or of ambrosia, but no further.
How unmeaning a sound was opium at that time ! what
solemn chords does it now strike upon my heart ! what
heart-quaking vibrations of sad and happy remembrances !
Reverting for a moment to these, I feel a mystic importance attached to the minutest circumstances connected
with the place, and the time, and the man (if man he
was), that first laid open to me the paradise of opium-
eaters. It was a Sunday afternoon, wet and cheerless ;
and a duller spectacle this earth of ours has not to show
than a rainy Sunday in London. My road homewards
lay through Oxford Street ; and near ‘ the *stately* Pantheon ’
(as Mr. Wordsworth has obligingly called it [1]) I saw a
druggist’s shop. The druggist (unconscious minister of
celestial pleasures !), as if in sympathy with the rainy
Sunday, looked dull and stupid, just as any mortal druggist
might be expected to look on a rainy London Sunday ;
and when I asked for the tincture of opium, he gave it to
me as any other man might do ; and, furthermore, out of

---

[1] ‘ *Stately* ’ :—It is but fair to say that Wordsworth meant to speak
of the *interior*, which could very little be inferred from the mean, un-
distinguished outside, as seen presenting itself endways in Oxford
Street.

my shilling returned to me what seemed to be real copper
halfpence, taken out of a real wooden drawer. Nevertheless, and notwithstanding all such indications of humanity,
he has ever since figured in my mind as a beatific vision of
an immortal druggist, sent down to earth on a special
mission to myself. And it confirms me in this way of
considering him that, when I next came up to London, I
sought him near the stately Pantheon, and found him not ;
and thus to me, who knew not his name (if, indeed, he
had one), he seemed rather to have vanished from Oxford
Street than to have flitted into any other locality, or (which
some abominable man suggested) to have absconded from
the rent. The reader may choose to think of him as,
possibly, no more than a sublunary druggist ; it may be
so, but my faith is better. I believe him to have
evanesced.[1] So unwillingly would I connect any mortal
remembrances with that hour, and place, and creature that
first brought me acquainted with the celestial drug.

Arrived at my lodgings, it may be supposed that I lost
not a moment in taking the quantity prescribed. I was
necessarily ignorant of the whole art and mystery of
opium-taking ; and what I took I took under every
disadvantage. But I took it ; and in an hour, O heavens !
what a revulsion ! what a resurrection, from its lowest
depths, of the inner spirit ! what an apocalypse of the
world within me ! That my pains had vanished was now
a trifle in my eyes ; this negative effect was swallowed up
in the immensity of those positive effects which had
opened before me, in the abyss of divine enjoyment thus
suddenly revealed. Here was a panacea, a $\phi\acute{a}\rho\mu\alpha\kappa\sigma\nu$
$\nu\eta\pi\epsilon\nu\theta\acute{\epsilon}s$, for all human woes ; here was the secret of

---

[1] 'Evanesced' :—This way of going off from the stage of life appears
to have been well known in the seventeenth century, but at that time
to have been considered a peculiar privilege of royalty, and by no means
open to the use of druggists. For, about the year 1686, a poet of rather
ominous name (and who, apparently, did justice to his name)—viz.,
Mr. FLAT-MAN—in speaking of the death of Charles II., expresses his
surprise that any prince should commit so vulgar an act as dying :
because, says he,

Kings should disdain to die, and only *disappear*.

happiness, about which philosophers had disputed for so many ages, at once discovered; happiness might now be bought for a penny, and carried in the waistcoat-pocket; portable ecstasies might be had corked up in a pint-bottle; and peace of mind could be sent down by the mail.

And, first, one word with respect to its bodily effects; for upon all that has been hitherto written on the subject of opium, whether by travellers in Turkey (who may plead their privilege of lying as an old immemorial right), or by professors of medicine writing *ex cathedra*, I have but one emphatic criticism to pronounce—Nonsense! I remember once, in passing a book-stall, to have caught these words from a page of some satiric author—'By this time I became convinced that the London newspapers spoke truth at least twice a week—viz., on Tuesday and Saturday[1]—and might safely be depended upon for—the list of bankrupts.' In like manner, I do by no means deny that some truths have been delivered to the world in regard to opium: thus, it has been repeatedly affirmed by the learned that opium is a tawny brown in colour—and this, take notice, I grant; secondly, that it is rather dear, which also I grant—for, in my time, East India opium has been three guineas a-pound, and Turkey eight; and, thirdly, that, if you eat a good deal of it, most probably you must do what is disagreeable to any man of regular habits—viz., die.[2] These weighty propositions are, all and singular, true; I cannot gainsay them; and truth ever was, and will be, commendable. But, in these three

---

[1] '*Tuesday and Saturday*': viz., the two days on which the *Gazette* is (or used to be) published.

[2] Of this, however, the learned appear latterly to have doubted; for, in a pirated edition of Buchan's *Domestic Medicine*, which I once saw in the hands of a farmer's wife, who was studying it for the benefit of her health, the doctor was made to caution his readers against taking more than 'twenty-five *ounces*' of laudanum at one dose. The true reading had doubtless been twenty-five *drops* or minims, which in a gross equation is held equivalent to one grain of average opium; but opium itself—crude opium—varies enormously in purity and strength; consequently the tincture prepared from it. And most of the medical connoisseurs whom I have known boiled their opium, so as to cleanse it from gross impurities.

theorems, I believe we have exhausted the stock of knowledge as yet accumulated by man on the subject of opium. And therefore, worthy doctors, as there seems to be room for further discoveries, stand aside, and allow me to come forward and lecture on this matter.

First, then, it is not so much affirmed as taken for granted by all who ever mention opium, formally or incidentally, that it does or can produce intoxication. Now, reader, assure yourself, *meo periculo*, that no quantity of opium ever did, or could, intoxicate. As to the tincture of opium (commonly called laudanum), *that* might certainly intoxicate, if a man could bear to take enough of it; but why? Because it contains so much proof spirits of wine, and not because it contains so much opium. But crude opium, I affirm peremptorily, is incapable of producing any state of body at all resembling that which is produced by alcohol; and not in *degree* only incapable, but even in *kind*; it is not in the quantity of its effects merely, but in the quality, that it differs altogether. The pleasure given by wine is always rapidly mounting, and tending to a crisis, after which as rapidly it declines; that from opium, when once generated, is stationary for eight or ten hours: the first, to borrow a technical distinction from medicine, is a case of acute, the second of chronic, pleasure; the one is a flickering flame, the other a steady and equable glow. But the main distinction lies in this—that, whereas wine disorders the mental faculties, opium, on the contrary (if taken in a proper manner), introduces amongst them the most exquisite order, legislation, and harmony. Wine robs a man of his self-possession; opium sustains and reinforces it. Wine unsettles the judgment, and gives a preternatural brightness and a vivid exaltation to the contempts and the admirations, to the loves and the hatreds, of the drinker; opium, on the contrary, communicates serenity and equipoise to all the faculties, active or passive; and, with respect to the temper and moral feelings in general, it gives simply that sort of vital warmth which is approved by the judgment, and which would probably always accompany a bodily constitution of primeval

or antediluvian health.   Thus, for instance, opium, like
wine, gives an expansion to the heart and the benevolent
affections; but, then, with this remarkable difference, that,
in the sudden development of kindheartedness which
accompanies inebriation, there is always more or less of a
maudlin and a transitory character, which exposes it to the
contempt of the bystander.   Men shake hands, swear
eternal friendship, and shed tears—no mortal knows why;
and the animal nature is clearly uppermost.   But the expansion of the benigner feelings incident to opium is no
febrile access, no fugitive paroxysm; it is a healthy restoration to that state which the mind would naturally recover
upon the removal of any deep-seated irritation from pain
that had disturbed and quarrelled with the impulses of a
heart originally just and good.   True it is, that even wine
up to a certain point, and with certain men, rather tends to
exalt and to steady the intellect; I myself, who have never
been a great wine-drinker, used to find that half a dozen
glasses of wine advantageously affected the faculties,
brightened and intensified the consciousness, and gave to
the mind a feeling of being '*ponderibus librata suis*'; and
certainly it is most absurdly said, in popular language, of
any man, that he is *disguised* in liquor; for, on the contrary,
most men are disguised by sobriety, and exceedingly disguised; and it is when they are drinking that men display
themselves in their true complexion of character; which
surely is not disguising themselves.   But still, wine constantly leads a man to the brink of absurdity and extravagance; and, beyond a certain point, it is sure to volatilise
and to disperse the intellectual energies; whereas opium
always seems to compose what had been agitated, and to
concentrate what had been distracted.   In short, to sum
up all in one word, a man who is inebriated, or tending to
inebriation, is, and feels that he is, in a condition which
calls up into supremacy the merely human, too often the
brutal, part of his nature; but the opium-eater (I speak of
him simply *as* such, and assume that he is in a normal
state of health) feels that the diviner part of his nature is
paramount—that is, the moral affections are in a state of

cloudless serenity; and high over all the great light of the majestic intellect.

This is the doctrine of the true church on the subject of opium : of which church I acknowledge myself to be the Pope (consequently infallible), and self-appointed *legate à latere* to all degrees of latitude and longitude. But then it is to be recollected that I speak from the ground of a large and profound personal experience, whereas most of the unscientific [1] authors who have at all treated of opium, and even of those who have written professionally on the *materia medica*, make it evident, by the horror they express of it, that their experimental knowledge of its action is none at all. I will, however, candidly acknowledge that I have met with one person who bore evidence to its intoxicating power, such as staggered my own incredulity; for he was a surgeon, and had himself taken opium largely for a most miserable affection (past all hope of cure) seated in one particular organ. This affection was a subtle inflammation, not acute, but chronic; and with this he fought for more (I believe) than twenty years; fought victoriously, if victory it were, to make life support-

[1] Amongst the great herd of travellers, etc., who show sufficiently by their thoughtlessness that they never held any intercourse with opium, I must caution my readers specially against the brilliant author of *Anastasius*. This gentleman, whose wit would lead one to presume him an opium-eater, has made it impossible to consider him in that character, from the grievous misrepresentation which he has given of its effects at pages 215-217 of Vol. I. Upon consideration, it must appear such to the author himself; for, waiving the errors I have insisted on in the text, which (and others) are adopted in the fullest manner, he will himself admit that an old gentleman, 'with a snow-white beard,' who eats 'ample doses of opium,' and is yet able to deliver what is meant and received as very weighty counsel on the bad effects of that practice, is but an indifferent evidence that opium either kills people prematurely, or sends them into a madhouse. But, for my part, I see into this old gentleman and his motives : the fact is, he was enamoured of 'the little golden receptacle of the pernicious drug' which Anastasius carried about him ; and no way of obtaining it so safe and so feasible occurred as that of frightening its owner out of his wits. This commentary throws a new light upon the case, and greatly improves it as a story ; for the old gentleman's speech, as a lecture on pharmacy, is absurd ; but, considered as a hoax on Anastasius, it reads excellently.

able for himself, and during all that time to maintain in respectability a wife and a family of children altogether dependent on him.[1] I happened to say to him, that his enemies (as I had heard) charged him with talking nonsense on politics, and that his friends apologised for him, by suggesting that he was constantly in a state of intoxication from opium. Now, the accusation, said I, is not *primâ facie* an absurd one ; but the defence *is*. To my surprise, however, he insisted that both his enemies and his friends were in the right. ' I will maintain,' said he, ' that I *do* talk nonsense ; and, secondly, I will maintain that I do not talk nonsense upon principle, or with any view to profit, but solely and simply,' said he—' solely and simply—solely and simply ' (repeating it three times over), ' because I am drunk with opium ; and that daily.' I re-

---

[1] This surgeon it was who first made me aware of the dangerous variability in opium as to strength under the shifting proportions of its combination with alien impurities. Naturally, as a man professionally alive to the danger of creating any artificial need of opium beyond what the anguish of his malady at any rate demanded, trembling every hour on behalf of his poor children, lest, by any indiscretion of his own, he should precipitate the crisis of his disorder, he saw the necessity of reducing the daily dose to a *minimum*. But to do this he must first obtain the means of measuring the quantities of opium ; not the apparent quantities as determined by weighing, but the *virtual* quantities after allowing for the alloy or varying amounts of impurity. This, however, was a visionary problem. To allow for it was simply impossible. The problem, therefore, changed its character. Not to measure the impurities was the object ; for, whilst entangled with the operative and efficient parts of the opium, they could not be measured. To separate and eliminate the impure (or inert) parts, this was now the object. And this was effected finally by a particular mode of boiling the opium. That done, the residuum became equable in strength ; and the daily doses could be nicely adjusted. About 18 grains formed his daily ration for many years. This, upon the common hospital equation, expresses 18 times 25 drops of laudanum. But, since 25 is $= \frac{100}{4}$, therefore 18 times one quarter of a hundred is = one quarter of 1800, and that, I suppose, is 450. So much this surgeon averaged upon each day for about twenty years. Then suddenly began a fiercer stage of the anguish from his disease. But then, also, the fight was finished, and the victory was won. All duties were fulfilled : his children prosperously launched in life ; and death, which to himself was becoming daily more necessary as a relief from torment, now fell injuriously upon nobody.

plied, that as to the allegation of his enemies, as it seemed
to be established upon such respectable testimony, seeing
that the three parties concerned all agreed so far, it did
not become me to question it; but the defence set up I must
demur to. He proceeded to discuss the matter, and to
lay down his reasons; but it seemed to me so impolite to
pursue an argument which must have presumed a man
mistaken in a point belonging to his own profession, that
I did not press him, even when his course of argument
seemed open to objection; not to mention that a man who
talks nonsense, even though 'with no view to profit,' is not
altogether the most agreeable respondent in a dispute. I
confess, however, that the authority of a surgeon, and one
who was reputed a good one, may seem a weighty one to
my prejudice; but still I must plead my experience, which
was greater than his greatest by more than seven thousand
drops a-day; and though it was not possible to suppose a
medical man unacquainted with the characteristic symptoms
of vinous intoxication, yet it struck me that he might
proceed on a logical error of using the word intoxication
with too careless a latitude, extending it generically to all
modes of nervous excitement, instead of restricting it to
one special quality of pleasurable elevation, distinguished
by well-known symptoms, and connected with tendencies
not to be evaded. Two of these tendencies I will mention
as diagnostic, or characteristic and inseparable marks of
ordinary alcoholic intoxication, but which no excess in the
use of opium ever develops. One is the loss of self-com-
mand, in relation to all one's acts and purposes, which
steals gradually (though with varying degrees of speed)
over *all* persons indiscriminately when indulging in wine
or distilled liquors beyond a certain limit. The tongue
and other organs become unmanageable: the intoxicated
man speaks inarticulately; and, with regard to certain
words, makes efforts ludicrously earnest, yet oftentimes
unavailing, to utter them. The eyes are bewildered, and
see double; grasping too little, and too much. The hand
aims awry. The legs stumble, and lose their power of
concurrent action. To this result *all* people tend, though

by varying rates of acceleration. Secondly, as another characteristic, it may be noticed that, in alcoholic intoxication, the movement is always along a kind of arch; the drinker rises through continual ascents to a summit or *apex*, from which he descends through corresponding steps of declension. There is a crowning point in the movement upwards, which once attained cannot be renewed : and it is the blind, unconscious, but always unsuccessful effort of the obstinate drinker to restore this supreme altitude of enjoyment which tempts him into excesses that become dangerous. After reaching this *acme* of genial pleasure, it is a mere necessity of the case to sink through corresponding stages of collapse. Some people have maintained, in my hearing, that they had been drunk upon green tea ; and a medical student in London, for whose knowledge in his profession I have reason to feel great respect, assured me, the other day, that a patient, in recovering from an illness, had got drunk on a beef-steak. All turns, in fact, upon a rigorous definition of intoxication.

Having dwelt so much on this first and leading error in respect to opium, I shall notice briefly a second and a third ; which are, that the elevation of spirits produced by opium is necessarily followed by a proportionate depression, and that the natural and even immediate consequence of opium is torpor and stagnation, animal as well as mental. The first of these errors I shall content myself with simply denying ; assuring my reader, that for ten years during which I took opium not regularly, but intermittingly, the day succeeding to that on which I allowed myself this luxury was always a day of unusually good spirits.

With respect to the torpor supposed to follow, or rather (if we were to credit the numerous pictures of Turkish opium-eaters) to accompany, the practice of opium-eating, I deny that also. Certainly, opium is classed under the head of narcotics, and some such effect it may produce in the end ; but the primary effects of opium are always, and in the highest degree, to excite and stimulate the system. This first stage of its action always lasted with me, during my novitiate, for upwards of eight hours ; so that it must be the fault of the opium-eater himself, if he does not so time his exhibition of the dose, as that the whole weight of its narcotic influence may descend upon his sleep.   Turkish opium-eaters, it seems, are absurd enough to sit, like so many equestrian statues, on logs of wood as stupid as themselves.   But, that the reader may judge of the degree in which opium is likely to stupefy the faculties of an Englishman, I shall (by way of treating the question illustratively, rather than argumentatively) describe the way in which I myself often passed an opium evening in London during the period between 1804 and 1812.   It will be seen, that at least opium did not move me to seek solitude, and much less to seek inactivity, or the torpid state of self-involution ascribed to the Turks.   I give this account at the risk of being pronounced a crazy enthusiast or visionary ; but I regard that little.   I must desire my reader to bear in mind that I was a hard student, and at severe studies for all the rest of my time ; and certainly I had a right occasionally to relaxations as well as other people.

The late Duke of Norfolk [1] used to say, ' Next Monday, wind and weather permitting, I purpose to be drunk ' ; and in like manner I used to fix beforehand how often within a given time, when, and with what accessory circumstances of festal joy, I would commit a debauch of opium. This was seldom more than once in three weeks ; for at that time I could not have ventured to call every day (as afterwards I did) for '*a glass of laudanum negus, warm, and without sugar.*'   No ; once in three weeks sufficed ; and the time selected was either a Tuesday or a Saturday

[1] ' *The late Duke of Norfolk* ' :—My authority was the late Sir George Beaumont, an old familiar acquaintance of the duke's.   But such expressions are always liable to grievous misapplication.   By ' the late ' duke Sir George meant that duke once so well known to the nation as the partisan friend of Fox, Burke, Sheridan, etc., at the era of the great French Revolution in 1789-93.   Since *his* time, I believe there have been three generations of ducal Howards — who are always interesting to the English nation, first, from the bloody historic traditions surrounding their great house ; secondly, from the fact of their being at the head of the British Peerage.

N

night; my reason for which was this:—Tuesday and Saturday were for many years the regular nights of performance at the King's Theatre (or Opera House); and there it was in those times that Grassini sang; and her voice (the richest of *contraltos*) was delightful to me beyond all that I had ever heard. Yes; or have since heard; or ever shall hear. I know not what may be the state of the opera-house now, having never been within its walls for seven or eight years; but at that time it was by much the most pleasant place of resort in London for passing an evening.[1] Half-a-guinea admitted you to the pit, under the troublesome condition, however, of being *en grande tenue*. But to the gallery five shillings admitted you; and that gallery was subject to far less annoyance than the pit of most theatres. The orchestra was distinguished by its sweet and melodious grandeur from all English orchestras; the composition of which, I confess, is not acceptable to my ear, from the predominance of the clangorous instruments, and in some instances from the tyranny of the violin. Thrilling was the pleasure with which almost always I heard this angelic Grassini. Shivering with expectation I sat, when the time drew near for her golden epiphany; shivering I rose from my seat, incapable of rest, when that heavenly and harp-like voice sang its own victorious welcome in its prelusive *threttánelo —threttánelo*[2] (θρεττάνελω — θρεττάνελω). The choruses

---

[1] I trust that my reader has not been so inattentive to the windings of my narrative as to fancy me speaking here of the Brown-Brunell and Pyment period. Naturally I had no money disposable at that period for the opera. I am speaking here of years stretching far beyond those boyish scenes—interludes in my Oxford life, or long after Oxford.

[2] '*Threttánelo—threttánelo*':—The beautiful representative echo by which Aristophanes expresses the sound of the Grecian *phorminx*, or of some other instrument, which conjecturally has been shown most to resemble our modern European harp. In the case of ancient Hebrew instruments used in the temple service, random and idle must be all the guesses through the Greek Septuagint or the Latin Vulgate to identify any one of them. But as to Grecian instruments the case is different; always there is a remote chance of digging up some marble sculpture of orchestral appurtenances and properties.

were divine to hear ; and, when Grassini [1] appeared in some interlude, as she often did, and poured forth her passionate soul as Andromache at the tomb of Hector, etc., I question whether any Turk, of all that ever entered the paradise of opium-eaters, can have had half the pleasure I had.   But, indeed, I honour the barbarians too much by supposing them capable of any pleasures approaching to the intellectual ones of an Englishman.   For music is an intellectual or a sensual pleasure, according to the temperament of him who hears it.   And, by the bye, with the exception of the fine extravaganza on that subject in *Twelfth Night*, I do not recollect more than one thing said adequately on the subject of music in all literature.   It is a passage in the *Religio Medici* [2] of Sir T. Browne, and, though chiefly remarkable for its sublimity, has also a philosophic value, inasmuch as it points to the true theory of musical effects.   The mistake of most people is, to suppose that it is by the ear they communicate with music, and therefore that they are purely passive as to its effects.   But this is not so ; it is by the reaction of the mind upon the notices of the ear (the *matter* coming by the senses, the *form* from the mind) that the pleasure is constructed ; and therefore it is that people of equally good ear differ so much in this point from one another.   Now opium, by greatly increasing the activity of the mind, generally increases, of necessity, that particular mode of its activity by which we are able to construct out of the raw material of organic sound an elaborate intellectual pleasure.   But, says a friend, a succession of musical sounds is to me like a collection of Arabic characters : I can attach

[1] Yet all things change : this same Grassini, whom once I adored. afterwards, when gorged with English gold, went off to Paris ; and when I heard on what terms she lived with a man so unmagnanimous as Napoleon, I came to hate her.   Did I complain of any man's hating England, or teaching a woman to hate her benefactress ?   Not at all ; but simply of his adopting at second-hand the malice of a jealous nation, with which originally he could have had no sincere sympathy. Hate us, if you please ; but not sycophantishly, by way of paying court to others.

[2] I have not the book at this moment to consult ; but I think the passage begins, 'And even that tavern music, which makes one man merry, another mad, in me strikes a deep fit of devotion,' etc.

no ideas to them. Ideas! my dear friend! there is no occasion for them; all that class of ideas which can be available in such a case has a language of representative feelings. But this is a subject foreign to my present purposes; it is sufficient to say that a chorus, etc., of elaborate harmony displayed before me, as in a piece of arras-work, the whole of my past life—not as if recalled by an act of memory, but as if present and incarnated in the music; no longer painful to dwell upon, but the detail of its incidents removed, or blended in some hazy abstraction, and its passions exalted, spiritualised, and sublimed. All this was to be had for five shillings—that being the price of admission to the gallery; or, if a man preferred the high-bred society of the pit, even this might be had for half-a-guinea; or, in fact, for half-a-crown less, by purchasing beforehand a ticket at the music shops. And over and above the music of the stage and the orchestra, I had all around me, in the intervals of the performance, the music of the Italian language talked by Italian women —for the gallery was usually crowded with Italians—and I listened with a pleasure such as that with which Weld, the traveller, lay and listened, in Canada, to the sweet laughter of Indian women; for the less you understand of a language, the more sensible you are to the melody or harshness of its sounds. For such a purpose, therefore, it was an advantage to me that in those days I was a poor Italian scholar, reading it but little, and not speaking it at all, nor understanding a tenth part of what I heard spoken.

These were my opera pleasures; but another pleasure I had, which, as it could be had only on a Saturday night, occasionally struggled with my love of the opera; for, in those years, Tuesday and Saturday were the regular opera nights. On this subject I am afraid I shall be rather obscure, but, I can assure the reader, not at all more so than Marinus in his *Life of Proclus*, or many other biographers and autobiographers of fair reputation. This pleasure, I have said, was to be had only on a Saturday night. What, then, was Saturday night to me more than any other night? I had no labours that I rested from ; no wages to receive ; what needed I to care for Saturday night, more than as it was a summons to hear Grassini? True, most logical reader ; what thou sayest is, and ever will be, unanswerable. And yet so it was, that, whereas different men throw their feelings into different channels, and most men are apt to show their interest in the concerns of the poor chiefly by sympathy with their distresses and sorrows, I at that time was disposed to express mine by sympathising with their pleasures. The pains of poverty I had lately seen too much of—more than I wished to remember ; but the pleasures of the poor, their hopes, their consolations of spirit, and their restings from toil, can never become oppressive to contemplate. Now, Saturday night is the season for the chief regular and periodic return of rest to the poor, and to all that live by bodily labour ; in this point the most hostile sects unite, and acknowledge a common link of brotherhood : almost all Christendom rests from its labours. It is a rest introductory to another rest ; and divided by a whole day and two nights from the renewal of toil. On this account I feel always, on a Saturday night, as though I also were released from some yoke of bondage, had some wages to receive, and some luxury of repose to enjoy. For the sake, therefore, of witnessing, upon as large a scale as possible, a spectacle with which my sympathy was so entire, I used often, on Saturday nights, after I had taken opium, to wander forth, without much regarding the direction or the distance, to all the markets, and other parts of London, whither the poor resort on a Saturday night, for laying out their wages. Many a family party, consisting of a man, his wife, and some-times one or two of their children, have I listened to, as they stood consulting on their ways and means, or the strength of their exchequer, or the price of household articles. Gradually I became familiar with their wishes, their difficulties, and their opinions. Sometimes there might be heard murmurs of discontent ; but far oftener expressions on the countenance, or uttered in words, of patience, of hope, and of reconciliation to their lot. Generally speaking, the impression left upon my mind was, that the poor are practically more philosophic than the rich; that they show a more ready and cheerful submission to what they consider as irremediable evils or irreparable losses. Whenever I saw occasion, or could do it without appearing to be intrusive, I joined their parties, and gave my opinion upon the matter in discussion, which, if not always judicious, was always received indulgently. If wages were a little higher, or were expected to be so—if the quartern loaf were a little lower, or it was reported that onions and butter were falling, I was glad; yet, if the contrary were true, I drew from opium some means of consolation. For opium (like the bee, that extracts its materials indiscriminately from roses and from the soot[1] of chimneys) can overrule all feelings into a compliance with the master-key. Some of these rambles led me to great distances; for an opium-eater is too happy to observe the motion of time. And sometimes, in my attempts to steer homewards, upon nautical principles, by fixing my eye on the pole-star, and seeking ambitiously for a north-west passage, instead of circumnavigating all the capes and headlands I had doubled in my outward voyage, I came suddenly upon such knotty problems of alleys, alleys without soundings, such enigmatical entries, and such sphinx's riddles of streets without obvious outlets or thoroughfares, as must baffle the audacity of porters, and confound the intellects of hackney coachmen. I could almost have believed, at times, that I must be the first discoverer of some of these *terræ incognitæ*, and doubted whether they had yet been laid down in the modern charts of London. Positively,

[1] 'Soot':—In the large capacious chimneys of the rustic cottages throughout the Lake district, you can see up the entire cavity from the seat which you occupy, as an honoured visitor, in the chimney corner. There I used often to hear (though not to see) bees. Their murmuring was audible, though their bodily forms were too small to be visible at that altitude. On inquiry, I found that soot (chiefly from wood and peats) was useful in some stage of their wax or honey manufacture.

in one line of communication to the south of Holborn, for foot passengers (known, I doubt not, to many of my London readers), the road lay through a man's kitchen ; and, as it was a small kitchen, you needed to steer cautiously, or else you might run foul of the dripping-pan. For all this, however, I paid a heavy price in distant years, when the human face tyrannised over my dreams, and the perplexities of my steps in London came back and haunted my sleep, with the feeling of perplexities, moral or intellectual, that brought confusion to the reason, that brought anguish and remorse to the conscience.

Thus I have shown, or tried to show, that opium does not of necessity produce inactivity or torpor ; but that, on the contrary, it often led me into markets and theatres. Yet, in candour, I will admit that markets and theatres are not the appropriate haunts of the opium-eater, when in the divinest state incident to his enjoyment. In that state, crowds become an oppression to him ; music, even, too sensual and gross. He naturally seeks solitude and silence, as indispensable conditions of those trances, or profoundest reveries, which are the crown and consummation of what opium can do for human nature. I, whose disease it was to meditate too much and to observe too little, and who, upon my first entrance at college, was nearly falling into a deep melancholy, from brooding too much on the sufferings which I had witnessed in London, was sufficiently aware of these tendencies in my own thoughts to do all I could to counteract them. I was, indeed, like a person, who, according to the old Pagan legend, had entered the cave of Trophonius ; and the remedies I sought were to force myself into society, and to keep my understanding in continual activity upon subtleties of philosophic speculation. But for these remedies, I should certainly have become hypochondriac-ally melancholy. In after years, however, when my cheerfulness was more fully re-established, I yielded to my natural inclination for a solitary life. At that time I often fell into such reveries after taking opium ; and

many a time it has happened to me on a summer night—
when I have been seated at an open window, from which
I could overlook the sea at a mile below me, and could at
the same time command a view of some great town
standing on a different radius of my circular prospect,
but at nearly the same distance—that from sunset to
sunrise, all through the hours of night, I have continued
motionless, as if frozen, without consciousness of myself
as of an object anywise distinct from the multiform scene
which I contemplated from above.　Such a scene in all its
elements was not unfrequently realised for me on the
gentle eminence of Everton.　Obliquely to the left lay
the many-languaged town of Liverpool; obliquely to
the right, the multitudinous sea.　The scene itself was
somewhat typical of what took place in such a reverie.
The town of Liverpool represented the earth, with its
sorrows and its graves left behind, yet not out of sight,
nor wholly forgotten.　The ocean, in everlasting but
gentle agitation, yet brooded over by dove-like calm,
might not unfitly typify the mind, and the mood which
then swayed it.　For it seemed to me as if then first I
stood at a distance aloof from the uproar of life; as if
the tumult, the fever, and the strife, were suspended; a
respite were granted from the secret burdens of the
heart; some sabbath of repose; some resting from
human labours.　Here were the hopes which blossom
in the paths of life, reconciled with the peace which is
in the grave; motions of the intellect as unwearied as
the heavens, yet for all anxieties a halcyon calm; tranquillity that seemed no product of inertia, but as if
resulting from mighty and equal antagonisms; infinite
activities, infinite repose.

　　O just, subtle, and all-conquering opium! that, to the
hearts of rich and poor alike, for the wounds that will
never heal, and for the pangs of grief that 'tempt the
spirit to rebel,' bringest an assuaging balm;—eloquent
opium! that with thy potent rhetoric stealest away the
purposes of wrath, pleadest effectually for relenting pity,
and through one night's heavenly sleep callest back to the

guilty man the visions of his infancy, and hands washed
pure from blood ;—O just and righteous opium ! that to
the chancery of dreams summonest, for the triumphs of
despairing innocence, false witnesses ; and confoundest
perjury ; and dost reverse the sentences of unrighteous
judges ;—thou buildest upon the bosom of darkness, out
of the fantastic imagery of the brain, cities and temples,
beyond the art of Phidias and Praxiteles—beyond the
splendours of Babylon and Hekatómpylos ;[1] and, 'from
the anarchy of dreaming sleep,' callest into sunny light
the faces of long-buried beauties, and the blessed household countenances, cleansed from the 'dishonours of the
grave.' Thou only givest these gifts to man ; and thou
hast the keys of Paradise, O just, subtle, and mighty
opium !

.   .   .   .

Courteous, and I hope indulgent reader, having accompanied me thus far, now let me request you to move
onwards for about eight years ; that is to say, from 1804
(when I said that my acquaintance with opium began) to
1812. The years of academic life are now over and gone
—almost forgotten ; the student's cap no longer presses
my temples ; if my cap exists at all, it presses those of
some youthful scholar, I trust, as happy as myself, and as
passionate a lover of knowledge. My gown is, by this
time, I dare to say, in the same condition with many
thousands of excellent books in the Bodleian,—viz.,
diligently perused by certain studious moths and worms ;
or departed, however (which is all that I know of its fate),
to that great reservoir of *somewhere*, to which all the tea-
cups, tea-caddies, tea-pots, tea-kettles, etc., have departed,
which occasional resemblances in the present generation of
tea-cups, etc., remind me of having once possessed, but of
whose departure and final fate I, in common with most

---

[1] *i.e.* the *hundred-gated* (from ἑκατόν, *hekaton*, a hundred, and
πύλη, *pyle*, a gate). This epithet of hundred-gated was applied to
the Egyptian Thebes in contradistinction to the ἑπτάπυλος (*heptápylos*,
or *seven-gated*) which designated the Grecian Thebes, within one day's
journey of Athens.

gownsmen of either university, could give but an obscure and conjectural history. The persecutions of the chapel bell, sounding its unwelcome summons to matins, interrupts my slumbers no longer; the porter who rang it is dead, and has ceased to disturb anybody; and I, with many others who suffered much from his tintinnabulous propensities, have now agreed to overlook his errors, and have forgiven him. Even with the bell I am now in charity; it rings, I suppose, as formerly, thrice a-day, and cruelly annoys, I doubt not, many worthy gentlemen, and disturbs their peace of mind; but, as to me, in this year 1812, I regard its treacherous voice no longer (treacherous, I call it, for, by some refinement of malice, it spoke in as sweet and silvery tones as if it had been inviting one to a party); its tones have no longer, indeed, power to reach me, let the wind sit as favourably as the malice of the bell itself could wish; for I am two hundred and fifty miles away from it, and buried in the depth of mountains.

And what am I doing amongst the mountains? Taking opium. Yes; but what else? Why, reader, in 1812, the year we are now arrived at, as well as for some years previous, I have been chiefly studying German metaphysics, in the writings of Kant, Fichte, Schelling, etc. And how, and in what manner, do I live? in short, what class or description of men do I belong to? I am at this period—viz., in 1812—living in a cottage; and with a single female servant (*honi soit qui mal y pense*), who, amongst my neighbours, passes by the name of my 'housekeeper.' And, as a scholar and a man of learned education, I may presume to class myself as an unworthy member of that indefinite body called *gentlemen*. Partly on the ground I have assigned—partly because, from having no visible calling or business, it is rightly judged that I must be living on my private fortune—I am so classed by my neighbours; and, by the courtesy of modern England, I am usually addressed on letters, etc., *Esquire*, though having, I fear, in the rigorous construction of heralds, antique or antic, dressed like the knaves of spades or diamonds, but slender pretensions to that distinguished

honour;—yes, in popular estimation, I am X. Y. Z.,
Esquire, but not Justice of the Peace, nor Custos
Rotulorum. Am I married? Not yet. And I still take
opium? On Saturday nights. And, perhaps, have taken
it unblushingly ever since 'the rainy Sunday,' and 'the
stately Pantheon,' and 'the beatific druggist' of 1804?
Even so. And how do I find my health after all this
opium-eating? in short, how do I do? Why, pretty
well, I thank you, reader. In fact, if I dared to say the
real and simple truth (though, in order to satisfy the
theories of some medical men, I ought to be ill), I was
never better in my life than in the spring of 1812; and I
hope sincerely, that the quantity of claret, port, or 'London
particular Madeira,' which, in all probability, you, good
reader, have taken, and design to take, for every term of
eight years during your natural life, may as little disorder
your health as mine was disordered by all the opium I had
taken (though in quantity such that I might well have
bathed and swum in it) for the eight years between 1804
and 1812. Hence you may see again the danger of taking
any medical advice from *Anastasius*;[1] in divinity, for
anything I know, he may be a safe counsellor, but not in
medicine. No; it is far better to consult Dr. Buchan, as
I did; for I never forgot that worthy man's excellent
suggestion, and I was 'particularly careful not to take
above five-and-twenty ounces of laudanum.' To this
moderation and temperate use of the article I may ascribe
it, I suppose, that as yet at least (that is, in 1812) I am
ignorant and unsuspicious of the avenging terrors which
opium has in store for those who abuse its long-suffering.
At the same time, as yet I had been only a *dilettante* eater
of opium; even eight years' practice, with the single pre-

[1] '*Anastasius*':—The reader of this generation will marvel at these
repeated references to *Anastasius*: it is now an almost forgotten book,
so vast has been the deluge of novel-writing talent, really original and
powerful, which has overflowed our literature during the lapse of thirty-
five years from the publication of these Confessions. *Anastasius* was
written by the famous and opulent Mr. Hope, and was in 1821 a book
both of high reputation and of great influence amongst the leading circles
of society.

caution of allowing sufficient intervals between every indulgence, has not been sufficient to make opium necessary to me as an article of daily diet. But now comes a different era. Move on, then, if you please, reader, to 1813. In the summer of the year we have just quitted, I had suffered much in bodily health from distress of mind connected with a melancholy event. This event, being nowise related to the subject now before me, further than through the bodily illness which it produced, I need not more particularly notice. Whether this illness of 1812 had any share in that of 1813, I know not; but so it was, that, in the latter year, I was attacked by a most appalling irritation of the stomach, in all respects the same as that which had caused me so much suffering in youth, and accompanied by a revival of all the old dreams. Now, then, it was—viz., in the year 1813—that I became a regular and confirmed (no longer an intermitting) opium-eater. And here I find myself in a perplexing dilemma. Either, on the one hand, I must exhaust the reader's patience by such a detail of my malady, and of my struggles with it, as might suffice to establish the fact of my inability to wrestle any longer with irritation and constant suffering; or, on the other hand, by passing lightly over this critical part of my story, I must forego the benefit of a stronger impression left on the mind of the reader, and must lay myself open to the mis-construction of having slipped by the easy and gradual steps of self-indulging persons, from the first to the final stage of opium eating (a misconstruction to which there will be a lurking predisposition in most readers, from my previous acknowledgments). This is the dilemma, the first horn of which is not to be thought of. It remains, then, that I *postulate* so much as is necessary for my purpose. And let me take as full credit for this as if I had demonstrated it, good reader, at the expense of your patience and my own. Be not so ungenerous as to let me suffer in your good opinion through my own forbearance and regard for your comfort. No; believe all that I ask of you—viz., that I could resist no longer—believe it

liberally, and as an act of grace, or else in mere prudence ;
for, if not, then in my next edition I will make you believe
and tremble ; and, *à force d'ennuyer*, by mere dint of
pandiculation, vulgarly called yawning, I will terrify all
readers of mine from ever again questioning any postulate
that I shall think fit to make.

This, then, let me repeat : I postulate that, at the time
I began to take opium daily, I could not have done otherwise. Whether, indeed, afterwards I might not have
succeeded in breaking off the habit, even when it seemed
to me that all efforts would be unavailing, and whether
many of the innumerable efforts which I *did* make might
not have been carried much further, and my gradual re-
conquests of lost ground might not have been followed up
much more energetically——these are questions which I must
decline. Perhaps I might make out a case of palliation ;
but (shall I speak ingenuously ?) I confess it, as a besetting
infirmity of mine, that I am too much of an Eudæmonist ;
I hanker too much after a state of happiness, both for
myself and others ; I cannot face misery, whether my own
or not, with an eye of sufficient firmness, and am little
capable of encountering present pain for the sake of any
reversionary benefit. On some other matters, I can agree
with the gentlemen of The Porch[1] at Manchester in
affecting the Stoic philosophy ; but not in this. Here I
take the liberty of an Eclectic philosopher, and I look out
for some courteous and considerate sect that will condescend
more to the infirm condition of an opium-eater ; that are
pleasant men and courteous, such as Chaucer describes, to
hear confession or to give absolution, and will show some
conscience in the penances they inflict, or the efforts of
abstinence they exact from poor sinners like myself. An
inhuman moralist I can no more endure, in my nervous
state, than opium that has not been boiled. At any rate,

[1] A handsome news-room, of which I was very courteously made
free, in passing through Manchester, by several gentlemen of that place,
is called either *The Porch* or *The Portico*, which in Greek is the *Stoa ;*
from which I, a stranger in Manchester, inferred that the subscribers
meant to profess themselves Stoics, or followers of Zeno. But I have
been since assured that this is a mistake.

he who summons me to send out a large freight of self-
denial and mortification upon any cruising voyage of
moral improvement, must make it clear to my understanding that the concern is a hopeful one. At my time
of life (six-and-thirty years of age[1]), it cannot be supposed
that I have much energy to spare; in fact, I find it all
little enough for the intellectual labours I have on my
hands; and, therefore, let no man expect to frighten me,
by a few hard words, into embarking any part of it upon
desperate adventures of morality.

Desperate or not, however, the issue of the struggle in
1813 was what I have mentioned; and from this date the
reader is to consider me as a regular and confirmed opium-
eater, of whom to ask whether on any particular day he
had or had not taken opium, would be to ask whether his
lungs had performed respiration, or the heart fulfilled its
functions. Now, then, reader, you understand what I am;
and you are by this time aware, that no old gentleman,
'with a snow-white beard,' will have any chance of per-
suading me (like Anastasius) to surrender 'the little
golden receptacle of the pernicious drug.' No; I give
notice to all, whether moralists or surgeons, that, whatever
be their pretensions and skill in their respective lines of
practice, they must not hope for any countenance from
me, if they think to begin by any savage proposition for a
Lent or Ramadan of abstinence from opium. This being
fully understood between us, we shall in future sail before
the wind; now, then, reader, from the year 1813, where
all this time we have been sitting down and loitering, rise
up, if you please, walk forward about three years more;
draw up the curtain, and you shall see me in a new
character.

If any man, poor or rich, were to say that he would
tell us what had been the happiest day in his life, and the
why and the wherefore, I suppose that we should all cry
out, Hear him! hear him! As to the happiest day, that
must be very difficult for any wise man to assign; because
any event that could occupy so distinguished a place in a

---

[1] This was written at the time of original publication.

man's retrospect of life, or be entitled to have shed a special,
separate, and supreme felicity on any one day, ought to be
of such an enduring character, as that (accidents apart) it
should have continued to shed the same felicity, or one
not distinguishably less, on very many years together.
To the happiest *lustrum*, however, or even to the happiest
year, a man may perhaps allowably point without discountenance from wisdom.   This year, in *my* case, reader,
was the one which we have now reached ; though it stood,
I confess, as a parenthesis between years of a gloomier
character.   It was a year of brilliant water (to speak after
the manner of jewellers), set, as it were, and insulated, in
the gloomy umbrage of opium.   Strange as it may sound,
I had a little before this time descended suddenly, and
without any considerable effort, from three hundred and
twenty grains of opium (that is, eight [1] thousand drops of
laudanum) per day, to forty grains, or one-eighth part.
Instantaneously, and as if by magic, the cloud of profoundest melancholy which rested upon my brain, like
some black vapours that I have seen roll away from the
summit of a mountain, drew off in one week ; passed away
with its murky banners as simultaneously as a ship that has
been stranded, and is floated off by a spring-tide,

> That moveth altogether, if it move at all.

Now, then, I was again happy : I now took only one
thousand drops of laudanum per day—and what was that ?
A latter spring had come to close up the season of youth.
My brain performed its functions as healthily as ever

---

[1] I here reckon twenty-five drops of laudanum as equivalent to one
grain of opium, which, I believe, is the common estimate.   However,
as both may be considered variable quantities (the crude opium varying
much in strength, and the tincture still more), I suppose that no
infinitesimal accuracy can be had in such a calculation.   Tea-spoons
vary as much in size as opium in strength.   Small ones hold about one
hundred drops ; so that eight thousand drops, which obviously read
into eighty hundred drops, fill a *small* tea-spoon eighty times.   But
large modern tea-spoons hold very much more.   Some even approach
in their capacity to dessert-spoons.   The reader sees how much I kept
within Dr. Buchan's indulgent allowance.

before. I read Kant again; and again I understood him,
or fancied that I did. Again my feelings of pleasure
expanded themselves to all around me; and, if any man
from Oxford or Cambridge, or from neither, had been
announced to me in my unpretending cottage, I should
have welcomed him with as sumptuous a reception as so
poor a man could offer. Whatever else might be wanting
to a wise man's happiness, of laudanum I would have given
him as much as he wished, and in a silver-gilt, if not
golden, cup. And, by the way, now that I speak of
giving laudanum away, I remember about this time a little
incident, which I mention because, trifling as it was, the
reader will soon meet it again in my dreams, which it
influenced more fearfully than could be imagined. One
day a Malay knocked at my door. What business a
Malay could have to transact amongst the recesses of
English mountains, is not my business to conjecture; but
possibly he was on his road to a seaport—viz., Whitehaven,
Workington, etc.—about forty miles distant.[1]

The servant who opened the door to him was a young
girl, born and bred amongst the mountains, who had never
seen an Asiatic dress of any sort: his turban, therefore,
confounded her not a little; and as it turned out that *his*
knowledge of English was exactly commensurate with *hers*
of Malay, there seemed to be an impassable gulf fixed
between all communication of ideas, if either party had

[1] Between the seafaring populations on the coast of Lancashire,
and the corresponding populations on the coast of Cumberland (such as
Ravenglass, Whitehaven, Workington, Maryport, etc.), there was a
slender current of interchange constantly going on, and especially in
the days of pressgangs—in part by sea, but in part also by land. By
the way, I may mention, as an interesting fact which I discovered from
an almanack and itinerary, dated about the middle of Queen Elizabeth's
reign (say 1579), that the official route in *her* days for queen's
messengers to the north of Ireland, and of course for travellers generally,
was not (as now) through Grasmere, and thence by St. John's Vale,
Threlkeld (for the short cut by Shoulthwaite Moss was then unknown),
Keswick, Cockermouth, and Whitehaven. Up to St. Oswald's Church,
Gresmere (so it was then spelled, in deference to its Danish original),
the route lay as at present. Thence it turned round the lake to the
left, crossed Hammerscar, up *Little* Langdale, across Wrynose to
Egremont, and from Egremont to Whitehaven.

happened to possess any. In this dilemma, the girl, recollecting the reputed learning of her master (and, doubtless, giving me credit for a knowledge of all the languages of the earth, besides, perhaps, a few of the lunar ones), came and gave me to understand that there was a sort of demon below, whom she clearly imagined that my art could exorcise from the house. The group which presented itself, arranged as it was by accident, though not very elaborate, took hold of my fancy and my eye more powerfully than any of the statuesque attitudes or groups exhibited in the ballets at the opera-house, though so ostentatiously complex. In a cottage kitchen, but not looking so much like *that* as a rustic hall of entrance, being pannelled on the wall with dark wood, that from age and rubbing resembled oak, stood the Malay, his turban and loose trousers of dingy white relieved upon the dark pannelling; he had placed himself nearer to the girl than she seemed to relish, though her native spirit of mountain intrepidity contended with the feeling of simple awe which her countenance expressed, as she gazed upon the tiger-cat before her. A more striking picture there could not be imagined, than the beautiful English face of the girl,[1] and its exquisite bloom, together with her erect and independent attitude, contrasted with the sallow and bilious skin of the Malay, veneered with mahogany tints by climate and marine air,

---

[1] This girl, Barbara Lewthwaite, was already at that time a person of some poetic distinction, being (unconsciously to herself) the chief speaker in a little pastoral poem of Wordsworth's. That she was really beautiful, and not merely so described by me for the sake of improving the picturesque effect, the reader will judge from this line in the poem, written perhaps ten years earlier, when Barbara might be six years old :—

'Twas little Barbara Lewthwaite, a child of beauty rare !

This, coming from William Wordsworth, both a fastidious judge and a truth-speaker of the severest literality, argues some real pretensions to beauty, or real at that time. But it is notorious that, in the anthologies of earth through all her zones, one flower beyond every other is liable to change, which flower is the countenance of woman. Whether in his fine stanzas upon 'Mutability,' where the most pathetic instances of this earthly doom are solemnly arrayed, Spenser has dwelt sufficiently upon this, the saddest of all, I do not remember.

his small, fierce, restless eyes, thin lips, slavish gestures and adorations. Half-hidden by the ferocious-looking Malay, was a little child from a neighbouring cottage, who had crept in after him, and was now in the act of reverting its head and gazing upwards at the turban and the fiery eyes beneath it, whilst with one hand he caught at the dress of the lovely girl for protection.

My knowledge of the Oriental tongues is not remarkably extensive, being, indeed, confined to two words— the Arabic word for barley, and the Turkish for opium (*madjoon*), which I have learned from *Anastasius*. And, as I had neither a Malay dictionary, nor even Adelung's *Mithridates*, which might have helped me to a few words, I addressed him in some lines from the *Iliad;* considering that, of such languages as I possessed, the Greek, in point of longitude, came geographically nearest to an Oriental one. He worshipped me in a devout manner, and replied in what I suppose to have been Malay. In this way I saved my reputation as a linguist with my neighbours ; for the Malay had no means of betraying the secret. He lay down upon the floor for about an hour, and then pursued his journey. On his departure, I presented him, *inter alia*, with a piece of opium. To him, as a native of the East, I could have no doubt that opium was not less familiar than his daily bread ; and the expression of his face convinced me that it was. Nevertheless, I was struck with some little consternation when I saw him suddenly raise his hand to his mouth, and bolt the whole, divided into three pieces, at one mouthful. The quantity was enough to kill some half dozen dragoons, together with their horses, supposing neither bipeds nor quadrupeds to be regularly trained opium-eaters. I felt some alarm for the poor creature ; but what could be done ? I had given him the opium in pure compassion for his solitary life, since, if he had travelled on foot from London, it must be nearly three weeks since he could have exchanged a thought with any human being. Ought I to have violated the laws of hospitality by having him seized and drenched with an emetic, thus frightening him into a notion that we were going to sacrifice him to some English idol? No : there was clearly no help for it. The mischief, if any, was done. He took his leave, and for some days I felt anxious ; but, as I never heard of any Malay, or of any man in a turban, being found dead on any part of the very slenderly peopled road between Grasmere and White-haven, I became satisfied that he was familiar with opium,[1] and that I must doubtless have done him the service I designed, by giving one night of respite from the pains of wandering.

This incident I have digressed to mention, because this Malay (partly from the picturesque exhibition he assisted to frame, partly from the anxiety I connected with his image for some days) fastened afterwards upon my fancy, and through *that* upon my dreams, bringing with him other Malays worse than himself, that ran 'a-muck '[2] at me, and led me into a world of nocturnal troubles. But to quit this episode, and to return to my intercalary year of happiness. I have said already that, on a subject so important to us all as happiness, we should listen with pleasure to any man's experience or experi-ments, even though he were but a ploughboy, who cannot be supposed to have ploughed very deep in such an intractable soil as that of human pains and pleasures, or to have conducted his researches upon any very enlightened principles. But I, who have taken happiness, both in a solid and a liquid shape, both boiled and unboiled, both East Indian and Turkish—who have conducted my experiments upon this interesting subject

---

[1] This, however, is not a necessary conclusion ; the varieties of effect produced by opium on different constitutions are infinite. A London magistrate (Hariott's *Struggles through Life*, vol. iii. p. 391, third edition) has recorded that, on the first occasion of his trying laudanum for the gout, he took FORTY drops ; the next night SIXTY, and on the fifth night EIGHTY, without any effect whatever ; and this at an advanced age.

[2] See the common accounts, in any eastern traveller or voyager, of the frantic excesses committed by Malays who have taken opium, or are reduced to desperation by ill luck at gambling.

with a sort of galvanic battery, and have, for the general benefit of the world, inoculated myself, as it were, with the poison of eight thousand drops of laudanum per day (and for the same reason as a French surgeon inoculated himself lately with a cancer, an English one, twenty years ago, with plague, and a third,[1] who was also English, with hydrophobia), I, it will be admitted, must surely now know what happiness is, if anybody does. And therefore I will here lay down an analysis of happiness ; and, as the most interesting mode of communicating it, I will give it, not didactically, but wrapped up and involved in a picture of one evening, as I spent every evening during the intercalary year, when laudanum, though taken daily, was to me no more than the elixir of pleasure.

Let there be a cottage, standing in a valley,[2] eighteen miles from any town ; no spacious valley, but about two miles long by three-quarters-of-a-mile in average width,—

[1] He was a surgeon at Brighton.

[2] The cottage and the valley concerned in this description were not imaginary : the valley was the lovely one, *in those days*, of Grasmere ; and the cottage was occupied for more than twenty years by myself, as immediate successor, in the year 1809, to Wordsworth. Looking to the limitation here laid down—viz., *in those days*—the reader will inquire in what way *Time* can have affected the beauty of Grasmere. Do the Westmoreland valleys turn grey-headed ? O reader ! this is a painful memento for some of us ! Thirty years ago, a gang of Vandals (nameless, I thank heaven, to me), for the sake of building a mail-coach road that never would be wanted, carried, at a cost or £3000 to the defrauded parish, a horrid causeway of sheer granite masonry, for three-quarters-of-a-mile, right through the loveliest succession of secret forest dells and shy recesses of the lake, margined by unrivalled ferns, amongst which was the *Osmunda regalis.* This sequestered angle of Grasmere is described by Wordsworth, as it unveiled itself on a September morning, in the exquisite poems on the ' Naming of Places.' From this also—viz., this spot of ground, and this magnificent crest (the Osmunda)—was suggested that unique line—the finest independent line through all the records of verse,

> Or lady of the lake,
> Sole-sitting by the shores of old romance.

Rightly, therefore, did I introduce this limitation. The Grasmere before and after this outrage were two different vales.

the benefit of which provision is, that all the families resident within its circuit will compose, as it were, one larger household, personally familiar to your eye, and more or less interesting to your affections. Let the mountains be real mountains, between three and four thousand feet high, and the cottage a real cottage, not (as a witty author has it) 'a cottage with a double coach-house'; let it be, in fact (for I must abide by the actual scene), a white cottage, embowered with flowering shrubs, so chosen as to unfold a succession of flowers upon the walls and clustering around the windows, through all the months of spring, summer, and autumn; beginning, in fact, with May roses, and ending with jasmine. Let it, however, *not* be spring, nor summer, nor autumn; but winter, in its sternest shape. This is a most important point in the science of happiness. And I am surprised to see people overlook it, as if it were actually matter of congratulation that winter is going, or, if coming, is not likely to be a severe one. On the contrary, I put up a petition, annually, for as much snow, hail, frost, or storm of one kind or other, as the skies can possibly afford. Surely everybody is aware of the divine pleasures which attend a winter fireside—candles at four o'clock, warm hearth-rugs, tea, a fair tea-maker, shutters closed, curtains flowing in ample draperies on the floor, whilst the wind and rain are raging audibly without,

> And at the doors and windows seem to call,
> As heaven and earth they would together mell;
> Yet the least entrance find they none at all;
> Whence sweeter grows our rest secure in massy hall.
> *Castle of Indolence.*

All these are items in the description of a winter evening which must surely be familiar to everybody born in a high latitude. And it is evident that most of these delicacies cannot be ripened, without weather stormy or inclement in some way or other. I am not '*particular*' whether it be snow, or black frost, or wind so strong that (as Mr. Anti-slavery Clarkson says) 'you may lean your back against it like a post.' I can put up even with rain,

provided that it rains cats and dogs, or, as sailors say,
'great guns and marlinespikes'; but something of the
sort I must have; and if I have it not, I think myself
in a manner ill-used: for why am I called on to pay
so heavily for winter in coals, candles, etc., if I am not
to have the article good of its kind! No: a Canadian
winter for my money, or a Russian one, where every
man is but a co-proprietor with the north wind in the
fee-simple of his own ears. Indeed, so great an epicure
am I in this matter that I cannot relish a winter night
fully, if it be much past St. Thomas's Day, and have
degenerated into disgusting tendencies towards vernal
indications: in fact, it must be divided by a thick wall
of dark nights from all return of light and sunshine.
Start, therefore, at the first week of November: thence
to the end of January, Christmas Eve being the meridian
line, you may compute the period when happiness is in
season, which in my judgment, enters the room with the
tea-tray. For tea, though ridiculed by those who are
naturally coarse in their nervous sensibilities, or are
become so from wine-drinking, and are not susceptible
of influence from so refined a stimulant, will always be
the favourite beverage of the intellectual; and, for my
part, I would have joined Dr. Johnson in a *bellum inter-
necinum* against Jonas Hanway, or any other impious
person who should have presumed to disparage it. But
here, to save myself the trouble of too much verbal
description, I will introduce a painter, and give him
directions for the rest of the picture. Painters do not
like white cottages, unless a good deal weather-stained;
but, as the reader now understands that it is a winter
night, his services will not be required except for the
inside of the house.

Paint me, then, a room seventeen feet by twelve, and
not more than seven and a half feet high. This, reader,
is somewhat ambitiously styled, in my family, the drawing-
room; but, being contrived 'a double debt to pay,' it is
also, and more justly, termed the library; for it happens
that books are the only article of property in which I

am richer than my neighbours. Of these I have about
five thousand, collected gradually since my eighteenth
year. Therefore, painter, put as many as you can into
this room. Make it populous with books ; and, furthermore, paint me a good fire ; and furniture plain and
modest, befitting the unpretending cottage of a scholar.
And near the fire paint me a tea-table ; and (as it is clear
that no creature can come to see one on such a stormy
night) place only two cups and saucers on the tea-tray ;
and, if you know how to paint such a thing, symbolically
or otherwise, paint me an eternal tea-pot—eternal *a parte
ante*, and *a parte post ;* for I usually drink tea from eight
o'clock at night to four in the morning. And, as it is
very unpleasant to make tea, or to pour it out for one's-
self, paint me a lovely young woman sitting at the table.
Paint her arms like Aurora's, and her smiles like Hebe's ;
but no, dear M——! not even in jest let me insinuate
that thy power to illuminate my cottage rests upon a
tenure so perishable as mere personal beauty ; or that
the witchcraft of angelic smiles lies within the empire
of any earthly pencil. Pass, then, my good painter, to
something more within its power ; and the next article
brought forward should naturally be myself—a picture
of the Opium-eater, with his 'little golden receptacle of
the pernicious drug' lying beside him on the table. As
to the opium, I have no objection to see a picture of
that ; you may paint it, if you choose ; but I apprise
you that no 'little' receptacle would, even in 1816,
answer *my* purpose, who was at a distance from the
'stately Pantheon' and all druggists (mortal or otherwise). No : you may as well paint the real receptacle,
which was not of gold, but of glass, and as much like
a sublunary wine-decanter as possible. In fact, one day,
by a series of happily-conceived experiments, I discovered
that it *was* a decanter. Into this you may put a quart
of ruby-coloured laudanum ; that, and a book of German
metaphysics placed by its side, will sufficiently attest my
being in the neighbourhood ; but, as to myself, there I
demur. I admit that, naturally, I ought to occupy the

foreground of the picture ; that, being the hero of the
piece, or (if you choose) the criminal at the bar, my
body should be had into court. This seems reasonable ;
but why should I confess on this point to a painter ? or
why confess it at all? If the public (into whose private
ear I am confidentially whispering my Confessions, and
not into any painter's) should chance to have framed some
agreeable picture for itself of the Opium-eater's exterior—
should have ascribed to him, romantically, an elegant
person or a handsome face—why should I barbarously
tear from it so pleasing a delusion ?—pleasing both to
the public and to me. No : paint me, if at all, according
to your own fancy ; and since a painter's fancy should
teem with beautiful creations, I cannot fail, in that way,
to be a gainer. And now, reader, we have run through
all the ten categories of my condition, as it stood about
1816-17, up to the middle of which latter year I judge
myself to have been a happy man ; and the elements of
that happiness I have endeavoured to place before you,
in the above sketch of the interior of a scholar's library,
in a cottage among the mountains, on a stormy winter
evening, rain driving vindictively and with malice afore-
thought against the windows, and darkness such that you
cannot see your own hand when held up against the sky.

But now farewell, a long farewell, to happiness,
winter or summer! farewell to smiles and laughter!
farewell to peace of mind, to tranquil dreams, and to the
blessed consolations of sleep! For more than three years
and a-half I am summoned away from these. Here
opens upon me an Iliad of woes : for I now enter upon

THE PAINS OF OPIUM

As when some great painter dips
His pencil in the gloom of earthquake and eclipse.
                                    SHELLEY's *Revolt of Islam.*

Reader, who have thus far accompanied me, I must
request your attention, before we go farther, to a few
explanatory notes.

1. You are already aware, I hope—else you must have a low opinion of my logic—that the opium miseries, which are now on the point of pressing forward to the front of this narrative, connect themselves with my early hardships in London (and therefore more remotely with those in Wales) by natural links of affiliation—that is, the early series of sufferings was the parent of the later. Otherwise, these Confessions would break up into two disconnected sections—first, a record of boyish calamities ; secondly, a record (totally independent) of sufferings consequent upon excesses in opium. And the two sections would have no link whatever to connect them, except the slight one of having both happened to the same person. But a little attention will show the strictness of the interconnexion. The boyish sufferings, whether in Wales or London, pressing upon an organ peculiarly weak in my bodily system—viz., the stomach—caused that subsequent distress and irritability of the stomach which drove me to the use of opium as the sole remedy potent enough to control it. Here already there is exposed a sufficient *causal* connexion between the two several sections of my experience. The opium would probably never have been promoted into the dignity of a daily and a life-long resource, had it not proved itself to be the one sole agent equal to the task of tranquillising the miseries left behind by the youthful privations. Thus far the *nexus*, as between cause and effect, is sufficiently established between the one experience and the other—between the boyish records and the records of mature life. There needed no other *nexus* to justify the unity of the entire Confessions. But, though not wanted, nevertheless it happens that there *is* another and a distinct link connecting the two separate records. The main phenomenon by which opium expressed itself permanently, and the sole phenomenon that was communicable, lay in the dreams (and in the peculiar dream-scenery) which followed the opium excesses. But naturally these dreams, and this dream-scenery, drew their outlines and materials—their great lights and shadows—from those profound revelations which had been ploughed so deeply

into the heart, from those *encaustic* records which in the mighty furnaces of London life had been burnt into the undying memory by the fierce action of misery. And thus in reality the early experiences of erring childhood not only led to the secondary experiences of opium, but also determined the particular form and pressure of the chief phenomena in those secondary experiences. Here is the briefest possible abstract of the total case :—The final object of the whole record lay in the dreams. For the sake of those the entire narrative arose. But what caused the dreams ? Opium used in unexampled excess. But what caused this excess in the use of opium ? Simply the early sufferings ; these, and these only, through the derangements which they left behind in the animal economy. On this mode of viewing the case, moving regressively from the end to the beginning, it will be seen that there is one uninterrupted bond of unity running through the entire succession of experiences—first and last: the dreams were an inheritance from the opium ; the opium was an inheritance from the boyish follies.

2. You will think, perhaps, that I am too confidential and communicative of my own private history. It may be so. But my way of writing is rather to think aloud, and follow my own humours, than much to inquire who is listening to me ; for, if once I stop to consider what is proper to be said, I shall soon come to doubt whether any part at all is proper. The fact is, I imagine myself writing at a distance of twenty—thirty—fifty years ahead of this present moment, either for the satisfaction of the few who may then retain any interest in myself, or of the many (a number that is sure to be continually growing) who will take an inextinguishable interest in the mysterious powers of opium. For opium *is* mysterious ; mysterious to the extent, at times, of apparent self-contradiction ; and *so* mysterious, that my own long experience in its use—sometimes even in its abuse—did but mislead me into conclusions ever more and more remote from what I now suppose to be the truth. Fifty-and-two years' experience of opium, as a magical resource under *all* modes of bodily

suffering, I may now claim to have had—allowing only for some periods of four and six months, during which, by unexampled efforts of self-conquest, I had accomplished a determined abstinence from opium.[1] These parentheses being subtracted, as also, and secondly, some off-and-on fits of tentative and intermitting dalliance with opium in the opening of my career—these deductions allowed for, I may describe myself as experimentally acquainted with opium for something more than half-a-century. What, then, is my final report upon its good and evil results? In particular, upon these two capital tendencies of habitual opium-eating under the popular misconceptions ; viz., its

[1] With what final result, I have much difficulty in saying. Invariably, after such victories, I returned, upon deliberate choice (after weighing all the consequences on this side and on that), to the daily use of opium. But with silent changes, many and great (worked apparently by these reiterated struggles), in the opium-eating habits. Amongst other changes was this, that the quantity required gradually fell by an enormous proportion. According to the modern slang phrase, I had in the meridian stage of my opium career used '*fabulous*' quantities. Stating the quantities—not in solid opium, but in the tincture (known to everybody as *laudanum*)—my daily ration was eight thousand drops. If you write down that amount in the ordinary way as 8000, you see at a glance that you may read it into eight quantities of a thousand, or into eight hundred quantities of ten, or lastly, into eighty quantities of one hundred. Now, a single quantity of one hundred will about fill a very old-fashioned obsolete tea-spoon, of that order which you find still lingering amongst the respectable poor. Eighty such quantities, therefore, would have filled eighty of such antediluvian spoons—that is, it would have been the common hospital dose for three hundred and twenty adult patients. But the ordinary tea-spoon of this present nineteenth century is nearly as capacious as the desert-spoon of our ancestors. Which I have heard accounted for thus :—Throughout the eighteenth century, when first tea became known to the working population, the tea-drinkers were almost exclusively women ; men, even in educated classes, very often persisting (down to the French Revolution) in treating such a beverage as an idle and effeminate indulgence. This obstinate twist in masculine habits it was that secretly controlled the manufacture of tea-spoons. Up to Waterloo, tea-spoons were adjusted chiefly to the calibre of female mouths. Since then, greatly to the benefit of the national health, the grosser and browner sex have universally fallen into the effeminate habit of tea-drinking ; and the capacity of tea-spoons has naturally conformed to the new order of cormorant mouths that have alighted by myriads upon the tea-trays of these later generations.

supposed necessity of continually clamouring for increasing quantities; secondly, its supposed corresponding declension in power and efficacy. Upon these ugly scandals, what is my most deliberate award? At the age of forty, the reader is aware that, under our ancestral proverb, every man is a fool or a physician. Apparently our excellent ancestors, aiming undeniably at alliteration, spelled *physician* with an *f*. And why not? A man's physic might be undeniable, although his spelling should be open to some slight improvements. But I presume that the proverb meant to exact from any man only so much medical skill as should undertake the responsibility of his own individual health. It is my duty, it seems, thus far to be a physician—to guarantee, so far as human foresight *can* guarantee, my own corporeal sanity. And this, trying the case by ordinary practical tests, I have accomplished. And I add solemnly, that without opium most certainly I could not have accomplished such a result. Thirty-five years ago, beyond all doubt, I should have been in my grave. And as to the two popular dilemmas—that either you must renounce opium, or else indefinitely augment the daily ration; and, secondly, that, even submitting to such a postulate, you must content yourself, under any scale of doses, with an effect continually decaying, in fact, that you must ultimately descend into the despairing condition of the martyr to dram-drinking—at this point, I make a resolute stand, in blank denial of the whole doctrine. Originally, when first entering upon my opium career, I did so with great anxiety: and before my eyes floated for ever the analogies—dim, or *not* dim, according to my spirits at the moment—of the poor, perishing brandy-drinker, often on the brink of *delirium tremens!* Opium I pursued under a harsh necessity, as an unknown, shadowy power, leading I knew not whither, and a power that might suddenly change countenance upon this un-known road. Habitually I lived under such an impression of awe as we have all felt from stories of fawns, or seem-ing fawns, that have run before some mounted hunter for many a league, until they have tempted him far into

the mazes of a boundless forest, and at that point, where
all regress had become lost and impossible, either suddenly
vanished, leaving the man utterly bewildered, or assumed
some more fearful shape.   A part of the evil which I
feared actually unfolded itself ; but all was due to my
own ignorance, to neglect of cautionary measures, or to
gross mismanagement of my health in points where I well
knew the risks, but grievously underrated their urgency
and pressure.   I was temperate : that solitary advantage
I had ; but I sank under the lulling seductions of opium
into total sedentariness, and *that* whilst holding firmly the
belief, that powerful exercise was omnipotent against all
modes of debility or obscure nervous irritations.   The
account of my depression, and almost of my helplessness,
in the next memorandum (No. 3), is faithful as a description to the real case.   But, in ascribing that case to opium,
as any transcendent and overmastering agency, I was
thoroughly wrong.   Twenty days of exercise, twenty
times twenty miles of walking, at the ordinary pace of
three and a-half miles an hour, or perhaps half that
amount, would have sent me up as buoyantly as a balloon
into regions of natural and healthy excitement, where
dejection is an impossible phenomenon.   O heavens! how
man abuses or neglects his natural resources!   Yes, the
thoughtful reader is disposed to say ; but very possibly
distinguishing between such *natural* resources and opium
as a resource that is *not* natural, but highly artificial, or
even absolutely unnatural.   I think otherwise : upon the
basis of my really vast, perhaps unequalled, experience (let
me add of my *tentative* experience, varying its trials in
every conceivable mode, so as to meet the question at issue
under every angle), I advance these three following propositions, all of them unsuspected by the popular mind,
and the last of them (as cannot much longer fail to be
discovered) bearing a national value—I mean, as meeting
our English hereditary complaint :—

    I. With respect to the morbid growth upon the
opium-eater of his peculiar habit, when once rooted in
the system, and throwing out *tentacula* like a cancer, it

is out of my power to deliver any such oracular judgment upon the case—*i.e.*, upon the apparent danger of such a course, and by what stages it might be expected to travel towards its final consummation—as naturally I should wish to do. Being an oracle, it is my wish to behave myself like an oracle, and not to evade any decent man's questions in the way that Apollo too often did at Delphi. But, in this particular instance before me, the accident of my own individual seamanship in presence of this storm interfered with the natural evolution of the problem in its extreme form of danger. I had become too uneasy under the consciousness of that intensely artificial condition into which I had imperceptibly lapsed through unprecedented quantities of opium ; the shadows of eclipse were too dark and lurid not to rouse and alarm me into a spasmodic effort for reconquering the ground which I had lost. Such an effort I made : every step by which I had gone astray did I patiently unthread. And thus I fought off the natural and spontaneous catastrophe, whatever *that* might be, which mighty Nature would else have let loose for redressing the wrongs offered to herself. But what followed ? In six or eight months more, upon fresh movements arising of insupportable nervous irritation, I fleeted back into the same opium lull. To and fro, up and down, did I tilt upon those mountainous seas, for year after year. 'See-saw,[1] like Margery Daw, that sold her bed and lay on straw.' Even so did I, led astray, perhaps, by the classical example of Miss Daw, see-saw for year after year, out and in, of manœuvres the most intricate, dances the most elaborate, receding or approaching, round my great central sun of opium. Sometimes I ran perilously close into my perihelion ; sometimes I became frightened, and wheeled off into a vast cometary aphelion, where for six months 'opium'

---

1 ' *See-saw*,' etc. :—O dear reader, surely you don't want an oracle to tell you that this is a good old nursery lyric, which through four centuries has stood the criticism—stood the anger against Daw's enemies—stood the pity for Daw herself, so infamously reduced to straw—of children through eighty generations, reckoning five years to each nursery succession.

was a word unknown. How nature stood all these see-sawings is quite a mystery to me : I must have led her a sad life in those days. Nervous irritation forced me, at times, upon frightful excesses ; but terror from anomalous symptoms sooner or later forced me back. This terror was strengthened by the vague hypotheses current at that period about spontaneous combustion. Might I not myself take leave of the literary world in that fashion ? According to the popular fancy, there were two modes of this spontaneity ; and really very little to choose between them. Upon one variety of this explosion, a man blew up in the dark, without match or candle near him, leaving nothing behind him but some bones, of no use to anybody, and which were supposed to be *his* only because nobody else ever applied for them. It was fancied that some volcanic agency—an unknown deposition—accumulated from some vast redundancy of brandy, furnished the self-exploding principle. But this startled the faith of most people ; and a more plausible scheme suggested itself, which depended upon the concurrence of a lucifer-match. Without an incendiary, a man could not take fire. We sometimes see the hands of inveterate dram-drinkers throw off an atmosphere of intoxicating vapours, strong enough to lay flies into a state of sleep or *coma ;* and on the same principle, it was supposed that the breath might be so loaded with spirituous particles, as to catch fire from a match applied to a pipe when held between the lips. If so, then what should hinder the 'devouring element' (as newspapers call fire) from spreading through the throat to the cavity of the chest : in which case, not being insured, the man would naturally become a total loss. Opium, however, it will occur to the reader, is not alcohol. That is true. But it might, for anything that was known experimentally, be ultimately worse. Coleridge, the only person known to the public as having dallied systematically and for many years with opium, could not be looked to for any candid report of its history and progress ; besides that, Coleridge was under a permanent craze of having nearly accomplished his own liberation from opium ; and thus he had come to have an *extra* reason for self-delusion. Finding myself, therefore, walking on a solitary path of bad repute, leading *whither* no man's experience could tell me, I became proportionably cautious ; and if nature had any plot for making an example of me, I was resolved to baulk her. Thus it was that I never followed out the seductions of opium to their final extremity. But, nevertheless, in evading that extremity, I stumbled upon as great a discovery as if I had *not* evaded it. After the first or second self-conquest in this conflict—although finding it impossible to persist through more than a few months in the abstinence from opium—I remarked, however, that the domineering tyranny of its exactions was at length steadily declining. Quantities noticeably less had now become sufficient : and after the fourth of these victories, won with continually decreasing efforts, I found that not only had the daily dose (upon relapsing) suffered a self-limitation to an enormous extent, but also that, upon any attempt obstinately to renew the old doses, there arose a new symptom —viz., an irritation on the surface of the skin—which soon became insupportable, and tended to distraction. In about four years, without any further efforts, my daily ration had fallen *spontaneously* from a varying quantity of eight, ten, or twelve thousand drops of laudanum to about three hundred. I describe the drug as *laudanum*, because another change ran along collaterally with this supreme change—viz., that the solid opium began to require a length of time, continually increasing, to expand its effects sensibly, oftentimes not less than four hours ; whereas the tincture manifested its presence instantaneously.

Thus, then, I had reached a position from which authoritatively it might be pronounced, as a result of long, anxious, and vigilant experience, that, on the assumption of earnest (even though intermitting) efforts towards recurrent abstinences on the part of the opium-eater, the practice of indulging to the very greatest excess in this narcotic tends to a natural (almost an inevitable) euthanasy. Many years ago, when briefly touching on this subject, I announced (as a fact even *then* made known to me) that no instance of abstinence, though it were but of three days' continuance, ever perishes. Ten grains, deducted from a daily ration of five hundred, will tell through a series of many weeks, and will be found again modifying the final result, even at the close of the year's reckoning. At this day, after a half-century of oscillating experience, and after no efforts or trying acts of self-denial beyond those severe ones attached to the several processes (five or six in all) of reconquering my freedom from the yoke of opium, I find myself pretty nearly at the same station which I occupied at that vast distance of time. It is recorded of Lord Nelson that, even after the Nile and Copenhagen, he still paid the penalty, on the first days of resuming his naval life, which is generally exacted by nature from the youngest little middy or the rawest griffin—viz., sea-sickness. And this happens to a considerable proportion of sailors : they do not recover their sea-legs till some days after getting afloat. The very same thing happens to veteran opium-eaters, when first, after long intermissions, resuming too abruptly their ancient familiarities with opium. It is a fact, which I mention as indicating the enormous revolutions passed through, that, within these five years, I have turned pale, and felt warnings, pointing towards such an uneasiness, after taking not more than twenty grains of opium. At present and for some years, I have been habitually content with five or six grains daily, instead of three hundred and twenty to four hundred grains. Let me wind up this retrospect with saying, that the powers of opium, as an anodyne, but still more as a tranquilliser of nervous and anomalous sensations, have not in the smallest degree decayed ; and that, if it has casually unveiled its early power of exacting slight penalties from any trivial inattention to accurate proportions, it has more than commensurately renewed its ancient privilege of lulling irritation and of supporting preternatural calls for exertion.

My first proposition, therefore, amounts to this—that the process of weaning one's-self from the deep bondage of opium, by many people viewed with despairing eyes, is not only a possible achievement, and one which grows easier in every stage of its progress, but is favoured and promoted by nature in secret ways that could not, without some experience, have been suspected. This, however, is but a sorry commendation of any resource making great pretensions, that, by a process confessedly trying to human firmness, it can ultimately be thrown aside. Certainly little would be gained by the negative service of cancelling a drawback upon any agency whatever, until it were shown that this drawback has availed to disturb and neutralise great positive blessings lying within the gift of that agency. What are the advantages connected with opium that can merit any such name as blessings?

II. Briefly let me say, in the *second* proposition, that if the reader had, in any South American forest, seen growing rankly some great febrifuge (such as the Jesuits' bark), he would probably have noticed it with slight regard. To understand its value, he must first have suffered from intermittent fever. Bark might strike him as an unnatural stimulant; but, when he came to see that tertian or quartan fever was also an unnatural pressure upon human energies, he would begin to guess that two counter unnaturals may terminate in one most natural and salubrious result. Nervous irritation is the secret desolator of human life; and for this there is probably no adequate controlling power but that of opium, taken daily, under steady regulation.

III. But even more momentous is the burden of my *third* proposition. Are you aware, reader, what it is that constitutes the scourge (physically speaking) of Great Britain and Ireland? All readers, who direct any part of their attention to medical subjects, must know that it is pulmonary consumption. If you walk through a forest at certain seasons, you will see what is called a *blaze* of white paint upon a certain *élite* of the trees marked out by the forester as ripe for the axe. Such a blaze, if the shadowy world could reveal its futurities, would be seen everywhere distributing its secret badges of cognisance amongst our

youthful men and women.   Of those that, in the expression
of Pericles, constitute the vernal section of our population,
what a multitudinous crowd would be seen to wear upon
their foreheads the same sad ghastly blaze, or some
equivalent symbol of dedication to an early grave.   How
appalling in its amount is this annual slaughter amongst
those that should by birthright be specially the children of
hope, and levied impartially from *every* rank of society!
Is the income-tax or the poor-rate, faithful as each is to
its regulating tide-tables, paid by *any* class with as much
punctuality as this premature *florilegium*, this gathering
and rendering up of blighted blossoms, by *all* classes?
Then comes the startling question—that pierces the breaking hearts of so many thousand afflicted relatives—Is there
no remedy?   Is there no palliation of the evil?   Waste
not a thought upon the idle question whether he that
speaks is armed with this form or that form of authorisa-
tion and sanction!   Think within yourself how infinite
would be the scorn of any poor sorrow-stricken mother, if
she—standing over the coffin of her daughter—could
believe or could imagine that any vestige of ceremonial
scruples, or of fool-born superstitions, or the terror of a
word, or old traditional prejudice, had been allowed to
neutralise one chance in a thousand for her daughter—
had by possibility (but, as I could tell her, had sometimes
to a certainty) stepped between patients and deliverance
from the grave, sure and perfect!   'What matter,' she
would cry out, indignantly, 'who it is that says the
thing, so long as the thing itself is true?'   It is the potent
and faithful *word* that is wanted, in perfect slight of the
organ through which it is uttered.   Let me premise this
notorious fact, that all consumption, though latent in the
constitution, and indicated often to the eye in bodily
conformation, does not therefore manifest itself as a disease,
until some form of 'cold' or bronchitis, some familiar
affection of the chest or of the lungs, arises to furnish a
starting-point for the morbid development.[1]   Now the

---

[1] Here is a parallel case, equally fatal where it occurs, but happily
moving within a far narrower circle.   About fifty years ago, Sir

one fatal blunder lies in suffering that development to occur; and the one counter-working secret for pre-arrestment of this evil lies in steadily, by whatever means, keeping up and promoting the insensible perspiration. In that one simple art of controlling a constant function of the animal economy, lies a magician's talisman for defeating the forces leagued against the great organs of respiration. Pulmonary affections, if not *previously* suffered to develop themselves, cannot live under the hourly counter-working of this magical force. Consequently, the one question in arrear is, what potent drug is that which possesses this power, a power like that of 'Amram's son,' for evoking salubrious streams, welling forth benignly from systems else parched and arid as rocks in the wilderness? There is none that I know of answering the need but opium. The powers of that great agent I first learned dimly to guess at from a remark made to me by a lady in London; then, for some time previously, she had been hospitably entertaining Coleridge, whom, indeed, she tended with the anxiety of a daughter. Consequently, she was familiarly acquainted with his opium habits; and on my asking, in reply to some remark of hers, how she could be so sure as her words implied, that Coleridge was just then likely to be incapacitated for writing (or, indeed, for any literary *exertion*), she said, 'Oh, I know it well by the glistening of his cheeks.' Coleridge's face, as is well known to his acquaintances, exposed a large surface of cheek; too large for the intellectual expression of his features generally, had not the final affect been redeemed by what Wordsworth styled his 'godlike forehead.' The result

Everard Home, a surgeon of the highest class, mentioned as a dreadful caution, that, within his own experience, many an indolent tumour in the face, not unfrequently the most trifling pimple, which for thirty or more years had caused no uneasiness whatever, suddenly might chance to receive the slightest possible wound from a razor in the act of shaving. What followed? Once disturbed, the trivial excrescence became an open cancer. Is the parallel catastrophe in the pulmonary system, when pushed forward into development, at all less likely to hide its importance from uninstructed eyes? Yet, on the other hand, it is a thousand times more likely to happen.

was, that no possible face so broadly betrayed and published any effects whatever, especially these lustrous effects from excesses in opium. For some years I failed to consider reflectively, or else, reflecting, I failed to decipher, this resplendent acreage of cheek. But at last, either *proprio marte*, or prompted by some medical hint, I came to understand that the glistening face, glorious from afar like the old Pagan face of the demigod Æsculapius, simply reported the gathering accumulations of insensible perspiration. In the very hour, a memorable hour, of making that discovery, I made another. My own history, medically speaking, involved a mystery. At the commencement of my opium career, I had myself been pronounced repeatedly a martyr-elect to pulmonary consumption. And although, in the common decencies of humanity, this opinion upon my prospects had always been accompanied with some formal words of encouragement— as, for instance, that constitutions, after all, varied by endless differences ; that nobody could fix limits to the powers of medicine, or, in default of medicine, to the healing resources of nature herself ; yet, without something like a miracle in my favour, I was instructed to regard myself as a condemned subject. That was the upshot of these agreeable communications ; alarming enough ; and they were rendered more so by these three facts :—first, that the opinions were pronounced by the highest authorities in Christendom —viz., the physicians at Clifton and the Bristol Hotwells, who saw more of pulmonary disorders in one twelvemonth than the rest of the profession through all Europe in a century ; for the disease, it must be remembered, was almost peculiar as a national scourge to Britain, interlinked with the local accidents of the climate and its restless changes ; so that only in England could it be studied ; and even there only in perfection at these Bristolian adjacencies—the reason being this, all opulent patients resorted to the Devonshire watering-places, where the balmy temperature of the air and prevailing winds allowed the myrtle and other greenhouse shrubs to stand out-of-doors all winter through ; and naturally on the road to

Devonshire all patients alike touched at Clifton. There I was myself continually resident. Many, therefore, and of supreme authority, were the prophets of evil that announced to me my doom. Secondly, they were countenanced by the ugly fact that I out of eight children was the one who most closely inherited the bodily conformation of a father who had died of consumption at the early age of thirty-nine. Thirdly, I offered at the first glance, to a medical eye, every symptom of *phthisis* broadly and conspicuously developed. The hectic colours on the face, the nocturnal perspirations, the growing embarrassment of the respiration, and other expressions of gathering feebleness under any attempts at taking exercise—all these symptoms were steadily accumulating between the age of twenty-two and twenty-four. What was it that first arrested them? Simply the use, continually becoming more regular, of opium. Nobody recommended this drug to me; on the contrary, under that ignorant horror which everywhere invested opium, I saw too clearly that any avowed use of it would expose me to a rabid persecution.[1] Under the sincere and unaffected hope of saving me from destruction, I should have been hunted into the grave within six months. I kept my own counsel; said nothing; awakened no suspicions; persevered more and more determinately in the use of opium; and finally effected so absolute a conquest over all pulmonary symptoms, as could not have failed to fix upon me the astonishment of Clifton, had not the sense of wonder been broken by the lingering time consumed in the several stages of the malady, and still

---

1 '*Rabid persecution*':—I do not mean that, in the circumstances of my individual position, any opening could have arisen to an opposition more than verbal; since it would have been easy for me at all times to withdraw myself by hundreds of leagues from controversies upon the case. But the reasons for concealment were not the less urgent. For it would have been painful to find myself reduced to the dilemma of either practising habitual and complex dissimulation, or, on the other hand, of throwing myself headlong into that fiery vortex of hotheaded ignorance upon the very name of opium, which to this hour (though with less of rancorous bigotry) makes it hazardous to avow any daily use of so potent a drug.

more effectually by my own personal withdrawal from Clifton and its neighbourhoods.

Finally, arose what will inevitably turn out a more decisive chapter in such a record.   I had always fixed my eyes and my expectations upon a revolution in the social history of opium, which could not (as I assured myself) by accident or by art be materially deferred.   The great social machinery of life - insurance, supposing no other agency to be brought into play, how would *that* affect the great medicinal interests of opium ?   I knew that insurance offices, and the ablest actuaries of such offices, were not less ignorant upon the real merits of the opium question, and (which was worse) not less profoundly *prejudiced*, or less fanatical in their prejudices, than the rest of society. But, then, there were interests, growing continually, which would very soon force them into relaxing these prejudices. It would be alleged, at first, that opium-eating increased the risk of a life-insurance.   Waiving the question whether it really *did* increase that risk, in any case that increase of risk, like other risks, could be valued, and *must* be valued. New habits were arising in society : that I well knew. And the old machineries for insuring life interests, under these or any other shifting conditions, would be obliged to adapt themselves to changing circumstances.   If the old offices should be weak enough to persist in their misdirected obstinacy, new ones would arise.   Meantime the history of this question moved through the following aspects :— Sixteen and seventeen years ago, the offices all looked with horror upon opium-eaters.   Thus far, all men must have disapproved the principles of their policy.   Habitual brandy-drinkers met with no repulse.   And yet alcohol leads into daily dangers—for instance, that of *delirium tremens*.   But no man ever heard of opium leading into *delirium tremens*.   In the one case, there are well-ascertained and notorious dangers besetting the path ; but, in the other, supposing any corresponding dangers to exist, they have yet to be discovered.   However, the offices would not look at us who came forward avowing ourselves to be opium-eaters.   Myself in particular they regarded, I believe,

as the abomination of desolation.   And fourteen offices in
succession, within a few months, repulsed me as a candidate
for insurance on that solitary ground of having owned
myself to be an opium-eater.   The insurance was of very
little consequence to myself, though involving some interest
to others.   And I contented myself with saying, 'Ten
years hence, gentlemen, you will have come to understand
your own interests better.'   In less than *seven* years I
received a letter from Mr. Tait, surgeon to the Police
Force in Edinburgh, reporting a direct investigation
officially pursued by him under private instructions received from two or more insurance offices.   I knew, at
the beginning of these seven years, or had strong reasons
for believing, that the habit of opium-eating was spreading
extensively, and through classes of society widely disconnected.   This diffusion would, beyond a doubt, as one of
its earliest consequences, coerce the insurance offices into a
strict revision of their old blind policy.   Accordingly it
had already done so ; and the earliest fruits of this revolution were now before me in the proof-sheets so obligingly
transmitted by Mr. Tait.   His object, as I understood it,
in sending these proofs to myself, was simply to collect
such additional notices, suggestions, or sceptical queries, as
might reasonably be anticipated from any reflective opium
experience so extensive as my own.   Most unhappily, this
gentleman, during the course of our brief correspondence,
was suddenly attacked by typhus fever ; and, after a short
illness, to my own exceeding regret, he died.   On all
accounts I had reason for sorrow.   Knowing him only
through his very interesting correspondence with myself, I
had learned to form high expectations from Mr. Tait's
philosophic spirit and his determined hostility to traditional
cant.   He had recorded, in the communications made to
myself, with great minuteness and anxiety for rigour of
accuracy, the cases of more than ninety patients.   And he
had shown himself inexorably deaf to all attempts at con-
founding evils specially belonging to opium as a stimulant,
as a narcotic, or as a poison, with those which belong to
opium merely as a cause of constipation or other ordinary

irregularities in the animal economy.   Most people of
sedentary habits, but amongst such people notoriously
those who think much, need some slight means of stimulating the watchwork of the animal system into action.
Neglect of such means will of course derange the health.
But in such derangements there is no special impeachment
of opium : many thousands of agents terminate in the
same or more obstinate derangements, unless vigilantly
counteracted.   The paramount mission of Mr. Tait, under
his instructions from insurance offices, as I interpreted his
own account of this mission, was, to report firmly and
decisively upon the tendencies of opium in relation to the
lengthening or shortening of life.   At that point where
his proof-sheets were interrupted by the fatal attack of
fever, he had not entirely finished his record of cases ; so
that his final judgment or summing up had not commenced.   It was, however, evident to me in what channel
this final judgment would have flowed.   To a certainty,
he would have authorised his clients (the insurance offices)
to dismiss all anxiety as to the life-abridging tendencies of
opium.   But he would have pointed their jealousy in
another direction—viz., this, that in some proportion of
cases there may always be a reasonable ground for suspecting, not the opium as separately in itself any cause of
mischief, but the opium as a conjectural indication of some
secret distress or irritation that had fastened upon the
system, and had in that way sought relief ; cases, in short,
which the use of opium had not caused, but which, on the
contrary, had caused the use of opium ;—opium having
been called in to redress or to relieve the affection.   In all
such circumstances, the insurance office is entitled to call
for a frank disclosure of the ailment ; but not, as hitherto,
entitled to assume the opium as itself an ailment.   It may
very easily have happened, that simply the genial restoration derived from opium, its power of qualifying a man
suddenly to face (that is, upon an hour's warning to face)
some twelve hours' unusual exertion, qualifying him both
as to spirits and as to strength ; or again, simply the
general purpose of seeking relief from ennui, or *tædium*

vitæ—any one of these motives may satisfactorily account for the applicant's having resorted to opium. He might reply to the office in Professor Wilson's word,[1] 'Gentlemen, I am a *Hedonist*; and, if you *must* know why I take opium, that's the reason why.' But still, upon every admission from a candidate that he took opium, it would be a prudent question and a just question on the part of the office, to ask '*why*'; and in what circumstances the practice had originated. If in any local uneasiness, then would arise a natural right on the part of the office to press for a surgical examination. But, apart from such special cases, it was evident that this acute and experienced surgeon saw no reason whatever in the simple practice of opium-eating for hesitating upon a life-insurance proposal, or for exacting a higher rate of premium.

Here I pause. The reader will infer, from what I have now said, that all passages, written at an earlier period under cloudy and uncorrected views of the evil agencies presumable in opium, stand retracted; although, shrinking from the labour of altering an error diffused so widely under my own early misconceptions of the truth, I have suffered them to remain as they were. My general views upon the powers and natural tendencies of opium were all supported and strengthened by this fortunate advantage of a professional correspondence. My special doctrine I now repeat at this point of valediction, and in a rememberable form. Lord Bacon said once, too boldly and hazardously, that he who discovers the secret of making myrrh soluble by human blood has discovered the secret of immortal life. I propose a more modest form of magic— that he who discovers the secret of stimulating and keeping up unintermittingly the insensible perspiration, has discovered the secret of intercepting pulmonary consumption. In my medical character, I here take leave of the reader, and fall back into the current of my regular narrative.

. . . . . .

[1] From the Greek word for *voluptuous pleasure*—viz., *Hedone* (ἡδονή) —Professor Wilson coined the English word *Hedonist*, which he sometimes applied in playful reproach to myself and others.

3. My studies have now been long interrupted. I
cannot read to myself with any pleasure, hardly with a
moment's endurance. Yet I sometimes read aloud for the
pleasure of others ; because reading is an accomplishment
of mine, and, in the slang use of the word *accomplishment*
as a superficial and ornamental attainment, almost the only
one I possess ; and formerly, if I had any vanity at all
connected with any endowment or attainment of mine, it
was with this ; for I had observed that no accomplishment
is more rare. Actors are the worst readers of all. John
Kemble is not effective as a reader, though he has the great
advantage of mature scholarship ; and his sister, the
immortal Siddons, with all her superiority to him in voice,
reads even less effectively. She reads nothing well but
dramatic works. In the *Paradise Lost*, which I heard her
attempt at Barley Wood, her failure was distressing ;
almost as distressing as the sycophantic applause of the
surrounding company—all lost, of course, in nearly speechless admiration. Yet I am sensible that this contemptuous
feeling for the circle of admirers is scarcely justified.
What *should* the poor creatures have done ? Already, in
the mere attempt to win their suffrages, in placing herself
once again upon trial, there was a condescension on the
part of Mrs. Siddons, after which free judgment became
impossible. I felt a wish to address Mrs. Siddons thus—
You that have read to royalty at Windsor, nay, have even
been desired to *sit down* at Windsor whilst reading, ever
afterwards are a privileged person, liable to no accent of
truth. Our feelings, as not free to take any natural
expression, can be of no value. Suffer us to be silent, if
only for the dignity of human nature. And do you yourself be silent, if only for the dignity of that once unequalled
voice. Neither Coleridge nor Southey is a good reader of
verse. Southey is admirable almost in all things, but not
in this. Both he and Coleridge read as if crying, or at
least wailing lugubriously. People in general either read
poetry without any passion at all, or else overstep the
modesty of nature. Of late, if I have felt moved by anything in books, it has been by the grand lamentations of

Samson Agonistes, or the great harmonies of the Satanic speeches in *Paradise Regained*, when read aloud by myself. We are far from towns ; but a young lady sometimes comes and drinks tea with us ; at her request and M——'s, I now and then read Wordsworth's poems to them. (Wordsworth, by the bye, is the only poet I ever met who could read his own verses; often, indeed, he reads admirably.)

For nearly two years I believe that I read nothing and studied nothing. Analytic studies are continuous studies, and not to be pursued by fits and starts, or fragmentary efforts. All these were become insupportable to me ; I shrank from them with a sense of powerless and infantine feebleness that gave me an anguish the greater from remembering the time when I grappled with them to my own hourly delight ; and for this further reason, because I had devoted the labour of my whole life, had dedicated my intellect, blossoms and fruits, to the slow and elaborate toil of constructing one single work, to which I had presumed to give the title of an unfinished work of Spinosa's —viz., *De Emendatione Humani Intellectûs*. This was now lying locked up as by frost, like any Spanish bridge or aqueduct begun upon too great a scale for the resources of the architect ; and, instead of surviving me, as a monument of wishes at least, and aspirations, and long labours, dedicated to the exaltation of human nature in that way in which God had best fitted me to promote so great an object, it was likely to stand a memorial to my children of hopes defeated, of baffled efforts, of materials uselessly accumulated, of foundations laid that were never to support a superstructure, of the grief and the ruin of the architect. In this state of imbecility, I had, for amusement, turned my attention to political economy ; my understanding, which formerly had been as active and restless as a panther, could not, I suppose (so long as I lived at all), sink into utter lethargy ; and political economy offers this advantage to a person in my state, that, though it is eminently an organic science (no part, that is to say, but what acts on the whole, as the whole

again reacts on and through each part), yet still the
several parts may be detached and contemplated singly.
Great as was the prostration of my powers at this time,
yet I could not forget my knowledge ; and my understanding had been for too many years intimate with severe
thinkers, with logic, and the great masters of knowledge,
not to be aware of a great call made by political economy
at this crisis for a new law and a transcendent legislator.
Suddenly, in 1818, a friend in Edinburgh sent me down
Mr. Ricardo's book ; and, recurring to my own prophetic
anticipation of some coming legislator for this science, I
said, before I had finished the first chapter, 'Thou art the
man !' Wonder and curiosity were emotions that had
long been dead in me. Yet I wondered once more—
wondered at myself that could once again be stimulated
to the effort of reading ; and much more I wondered at
the book. Had this profound work been really written
during the tumultuous hurry of the nineteenth century ?
Could it be that an Englishman, and he not in academic
bowers, but oppressed by mercantile and senatorial cares,
had accomplished what all the universities of Europe, and
a century of thought, had failed even to advance by one
hair's-breadth? Previous writers had been crushed and
overlaid by the enormous weights of facts, details, and
exceptions ; Mr. Ricardo had deduced, *a priori*, from the
understanding itself, laws which first shot arrowy light
into the dark chaos of materials, and had thus constructed
what hitherto was but a collection of tentative discussions
into a science of regular proportions, now first standing
upon an eternal basis.

Thus did one simple work of a profound understanding avail to give me a pleasure and an activity which I
had not known for years ; it roused me even to write, or,
at least, to dictate what M——— wrote for me. It seemed
to me that some important truths had escaped even 'the
inevitable eye' of Mr. Ricardo ; and, as these were, for
the most part, of such a nature that I could express or
illustrate them briefly and elegantly by algebraic symbols,
the whole would hardly have reached the bulk of a

pamphlet. With M—— for my amanuensis, even at this time, incapable as I was of all general exertion, I drew up, therefore, my *Prolegomena to all Future Systems of Political Economy.*

This exertion, however, was but a momentary flash, as the sequel showed. Arrangements were made at a provincial press, about eighteen miles distant, for printing it. An additional compositor was retained for some days, on this account. The work was even twice advertised; and I was, in a manner, pledged to the fulfilment of my intention. But I had a preface to write, and a dedication, which I wished to make impressive, to Mr. Ricardo. I found myself quite unable to accomplish all this. The arrangements were countermanded, the compositor dismissed, and my *Prolegomena* rested peacefully by the side of its elder and more dignified brother.

In thus describing and illustrating my intellectual torpor, I use terms that apply, more or less, to every part of the years during which I was under the Circean spells of opium. But for misery and suffering, I might, indeed, be said to have existed in a dormant state. I seldom could prevail on myself to write a letter; an answer of a few words, to any that I received, was the utmost that I could accomplish; and often *that* not until the letter had lain for weeks, or even months, on my writing-table. Without the aid of M——, my whole domestic economy, whatever became of political economy, must have gone into irretrievable confusion. I shall not afterwards allude to this part of the case; it is one, however, which the opium-eater will find, in the end, most oppressive and tormenting, from the sense of incapacity and feebleness, from the direct embarrassments incident to the neglect or procrastination of each day's appropriate labours, and from the remorse which must often exasperate the stings of these evils to a conscientious mind. The opium-eater loses none of his moral sensibilities or aspirations; he wishes and longs as earnestly as ever to realise what he believes possible, and feels to be exacted by duty; but his intellectual apprehension of what is possible infinitely

outruns his power, not of execution only, but even of
proposing or willing.   He lies under a world's weight of
incubus and nightmare ; he lies in sight of all that he
would fain perform, just as a man forcibly confined to his
bed by the mortal languor of paralysis, who is compelled
to witness injury or outrage offered to some object of his
tenderest love :—he would lay down his life if he might
but rise and walk ; but he is powerless as an infant, and
cannot so much as make an effort to move.

But from this I now pass to what is the main subject
of these latter Confessions—to the history and journal of
what took place in my dreams ; for these were the immediate and proximate cause of shadowy terrors that
settled and brooded over my whole waking life.

The first notice I had of any important change going
on in this part of my physical economy, was from the
re-awaking of a state of eye oftentimes incident to childhood.   I know not whether my reader is aware that
many children have a power of painting, as it were, upon
the darkness all sorts of phantoms ; in some that power
is simply a mechanic affection of the eye ; others have a
voluntary or semi-voluntary power to dismiss or summon
such phantoms ; or, as a child once said to me, when I
questioned him on this matter, 'I can tell them to go,
and they go ; but sometimes they come when I don't tell
them to come.'   He had by one-half as unlimited a
command over apparitions as a Roman centurion over his
soldiers.   In the middle of 1817 this faculty became
increasingly distressing to me : at night, when I lay awake
in bed, vast processions moved along continually in
mournful pomp ; friezes of never-ending stories, that to
my feelings were as sad and solemn as stories drawn from
times before Œdipus or Priam, before Tyre, before
Memphis.   And, concurrently with this, a corresponding
change took place in my dreams ; a theatre seemed
suddenly opened and lighted up within my brain, which
presented nightly spectacles of more than earthly splendour.
And the four following facts may be mentioned, as noticeable at this time :—

1. That, as the creative state of the eye increased, a sympathy seemed to arise between the waking and the dreaming states of the brain in one point—that whatsoever I happened to call up and to trace by a voluntary act upon the darkness was very apt to transfer itself to my dreams; and at length I feared to exercise this faculty; for, as Midas turned all things to gold that yet baffled his hopes and defrauded his human desires, so whatsoever things capable of being visually represented I did but think of in the darkness, immediately shaped themselves into phantoms for the eye; and, by a process apparently no less inevitable, when thus once traced in faint and visionary colours, like writings in sympathetic ink, they were drawn out, by the fierce chemistry of my dreams, into insufferable splendour that fretted my heart.

2. This and all other changes in my dreams were accompanied by deep-seated anxiety and funereal melancholy, such as are wholly incommunicable by words. I seemed every night to descend—not metaphorically, but literally to descend—into chasms and sunless abysses, depths below depths, from which it seemed hopeless that I could ever re-ascend. Nor did I, by waking, feel that I *had* re-ascended. Why should I dwell upon this? For indeed the state of gloom which attended these gorgeous spectacles, amounting at last to utter darkness, as of some suicidal despondency, cannot be approached by words.

3. The sense of space, and in the end the sense of time, were both powerfully affected. Buildings, landscapes, etc., were exhibited in proportions so vast as the bodily eye is not fitted to receive. Space swelled, and was amplified to an extent of unutterable and self-repeating infinity. This disturbed me very much less than the vast expansion of time. Sometimes I seemed to have lived for seventy or a hundred years in one night; nay, sometimes had feelings representative of a duration far beyond the limits of any human experience.

4. The minutest incidents of childhood, or forgotten scenes of later years, were often revived. I could not be said to recollect them; for, if I had been told of them

when waking, I should not have been able to acknowledge them as parts of my past experience. But placed as they were before me, in dreams like intuitions, and clothed in all their evanescent circumstances and accompanying feelings, I *recognised* them instantaneously. I was once told by a near relative of mine, that having in her child-hood fallen into a river, and being on the very verge of death but for the assistance which reached her at the last critical moment, she saw in a moment her whole life, clothed in its forgotten incidents, arrayed before her as in a mirror, not successively, but simultaneously ; and she had a faculty developed as suddenly for compre-hending the whole and every part.[1] This, from some

[1] The heroine of this remarkable case was a girl about nine years old ; and there can be little doubt that she looked down as far within the *crater* of death—that awful volcano—as any human being ever *can* have done that has lived to draw back and to report her experience. Not less than ninety years did she survive this memorable escape ; and I may describe her as in all respects a woman of remarkable and interesting qualities. She enjoyed throughout her long life, as the reader will readily infer, serene and cloudless health ; had a masculine understanding ; reverenced truth not less than did the Evangelists ; and led a life of saintly devotion, such as might have glorified '*Hilarion or Paul.*'—(The words in italic are Ariosto's.)—I mention these traits as characterising her in a memorable extent, that the reader may not suppose himself relying upon a dealer in exaggerations, upon a credulous enthusiast, or upon a careless wielder of language. Forty-five years had intervened between the first time and the last time of her telling me this anecdote, and not one iota had shifted its ground amongst the incidents, nor had any the most trivial of the circum-stantiations suffered change. The scene of the accident was the least of valleys, what the Greeks of old would have called an ἄγκος, and we English should properly call a dell. Human tenant it had none : even at noonday it was a solitude ; and would oftentimes have been a silent solitude but for the brawling of a brook — not broad, but occasionally deep—which ran along the base of the little hills. Into this brook, probably into one of its dangerous pools, the child fell : and, according to the ordinary chances, she could have had but a slender prospect indeed of any deliverance ; for, although a dwelling-house was close by, it was shut out from view by the undulations of the ground. How long the child lay in the water was probably never inquired earnestly until the answer had become irrecoverable : for a servant, to whose care the child was then confided, had a natural interest in suppressing the whole case. From the child's own account, it should seem that *asphyxia* must have announced its commencement.

opium experiences, I can believe ; I have, indeed, seen
the same thing asserted twice in modern books, and
accompanied by a remark which probably is true—viz.,
that the dread book of account, which the Scriptures
speak of, is, in fact, the mind itself of each individual.
Of this, at least, I feel assured, that there is no such
thing as ultimate *forgetting* ; traces once impressed upon
the memory are indestructible ; a thousand accidents may
and will interpose a veil between our present consciousness and the secret inscriptions on the mind. Accidents
of the same sort will also rend away this veil. But alike,
whether veiled or unveiled, the inscription remains for
ever ; just as the stars seem to withdraw before the
common light of day, whereas, in fact, we all know that
it is the light which is drawn over them as a veil ; and
that they are waiting to be revealed, whenever the
obscuring daylight itself shall have withdrawn.

Having noticed these four facts as memorably distinguishing my dreams from those of health, I shall now
cite a few illustrative cases ; and shall then cite such
others as I remember, in any order that may give them
most effect as pictures to the reader.

I had been in youth, and ever since, for occasional
amusement, a great reader of Livy, whom I confess that
I prefer, both for style and matter, to any other of the
Roman historians ; and I had often felt as solemn and
appalling sounds, emphatically representative of Roman

A process of struggle and deadly suffocation was passed through half
consciously. This process terminated by a sudden blow apparently *on*
or *in* the brain, after which there was no pain or conflict ; but in an
instant succeeded a dazzling rush of light ; immediately after which
came the solemn apocalypse of the entire past life. Meantime, the
child's disappearance in the water had happily been witnessed by a
farmer who rented some fields in this little solitude, and by a rare
accident was riding through them at the moment. Not being very
well mounted, he was retarded by the hedges and other fences in
making his way down to the water ; some time was thus lost ; but
once at the spot, he leaped in, booted and spurred, and succeeded in
delivering one that must have been as nearly counted amongst the
populations of the grave as perhaps the laws of the shadowy world can
suffer to return !

majesty, the two words so often occurring in Livy, *Consul Romanus*; especially when the consul is introduced in his military character. I mean to say, that the words king, sultan, regent, etc., or any other titles of those who embody in their own persons the collective majesty of a great people, had less power over my reverential feelings. I had also, though no great reader of history, made myself critically familiar with one period of English history— viz., the period of the Parliamentary War—having been attracted by the moral grandeur of some who figured in that day, and by the interesting memoirs which survive those unquiet times. Both these parts of my lighter reading, having furnished me often with matter of reflection, now furnished me with matter for my dreams. Often I used to see, after painting upon the blank darkness a sort of rehearsal whilst waking, a crowd of ladies, and perhaps a festival and dances. And I heard it said, or I said to myself, 'These are English ladies from the unhappy times of Charles I. These are the wives and daughters of those who met in peace, and sat at the same tables, and were allied by marriage or by blood; and yet, after a certain day in August 1642,[1] never smiled upon each other again, nor met but in the field of battle ; and at Marston Moor, at Newbury, or at Naseby, cut asunder all ties of love by the cruel sabre, and washed away in blood the memory of ancient friendship.' The ladies danced, and looked as lovely as at the court of George IV. Yet even in my dream I knew that they had been in the grave for nearly two centuries. This pageant would suddenly dissolve ; and, at a clapping of hands, would be

---

[1] I think (but at the moment have no means of verifying my conjecture) that this day was the 24th of August. On or about that day Charles raised the royal standard at Nottingham ; which, ominously enough (considering the strength of such superstitions in the seventeenth century, and, amongst the generations of that century, more especially in this particular generation of the Parliamentary War), was blown down during the succeeding night. Let me remark, in passing, that no falsehood can virtually be greater or more malicious than that which imputes to Archbishop Laud a special or exceptional faith in such mute warnings.

heard the heart-shaking sound of *Consul Romanus*; and immediately came 'sweeping by,' in gorgeous paludaments, Paullus or Marius, girt around by a company of centurions, with the crimson tunic[1] hoisted on a spear, and followed by the *alalagmos*[2] of the Roman legions.

Many years ago, when I was looking over Piranesi's *Antiquities of Rome*, Coleridge, then standing by, described to me a set of plates from that artist, called his *Dreams*, and which record the scenery of his own visions during the delirium of a fever. Some of these (I describe only from memory of Coleridge's account) represented vast Gothic halls; on the floor of which stood mighty engines and machinery, wheels, cables, catapults, etc., expressive of enormous power put forth, or resistance overcome. Creeping along the sides of the walls, you perceived a staircase; and upon this, groping his way upwards, was Piranesi himself. Follow the stairs a little farther, and you perceive them reaching an abrupt termination, without any balustrade, and allowing no step onwards to him who should reach the extremity, except into the depths below. Whatever is to become of poor Piranesi, at least you suppose that his labours must now in some way terminate. But raise your eyes, and behold a second flight of stairs still higher, on which again Piranesi is perceived, by this time standing on the very brink of the abyss. Once again elevate your eye, and a still more aërial flight is descried; and there, again, is the delirious Piranesi, busy on his aspiring labours: and so on, until the unfinished stairs and the hopeless Piranesi both are lost in the upper gloom of the hall. With the same power of endless growth and self-reproduction did my architecture proceed in dreams. In the early stage of the malady, the splendours of my dreams were indeed chiefly architectural; and I beheld such pomp of cities and palaces as never yet was beheld by the waking eye, unless

---

[1] '*The crimson tunic*':—The signal which announced a day of battle.

[2] '*Alalagmos*':—A word expressing collectively the gathering of the Roman war-cries—*Alála, Alála!*

in the clouds. From a great modern poet[1] I cite the part
of a passage which describes, as an appearance actually
beheld in the clouds, what in many of its circumstances I
saw frequently in sleep :—

> The appearance, instantaneously disclosed,
> Was of a mighty city—boldly say
> A wilderness of building, sinking far
> And self-withdrawn into a wondrous depth,
> Far sinking into splendour without end !
> Fabric it seem'd of diamond and of gold,
> With alabaster domes and silver spires,
> And blazing terrace upon terrace, high
> Uplifted ; here, serene pavilions bright,
> In avenues disposed ; there towers begirt
> With battlements that on their restless fronts
> Bore stars—illumination of all gems !
> By earthly nature had the effect been wrought
> Upon the dark materials of the storm
> Now pacified ; on them, and on the coves,
> And mountain-steeps and summits, whereunto
> The vapours had receded—taking there
> Their station under a cerulean sky.

The sublime circumstance—'that on their *restless* fronts
bore stars'—might have been copied from my own
architectural dreams, so often did it occur. We hear it
reported of Dryden, and in later times of Fuseli, that they
ate raw meat for the sake of obtaining splendid dreams :

[1] '*From a great modern poet*' :—What poet ? It was Wordsworth ;
and why did I not formerly name him ? This throws a light backwards upon the strange history of Wordsworth's reputation. The year
in which I wrote and published these Confessions was 1821 ; and at
that time the name of Wordsworth, though beginning to emerge from
the dark cloud of scorn and contumely which had hitherto overshadowed it, was yet most imperfectly established. Not until ten
years later was his greatness cheerfully and generally acknowledged.
I, therefore, as the very earliest (without one exception) of all who
came forward, in the beginning of his career, to honour and welcome
him, shrank with disgust from making any sentence of mine the
occasion for an explosion of vulgar malice against him. But the
grandeur of the passage here cited inevitably spoke for itself ; and he
that would have been most scornful on hearing the name of the poet
coupled with this epithet of 'great' could not but find his malice
intercepted, and himself cheated into cordial admiration, by the
splendour of the verses.

how much better, for such a purpose, to have eaten
opium, which yet I do not remember that any poet is
recorded to have done, except the dramatist Shadwell;
and in ancient days, Homer is, I think, rightly reputed
to have known the virtues of opium as a φάρμακον
νηπενθές—*i.e.*, as an anodyne.

To my architecture succeeded dreams of lakes and
silvery expanses of water : these haunted me so much,
that I feared lest some dropsical state or tendency of
the brain might thus be making itself (to use a metaphysical word) *objective* ;[1] and that the sentient organ
might be projecting itself as its own object. For two
months I suffered greatly in my head—a part of my
bodily structure which had hitherto been so clear from
all touch or taint of weakness (physically, I mean), that
I used to say of it, as the last Lord Oxford said of his
stomach, that it seemed likely to survive the rest of my
person. Till now, I had never felt a headache even, or
any the slightest pain, except rheumatic pains caused by
my own folly.

The waters gradually changed their character—from
translucent lakes, shining like mirrors, they became seas
and oceans. And now came a tremendous change,
which, unfolding itself slowly like a scroll, through
many months, promised an abiding torment ; and, in
fact, it never left me, though recurring more or less
intermittingly. Hitherto the human face had often
mixed in my dreams, but not despotically, nor with any
special power of tormenting. But now that affection,
which I have called the tyranny of the human face,
began to unfold itself. Perhaps some part of my London
life (the searching for Ann amongst fluctuating crowds)
might be answerable for this. Be that as it may, now
it was that upon the rocking waters of the ocean the

[1] '*Objective*' :—This word, so nearly unintelligible in 1821, so
intensely scholastic, and, consequently, when surrounded by familiar
and vernacular words, so apparently pedantic, yet, on the other hand,
so indispensable to accurate thinking, and to *wide* thinking, has since
1821 become too common to need any apology.

human face began to reveal itself; the sea appeared
paved with innumerable faces, upturned to the heavens;
faces, imploring, wrathful, despairing; faces that surged
upwards by thousands, by myriads, by generations:
infinite was my agitation; my mind tossed, as it seemed,
upon the billowy ocean, and weltered upon the weltering
waves.

May 1818.—The Malay has been a fearful enemy
for months. Every night, through his means, I have
been transported into Asiatic scenery. I know not
whether others share in my feelings on this point; but
I have often thought that if I were compelled to forego
England, and to live in China, among Chinese manners
and modes of life and scenery, I should go mad. The
causes of my horror lie deep, and some of them must
be common to others. Southern Asia, in general, is
the seat of awful images and associations. As the cradle
of the human race, if on no other ground, it would have
a dim, reverential feeling connected with it. But there
are other reasons. No man can pretend that the wild,
barbarous, and capricious superstitions of Africa, or of
savage tribes elsewhere, affect him in the way that he is
affected by the ancient, monumental, cruel, and elaborate
religions of Hindostan. The mere antiquity of Asiatic
things, of their institutions, histories, above all, of their
mythologies, &c., is so impressive, that to me the vast age
of the race and name overpowers the sense of youth in
the individual. A young Chinese seems to me an antediluvian man renewed. Even Englishmen, though not
bred in any knowledge of such institutions, cannot but
shudder at the mystic sublimity of *castes* that have flowed
apart, and refused to mix, through such immemorial tracts
of time; nor can any man fail to be awed by the sanctity
of the Ganges, or by the very name of the Euphrates. It
contributes much to these feelings that South-eastern Asia
is, and has been for thousands of years, the part of the
earth most swarming with human life, the great *officina
gentium*. Man is a weed in those regions. The vast
empires, also, into which the enormous population of Asia

has always been cast, give a further sublimity to the
feelings associated with all oriental names or images. In
China, over and above what it has in common with the
rest of Southern Asia, I am terrified by the modes of life,
by the manners, by the barrier of utter abhorrence placed
between myself and *them*, by counter-sympathies deeper
than I can analyse. I could sooner live with lunatics,
with vermin, with crocodiles or snakes. All this, and
much more than I can say, the reader must enter into
before he can comprehend the unimaginable horror which
these dreams of oriental imagery and mythological tortures
impressed upon me. Under the connecting feeling of
tropical heat and vertical sunlights, I brought together
all creatures, birds, beasts, reptiles, all trees and plants,
usages and appearances, that are found in all tropical
regions, and assembled them together in China or
Hindostan. From kindred feelings, I soon brought
Egypt and her gods under the same law. I was stared
at, hooted at, grinned at, chattered at, by monkeys, by
paroquets, by cockatoos. I ran into pagodas, and was
fixed for centuries at the summit, or in secret rooms ;
I was the idol ; I was the priest ; I was worshipped ;
I was sacrificed. I fled from the wrath of Brama through
all the forests of Asia ; Vishnu hated me ; Seeva lay in
wait for me. I came suddenly upon Isis and Osiris :
I had done a deed, they said, which the ibis and the
crocodile trembled at. Thousands of years I lived and
was buried in stone coffins, with mummies and sphinxes,
in narrow chambers at the heart of eternal pyramids. I
was kissed, with cancerous kisses by crocodiles, and was
laid, confounded with all unutterable abortions, amongst
reeds and Nilotic mud.

Some slight abstraction I thus attempt of my oriental
dreams, which filled me always with such amazement at
the monstrous scenery, that horror seemed absorbed for
a while in sheer astonishment. Sooner or later came a
reflux of feeling that swallowed up the astonishment,
and left me, not so much in terror, as in hatred and
abomination of what I saw. Over every form, and

threat, and punishment, and dim sightless incarceration,
brooded a killing sense of eternity and infinity. Into
these dreams only it was, with one or two slight exceptions, that any circumstances of physical horror entered.
All before had been moral and spiritual terrors. But
here the main agents were ugly birds, or snakes, or
crocodiles, especially the last. The cursed crocodile
became to me the object of more horror than all the
rest. I was compelled to live with him ; and (as was
always the case in my dreams) for centuries. Sometimes
I escaped, and found myself in Chinese houses. All the
feet of the tables, sofas, &c., soon became instinct with
life : the abominable head of the crocodile, and his leering
eyes, looked out at me, multiplied into ten thousand
repetitions ; and I stood loathing and fascinated. So
often did this hideous reptile haunt my dreams, that
many times the very same dream was broken up in the
very same way : I heard gentle voices speaking to me
(I hear everything when I am sleeping), and instantly
I awoke ; it was broad noon, and my children were
standing, hand in hand, at my bedside, come to show
me their coloured shoes, or new frocks, or to let me
see them dressed for going out. No experience was
so awful to me, and at the same time so pathetic,
as this abrupt translation from the darkness of the
infinite to the gaudy summer air of highest noon, and
from the unutterable abortions of miscreated gigantic
vermin to the sight of infancy, and innocent *human*
natures.

June 1819. — I have had occasion to remark, at
various periods of my life, that the deaths of those
whom we love, and, indeed, the contemplation of death
generally, is (*cæteris paribus*) more affecting in summer
than in any other season of the year. And the reasons
are these three, I think : first, that the visible heavens
in summer appear far higher, more distant, and (if such
a solecism may be excused) more infinite ; the clouds
by which chiefly the eye expounds the distance of the
blue pavilion stretched over our heads are in summer

more voluminous, more massed, and are accumulated in
far grander and more towering piles; secondly, the light
and the appearances of the declining and the setting sun
are much more fitted to be types and characters of the
infinite; and, thirdly (which is the main reason), the
exuberant and riotous prodigality of life naturally forces
the mind more powerfully upon the antagonist thought
of death, and the wintery sterility of the grave. For
it may be observed generally, that wherever two thoughts
stand related to each other by a law of antagonism, and
exist, as it were, by mutual repulsion, they are apt to
suggest each other. On these accounts it is that I find
it impossible to banish the thought of death when I am
walking alone in the endless days of summer; and any
particular death, if not actually more affecting, at least
haunts my mind more obstinately and besiegingly, in
that season. Perhaps this cause, and a slight incident
which I omit, might have been the immediate occasions
of the following dream, to which, however, a predisposition must always have existed in my mind; but, having
been once roused, it never left me, and split into a
thousand fantastic variations, which often suddenly re-
combined; locked back into startling unity, and restored
the original dream.

I thought that it was a Sunday morning in May;
that it was Easter Sunday, and as yet very early in the
morning. I was standing, as it seemed to me, at the
door of my own cottage. Right before me lay the very
scene which could really be commanded from that situation, but exalted, as was usual, and solemnised by the
power of dreams. There were the same mountains, and
the same lovely valley at their feet; but the mountains
were raised to more than Alpine height, and there was
interspace far larger between them of savannahs and forest
lawns; the hedges were rich with white roses; and no
living creature was to be seen, excepting that in the green
churchyard there were cattle tranquilly reposing upon the
verdant graves, and particularly round about the grave of
a child whom I had once tenderly loved, just as I had

really beheld them, a little before sunrise, in the same summer when that child died. I gazed upon the well-known scene, and I said to myself, 'It yet wants much of sunrise; and it is Easter Sunday; and that is the day on which they celebrate the first-fruits of Resurrection. I will walk abroad; old griefs shall be forgotten to-day: for the air is cool and still, and the hills are high, and stretch away to heaven; and the churchyard is as verdant as the forest lawns, and the forest lawns are as quiet as the churchyard; and with the dew I can wash the fever from my forehead; and then I shall be unhappy no longer." I turned, as if to open my garden gate, and immediately I saw upon the left a scene far different; but which yet the power of dreams had reconciled into harmony. The scene was an oriental one; and there also it was Easter Sunday, and very early in the morning. And at a vast distance were visible, as a stain upon the horizon, the domes and cupolas of a great city—an image or faint abstraction, caught perhaps in childhood from some picture of Jerusalem. And not a bow-shot from me, upon a stone, shaded by Judean palms, there sat a woman; and I looked, and it was—Ann! She fixed her eyes upon me earnestly; and I said to her at length, 'So, then, I have found you at last.' I waited; but she answered me not a word. Her face was the same as when I saw it last; the same, and yet, again, how different! Seventeen years ago, when the lamp-light of mighty London fell upon her face, as for the last time I kissed her lips (lips, Ann, that to me were not polluted!), her eyes were streaming with tears. The tears were now no longer seen. Sometimes she seemed altered; yet again sometimes *not* altered; and hardly older. Her looks were tranquil, but with unusual solemnity of expression, and I now gazed upon her with some awe. Suddenly her countenance grew dim; and, turning to the mountains, I perceived vapours rolling between us; in a moment all had vanished; thick darkness came on; and in the twinkling of an eye I was far away from mountains, and by lamp-light in London, walking again with Ann—just as we had walked, when both children, eighteen years before, along the endless terraces of Oxford Street.

Then suddenly would come a dream of far different character—a tumultuous dream—commencing with a music such as now I often heard in sleep—music of preparation and of awakening suspense. The undulations of fast-gathering tumults were like the opening of the Coronation Anthem ; and, like *that*, gave the feeling of a multitudinous movement, of infinite cavalcades filing off, and the tread of innumerable armies. The morning was come of a mighty day—a day of crisis and of ultimate hope for human nature, then suffering mysterious eclipse, and labouring in some dread extremity. Somewhere, but I knew not where—somehow, but I knew not how—by some beings, but I knew not by whom—a battle, a strife, an agony, was travelling through all its stages—was evolving itself, like the catastrophe of some mighty drama, with which my sympathy was the more insupportable, from deepening confusion as to its local scene, its cause, its nature, and its undecipherable issue. I (as is usual in dreams where, of necessity, we make ourselves central to every movement) had the power, and yet had not the power, to decide it. I had the power, if I could raise myself to will it ; and yet again had not the power, for the weight of twenty Atlantics was upon me, or the oppression of inexpiable guilt. 'Deeper than ever plummet sounded,' I lay inactive. Then, like a chorus, the passion deepened. Some greater interest was at stake, some mightier cause, than ever yet the sword had pleaded, or trumpet had proclaimed. Then came sudden alarms ; hurryings to and fro ; trepidations of innumerable fugitives, I knew not whether from the good cause or the bad ; darkness and lights ; tempest and human faces ; and at last, with the sense that all was lost, female forms, and the features that were worth all the world to me ; and but a moment allowed—and clasped hands, with heart-breaking partings, and then—everlasting farewells ! and, with a sigh such as the caves of hell sighed when the incestuous mother uttered the abhorred name of Death, the sound was reverberated—everlasting farewells! and again, and yet again reverberated—everlasting farewells!

And I awoke in struggles, and cried aloud, 'I will sleep no more!'

Now, at last, I had become awestruck at the approach of sleep, under the condition of visions so afflicting, and so intensely life-like as those which persecuted my phantom-haunted brain. More and more also I felt violent palpitations in some internal region, such as are commonly, but erroneously, called palpitations of the heart—being, as I suppose, referable exclusively to derangements in the stomach. These were evidently increasing rapidly in frequency and in strength. Naturally, therefore, on considering how important my life had become to others besides myself, I became alarmed; and I paused seasonably; but with a difficulty that is past all description. Either way it seemed as though death had, in military language, 'thrown himself astride of my path.' Nothing short of mortal anguish, in a physical sense, it seemed, to wean myself from opium; yet, on the other hand, death through overwhelming nervous terrors — death by brain fever or by lunacy—seemed too certainly to besiege the alternative course. Fortunately I had still so much of firmness left as to face that choice, which, with most of instant suffering, showed in the far distance a possibility of final escape.

This possibility was realised: I *did* accomplish my escape. And the issue of that particular stage in my opium experiences (for such it was—simply a provisional stage, that paved the way subsequently for many milder stages, to which gradually my constitutional system accommodated itself) was, pretty nearly in the following words, communicated to my readers in the earliest edition of these Confessions:—

I triumphed. But infer not, reader, from this word '*triumphed*,' a condition of joy or exultation. Think of me as of one, even when four months had passed, still agitated, writhing, throbbing, palpitating, shattered; and much, perhaps, in the situation of him who has been

racked, as I collect the torments of that state from the
affecting account of them left by a most innocent sufferer [1]
(in the time of James I.).   Meantime, I derived no benefit
from any medicine whatever, except ammoniated tincture
of valerian.   The moral of the narrative is addressed to
the opium-eater ; and therefore, of necessity, limited in
its application.   If he is taught to fear and tremble,
enough has been effected.   But he may say that the issue
of my case is at least a proof that opium, after an eighteen
years' use, and an eight years' abuse of its powers, may
still be renounced ; and that he may chance to bring to
the task greater energy than I did, or that, with a stronger
constitution, he may obtain the same results with less.
This may be true ; I would not presume to measure the
efforts of other men by my own.   Heartily I wish him
more resolution ; heartily I wish him an equal success.
Nevertheless, I had motives external to myself which he
may unfortunately want ; and these supplied me with
conscientious supports, such as merely selfish interests
might fail in supplying to a mind debilitated by opium.

Lord Bacon conjectures that it may be as painful to
be born as to die. [2]   That seems probable ; and, during
the whole period of diminishing the opium, I had the
torments of a man passing out of one mode of existence
into another, and liable to the mixed or the alternate pains
of birth and death.   The issue was not death, but a sort
of physical regeneration ; and I may add, that ever since,
at intervals, I have had a restoration of more than youthful
spirits.

[1] William Lithgow. His book (Travels, etc.) is tedious and not
well written ; but the account of his own sufferings on the rack at
Malaga, and subsequently, is overpoweringly affecting. Less circumstantial, but the same in tendency, is the report of the results from
torture published in 1830 by Juan Van Halen.

[2] In all former editions, I had ascribed this sentiment to Jeremy
Taylor. On a close search, however, wishing to verify the quotation,
it appeared that I had been mistaken. Something very like it occurs
more than once in the bishop's voluminous writings : but the exact
passage moving in my mind had evidently been this which follows,
from Lord Bacon's *Essay on Death :*—'It is as natural to die as to be
born ; and to a little infant perhaps the one is as painful as the other.'

One memorial of my former condition nevertheless remains : my dreams are not calm ; the dread swell and agitation of the storm have not wholly subsided ; the legions that encamped in them are drawing off, but not departed ; my sleep is still tumultuous ; and, like the gates of Paradise to our first parents when looking back from afar, it is still (in the tremendous line of Milton)—

With dreadful faces thronged and fiery arms.

THE DAUGHTER OF LEBANON

THE DAUGHTER OF LEBANON

DAMASCUS, first-born of cities, *Om el Denia*,[1] mother of
generations, that wast before Abraham, that wast before
the Pyramids! what sounds are those that, from a postern
gate, looking eastwards over secret paths that wind away
to the far distant desert, break the solemn silence of an
oriental night? Whose voice is that which calls upon
the spearmen, keeping watch for ever in the turret surmounting the gate, to receive him back into his Syrian
home? Thou knowest him, Damascus, and hast known
him in seasons of trouble as one learned in the afflictions
of man; wise alike to take counsel for the suffering spirit
or for the suffering body. The voice that breaks upon
the night is the voice of a great evangelist—one of the
four; and he is also a great physician. This do the
watchmen at the gate thankfully acknowledge, and joyfully
they give him entrance. His sandals are white with dust;
for he has been roaming for weeks beyond the desert,
under the guidance of Arabs, on missions of hopeful
benignity to Palmyra;[2] and in spirit he is weary of all

---

[1] '*Om el Denia*':—Mother of the World is the Arabic title of
Damascus. That it was before Abraham—*i.e.*, already an old establishment much more than a thousand years before the siege of Troy, and
than two thousand years before our Christian era—may be inferred
from Gen. xv. 2; and by the general consent of all eastern races,
Damascus is accredited as taking precedence in age of all cities to the
west of the Indus.

[2] Palmyra had not yet reached its meridian splendour of Grecian
development, as afterwards near the age of Aurelian, but it was already
a noble city.

things, except faithfulness to God, and burning love to man.

Eastern cities are asleep betimes ; and sounds few or none fretted the quiet of all around him, as the evangelist paced onward to the market-place ; but there another scene awaited him. On the right hand, in an upper chamber, with lattices widely expanded, sat a festal company of youths, revelling under a noonday blaze of light, from cressets and from bright tripods that burned fragrant woods—all joining in choral songs, all crowned with odorous wreaths from Daphne and the banks of the Orontes. Them the evangelist heeded not ; but far away upon the left, close upon a sheltered nook, lighted up by a solitary vase of iron fretwork filled with cedar boughs, and hoisted high upon a spear, behold there sat a woman of loveliness so transcendent, that, when suddenly revealed, as now, out of deepest darkness, she appalled men as a mockery, or a birth of the air. Was she born of woman ? Was it perhaps the angel—so the evangelist argued with himself—that met him in the desert after sunset, and strengthened him by secret talk ? The evangelist went up, and touched her forehead ; and when he found that she was indeed human, and guessed, from the station which she had chosen, that she waited for some one amongst this dissolute crew as her companion, he groaned heavily in spirit, and said, half to himself, but half to her, ' Wert thou, poor ruined flower, adorned so divinely at thy birth—glorified in such excess that not Solomon in all his pomp—no, nor even the lilies of the field—can approach thy gifts—only that thou shouldest grieve the holy spirit of God ? ' The woman trembled exceedingly, and said, ' Rabbi, what should I do ? For behold ! all men forsake me.' The evangelist mused a little, and then secretly to himself he said, ' Now will I search this woman's heart—whether in very truth it inclineth itself to God, and hath strayed only before fiery compulsion.' Turning therefore to the woman, the Prophet[1] said, ' Listen : I am the messenger of Him

1 ' The Prophet ' :—Though a Prophet was not therefore and in

whom thou hast not known ; of Him that made Lebanon
and the cedars of Lebanon ; that made the sea, and the
heavens, and the host of the stars ; that made the light ;
that made the darkness ; that blew the spirit of life into
the nostrils of man. His messenger I am : and from Him
all power is given me to bind and to loose, to build and
to pull down. Ask, therefore, whatsoever thou wilt—
great or small—and through me thou shalt receive it
from God. But, my child, ask not amiss. For God is
able out of thy own evil asking to weave snares for thy
footing. And oftentimes to the lambs whom He loves,
He gives by seeming to refuse ; gives in some better
sense, or ' (and his voice swelled into the power of
anthems) ' in some far happier world. Now, therefore,
my daughter, be wise on thy own behalf ; and say what
it is that I shall ask for thee from God.' But the
Daughter of Lebanon needed not his caution ; for immediately dropping on one knee to God's ambassador,
whilst the full radiance from the cedar torch fell upon the
glory of a penitential eye, she raised her clasped hands in
supplication, and said, in answer to the evangelist asking
for a second time what gift he should call down upon her
from Heaven, ' Lord, that thou wouldest put me back
into my father's house.' And the evangelist, because he
was human, dropped a tear as he stooped to kiss her forehead, saying, ' Daughter, thy prayer is heard in heaven ;
and I tell thee that the daylight shall not come and go for
thirty times, not for the thirtieth time shall the sun drop
behind Lebanon, before I will put thee back into thy
father's house.'

virtue of that character an Evangelist, yet every Evangelist was
necessarily in the scriptural sense a Prophet. For let it be remembered that a Prophet did not mean a *Pre*dicter, or *Fore*shower of
events, except derivatively and inferentially. What *was* a Prophet in
the uniform scriptural sense ? He was a man, who drew aside the
curtain from the secret counsels of Heaven. He declared, or made
public, the previously hidden truths of God : and because future
events might chance to involve divine truth, therefore a revealer of
future events might happen so far to be a Prophet. Yet still small
was that part of a Prophet's functions which concerned the fore-
showing of events ; and not necessarily *any* part.

Thus the lovely lady came into the guardianship of the evangelist. She sought not to varnish her history, or to palliate her own transgressions. In so far as she had offended at all, her case was that of millions in every generation. Her father was a prince in Lebanon, proud, unforgiving, austere. The wrongs done to his daughter by her dishonourable lover, because done under favour of opportunities created by her confidence in his integrity, her father persisted in resenting as wrongs done by this injured daughter herself; and, refusing to her all protection, drove her, whilst yet confessedly innocent, into criminal compliances under sudden necessities of seeking daily bread from her own uninstructed efforts. Great was the wrong she suffered both from father and lover; great was the retribution. She lost a churlish father and a wicked lover; she gained an apostolic guardian. She lost a princely station in Lebanon; she gained an early heritage in heaven. For this heritage is hers within thirty days, if she will not defeat it herself. And, whilst the stealthy motion of time travelled towards this thirtieth day, behold! a burning fever desolated Damascus, which also laid its arrest upon the Daughter of Lebanon, yet gently, and so that hardly for an hour did it withdraw her from the heavenly teachings of the evangelist. And thus daily the doubt was strengthened—would the holy apostle suddenly touch her with his hand, and say, 'Woman, be thou whole!' or would he present her on the thirtieth day as a pure bride to Christ? But perfect freedom belongs to Christian service, and she only must make the election.

Up rose the sun on the thirtieth morning in all his pomp, but suddenly was darkened by driving storms. Not until noon was the heavenly orb again revealed; then the glorious light was again unmasked, and again the Syrian valleys rejoiced. This was the hour already appointed for the baptism of the new Christian daughter. Heaven and earth shed gratulation on the happy festival; and, when all was finished, under an awning raised above the level roof of her dwelling-house, the regenerate daughter of Lebanon, looking over the rose-gardens of Damascus, with amplest prospect of her native hills, lay in blissful trance, making proclamation, by her white baptismal robes, of recovered innocence and of reconciliation with God. And, when the sun was declining to the west, the evangelist, who had sat from noon by the bed-side of his spiritual daughter, rose solemnly, and said, ' Lady of Lebanon, the day is already come, and the hour is coming, in which my covenant must be fulfilled with thee. Wilt thou, therefore, being now wiser in thy thoughts, suffer God, thy new Father, to give by seeming to refuse ; to give in some better sense, or in some far happier world ? ' But the Daughter of Lebanon sorrowed at these words ; she yearned after her native hills ; not for themselves, but because there it was that she had left that sweet twin-born sister with whom from infant days hand-in-hand she had wandered amongst the everlasting cedars. And again the evangelist sat down by her bed-side ; whilst she by intervals communed with him, and by intervals slept gently under the oppression of her fever. But, as evening drew nearer, and it wanted now but a brief space to the going down of the sun, once again, and with deeper solemnity, the evangelist rose to his feet, and said, ' O daughter ! this is the thirtieth day, and the sun is drawing near to his rest ; brief, therefore, is the time within which I must fulfil the word that God spoke to thee by me.' Then, because light clouds of delirium were playing about her brain, he raised his pastoral staff, and pointing it to her temples, rebuked the clouds, and bade that no more they should trouble her vision, or stand between her and the forests of Lebanon. And the delirious clouds parted asunder, breaking away to the right and to the left. But upon the forests of Lebanon there hung a mighty mass of overshadowing vapours, bequeathed by the morning's storm. And a second time the evangelist raised his pastoral staff, and, pointing it to the gloomy vapours, rebuked them, and bade that no more they should stand between his daughter and her father's house, and immediately the dark vapours broke away from

Lebanon to the right and to the left; and the farewell radiance of the sun lighted up all the paths that ran between the everlasting cedars and her father's palace. But vainly the lady of Lebanon searched every path with her eyes for memorials of her sister. And the evangelist, pitying her sorrow, turned away her eyes to the clear blue sky, which the departing vapours had exposed. And he showed her the peace that was there. And then he said, 'O daughter! this also is but a mask.' And immediately for the third time he raised his pastoral staff, and, pointing it to the fair blue sky, he rebuked it, and bade that no more it should stand between her and the vision of God. Immediately the blue sky parted to the right and to the left, laying bare the infinite revelations that can be made visible only to dying eyes. And the Daughter of Lebanon said to the evangelist, 'O father! what armies are these that I see mustering within the infinite chasm?' And the evangelist replied, 'These are the armies of Christ, and they are mustering to receive some dear human blossom, some first-fruits of Christian faith, that shall rise this night to Christ from Damascus.' Suddenly, as thus the child of Lebanon gazed upon the mighty vision, she saw bending forward from the heavenly host, as if in gratulation to herself, the one countenance for which she hungered and thirsted. The twin sister, that should have waited for her in Lebanon, had died of grief, and was waiting for her in Paradise. Immediately in rapture she soared upwards from her couch; immediately in weakness she fell back; and being caught by the evangelist, she flung her arms around his neck; whilst he breathed into her ear his final whisper, 'Wilt thou now suffer that God should give by seeming to refuse?'—'Oh yes—yes—yes,' was the fervent answer from the Daughter of Lebanon. Immediately the evangelist gave the signal to the heavens, and the heavens gave the signal to the sun; and in one minute after the Daughter of Lebanon had fallen back a marble corpse amongst her white baptismal robes; the solar orb dropped behind Lebanon; and the evangelist, with eyes glorified by mortal and immortal tears, rendered thanks to God that had thus accomplished the word which he spoke through himself to the Magdalen of Lebanon— that not for the thirtieth time should the sun go down behind her native hills, before he had put her back into her Father's house.

APPENDIX

De Quincey.—Page 69.

THIS family, which split (or, as a grammatical purist lately said to me in a tone of expostulation, *splat*) into three national divisions—English, French, and American—originally was Norwegian : and in the year of our Christian era *one thousand*, spoke (I believe) the most undeniable Norse. Throughout the eleventh century the heads of this family (in common with all the ruffians and martial vagabonds of Europe that had Venetian sequins enough disposable for such a trip) held themselves in readiness to join any *likely* leader ; and did join William the Norman. Very few indeed, or probably none, of his brigands were Frenchmen, or native Neustrians ; Normans being notoriously a name not derived *from* any French province, but imported *into* that province by trans-Baltic, and in a smaller proportion by cis-Baltic, aliens. This Norwegian family, having assumed a territorial denomination from the district or village of Quincy, in the province now called Normandy, transplanted themselves to England : where, and subsequently by marriage in Scotland, they ascended to the highest rank in both kingdoms, and held the highest offices open to a subject. A late distinguished writer, Mr. Moir of Musselburgh, the 'Delta' of *Blackwood's Magazine*, took the trouble (which must have been considerable) of tracing their aspiring movements in Scotland, through a period when Normans transferred themselves from England to Scotland in considerable numbers, and with great advantages. This elaborate paper, published many years ago in *Blackwood's Magazine*, first made known the leading facts of their career in Scotland. Meantime in England they continued to flourish through nine or ten generations ; took a distinguished part in one, at least, of the Crusades ; and a still more perilous share in the Barons Wars under Henry III. No family drank more deeply or more frequently from the cup of treason ; which in those days was not always a very grave offence in people who, having much territorial influence, had also much money. But, happening to drink once too often, or taking too long a 'pull' at the cup, the Earls of Winchester suddenly came to grief. Amongst the romances of astronomy there is one, I believe, which has endeavoured to account for the little asteroids of our system by supposing them fragments of some great planet that had, under internal convulsion or external collision, at some period suddenly exploded. In our own planet Tellus such a county as York, under a similar catastrophe, would make a very pretty little asteroid. And, with some miniature resemblance to such a case, sometimes benefiting by the indulgence of the crown, sometimes by legal devices, sometimes by aid of matrimonial alliances, numerous descendants, confessedly innocent, from the guilty earl projected themselves by successive efforts, patiently watching their opportunities, from the smoking ruins of the great feudal house : stealthily through two generations creeping out of their lurking holes ; timidly, when the great shadows from the threatening throne had passed over, re-assuming the family name. Concurrently with these *personal* fragments projected from the ancient house, flew off random splinters and fragments from the great planetary disk of the Winchester estates, little asteroids that formed ample inheritances for the wants of this or that provincial squire, of this or that tame villatic squireen.[1]

The kingly old oak, that had been the leader of the forest, was thus suddenly (in the technical language of woodcraft) cut down into a 'pollard.' This mutilation for ever prevented it from aspiring cloudwards by means of some mighty stem, such as grows upon Norwegian hills, fit to be the mast of 'some great ammiral.' Nevertheless, we see daily amongst the realities of nature that a tree, after passing through such a process of degradation, yet manifests the great arrears of vindictive life lurking within it by throwing out a huge radiation of slender boughs and miniature shoots, small but many, so that we are forced exactly to invert the fine words of Lucan, saying no longer *trunco, non frondibus, efficit umbram*, but, on the contrary, *non trunco sed frondibus efficit umbram*. This great cabbage-head of this ancient human tree threw a broad massy umbrage over more villages than one ; sometimes yielding representatives moody and mutinous, sometimes vivacious and inventive, sometimes dull and lethargic, until at last, one fine morning, on rubbing their eyes, they found themselves actually in the sixteenth century abreast of Henry VIII. and his fiery children. Ah, what a century was that ! Sculptured as only Froude can sculpture those that fight across the chasms of eternity, grouped as only Froude can group the mighty factions, acting or suffering, arraigning before chanceries of man, or protesting before chanceries of God—what vast arrays of marble gladiators fighting for truth, real or imagined, throng the arenas in each generation of that and the succeeding century. And how ennobling a distinction of modern humanity, that in Pagan antiquity no truth as yet existed, none had

---

[1] This last variety of the rustic *regulus* is of Hibernian origin, and, as regards the name, was unknown to us in England until Miss Edgeworth had extended the horizon of our social experience. Yet, without the name, I presume that the *thing* must have been known occasionally even in England.

been revealed, none emblazoned, on behalf of which man *could* have fought! As Lord Bacon remarks—though strangely, indeed, publishing in the very terms of this remark his own blindness to the causes and consequences—religious wars were unknown to antiquity. Personal interests, and those only, did or could furnish a subject of conflict. But throughout the sixteenth century, whether in England, in France, or in Germany, it was a spiritual interest, shadowy and aerial, which embattled armies against armies. Simply the nobility of this interest it was, simply the grandeur of a cause moving by springs transcendent to all vulgar and mercenary collisions of prince with prince, or family with family, that arrayed man against man, not upon petty combinations of personal intrigue, but upon questions of everlasting concern—this majestic principle of the strife it was that constituted for the noblest minds its secret magnetism. Early in the seventeenth century, when it seemed likely that the interests of a particular family would be entangled with the principles at issue, multitudes became anxious to evade the strife by retiring to the asylum of forests. Amongst these was one branch of the De Quinceys. Enamoured of democracy, this family, laying aside the aristocratic *De* attached to their name, settled in New England, where they subsequently rose, through long public services, to the highest moral rank —as measured by all possible expressions of public esteem that are consistent with the simplicities of the great republic. Mr. Josiah Quincy, as head of this distinguished family, is appealed to as one who takes rank by age and large political experience with the founders of the American Union. Another branch of the same family had at a much earlier period settled in France. Finally, the squires and squireens—*i.e.*, those who benefited in any degree by those 'asteroids' which I have explained as exploded from the ruins of the Winchester estates—naturally remained in England. The last of them who enjoyed any relics whatever of that ancient territorial domain was an elder kinsman of my father. I never had the honour of seeing him; in fact, it was impossible that I *should* have such an honour, since he died during the American War, which war had closed, although it had not paid its bills, some time before my birth. He enacted the part of squireen, I have been told, creditably enough in a village belonging either to the county of Leicester, Nottingham, or Rutland. Sir Andrew Aguecheek observes as one of his sentimental remembrances, that he also at one period of his life had been 'adored': 'I was adored once,' says the knight, seeming to acknowledge that he was not adored then. But the squireen was 'adored' in a limited way to the last. This fading representative of a crusading house declined gradually into the oracle of the bar at the Red Lion, and was adored by two persons at the least (not counting himself)—viz., the landlord, and occasionally the waiter. Mortgages had eaten up the last vestiges of the old territorial wrecks; and with his death a new era commenced for this historical family, which now (as if expressly to irritate its ambition) finds itself distributed amongst three mighty nations—France, America, and England—and precisely those three that are usually regarded as the leaders of civilisation.[1]

BARBARA LEWTHWAITE.—Page 193.

Already Barbara Lewthwaite had contributed to the composition of two impressive pictures : first, in her infancy, with her pet lamb, under the evening shadows of the mighty Fairfield ; secondly, in her girlhood, with the turbaned Malay and the little cottage child. But subsequently, when a young woman, she entered unconsciously into the composition of another picture even more rememberable, suggesting great names, connected with the greatest of themes ; the names being those of Plato, and, in this instance at least, of a mightier than Plato—viz., William Wordsworth ; and the theme concerned being that problem which, measured by its interest to man, by its dependencies, by the infinite jewel staked upon the verdict, we should all confess to be the most solemn and heart-shaking that is hung out by golden chains from the heaven of heavens to human investigation— viz., Is the spirit of man numbered amongst things naturally perishable ? The doctrine of our own Dodwell (a most orthodox man) was that naturally and *per se* it was perishable, but that by supernatural endowment it was made immortal. Apparently the ancient oracles of the Hebrew literature had all and everywhere assumed the soul's natural mortality. The single passage in Job that *seemed* to look in the counter direction has long since received an interpretation painfully alien from such a meaning ; not to mention that the same objection would apply to this passage, if read into a Christian sense, as applies to the ridiculous interpolation in Josephus describing Christ's personal appearance—viz., Once suppose it genuine, and why were there not myriads of other passages in the same key ? Imagine, for a moment, the writer so penetrated with premature Christian views, by what inexplicable rigour of abstinence had he forborne to meet ten thousand calls, at other turns of his work, for similar utterances of Christian sentiment ? It must not be supposed that the objections to this Christian interpretation of Job rest solely with German scholars. Coleridge, one of the most devout and evangelical amongst modern theologians, took the same view, and has expressed it with decision. But Job is of slight importance in comparison with Moses. Now Warburton, in his well-known argument, held not only that Moses *did* (as a fact) assume the mortality of the soul, but that, as a necessity, he did so, since upon this assumption rests the weightiest argument for his own divine mission. That Moses could dispense with a support

---

[1] The omission of the *De*, as an addition looking better at a tournament than as an indorsement on a bill of exchange, began, as to many hundreds of English names, full three hundred years ago. Many English families have disused this affix simply from indolence. As to the terminal variations, *cy*, *cie*, *cey*, those belong, as natural and inevitable exponents of a transitional condition, to the unsettled spelling that characterises the early stages of literature in all countries alike.

which Warburton fancied all other legislators had needed and postu-
lated argued, in the bishop's opinion, a vicarious support—a secret and
divine support.   This extreme view will be rejected, perhaps, by most
people.   But, in the meantime, the very existence of such a sect as
the Sadducees proves sufficiently that no positive affirmation of the
soul's immortality could have been accredited amongst the Hebrew
nation as a Mosaic doctrine.   The rise of a counter sect, the Pharisees,
occurred in later days, clearly under a principle of 'development'
applied to old traditions current among the Jews.   It was not alleged
as a Mosaic doctrine, but as something deducible from traditions
countenanced by Moses.   From Hebrew literature, therefore, no help
is to be looked for on this great question.   Pagan literature first of all
furnishes any response upon it favourable to human yearnings.   But,
unhappily, the main argument upon which the sophist in the *Phædo*
relies is a pure scholastic conundrum, baseless and puerile.   The
homogeneity of human consciousness, upon which is made to rest its
indestructibility, is not established or made probable by any plausible
logic.   If we should figure to ourselves some mighty angel mounting
guard upon human interests twenty-three centuries ago, this tutelary
spirit would have smiled derisively upon the advent and the departure
of Plato.   At length, once again, after many centuries, was heard the
clarion of immortality—not as of any preternatural gift, but as a
natural prerogative of the human spirit.   This time the angel would
have paused and hearkened.   The auguries for immortality which
Wordsworth drew from indications running along the line of daily
human experience were two.

   The first was involved in the exquisite little poem of *We are
Seven*.   That authentic voice, said Wordsworth, which affirmed life
as a necessity inalienable from man's consciousness was a revelation
through the lips of childhood.   Life in its torrent fulness—that is,
life in its earliest stage—affirmed itself; whereas the voice which
whispered doubts was an adventitious and secondary voice consequent
upon an earthly experience.   The child in this little poem is unable
to admit the thought of death, though, in compliance with custom, she
uses the word :—

> 'The first that *died* was little Jane;
>   In bed she moaning lay,
> Till God released her from her pain;
>   And then she went away.'

The graves of her brother and sister she is so far from regarding as
any argument of their having died that she supposes the stranger
simply to doubt her statement, and she reiterates her assertion of their
graves as lying in the churchyard, in order to prove that they were
living :—

> 'Their graves are green, they may be seen,'
>   The little maid replied,
> 'Twelve steps or more from my mother's door,
>   And they are side by side.

> And often after sunset, sir,
>   When it is light and fair,
> I take my little porringer,
>   And eat my supper there.
> My stockings there I often knit,
>   My kerchief there I hem :
> And there upon their graves I sit—
>   I sit, and sing to them.'

The other argument was developed in the sublime *Ode upon the Intimations of Immortality*, etc.   Man in his infancy stood *nearest* (so much was matter of fact) to the unseen world of the Infinite.   What voices he heard most frequently, murmuring through the cells of his infantine brain, were echoes of the great realities which, as a new-born infant, he had just quitted.   Hanging upon his mother's breast, he heard dim prolongations of a music which belonged to a life ever more and more receding into a distance buried in clouds and vapours. Man's orient, in which lie the fountains of the dawn, must be sought for in that Eden of infancy which first received him as a traveller emerging from a world now daily becoming more distant.   And it is a great argument of the divine splendour investing man's natural home that the heavenly lights which burned in his morning grow fainter and fainter as he ' travels farther from the East.'

The little Carnarvonshire child in *We are Seven*, who is repre-sented as repelling the idea of death under an absolute inability to receive it, had completed her eighth year.   But this might be an ambitious exaggeration, such as aspiring female children are generally disposed to practise.   It is more probable that she might be in the currency of her eighth year.   Naturally we must not exact from Wordsworth any pedantic rigour of accuracy in such a case ; but assuredly we have a right to presume that his principle, if tenable at all, must apply to all children below the age of *five*.   However I will say *four*.   In that case the following anecdote seems to impeach the philosophic truth of this doctrine.   I give the memorandum as it was drawn up by myself at the time :—

My second child, but eldest daughter, little M——, is between two and three weeks less than two years old ; and from the day of her birth she has been uniformly attended by Barbara Lewthwaite.   We are now in the first days of June ; but, about three weeks since, con-sequently in the earlier half of May, some one of our neighbours gave to M—— a little bird.   I am no great ornithologist.   ' Perhaps only a tenth-rate one,' says some too flattering reader.   Oh dear, no, nothing near it : I fear, no more than a 510th rater.   Consequently, I cannot ornithologically describe or classify the bird.   But I believe that it belonged to the family of finches—either a goldfinch, bullfinch, or at least something ending in *inch*.   The present was less splendid than at first it seemed.   For the bird was wounded, though not in a way that made the wound apparent ; and too sensibly as the evening wore away it drooped.   None of us knew what medical treatment to suggest ; and all that occurred was to place it with free access to birdseed and water. At length sunset arrived, which was the signal for M——'s departure to bed. She came therefore as usual to me, threw her arms round my neck, and went through her ordinary routine of prayers : viz., first, the Lord's Prayer, and finally the four following lines (a Roman Catholic bequest to the children of Northern England) :—

> Holy[1] Jesus, meek and mild,
> Look on me, a little child :
> Pity my simplicity ;
> Grant that I may come to thee.

M——, as she was moving off to bed, whispered to me that I was to 'mend' the bird with 'yoddonum.' Having always seen *me* taking laudanum, and for the purpose (as she was told) of growing better in health, reasonably it struck her that the little bird would improve under the same regimen. For her satisfaction, I placed a little diluted laudanum near to the bird; and she then departed to bed, though with uneasy looks reverting to her sick little pet. Occupied with some point of study, it happened that I sat up through the whole night : and long before seven o'clock in the morning she had summoned Barbara to dress her, and soon I heard the impatient little foot descending the stairs to my study. I had such a Jesuitical *bulletin* ready, by way of a report upon the bird's health, as might not seem absolutely despairing, though not too dangerously sanguine. And, as the morning was one of heavenly splendour, I proposed that we should improve the bird's chances by taking it out-of-doors into the little orchard at the foot of Fairfield—our loftiest Grasmere mountain. Thither moved at once Barbara Lewthwaite, little M——, myself, and the poor languishing bird. By that time in May, in any far southern county, perhaps the birds would be ceasing to sing; but not so with us dilatory people in Westmoreland. Suddenly, as we all stood around the little perch on which the bird rested, one thrilling song, louder than the rest, arose from a neighbouring hedge. Immediately the bird's eye, previously dull, kindled into momentary fire ; the bird rose on its perch, struggled for an instant, seemed to be expanding its wings, made one aspiring movement upwards, in doing so fell back, and in another moment was dead. Too certainly and apparently all these transitions symbolically interpreted themselves, and to all of us alike : the proof of which was that man, woman, and child spontaneously shed tears : a weakness, perhaps, but more natural under the regular processional evolution of the scenical stages than when simply read as a narrative : for too evident it was, to one and all of us, without needing to communicate by words, *what* vision had revealed itself to all alike—to the child under two years old, not less than to the adults : too evident it was that, on this magnificent May

---

[1] '*Holy Jesus*' :—This was a very judicious correction introduced by Wordsworth. Originally the traditional line had stood—'Gentle Jesus, meek and mild.' But Wordsworth, offended by the idle iteration of one idea in the words gentle, meek, mild, corrected the text into *Holy*.

morning, there had been exhibited, as on the stage of a theatre—there had passed before the eyes of us all—passed, and was finished—the everlasting mystery of death! It seemed to me that little M——, by her sudden burst of tears, must have read this saddest of truths—must have felt that the bird's fate was sealed—not less clearly than Barbara or myself.

ON MURDER

CONSIDERED AS ONE OF THE FINE ARTS

ON MURDER

CONSIDERED AS ONE OF THE FINE ARTS

Advertisement of a Man Morbidly Virtuous

Most of us, who read books, have probably heard of a Society for the Promotion of Vice, of the Hell-Fire Club, founded in the last century by Sir Francis Dashwood, etc. At Brighton I think it was, that a Society was formed for the Suppression of Virtue. That society was itself suppressed ; but I am sorry to say that another exists in London, of a character still more atrocious. In tendency, it may be denominated a Society for the Encouragement of Murder ; but, according to their own delicate εὐφημισμός, it is styled, the Society of Connoisseurs in Murder. They profess to be curious in homicide ; amateurs and dilettanti in the various modes of carnage ; and, in short, Murder-Fanciers. Every fresh atrocity of that class which the police annals of Europe bring up, they meet and criticise as they would a picture, statue, or other work of art. But I need not trouble myself with any attempt to describe the spirit of their proceedings, as the reader will collect *that* much better from one of the Monthly Lectures read before the society last year. This has fallen into my hands accidentally, in spite of all the vigilance exercised to keep their transactions from the public eye. The publication of it will alarm them ; and my purpose is, that it should. For I would much rather put them down quietly, by an appeal to public opinion, than by such an exposure of names as would follow an appeal to Bow Street; which last appeal, however, if this should fail, I must really resort to. For my intense virtue will not put up with such things in a Christian land. Even in a heathen land, the toleration of murder—viz., in the dreadful shows of the amphitheatre—was felt by a Christian writer to be the most crying reproach of the public morals. This writer was Lactantius; and with his words, as singularly applicable to the present occasion, I shall conclude :—'Quid tam horribile,' says he, 'tam tetrum, quam hominis trucidatio? Ideo severissimis legibus vita nostra munitur; ideo bella execrabilia sunt. Invenit tamen consuetudo quatenus homicidium sine bello ac sine legibus faciat : et hoc sibi voluptas quod scelus vindicavit. Quod si interesse homicidio sceleris con-scientia est,—et eidem facinori spectator obstrictus est cui et admissor; ergo et in his gladiatorum cædibus non minus cruore profunditur qui spectat, quam ille qui facit : nec potest esse immunis à sanguine qui voluit effundi; aut videri non interfecisse, qui interfectori et favit et prœmium postulavit.' 'What is so dreadful,' says Lac-tantius, 'what so dismal and revolting, as the murder of a human creature? Therefore it is, that life for us is pro-tected by laws the most rigorous : therefore it is, that wars are objects of execration. And yet the traditional usage of Rome has devised a mode of authorising murder apart from war, and in defiance of law; and the demands of taste (voluptas) are now become the same as those of abandoned guilt.' Let the Society of Gentlemen Amateurs consider this; and let me call their especial attention to the last sentence, which is so weighty, that I shall attempt to convey it in English : 'Now, if merely to be present at a murder fastens on a man the character of an accom-plice; if barely to be a spectator involves us in one common guilt with the perpetrator, it follows, of necessity, that, in these murders of the amphitheatre, the hand which inflicts the fatal blow is not more deeply imbrued in blood than his who passively looks on; neither can *he* be clear of blood who has countenanced its shedding; nor that man seem other than a participator in murder, who gives his applause to the murderer, and calls for prizes on his behalf.' The '*præmia postulavit*' I have not yet heard charged upon the Gentlemen Amateurs of London, though undoubtedly their proceedings tend to that; but the '*interfectori favit*' is implied in the very title of this association, and expressed in every line of the lecture which follows.

X. Y. Z.

LECTURE

GENTLEMEN—I have had the honour to be appointed by your committee to the trying task of reading the Williams Lecture on Murder, considered as one of the Fine Arts; a task which might be easy enough three or four centuries ago, when the art was little understood, and few great models had been exhibited; but in this age, when masterpieces of excellence have been executed by professional men, it must be evident, that in the style of criticism applied to them, the public will look for something of a corresponding improvement. Practice and theory must advance *pari passu*. People begin to see that something more goes to the composition of a fine murder than two blockheads to kill and be killed—a knife—a purse—and a dark lane. Design, gentlemen, grouping, light and shade, poetry, sentiment, are now deemed indispensable to attempts of this nature. Mr. Williams has exalted the ideal of murder to all of us; and to me, therefore, in particular, has deepened the arduousness of my task. Like Æschylus or Milton in poetry, like Michael Angelo in painting, he has carried his art to a point of colossal sublimity; and, as Mr. Wordsworth observes, has in a manner 'created the taste by which he is to be enjoyed.' To sketch the history of the art, and to examine its principles critically, now remains as a duty for the connoisseur, and for judges of quite another stamp from his Majesty's Judges of Assize.

Before I begin, let me say a word or two to certain prigs, who affect to speak of our society as if it were in

some degree immoral in its tendency.   Immoral! Jupiter
protect me, gentlemen, what is it that people mean?   I
am for morality, and always shall be, and for virtue, and
all that ; and I do affirm, and always shall (let what will
come of it), that murder is an improper line of conduct,
highly improper ; and I do not stick to assert, that any
man who deals in murder, must have very incorrect ways
of thinking, and truly inaccurate principles ; and so far
from aiding and abetting him by pointing out his victim's
hiding-place, as a great moralist of Germany[1] declared it
to be every good man's duty to do, I would subscribe one
shilling and sixpence to have him apprehended, which is
more by eighteenpence than the most eminent moralists
have hitherto subscribed for that purpose.   But what
then?   Everything in this world has two handles.   Murder, for instance, may be laid hold of by its moral handle
(as it generally is in the pulpit, and at the Old Bailey) ;
and *that*, I confess, is its weak side ; or it may also be
treated *æsthetically*, as the Germans call it—that is, in
relation to good taste.

   To illustrate this, I will urge the authority of three
eminent persons—viz., S. T. Coleridge, Aristotle, and
Mr. Howship the surgeon.   To begin with S. T. C.
One night, many years ago, I was drinking tea with him
in Berners Street (which, by the way, for a short street,
has been uncommonly fruitful in men of genius).   Others
were there besides myself ; and, amidst some carnal considerations of tea and toast, we were all imbibing a dis-
sertation on Plotinus from the Attic lips of S. T. C.
Suddenly a cry arose of ' *Fire—fire !* ' upon which all of
us, master and disciples, Plato and οἱ περὶ τὸν Πλάτωνα,
rushed out, eager for the spectacle.   The fire was in

   [1] Kant—who carried his demands of unconditional veracity to so
extravagant a length as to affirm, that, if a man were to see an innocent
person escape from a murderer, it would be his duty, on being questioned
by the murderer, to tell the truth, and to point out the retreat of the
innocent person, under any certainty of causing murder.   Lest this
doctrine should be supposed to have escaped him in any heat of
dispute, on being taxed with it by a celebrated French writer, he
solemnly re-affirmed it, with his reasons.

Oxford Street, at a pianoforte-maker's ; and, as it promised to be a conflagration of merit, I was sorry that my engagements forced me away from Mr. Coleridge's party, before matters had come to a crisis. Some days after, meeting with my Platonic host, I reminded him of the case, and begged to know how that very promising exhibition had terminated. 'Oh, sir,' said he, 'it turned out so ill that we damned it unanimously.' Now, does any man suppose that Mr. Coleridge—who, for all he is too fat to be a person of active virtue, is undoubtedly a worthy Christian—that this good S. T. C., I say, was an incendiary, or capable of wishing any ill to the poor man and his pianofortes (many of them, doubtless, with the additional keys)? On the contrary, I know him to be that sort of man, that I durst stake my life upon it, he would have worked an engine in a case of necessity, although rather of the fattest for such fiery trials of his virtue. But how stood the case? Virtue was in no request. On the arrival of the fire engines, morality had devolved wholly on the insurance office. This being the case, he had a right to gratify his taste. He had left his tea. Was he to have nothing in return?

I contend that the most virtuous man, under the premises stated, was entitled to make a luxury of the fire, and to hiss it, as he would any other performance that raised expectations in the public mind which afterwards it disappointed. Again, to cite another great authority, what says the Stagirite? He (in the Fifth Book, I think it is, of his Metaphysics) describes what he calls κλεπτὴν τέλειον—*i.e.*, *a perfect thief*; and, as to Mr. Howship, in a work of his on Indigestion, he makes no scruple to talk with admiration of a certain ulcer which he had seen, and which he styles 'a beautiful ulcer.' Now, will any man pretend, that, abstractedly considered, a thief could appear to Aristotle a perfect character, or that Mr. Howship could be enamoured of an ulcer? Aristotle, it is well known, was himself so very moral a character, that, not content with writing his Nichomachéan Ethics, in one volume octavo, he also wrote another system, called *Magna*

Moralia, or Big Ethics.   Now, it is impossible that a man who composes any ethics at all, big or little, should admire a thief *per se;* and as to Mr. Howship, it is well known that he makes war upon all ulcers, and, without suffering himself to be seduced by their charms, endeavours to banish them from the county of Middlesex.   But the truth is, that, however objectionable *per se*, yet, relatively to others of their class, both a thief and an ulcer may have infinite degrees of merit.   They are both imperfections, it is true; but, to be imperfect being their essence, the very greatness of their imperfection becomes their perfection. *Spartam nactus es, hanc exorna.*   A thief like Autolycus or the once famous George Barrington, and a grim phage-dænic ulcer, superbly defined, and running regularly through all its natural stages, may no less justly be regarded as ideals after *their* kind, than the most faultless moss-rose amongst flowers, in its progress from bud to 'bright consummate flower;' or, amongst human flowers, the most magnificent young female, apparelled in the pomp of womanhood.   And thus not only the ideal of an inkstand may be imagined (as Mr. Coleridge illustrated in his celebrated correspondence with Mr. Blackwood), in which, by the way, there is not so much, because an ink-stand is a laudable sort of thing, and a valuable member of society ; but even imperfection itself may have its ideal or perfect state.

Really, gentlemen, I beg pardon for so much philo-sophy at one time ; and now let me apply it.   When a murder is in the paulo-post-futurum tense—not done, not even (according to modern purism) *being* done, but only going to be done—and a rumour of it comes to our ears, by all means let us treat it morally.   But suppose it over and done, and that you can say of it, Τετέλεσται, It is finished, or (in that adamantine molossus of *Medea*) εἴργασται, Done it is : it is a *fait accompli;* suppose the poor murdered man to be out of his pain, and the rascal that did it off like a shot, nobody knows whither ; sup-pose, lastly, that we have done our best, by putting out our legs, to trip up the fellow in his flight, but all to no

purpose—'abiit, evasit, excessit, erupit,' etc.—why, then,
I say, what's the use of any more virtue? Enough has
been given to morality; now comes the turn of Taste
and the Fine Arts. A sad thing it was, no doubt, very
sad; but *we* can't mend it. Therefore let us make the
best of a bad matter; and, as it is impossible to hammer
anything out of it for moral purposes, let us treat it
æsthetically, and see if it will turn to account in that way.
Such is the logic of a sensible man, and what follows?
We dry up our tears, and have the satisfaction, perhaps,
to discover that a transaction, which, morally considered,
was shocking, and without a leg to stand upon, when tried
by principles of Taste, turns out to be a very meritorious
performance. Thus all the world is pleased; the old
proverb is justified, that it is an ill wind which blows
nobody good; the amateur, from looking bilious and
sulky, by too close an attention to virtue, begins to pick
up his crumbs; and general hilarity prevails. Virtue has
had her day; and henceforward, *Virtù*, so nearly the same
thing as to differ only by a single letter (which surely is
not worth haggling or higgling about)—*Virtù*, I repeat,
and Connoisseurship have leave to provide for themselves.
Upon this principle, gentlemen, I propose to guide your
studies, from Cain to Mr. Thurtell. Through this great
gallery of murder, therefore, together let us wander hand
in hand, in delighted admiration; while I endeavour to
point your attention to the objects of profitable criticism.

The first murder is familiar to you all. As the in-
ventor of murder, and the father of the art, Cain must
have been a man of first-rate genius. All the Cains were
men of genius. Tubal Cain invented tubes, I think, or
some such thing. But, whatever might be the originality
and genius of the artist, every art was then in its infancy,
and the works turned out from each several *studio*, must
be criticised with a recollection of that fact. Even Tubal's
work would probably be little approved at this day in
Sheffield; and therefore of Cain (Cain senior, I mean) it
is no disparagement to say, that his performance was but

so-so.   Milton, however, is supposed to have thought
differently.   By his way of relating the case, it should
seem to have been rather a pet murder with him, for he
retouches it with an apparent anxiety for its picturesque
effect :—

> Whereat he inly raged ; and, as they talk'd,
> Smote him into the midriff with a stone
> That beat out life : he fell ; and, deadly pale,
> Groan'd out his soul *with gushing blood effused.*
>
> *Par. Lost*, Bk. **XI.**

Upon this, Richardson the painter, who had an eye for
effect, remarks as follows, in his 'Notes on Paradise Lost,'
p. 497 :—'It has been thought,' says he, 'that Cain beat
(as the common saying is) the breath out of his brother's
body with a great stone ; Milton gives in to this, with the
addition, however, of a large wound.'   In this place it was
a judicious addition ; for the rudeness of the weapon,
unless raised and enriched by a warm, sanguinary colouring,
has too much of the naked air of the savage school ; as if
the deed were perpetrated by a Polypheme without science,
premeditation, or anything but a mutton-bone.   However,
I am chiefly pleased with the improvement, as it implies
that Milton was an amateur.   As to Shakespeare, there
never was a better ; witness his description of the murdered
Duncan, Banquo, etc. ; and above all, witness his incomparable miniature, in 'Henry VI.,' of the murdered
Gloucester.[1]

---

[1] The passage occurs in the *second* part (act 3) of 'Henry VI.,' and
is doubly remarkable—first, for its critical fidelity to nature, were the
description meant only for *poetic* effect ; but, secondly, for the *judicial*
value impressed upon it when offered (as here it *is* offered) in silent
corroboration legally of a dreadful whisper, all at once arising, that foul
play had been dealing with a great prince, clothed with an official state
character.   It is the Duke of Gloucester, faithful guardian and loving
uncle of the simple and imbecile king, who has been found dead in
his bed.   How shall this event be interpreted ?   Had he died under
some natural visitation of Providence, or by violence from his enemies ?
The two court factions read the circumstantial indications of the case
into opposite constructions.   The affectionate and afflicted young king,
whose position almost pledges him to neutrality, cannot, nevertheless,
disguise his overwhelming suspicions of hellish conspiracy in the back-

The foundation of the art having been once laid, it is pitiable to see how it slumbered without improvement for ages. In fact, I shall now be obliged to leap over all murders, sacred and profane, as utterly unworthy of notice, until long after the Christian era. Greece, even in the age of Pericles, produced no murder, or at least none is recorded, of the slightest merit ; and Rome had too little originality of genius in any of the arts to succeed where

ground. Upon this, a leader of the opposite faction endeavours to break the force of this royal frankness, countersigned and echoed most impressively by Lord Warwick. 'What *instance*,' he asks—meaning by *instance* not example or illustration, as thoughtless commentators have constantly supposed, but in the common scholastic sense—what *instantia*, what pressure of argument, what urgent plea, can Lord Warwick put forward in support of his 'dreadful oath'—an oath, namely, that, as surely as he hopes for the life eternal, so surely

> I do believe that violent hands were laid
> Upon the life of this thrice faméd duke.

Ostensibly the challenge is to Warwick, but substantially it is meant for the king. And the reply of Warwick, the argument on which he builds, lies in a solemn array of all the changes worked in the duke's features by death, as irreconcilable with any other hypothesis than that this death had been a violent one. What argument have I that Gloucester died under the hands of murderers ? Why the following roll-call of awful changes, affecting head, face, nostrils, eyes, hands, etc., which do not belong indifferently to *any* mode of death, but exclusively to a death by violence :—

> But see, his face is black and full of blood ;
> His eyeballs farther out than when he lived,
> Staring full ghastly, like a strangled man ;
> His hair uprear'd, his nostrils stretch'd with struggling ;
> His hands abroad display'd, as one that grasp'd
> And tugg'd for life, and was by strength subdued.
> Look on the sheets :—his hair, you see, is sticking ;
> His well-proportion'd beard made rough and rugged,
> Like to the summer's corn by tempest lodged.
> It cannot be but he was murder'd here ;
> The least of all these signs were probable.

As the logic of the case, let us not for a moment forget, that, to be of any value, the signs and indications pleaded must be sternly *diagnostic*. The discrimination sought for is between death that is natural, and death that is violent. All indications, therefore, that belong equally and indifferently to either, are equivocal, useless, and alien from the very purpose of the signs here registered by Shakespeare.

her model failed her.[1]   In fact, the Latin language sinks
under the very idea of murder. 'The man was murdered;'
—how will this sound in Latin? *Interfectus est, interemptus
est*—which simply expresses a homicide; and hence the
Christian Latinity of the middle ages was obliged to introduce a new word, such as the feebleness of classic
conceptions never ascended to. *Murdratus est*, says
the sublimer dialect of Gothic ages. Meantime, the Jewish
school of murder kept alive whatever was yet known in the
art, and gradually transferred it to the Western World.
Indeed, the Jewish school was always respectable, even in
its medieval stages, as the case of Hugh of Lincoln shows,
which was honoured with the approbation of Chaucer, on
occasion of another performance from the same school,
which, in his Canterbury Tales, he puts into the mouth of
the Lady Abbess.

Recurring, however, for one moment, to classical
antiquity, I cannot but think that Catiline, Clodius, and
some of that coterie, would have made first-rate artists;
and it is on all accounts to be regretted, that the priggism
of Cicero robbed his country of the only chance she had
for distinction in this line. As the *subject* of a murder, no
person could have answered better than himself. Oh
Gemini! how he would have howled with panic, if he had
heard Cethegus under his bed. It would have been truly
diverting to have listened to him; and satisfied I am,
gentlemen, that he would have preferred the *utile* of creep-

---

[1] At the time of writing this I held the common opinion upon
that subject. Mere inconsideration it was that led to so erroneous
a judgment. Since then, on closer reflection, I have seen ample
reason to retract it: satisfied I now am, that the Romans, in every art
which allowed to them any parity of advantages, had merits as racy,
native, and characteristic, as the best of the Greeks. Elsewhere I shall
plead this cause circumstantially, with the hope of converting the
reader. In the meantime I was anxious to lodge my protest against
this ancient error; an error which commenced in the time-serving
sycophancy of Virgil the court-poet. With the base purpose of grati-
fying Augustus in his vindictive spite against Cicero, and by way of
introducing, therefore, the little clause, *orabunt causas melius* as applying
to all Athenian against all Roman orators, Virgil did not scruple to
sacrifice by wholesale the just pretensions of his compatriots collectively.

ing into a closet, or even into a *cloaca*, to the *honestum* of facing the bold artist.

To come now to the dark ages—(by which we that speak with precision mean, *par excellence*, the tenth century as a meridian line, and the two centuries immediately before and after, full midnight being from A.D. 888 to A.D. 1111) —these ages ought naturally to be favourable to the art of murder, as they were to church architecture, to stained glass, etc. ; and, accordingly, about the latter end of this period, there arose a great character in our art, I mean the Old Man of the Mountains. He was a shining light, indeed, and I need not tell you, that the very word 'assassin' is deduced from him. So keen an amateur was he, that on one occasion, when his own life was attempted by a favourite assassin, he was so much pleased with the talent shown, that, notwithstanding the failure of the artist, he created him a duke upon the spot, with remainder to the female line, and settled a pension on him for three lives. Assassination is a branch of the art which demands a separate notice ; and it is possible that I may devote an entire lecture to it. Meantime, I shall only observe how odd it is, that this branch of the art has flourished by intermitting fits. It never rains, but it pours. Our own age can boast of some fine specimens, such, for instance, as Bellingham's affair with the prime minister Perceval, the Duc de Berri's case at the Parisian Opera House, the Maréchal Bessieres's case at Avignon ; and about two and a half centuries ago, there was a most brilliant constellation of murders in this class. I need hardly say, that I allude especially to those seven splendid works—the assassinations of William I., of Orange ; of the three French Henries, viz.—Henri, Duke of Guise, that had a fancy for the throne of France ; of Henri III., last prince in the line of Valois, who then occupied that throne ; and finally of Henri IV., his brother-in-law, who succeeded to that throne as first prince in the line of Bourbon ; not eighteen years later came the 5th on the roll, viz., that of our Duke of Buckingham (which you will find excellently described in the letters published by

Sir Henry Ellis, of the British Museum), 6thly of
Gustavus Adolphus, and 7thly of Wallenstein. What a
glorious Pleiad of murders! And it increases one's
admiration—that this bright constellation of artistic dis-
plays, comprehending 3 Majesties, 3 Serene Highnesses,
and 1 Excellency, all lay within so narrow a field of time
as between A.D. 1588 and 1635. The King of Sweden's
assassination, by the bye, is doubted by many writers,
Harte amongst others; but they are wrong. He was
murdered; and I consider his murder unique in its
excellence; for he was murdered at noon-day, and on the
field of battle—a feature of original conception, which
occurs in no other work of art that I remember. To
conceive the idea of a secret murder on private account,
as enclosed within a little parenthesis on a vast stage of
public battle-carnage, is like Hamlet's subtle device of a
tragedy within a tragedy. Indeed, all of these assassinations may be studied with profit by the advanced connoisseur. They are all of them *exemplaria*, model murders,
pattern murders, of which one may say—

> Nocturnâ versate manu, versate diurna;

especially *nocturnâ*.

In these assassinations of princes and statesmen, there
is nothing to excite our wonder; important changes often
depend on their deaths; and, from the eminence on which
they stand, they are peculiarly exposed to the aim of every
artist who happens to be possessed by the craving for
scenical effect. But there is another class of assassinations, which has prevailed from an early period of the
seventeenth century, that really *does* surprise me; I mean
the assassination of philosophers. For, gentlemen, it is a
fact, that every philosopher of eminence for the two last
centuries has either been murdered, or, at the least, been
very near it; insomuch, that if a man calls himself a
philosopher, and never had his life attempted, rest assured
there is nothing in him; and against Locke's philosophy
in particular, I think it an unanswerable objection (if we
needed any), that, although he carried his throat about

with him in this world for seventy-two years, no man ever condescended to cut it. As these cases of philosophers are not much known, and are generally good and well composed in their circumstances, I shall here read an excursus on that subject, chiefly by way of showing my own learning.

The first great philosopher of the seventeenth century (if we except Bacon and Galileo) was Des Cartes ; and if ever one could say of a man that he was all *but* murdered —murdered within an inch—one must say it of him. The case was this, as reported by Baillet in his *Vie de M. Des Cartes*, tom. i. pp. 102-3. In the year 1621, when Des Cartes might be about twenty-six years old, he was touring about as usual (for he was as restless as a hyena); and, coming to the Elbe, either at Gluckstadt or at Hamburgh, he took shipping for East Friezland. What he could want in East Friezland no man has ever discovered ; and perhaps he took this into consideration himself; for, on reaching Embden, he resolved to sail instantly for *West* Friezland ; and being very impatient of delay, he hired a bark, with a few mariners to navigate it. No sooner had he got out to sea, than he made a pleasing discovery, viz., that he had shut himself up in a den of murderers. His crew, says M. Baillet, he soon found out to be 'des scélérats'— not *amateurs*, gentlemen, as we are, but professional men — the height of whose ambition at that moment was to cut his individual throat. But the story is too pleasing to be abridged ; I shall give it, therefore, accurately, from the French of his biographer : 'M. Des Cartes had no company but that of his servant, with whom he was conversing in French. The sailors, who took him for a foreign merchant, rather than a cavalier, concluded that he must have money about him. Accordingly, they came to a resolution by no means advantageous to his purse. There is this difference, however, between sea-robbers and the robbers in forests, that the latter may, without hazard, spare the lives of their victims ; whereas the others cannot put a passenger on shore in such a case without running the risk of being

T

apprehended.   The crew of M. Des Cartes arranged their measures with a view to evade any danger of that sort. They observed that he was a stranger from a distance, without acquaintance in the country, and that nobody would take any trouble to inquire about him, in case he should never come to hand (*quand il viendroit à manquer*).' Think, gentlemen, of these Friezland dogs discussing a philosopher as if he were a puncheon of rum consigned to some shipbroker.   'His temper, they remarked, was very mild and patient ; and, judging from the gentleness of his deportment, and the courtesy with which he treated themselves, that he could be nothing more than some green young man, without station or root in the world, they concluded that they should have all the easier task in disposing of his life.   They made no scruple to discuss the whole matter in his presence, as not supposing that he understood any other language than that in which he conversed with his servant ; and the amount of their deliberation was—to murder him, then to throw him into the sea, and to divide his spoils.'

Excuse my laughing, gentlemen ; but the fact is, I always *do* laugh when I think of this case—two things about it seem so droll.   One is, the horrid panic or 'funk' (as the men of Eton call it) in which Des Cartes must have found himself, upon hearing this regular drama sketched for his own death — funeral — succession and administration to his effects.   But another thing which seems to me still more funny about this affair is, that if these Friezland hounds had been 'game,' we should have no Cartesian philosophy ; and how we could have done without *that*, considering the world of books it has produced, I leave to any respectable trunk-maker to declare.

However, to go on : spite of his enormous funk, Des Cartes showed fight, and by that means awed these Anti-Cartesian rascals.   'Finding,' says M. Baillet, 'that the matter was no joke, M. Des Cartes leaped upon his feet in a trice, assumed a stern countenance that these cravens had never looked for, and, addressing them in their own language, threatened to run them through on the spot if they dared to give him any insult.' Certainly, gentlemen, this would have been an honour far above the merits of such inconsiderable rascals—to be spitted like larks upon a Cartesian sword; and therefore I am glad M. Des Cartes did not rob the gallows by executing his threat, especially as he could not possibly have brought his vessel to port, after he had murdered his crew; so that he must have continued to cruise for ever in the Zuyder Zee, and would probably have been mistaken by sailors for the *Flying Dutchman*, homeward bound. 'The spirit which M. Des Cartes manifested,' says his biographer, 'had the effect of magic on these wretches. The suddenness of their consternation struck their minds with a confusion which blinded them to their advantage, and they conveyed him to his destination as peaceably as he could desire.'

Possibly, gentlemen, you may fancy that, on the model of Cæsar's address to his poor ferryman—'*Cæsarem vehis et fortunas ejus*'—M. Des Cartes needed only to have said, 'Dogs, you cannot cut my throat, for you carry Des Cartes and his philosophy,' and might safely have defied them to do their worst. A German emperor had the same notion, when, being cautioned to keep out of the way of a cannonading, he replied, 'Tut! man. Did you ever hear of a cannon-ball that killed an emperor?'[1] As to an emperor I cannot say, but a less thing has sufficed to smash a philosopher; and the next great philosopher of Europe undoubtedly *was* murdered. This was Spinosa.

I know very well the common opinion about him is, that he died in his bed. Perhaps he did, but he was murdered for all that; and this I shall prove by a book published at Brussels in the year 1731, entitled 'La Vie de Spinosa, par M. Jean Colerus,' with many additions, from a MS. life, by one of his friends. Spinosa died on

[1] This same argument has been employed at least once too often: some centuries back a dauphin of France, when admonished of his risk from small-pox, made the same demand as the emperor—'Had any gentleman heard of a dauphin killed by small-pox?' No; not any gentleman *had* heard of such a case. And yet, for all that, this dauphin died of that same small-pox.

the 21st February 1677, being then little more than
forty-four years old.   This, of itself, looks suspicious ;
and M. Jean admits, that a certain expression in the MS.
life of him would warrant the conclusion, ' que sa mort
n'a pas été tout-à-fait naturelle.'   Living in a damp
country, and a sailor's country, like Holland, he may be
thought to have indulged a good deal in grog, especially
in punch,[1] which was then newly discovered. Undoubtedly
he might have done so ; but the fact is, that he did not.
M. Jean calls him ' extrêmement sobre en son boire et en
son manger.'   And though some wild stories were afloat
about his using the juice of mandragora (p. 140) and
opium (p. 144), yet neither of these articles is found in
his druggist's bill.   Living, therefore, with such sobriety,
how was it possible that he should die a natural death at
forty-four ?   Hear his biographer's account :—' Sunday
morning, the 21st of February, before it was church time,
Spinosa came down stairs, and conversed with the master
and mistress of the house.'   At this time, therefore,
perhaps ten o'clock on Sunday morning, you see that
Spinosa was alive, and pretty well.   But it seems ' he had
summoned from Amsterdam a certain physician, whom,'
says the biographer, ' I shall not otherwise point out to
notice than by these two letters, L. M.'   This L. M. had
directed the people of the house to purchase ' an ancient
cock,' and to have him boiled forthwith, in order that
Spinosa might take some broth about noon ; which in
fact he did ; and ate some of the *old cock* with a good
appetite, after the landlord and his wife had returned
from church.

' In the afternoon, L. M. staid alone with Spinosa,
the people of the house having returned to church ; on

---

[1] ' June 1, 1675.—Drinke part of three boules of punch (a liquor
very strainge to me),' says the Rev. Mr. Henry Teonge, in his Diary
published by C. Knight.   In a note on this passage, a reference is
made to Fryer's Travels to the East Indies, 1672, who speaks of ' that
enervating liquor called *paunch* (which is Hindostanee for five), from
five ingredients.'   Made thus, it seems the medical men called it
diapente ; if with four only, diatessaron.   No doubt, it was this
evangelical name that recommended it to the Rev. Mr. Teonge.

coming out from which, they learned, with much surprise, that Spinosa had died about three o'clock, in the presence of L. M., who took his departure for Amsterdam that same evening, by the night-boat, without paying the least attention to the deceased,' and probably without paying very much attention to the payment of his own little account. 'No doubt he was the readier to dispense with these duties, as he had possessed himself of a ducatoon, and a small quantity of silver, together with a silver-hafted knife, and had absconded with his pillage.' Here you see, gentlemen, the murder is plain, and the manner of it. It was L. M. who murdered Spinosa for his money. Poor Spinosa was an invalid, meagre and weak : as no blood was observed, L. M. no doubt threw him down, and smothered him with pillows—the poor man being already half-suffocated by his infernal dinner. After masticating that 'ancient cock,' which I take to mean a cock of the preceding century, in what condition could the poor invalid find himself for a stand-up fight with L. M.? But who was L. M.? It surely never could be Lindley Murray, for I saw him at York in 1825 ; and, besides, I do not think he would do such a thing—at least, not to a brother grammarian : for you know, gentlemen, that Spinosa wrote a very respectable Hebrew grammar.

Hobbes—but why, or on what principle, I never could understand—was not murdered. This was a capital oversight of the professional men in the seventeenth century ; because in every light he was a fine subject for murder, except, indeed, that he was lean and skinny ; for I can prove that he had money, and (what was very funny) he had no right to make the least resistance; since, according to himself, irresistible power creates the very highest species of right, so that it is rebellion of the blackest dye to refuse to be murdered, when a competent force appears to murder you. However, gentlemen, though he was not murdered, I am happy to assure you that (by his own account) he was three times very near being murdered, which is consolatory. The first time was in the spring of 1640, when he pretends to have circulated a little MS. on the king's behalf against the Parliament; he never could produce this MS., by the bye; but he says, that, 'Had not His Majesty dissolved the Parliament' (in May), 'it had brought him into danger of his life.' Dissolving the Parliament, however, was of no use; for in November of the same year the Long Parliament assembled, and Hobbes, a second time fearing he should be murdered, ran away to France. This looks like the madness of John Dennis, who thought that Louis XIV. would never make peace with Queen Anne, unless he (Dennis to wit) were given up to French vengeance; and actually ran away from the sea-coast under that belief. In France, Hobbes managed to take care of his throat pretty well for ten years; but at the end of that time, by way of paying court to Cromwell, he published his 'Leviathan.' The old coward now began to 'funk' horribly for the third time; he fancied the swords of the cavaliers were constantly at his throat, recollecting how they had served the Parliament ambassadors at the Hague and Madrid. 'Tum,' says he, in his dog-Latin life of himself,

> Tum venit in mentem mihi Dorislaus et Ascham;
> Tanquam proscripto terror ubique aderat.

And accordingly he ran home to England. Now, certainly, it is very true that a man deserved a cudgelling for writing 'Leviathan'; and two or three cudgellings for writing a pentameter ending so villainously as 'terror ubique aderat!' But no man ever thought him worthy of anything beyond cudgelling. And, in fact, the whole story is a bounce of his own. For, in a most abusive letter which he wrote 'to a learned person' (meaning Wallis the mathematician), he gives quite another account of the matter, and says (p. 8), he ran home 'because he would not trust his safety with the French clergy;' insinuating that he was likely to be murdered for his religion, which would have been a high joke indeed— Tom's being brought to the stake for religion.

Bounce or not bounce, however, certain it is that Hobbes, to the end of his life, feared that somebody would murder him. This is proved by the story I am going to tell you : it is not from a manuscript, but (as Mr. Coleridge says) it is as good as manuscript ; for it comes from a book now entirely forgotten, viz., 'The Creed of Mr. Hobbes Examined : in a Conference between him and a Student in Divinity' (published about ten years before Hobbes's death). The book is anonymous, but it was written by Tennison, the same who, about thirty years after, succeeded Tillotson as Archbishop of Canterbury. The introductory anecdote is as follows : —'A certain divine' (no doubt Tennison himself) 'took an annual tour of one month to different parts of the island.' In one of these excursions (1670), he visited the Peak in Derbyshire, partly in consequence of Hobbes's description of it. Being in that neighbourhood, he could not but pay a visit to Buxton ; and at the very moment of his arrival, he was fortunate enough to find a party of gentlemen dismounting at the inn-door, amongst whom was a long thin fellow, who turned out to be no less a person than Mr. Hobbes, who probably had ridden over from Chatsworth.[1] Meeting so great a lion, a tourist, in search of the picturesque, could do no less than present himself in the character of bore. And luckily for this scheme, two of Mr. Hobbes's companions were suddenly summoned away by express ; so that, for the rest of his stay at Buxton, he had Leviathan entirely to himself, and had the honour of bowsing with him in the evening. Hobbes, it seems, at first showed a good deal of stiffness, for he was shy of divines ; but this wore off, and he became very sociable and funny, and they agreed to go

[1] Chatsworth was then, as now, the superb seat of the Cavendishes in their highest branch—in those days Earl, at present Duke, of Devonshire. It is to the honour of this family that, through two generations, they gave an asylum to Hobbes. It is noticeable that Hobbes was born in the year of the Spanish Armada, *i.e.* in 1588 : such, at least, is my belief [5th April 1588, the day being the Good Friday of that year]. And, therefore, at this meeting with Tennison in 1670, he must have been about 82 years old.

into the bath together. How Tennison could venture
to gambol in the same water with Leviathan, I cannot
explain ; but so it was : they frolicked about like two
dolphins, though Hobbes must have been as old as the
hills ; and 'in those intervals wherein they abstained from
swimming and plunging themselves' (*i.e.*, diving), 'they
discoursed of many things relating to the baths of the
Ancients, and the Origine of Springs. When they had in
this manner passed away an hour, they stepped out of the
bath ; and, having dried and cloathed themselves, they
sate down in expectation of such a supper as the place
afforded ; designing to refresh themselves like the *Deipno-
sophistæ*, and rather to reason than to drink profoundly.
But in this innocent intention they were interrupted by
the disturbance arising from a little quarrel, in which some
of the ruder people in the house were for a short time
engaged. At this Mr. Hobbes seemed much concerned,
though he was at some distance from the persons.' And
why was he concerned, gentlemen ? No doubt, you fancy,
from some benign and disinterested love of peace, worthy
of an old man and a philosopher. But listen—'For
awhile he was not composed, but related it once or twice
as to himself, with a low and careful, *i.e.*, anxious, tone,
how Sextus Roscius was murthered after supper by the
Balneæ Palatinæ. Of such general extent is that remark
of Cicero, in relation to Epicurus the Atheist, of whom
he observed, that he of all men dreaded most those things
which he contemned—Death and the Gods.' Merely
because it was supper time, and in the neighbourhood
of a bath, Mr. Hobbes must have the fate of Sextus
Roscius. He must be mur*th*ered, because Sextus Roscius
was mur*th*ered. What logic was there in this, unless to
a man who was always dreaming of murder ? Here was
Leviathan, no longer afraid of the daggers of English
cavaliers or French clergy, but 'frightened from his propriety' by a row in an alehouse between some honest
clod-hoppers of Derbyshire, whom his own gaunt scarecrow of a person, that belonged to quite another century,
would have frightened out of their wits.

Malebranche, it will give you pleasure to hear, was murdered. The man who murdered him is well known : it was Bishop Berkeley. The story is familiar, though hitherto not put in a proper light. Berkeley, when a young man, went to Paris, and called on Père Malebranche. He found him in his cell cooking. Cooks have ever been a *genus irritabile*; authors still more so : Malebranche was both : a dispute arose ; the old father, warm already, became warmer ; culinary and metaphysical irritations united to derange his liver : he took to his bed, and died. Such is the common version of the story : ' So the whole ear of Denmark is abused.' The fact is, that the matter was hushed up, out of consideration for Berkeley, who (as Pope justly observes) had 'every virtue under heaven :' else it was well known that Berkeley, feeling himself nettled by the waspishness of the old Frenchman, squared at him ; a *turn-up* was the consequence : Malebranche was floored in the first round ; the conceit was wholly taken out of him ; and he would perhaps have given in ; but Berkeley's blood was now up, and he insisted on the old Frenchman's retracting his doctrine of Occasional Causes. The vanity of the man was too great for this ; and he fell a sacrifice to the impetuosity of Irish youth, combined with his own absurd obstinacy.

Leibnitz being every way superior to Malebranche, one might, *a fortiori*, have counted on *his* being murdered ; which, however, was not the case. I believe he was nettled at this neglect, and felt himself insulted by the security in which he passed his days. In no other way can I explain his conduct at the latter end of his life, when he chose to grow very avaricious, and to hoard up large sums of gold, which he kept in his own house. This was at Vienna, where he died ; and letters are still in existence, describing the immeasurable anxiety which he entertained for his throat. Still his ambition, for being *attempted* at least, was so great, that he would not forego the danger. A late English pedagogue, of Birmingham manufacture— viz., Dr. Parr—took a more selfish course under the same circumstance. He had amassed a considerable quantity

of gold and silver plate, which was for some time deposited
in his bedroom at his parsonage house, Hatton. But
growing every day more afraid of being murdered, which
he knew that he could not stand (and to which, indeed,
he never had the slightest pretensions), he transferred the
whole to the Hatton blacksmith ; conceiving, no doubt,
that the murder of a blacksmith would fall more lightly
on the *salus reipublicæ*, than that of a pedagogue. But
I have heard this greatly disputed ; and it seems now
generally agreed, that one good horseshoe is worth about
two and a quarter Spital sermons.[1]

As Leibnitz, though not murdered, may be said to
have died partly of the fear that he should be murdered,
and partly of vexation that he was not, Kant, on the other
hand—who manifested no ambition in that way—had a
narrower escape from a murderer than any man we read of,
except Des Cartes. So absurdly does fortune throw about
her favours ! The case is told, I think, in an anonymous
life of this very great man. For health's sake, Kant
imposed upon himself, at one time, a walk of six miles
every day along a high-road. This fact becoming known
to a man who had his private reasons for committing
murder, at the third milestone from Königsberg, he waited
for his 'intended,' who came up to time as duly as a mail-
coach.

But for an accident, Kant was a dead man. This
accident lay in the scrupulous, or what Mrs. Quickly
would have called the *peevish*, morality of the murderer.
An old professor, he fancied, might be laden with sins.
Not so a young child. On this consideration, he turned
away from Kant at the critical moment, and soon after
murdered a child of five years old. Such is the German
account of the matter ; but my opinion is, that the mur-

---

[1] '*Spital Sermons :*' Dr. Parr's chief public appearances as an
author, after his original appearance in the famous Latin preface to
Bellendēnus (don't say Bellendĕnus), occurred in certain sermons at
periodic intervals, delivered on behalf of some hospital (I really forget
what) which retained for its official designation the old word *Spital;*
and thus it happened that the sermons themselves were generally known
by the title of *Spital* Sermons.

derer was an amateur, who felt how little would be gained
to the cause of good taste by murdering an old, arid, and
adust metaphysician ; there was no room for display, as
the man could not possibly look more like a mummy when
dead, than he had done alive.

Thus, gentlemen, I have traced the connection between
philosophy and our art, until insensibly I find that I have
wandered into our own era. This I shall not take any
pains to characterise apart from that which preceded it,
for, in fact, they have no distinct character. The seventeenth and eighteenth centuries, together with so much of
the nineteenth as we have yet seen, jointly compose the
Augustan age of murder. The finest work of the seventeenth century is, unquestionably, the murder of Sir
Edmondbury Godfrey, which has my entire approbation.
In the grand feature of *mystery*, which in some shape or other
ought to colour every judicious attempt at murder, it is excellent ; for the mystery is not yet dispersed. The attempt to
fasten the murder upon the Papists, which would injure it
as much as some well-known Correggios have been injured
by the professional picture-cleaners, or would even ruin it
by translating it into the spurious class of mere political
or partisan murders, thoroughly wanting in the murderous
animus, I exhort the society to discountenance. In fact,
this notion is altogether baseless, and arose in pure Protestant fanaticism. Sir Edmondbury had not distinguished
himself amongst the London magistrates by any severity
against the Papists, or in favouring the attempts of zealots
to enforce the penal laws against individuals. He had
not armed against himself the animosities of any religious
sect whatever. And as to the droppings of wax-lights
upon the dress of the corpse when first discovered in a
ditch, from which it was inferred at the time that the
priests attached to the Popish Queen's Chapel had been
concerned in the murder, either these were mere fraudulent
artifices devised by those who wished to fix the suspicion
upon the Papists, or else the whole allegation—wax-drop-
pings, and the suggested cause of the droppings—might
be a bounce or fib of Bishop Burnet ; who, as the Duchess

of Portsmouth used to say, was the one great master of fibbing and romancing in the seventeenth century. At the same time, it must be observed that the quantity of murder was not great in Sir Edmondbury's century, at least amongst our own artists; which, perhaps, is attributable to the want of enlightened patronage. *Sint Mæcenates, non deerunt, Flacce, Marones.* Consulting Grant's *Observations on the Bills of Mortality* (4th edition, Oxford, 1665), I find, that, out of 229,250, who died in London during one period of twenty years in the seventeenth century, not more than eighty-six were murdered; that is, about four three-tenths per annum. A small number this, gentlemen, to found an academy upon; and certainly, where the quantity is so small, we have a right to expect that the quality should be first-rate. Perhaps it was; yet still I am of opinion that the best artist in this century was not equal to the best in that which followed. For instance, however praiseworthy the case of Sir Edmondbury Godfrey may be (and nobody can be more sensible of its merits than I am), still, I cannot consent to place it on a level with that of Mrs. Ruscombe of Bristol, either as to originality of design, or boldness and breadth of style. This good lady's murder took place early in the reign of George III.—a reign which was notoriously favourable to the arts generally. She lived in College Green, with a single maid-servant, neither of them having any pretension to the notice of history but what they derived from the great artist whose workmanship I am recording. One fine morning, when all Bristol was alive and in motion, some suspicion arising, the neighbours forced an entrance into the house, and found Mrs. Ruscombe murdered in her bedroom, and the servant murdered on the stairs: this was at noon; and, not more than two hours before, both mistress and servant had been seen alive. To the best of my remembrance, this was in 1764; upwards of sixty years, therefore, have now elapsed, and yet the artist is still undiscovered. The suspicions of posterity have settled upon two pretenders—a baker and a chimney-sweeper. But posterity is wrong; no un-

practised artist could have conceived so bold an idea as
that of a noonday murder in the heart of a great city.   It
was no obscure baker, gentlemen, or anonymous chimney-
sweeper, be assured, that executed this work.   I know who
it was.   (*Here there was a general buzz, which at length
broke out into open applause; upon which the lecturer blushed,
and went on with much earnestness.*)   For heaven's sake,
gentlemen, do not mistake me ; it was not I that did it.
I have not the vanity to think myself equal to any such
achievement ; be assured that you greatly overrate my
poor talents ; Mrs. Ruscombe's affair was far beyond my
slender abilities.   But I came to know who the artist was,
from a celebrated surgeon who assisted at his dissection.
This gentleman had a private museum in the way of his
profession, one corner of which was occupied by a cast
from a man of remarkably fine proportions.

' That,' said the surgeon, ' is a cast from the celebrated
Lancashire highwayman, who concealed his profession for
some time from his neighbours, by drawing woollen stock-
ings over his horse's legs, and in that way muffling the
clatter which he must else have made in riding up a flagged
alley that led to his stable.   At the time of his execution
for highway robbery, I was studying under Cruickshank :
and the man's figure was so uncommonly fine, that no
money or exertion was spared to get into possession of
him with the least possible delay.   By the connivance of
the under-sheriff, he was cut down within the legal time,
and instantly put into a chaise-and-four ; so that, when he
reached Cruickshank's, he was positively not dead.   Mr.
——, a young student at that time, had the honour of
giving him the *coup de grâce*, and finishing the sentence of
the law.'   This remarkable anecdote, which seemed to
imply that all the gentlemen in the dissecting-room were
amateurs of our class, struck me a good deal ; and I was
repeating it one day to a Lancashire lady, who thereupon
informed me, that she had herself lived in the neighbourhood of that highwayman, and well remembered two
circumstances, which combined, in the opinion of all his
neighbours, to fix upon him the credit of Mrs. Ruscombe's

affair. One was, the fact of his absence for a whole fortnight at the period of that murder ; the other, that, within
a very little time after, the neighbourhood of this highwayman was deluged with dollars : now, Mrs. Ruscombe
was known to have hoarded about two thousand of that
coin. Be the artist, however, who he might, the affair
remains a durable monument of his genius ; for such was
the impression of awe, and the sense of power left behind,
by the strength of conception manifested in this murder,
that no tenant (as I was told in 1810) had been found up
to that time for Mrs. Ruscombe's house.

But, whilst I thus eulogise the Ruscombian case, let
me not be supposed to overlook the many other specimens
of extraordinary merit spread over the face of this century.
Such cases, indeed, as that of Miss Bland, or of Captain
Donnellan and Sir Theophilus Boughton, shall never have
any countenance from me. Fie on these dealers in poison,
say I : can they not keep to the old honest way of cutting
throats, without introducing such abominable innovations
from Italy ?   I consider all these poisoning cases, compared
with the legitimate style, as no better than waxwork by
the side of sculpture, or a lithographic print by the side
of a fine Volpato. But, dismissing these, there remain
many excellent works of art in a pure style, such as
nobody need be ashamed to own ; and this every candid
connoisseur will admit. *Candid*, observe, I say ; for great
allowances must be made in these cases ; no artist can
ever be sure of carrying through his own fine preconcep-
tion. Awkward disturbances will arise ; people will not
submit to have their throats cut quietly ; they will run,
they will kick, they will bite ; and whilst the portrait
painter often has to complain of too much torpor in his
subject, the artist in our line is generally embarrassed by
too much animation. At the same time, however disagreeable to the artist, this tendency in murder to excite
and irritate the subject is certainly one of its advantages
to the world in general, which we ought not to overlook,
since it favours the development of latent talent. Jeremy
Taylor notices with admiration the extraordinary leaps

which people will take under the influence of fear.   There
was a striking instance of this in the recent case of the
M'Keans : the boy cleared a height, such as he will never
clear again to his dying day.   Talents also of the most
brilliant description for thumping, and, indeed, for all the
gymnastic exercises, have sometimes been developed by the
panic which accompanies our artists ; talents else buried
and hid under a bushel, to the possessors, as much as to
their friends.   I remember an interesting illustration of
this fact, in a case of which I learned in Germany.

Riding one day in the neighbourhood of Munich,
I overtook a distinguished amateur of our society, whose
name, for obvious reasons, I shall conceal.   This gentleman informed me that, finding himself wearied with the
frigid pleasures (such he esteemed them) in mere amateur-
ship, he had quitted England for the Continent—meaning
to practise a little professionally.   For this purpose he
resorted to Germany, conceiving the police in that part
of Europe to be more heavy and drowsy than elsewhere.
His *début* as a practitioner took place at Mannheim ; and,
knowing me to be a brother amateur, he freely communicated the whole of his maiden adventure.   'Opposite to
my lodging,' said he, lived a baker : he was somewhat
of a miser, and lived quite alone.   Whether it were his
great expanse of chalky face, or what else, I know not,
but the fact was, I "fancied" him, and resolved to
commence business upon his throat, which, by the way,
he always carried bare—a fashion which is very irritating
to my desires.   Precisely at eight o'clock in the evening,
I observed that he regularly shut up his windows.   One
night I watched him when thus engaged—bolted in after
him—locked the door—and, addressing him with great
suavity, acquainted him with the nature of my errand ; at
the same time advising him to make no resistance, which
would be mutually unpleasant.   So saying, I drew out
my tools ; and was proceeding to operate.   But at this
spectacle the baker, who seemed to have been struck by
catalepsy at my first announcement, awoke into tremendous
agitation.   "I will *not* be murdered !" he shrieked aloud ;

"what for will I" (meaning *shall* I) "lose my precious
throat ?"—"What for ?" said I; "if for no other reason,
for this—that you put alum into your bread. But no
matter, alum or no alum (for I was resolved to forestall
any argument on that point), know that I am a virtuoso
in the art of murder—am desirous of improving myself
in its details—and am enamoured of your vast surface of
throat, to which I am determined to be a customer."—
"Is it so ?" said he, "but I'll find you a customer in
another line;" and so saying, he threw himself into a
boxing attitude. The very idea of his boxing struck me
as ludicrous. It is true, a London baker had distinguished
himself in the ring, and became known to fame under the
title of the Master of the Rolls; but he was young and
unspoiled: whereas, this man was a monstrous feather-
bed in person, fifty years old, and totally out of condition.
Spite of all this, however, and contending against me, who
am a master in the art, he made so desperate a defence,
that many times I feared he might turn the tables upon
me; and that I, an amateur, might be murdered by a
rascally baker. What a situation! Minds of sensibility
will sympathise with my anxiety. How severe it was,
you may understand by this, that for the first thirteen
rounds the baker positively had the advantage. Round
the 14th, I received a blow on the right eye, which closed
it up; in the end, I believe, this was my salvation; for
the anger it roused in me was so great, that, in the next,
and every one of the three following rounds, I floored the
baker.

'Round 19th. The baker came up piping, and mani-
festly the worse for wear. His geometrical exploits in the
four last rounds had done him no good. However, he
showed some skill in stopping a message which I was sending to his cadaverous mug; in delivering which, my foot
slipped, and I went down.

'Round 20th. Surveying the baker, I became
ashamed of having been so much bothered by a shapeless mass of dough; and I went in fiercely, and
administered some severe punishment. A rally took

place—both went down—baker undermost—ten to three
on amateur.

'Round 21st. The baker jumped up with surprising
agility ; indeed, he managed his pins capitally, and fought
wonderfully, considering that he was drenched in perspiration ; but the shine was now taken out of him, and his
game was the mere effect of panic. It was now clear that
he could not last much longer. In the course of this
round we tried the weaving system, in which I had greatly
the advantage, and hit him repeatedly on the conk. My
reason for this was, that his conk was covered with car-
buncles ; and I thought I should vex him by taking such
liberties with his conk, which in fact I did.

'The three next rounds, the master of the rolls staggered
about like a cow on the ice. Seeing how matters stood, in
round 24th I whispered something into his ear, which sent
him down like a shot. It was nothing more than my
private opinion of the value of his throat at an annuity
office. This little confidential whisper affected him greatly ;
the very perspiration was frozen on his face, and for the
next two rounds I had it all my own way. And when
I called *time* for the 27th round, he lay like a log on the
floor.'

After which, said I to the amateur, 'It may be presumed that you accomplished your purpose.'—'You are
right,' said he mildly, 'I did ; and a great satisfaction, you
know, it was to my mind, for by this means I killed two
birds with one stone' ; meaning that he had both thumped
the baker and murdered him. Now, for the life of me, I
could not see *that* ; for, on the contrary, to my mind it
appeared that he had taken two stones to kill one bird,
having been obliged to take the conceit out of him first
with his fist, and then with his tools. But no matter for
his logic. The moral of his story was good, for it showed
what an astonishing stimulus to latent talent is contained
in any reasonable prospect of being murdered. A pursy,
unwieldy, half cataleptic baker of Mannheim had absolutely
fought seven-and-twenty rounds with an accomplished
English boxer, merely upon this inspiration ; so greatly

was natural genius exalted and sublimed by the genial presence of his murderer.

Really, gentlemen, when one hears of such things as these, it becomes a duty, perhaps, a little to soften that extreme asperity with which most men speak of murder. To hear people talk, you would suppose that all the disadvantages and inconveniences were on the side of being murdered, and that there were none at all in *not* being murdered. But considerate men think otherwise. 'Certainly,' says Jeremy Taylor, 'it is a less temporal evil to fall by the rudeness of a sword than the violence of a fever : and the axe' (to which he might have added the ship-carpenter's mallet and the crowbar), 'a much less affliction than a strangury.' Very true ; the bishop talks like a wise man and an amateur, as I am sure he was ; and another great philosopher, Marcus Aurelius, was equally above the vulgar prejudices on this subject. He declares it to be one of 'the noblest functions of reason to know whether it is time to walk out of the world or not' (Book III., Collier's Translation). No sort of knowledge being rarer than this, surely *that* man must be a most philanthropic character, who undertakes to instruct people in this branch of knowledge gratis, and at no little hazard to himself. All this, however, I throw out only in the way of speculation to future moralists ; declaring in the meantime my own private conviction, that very few men commit murder upon philanthropic or patriotic principles, and repeating what I have already said once at least—that, as to the majority of murderers, they are very incorrect characters.

With respect to the Williams murders, the sublimest and most entire in their excellence that ever were committed, I shall not allow myself to speak incidentally. Nothing less than an entire lecture, or even an entire course of lectures, would suffice to expound their merits. But one curious fact connected with his case I shall mention, because it seems to imply that the blaze of his genius absolutely dazzled the eye of criminal justice. You all remember, I doubt not, that the instruments

with which he executed his first great work (the murder
of the Marrs) were a ship-carpenter's mallet and a knife.
Now, the mallet belonged to an old Swede, one John
Peterson, and bore his initials.   This instrument Williams
left behind him in Marr's house, and it fell into the hands
of the magistrates.   But, gentlemen, it is a fact that the
publication of this circumstance of the initials led immediately to the apprehension of Williams, and, if made earlier,
would have prevented his second great work (the murder
of the Williamsons), which took place precisely twelve
days after.   Yet the magistrates kept back this fact from
the public for the entire twelve days, and until that second
work was accomplished.   That finished, they published it,
apparently feeling that Williams had now done enough for
his fame, and that his glory was at length placed beyond
the reach of accident.

As to Mr. Thurtell's case, I know not what to say.
Naturally, I have every disposition to think highly of my
predecessor in the chair of this society ; and I acknowledge that his lectures were unexceptionable.   But, speaking
ingenuously, I do really think that his principal performance, as an artist, has been much overrated.   I admit,
that at first I was myself carried away by the general
enthusiasm.   On the morning when the murder was made
known in London, there was the fullest meeting of
amateurs that I have ever known since the days of
Williams ; old bedridden connoisseurs, who had got into
a peevish way of sneering and complaining 'that there
was nothing doing,' now hobbled down to our club-room :
such hilarity, such benign expression of general satisfaction, I have rarely witnessed.   On every side you saw
people shaking hands, congratulating each other, and
forming dinner parties for the evening ; and nothing was
to be heard but triumphant challenges of—'Well ! will
this do?'   'Is *this* the right thing?'   'Are you satisfied
at last?'   But, in the middle of the row, I remember, we
all grew silent, on hearing the old cynical amateur L.
S—— stumping along with his wooden leg ; he entered
the room with his usual scowl ; and, as he advanced, he

continued to growl and stutter the whole way—'Mere
plagiarism—base plagiarism from hints that I threw out!
Besides, his style is as harsh as Albert Durer, and as
coarse as Fuseli.' Many thought that this was mere
jealousy, and general waspishness; but I confess that,
when the first glow of enthusiasm had subsided, I have
found most judicious critics to agree that there was something *falsetto* in the style of Thurtell. The fact is, he
was a member of our society, which naturally gave a
friendly bias to our judgments; and his person was universally familiar to the 'fancy,' which gave him, with the
whole London public, a temporary popularity, that his
pretensions are not capable of supporting; for *opinionum
commenta delet dies, naturæ judicia confirmat.* There was,
however, an unfinished design of Thurtell's for the murder
of a man with a pair of dumb-bells, which I admired
greatly; it was a mere outline, that he never filled in;
but to my mind it seemed every way superior to his chief
work. I remember that there was great regret expressed
by some amateurs that this sketch should have been left
in an unfinished state: but there I cannot agree with
them; for the fragments and first bold outlines of original
artists have often a felicity about them which is apt to
vanish in the management of the details.

The case of the M'Keans I consider far beyond the
vaunted performance of Thurtell — indeed, above all
praise; and bearing that relation, in fact, to the immortal
works of Williams, which the 'Æneid' bears to the
'Iliad.'

But it is now time that I should say a few words about
the principles of murder, not with a view to regulate your
practice, but your judgment: as to old women, and the
mob of newspaper readers, they are pleased with anything,
provided it is bloody enough. But the mind of sensibility
requires something more. *First*, then, let us speak of the
kind of person who is adapted to the purpose of the
murderer; *secondly*, of the place where; *thirdly*, of the
time when, and other little circumstances.

As to the person, I suppose it is evident that he ought

to be a good man, because, if he were not, he might himself, by possibility, be contemplating murder at the very
time ; and such 'diamond-cut-diamond' tussles, though
pleasant enough where nothing better is stirring, are really
not what a critic can allow himself to call murders. I
could mention some people (I name no names) who have
been murdered by other people in a dark lane ; and so
far all seemed correct enough ; but, on looking further
into the matter, the public have become aware that the
murdered party was himself, at the moment, planning to
rob his murderer, at the least, and possibly to murder him,
if he had been strong enough. Whenever that is the case,
or may be thought to be the case, farewell to all the
genuine effects of the art. For the final purpose of
murder, considered as a fine art, is precisely the same as
that of tragedy, in Aristotle's account of it ; viz., 'to
cleanse the heart by means of pity and terror.' Now,
terror there may be, but how can there be any pity for
one tiger destroyed by another tiger ?

It is also evident that the person selected ought not
to be a public character. For instance, no judicious artist
would have attempted to murder Abraham Newland.[1] For
the case was this : everybody read so much about Abraham
Newland, and so few people ever saw him, that to the general
belief he was a mere abstract idea. And I remember,
that once, when I happened to mention that I had dined
at a coffee-house in company with Abraham Newland,
everybody looked scornfully at me, as though I had
pretended to have played at billiards with Prester John,
or to have had an affair of honour with the Pope. And,
by the way, the Pope would be a very improper person to
murder : for he has such a virtual ubiquity as the father

---

[1] Abraham Newland [chief cashier of the Bank of England, who
died 1807] is now utterly forgotten. But when this was written
[1827], his name had not ceased to ring in British ears, as the most
familiar and most significant that perhaps has ever existed. It was the
name which appeared on the face of all Bank of England notes, great
or small ; and had been, for more than a quarter of a century (especially through the whole career of the French Revolution), a short-hand
expression for paper money in its safest form.

of Christendom, and, like the cuckoo, is so often heard but never seen, that I suspect most people regard *him* also as an abstract idea. Where, indeed, a public man is in the habit of giving dinners, ' with every delicacy of the season,' the case is very different : every person is satisfied that *he* is no abstract idea ; and, therefore, there can be no impropriety in murdering him ; only that his murder will fall into the class of assassinations, which I have not yet treated.

Thirdly. The subject chosen ought to be in good health : for it is absolutely barbarous to murder a sick person, who is usually quite unable to bear it. On this principle, no tailor ought to be chosen who is above twenty-five, for after that age he is sure to be dyspeptic. Or at least, if a man will hunt in that warren, he will of course think it his duty, on the old established equation, to murder some multiple of 9—say 18, 27, or 36. And here, in this benign attention to the comfort of sick people, you will observe the usual effect of a fine art to soften and refine the feelings. The world in general, gentlemen, are very bloody-minded ; and all they want in a murder is a copious effusion of blood ; gaudy display in this point is enough for *them*. But the enlightened connoisseur is more refined in his taste ; and from our art, as from all the other liberal arts when thoroughly mastered, the result is, to humanise the heart ; so true is it, that

Ingenuas didicisse fideliter artes,
Emollit mores, nec sinit esse feros.

A philosophic friend, well known for his philanthropy and general benignity, suggests that the subject chosen ought also to have a family of young children wholly dependent on his exertions, by way of deepening the pathos. And, undoubtedly, this is a judicious caution. Yet I would not insist too keenly on such a condition. Severe good taste unquestionably suggests it ; but still, where the man was otherwise unobjectionable in point of morals and health, I would not look with too curious a jealousy to a restriction which might have the effect of narrowing the artist's sphere.

So much for the person. As to the time, the place, and the tools, I have many things to say, which at present I have no room for. The good sense of the practitioner has usually directed him to night and privacy. Yet there have not been wanting cases where this rule was departed from with excellent effect. In respect to time, Mrs. Ruscombe's case is a beautiful exception, which I have already noticed ; and in respect both to time and place, there is a fine exception in the annals of Edinburgh (year 1805), familiar to every child in Edinburgh, but which has unaccountably been defrauded of its due portion of fame amongst English amateurs. The case I mean is that of a porter to one of the banks, who was murdered, whilst carrying a bag of money, in broad daylight, on turning out of the High Street, one of the most public streets in Europe ; and the murderer is to this hour undiscovered.

> Sed fugit interea, fugit irreparabile tempus,
> Singula dum capti circumvectamur amore.

And now, gentlemen, in conclusion, let me again solemnly disclaim all pretensions on my part to the character of a professional man. I never attempted any murder in my life, except in the year 1801, upon the body of a tom-cat ; and *that* turned out differently from my intention. My purpose, I own, was downright murder. ' Semper ego auditor tantum ? ' said I, ' nun- quamne reponam ? ' And I went down-stairs in search of Tom at one o'clock on a dark night, with the ' animus,' and no doubt with the fiendish looks, of a murderer. But when I found him, he was in the act of plundering the pantry of bread and other things. Now this gave a new turn to the affair ; for the time being one of general scarcity, when even Christians were reduced to the use of potato-bread, rice-bread, and all sorts of things, it was downright treason in a tom-cat to be wasting good wheaten-bread in the way he was doing. It instantly became a patriotic duty to put him to death ; and, as I raised aloft

and shook the glittering steel, I fancied myself rising, like
Brutus, effulgent from a crowd of patriots, and, as I
stabbed him, I

> Call'd aloud on Tully's name,
> And bade the father of his country hail !

Since then, what wandering thoughts I may have had
of attempting the life of an ancient ewe, of a superannuated
hen, and such ' small deer,' are locked up in the secrets of
my own breast ; but, for the higher departments of the
art, I confess myself to be utterly unfit. My ambition
does not rise so high. No, gentlemen, in the words of
Horace,

> Fungar vice cotis, acutum
> Reddere quæ ferrum valet, exsors ipsa secandi.

SUPPLEMENTARY PAPER ON MURDER
CONSIDERED AS ONE OF THE FINE ARTS

A GOOD many years ago, the reader may remember that I
came forward in the character of a *dilettante* in murder.
Perhaps *dilettante* is too strong a word. *Connoisseur* is
better suited to the scruples and infirmity of public taste.
I suppose there is no harm in *that*, at least. A man is not
bound to put his eyes, ears, and understanding into his
breeches-pocket when he meets with a murder. If he is
not in a downright comatose state, I suppose he must see
that one murder is better or worse than another, in point
of good taste. Murders have their little differences and
shades of merit, as well as statues, pictures, oratorios,
cameos, intaglios, or what not. You may be angry with
the man for talking too much, or too publicly (as to the
too much, that I deny—a man can never cultivate his taste
too highly) ; but you must allow him to think, at any rate.
Well, would you believe it? all my neighbours came to
hear of that little æsthetic essay which I had published ;
and, unfortunately, hearing at the very same time of a club
that I was connected with, and a dinner at which I presided
—both tending to the same little object as the essay, viz.,
the diffusion of a just taste among Her [1] Majesty's subjects,
they got up the most barbarous calumnies against me. In

[1] *Her* Majesty : In the lecture, having occasion to refer to the
reigning sovereign, I ⸻ '*His* Majesty'; for at that time [1827]
William IV. was on the throne [no : George IV.] : but between the
lecture and this supplement had occurred the accession of our present
Queen.

particular, they said that I, or that the club (which comes to the same thing), had offered bounties on well-conducted homicides—with a scale of drawbacks, in case of any one defect or flaw, according to a table issued to private friends. Now, let me tell the whole truth about the dinner and the club, and it will be seen how malicious the world is. But first, confidentially, allow me to say what my real principles are upon the matter in question.

As to murder, I never committed one in my life. It's a well-known thing amongst all my friends. I can get a paper to certify as much, signed by lots of people. Indeed, if you come to that, I doubt whether many people could produce as strong a certificate. Mine would be as big as a breakfast tablecloth. There is indeed one member of the club, who pretends to say he caught me once making too free with his throat on a club night, after everybody else had retired. But, observe, he shuffles in his story according to his state of civilation. When not far gone, he contents himself with saying that he caught me ogling his throat ; and that I was melancholy for some weeks after, and that my voice sounded in a way expressing, to the nice ear of a connoisseur, *the sense of opportunities lost;* but the club all know that he is a disappointed man himself, and that he speaks querulously at times about the fatal neglect of a man's coming abroad without his tools. Besides, all this is an affair between two amateurs, and everybody makes allowances for little asperities and fibs in such a case. ' But,' say you, ' if no murderer, you may have encouraged, or even have bespoken a murder.' No, upon my honour —no. And that was the very point I wished to argue for your satisfaction. The truth is, I am a very particular man in everything relating to murder ; and perhaps I carry my delicacy too far. The Stagirite most justly, and possibly with a view to my case, placed virtue in the τὸ μέσον, or middle point between two extremes. A golden mean is certainly what every man should aim at. But it is easier talking than doing ; and, my infirmity being notoriously too much milkiness of heart, I find it difficult to maintain that steady equatorial line between the two poles of too much murder on the one hand, and too little on the other. I am too soft—and people get excused through me—nay, go through life without an attempt made upon them, that ought *not* to be excused. I believe, if I had the management of things, there would hardly be a murder from year's end to year's end. In fact, I'm for peace, and quietness, and fawningness, and what may be styled *knocking-underness*. A man came to me as a candidate for the place of my servant, just then vacant. He had the reputation of having dabbled a little in our art ; some said, not without merit. What startled me, however, was that he supposed this art to be part of his regular duties in my service, and talked of having it considered in his wages. Now, that was a thing I would not allow ; so I said at once, 'Richard (or James, as the case might be), you misunderstand my character. If a man will and must practise this difficult (and allow me to add, dangerous) branch of art—if he has an overruling genius for it—why, in that case, all I say is, that he might as well pursue his studies whilst living in my service as in another's. And also, I may observe, that it can do no harm either to himself or to the subject on whom he operates, that he should be guided by men of more taste than himself. Genius may do much, but long study of the art must always entitle a man to offer advice. So far I will go—general principles I will suggest. But as to any particular case, once for all I will have nothing to do with it. Never tell me of any special work of art you are meditating—I set my face against it *in toto*. For, if once a man indulges himself in murder, very soon he comes to think little of robbing ; and from robbing he comes next to drinking and Sabbath-breaking, and from that to incivility and procrastination. Once begin upon this downward path, you never know where you are to stop. Many a man has dated his ruin from some murder or other that perhaps he thought little of at the time. *Principiis obsta*—that's my rule.' Such was my speech, and I have always acted up to it ; so, if that is not being virtuous, I should be glad to know what is. But now about the dinner and the club. The club was

not particularly of my creation ; it arose pretty much as
other similar associations, for the propagation of truth and
the communication of new ideas ; rather from the necessities
of things, than upon any one man's suggestion. As to the
dinner, if any man more than another could be held
responsible for that, it was a member known amongst us
by the name of *Toad-in-the-hole*. He was so called from
his gloomy misanthropical disposition, which led him into
constant disparagements of all modern murders as vicious
abortions, belonging to no authentic school of art.   The
finest performances of our own age he snarled at cynically ;
and at length this querulous humour grew upon him so
much, and he became so notorious as a *laudator temporis
acti*, that few people cared to seek his society.   This made
him still more fierce and truculent.   He went about
muttering and growling ; wherever you met him, he was
soliloquising, and saying, 'Despicable pretender—without
grouping—without two ideas upon handling—without
——' and there you lost him. At length existence seemed
to be painful to him ; he rarely spoke, he seemed conversing with phantoms in the air ; his housekeeper informed
us that his reading was nearly confined to 'God's Revenge
upon Murder,' by Reynolds, and a more ancient book of
the same title, noticed by Sir Walter Scott in his 'Fortunes
of Nigel.' Sometimes, perhaps, he might read in the
'Newgate Calendar' down to the year 1788, but he never
looked into a book more recent.   In fact, he had a theory
with regard to the French Revolution, as having been the
great cause of degeneration in murder. 'Very soon, sir,'
he used to say, 'men will have lost the art of killing
poultry : the very rudiments of the art will have perished !'
In the year 1811, he retired from general society.   Toad-
in-the-hole was no more seen in any public resort.   We
missed him from his wonted haunts—'nor up the lawn,
nor at the wood was he.' By the side of the main conduit
his listless length at noontide he would stretch, and pore
upon the filth that muddled by. 'Even dogs,' this pensive
moralist would say, 'are not what they were, sir—not what
they should be.   I remember in my grandfather's time

that some dogs had an idea of murder. I have known a
mastiff, sir, that lay in ambush for a rival, yes, sir, and
finally murdered him, with pleasing circumstances of good
taste. I also was on intimate terms of acquaintance with
a tom-cat that was an assassin. But now——' and then,
the subject growing too painful, he dashed his hand to his
forehead, and went off abruptly in a homeward direction
towards his favourite conduit, where he was seen by an
amateur in such a state, that he thought it dangerous to
address him. Soon after Toad shut himself entirely up ;
it was understood that he had resigned himself to melancholy ; and at length the prevailing notion was, that Toad-
in-the-hole had hanged himself.

The world was wrong *there*, as it had been on some
other questions. Toad-in-the-hole might be sleeping,
but dead he was not ; and of that we soon had ocular
proof. One morning in 1812, an amateur surprised us
with the news that he had seen Toad-in-the-hole brushing
with hasty steps the dews away, to meet the postman by
the conduit side. Even that was something : how much
more, to hear that he had shaved his beard—had laid
aside his sad-coloured clothes, and was adorned like a
bridegroom of ancient days. What could be the meaning
of all this ? Was Toad-in-the-hole mad ? or how ? Soon
after the secret was explained—in more than a figurative
sense 'the murder was out.' For in came the London
morning papers, by which it appeared that but three days
before a murder, the most superb of the century by many
degrees, had occurred in the heart of London. I need
hardly say, that this was the great exterminating *chef-
d'œuvre* of Williams at Mr. Marr's, No. 29 Ratcliffe
Highway. That was the *début* of the artist ; at least
for anything the public knew. What occurred at Mr.
Williamson's twelve nights afterwards—the second work
turned out from the same chisel—some people pronounced
even superior. But Toad-in-the-hole always 'reclaimed,'
he was even angry, at such comparisons. 'This vulgar
gout de comparaison, as La Bruyère calls it,' he would
often remark, 'will be our ruin ; each work has its

own separate characteristics—each in and for itself is
incomparable. One, perhaps, might suggest the *Iliad*—
the other the *Odyssey*: but what do you get by such
comparisons? Neither ever was, or will be surpassed;
and when you've talked for hours, you must still come
back to that.' Vain, however, as all criticism might be,
he often said that volumes might be written on each case
for itself; and he even proposed to publish in quarto on
the subject.

Meantime, how had Toad-in-the-hole happened to
hear of this great work of art so early in the morning?
He had received an account by express, despatched by
a correspondent in London, who watched the progress
of art on *Toad's* behalf, with a general commission to
send off a special express, at whatever cost, in the event
of any estimable works appearing. The express arrived
in the night-time; Toad-in-the-hole was then gone to
bed; he had been muttering and grumbling for hours,
but of course he was called up. On reading the account,
he threw his arms round the express, declared him his
brother and his preserver, and expressed his regret at
not having it in his power to knight him. We, amateurs,
having heard that he was abroad, and therefore had *not*
hanged himself, made sure of soon seeing him amongst
us. Accordingly he soon arrived; seized every man's
hand as he passed him—wrung it almost frantically, and
kept ejaculating, 'Why, now, here's something like a
murder!—this is the real thing—this is genuine—this is
what you can approve, can recommend to a friend: this
—says every man, on reflection—this is the thing that
ought to be! Such works are enough to make us all
young.' And in fact the general opinion is, that Toad-
in-the-hole would have died but for this regeneration of
art, which he called a second age of Leo the Tenth; and
it was our duty, he said, solemnly to commemorate it.
At present, and *en attendant*, he proposed that the club
should meet and dine together. A dinner, therefore,
was given by the club; to which all amateurs were
invited from a distance of one hundred miles.

Of this dinner, there are ample shorthand notes amongst the archives of the club. But they are not 'extended,' to speak diplomatically; and the reporter, who only could give the whole report *in extenso*, is missing—I believe murdered. Meantime, in years long after that day, and on an occasion perhaps equally interesting, viz., the turning up of Thugs and Thuggism, another dinner was given. Of this I myself kept notes, for fear of another accident to the shorthand reporter. And I here subjoin them. Toad-in-the-hole, I must mention, was present at this dinner. In fact, it was one of its sentimental incidents. Being as old as the valleys at the dinner of 1812, naturally he was as old as the hills at the Thug dinner of 1838. He had taken to wearing his beard again; why, or with what view, it passes my persimmon to tell you. But so it was. And his appearance was most benign and venerable. Nothing could equal the angelic radiance of his smile, as he inquired after the unfortunate reporter (whom, as a piece of private scandal, I should tell you that he was himself supposed to have murdered in a rapture of creative art): the answer was, with roars of laughter, from the under-sheriff of our county—'Non est inventus.' Toad-in-the-hole laughed outrageously at this: in fact, we all thought he was choking; and, at the earnest request of the company, a musical composer furnished a most beautiful glee upon the occasion, which was sung five times after dinner, with universal applause and inextinguishable laughter, the words being these (and the chorus so contrived, as most beautifully to mimic the peculiar laughter of Toad-in-the-hole) :—

Et interrogatum est à Toad-in-the-hole—Ubi est ille reporter?
Et responsum est cum cachinno—*Non est inventus.*

Chorus.

Deinde iteratum est ab omnibus, cum cachinnatione undulante
 trepidante—*Non est inventus.*

Toad-in-the-hole, I ought to mention, about nine years before, when an express from Edinburgh brought him the earliest intelligence of the Burke-and-Hare revolution in the art, went mad upon the spot; and, instead of a pension to the express for even one life, or a knighthood, endeavoured to Burke him; in consequence of which he was put into a strait-waistcoat. And that was the reason we had no dinner then. But now all of us were alive and kicking, strait-waistcoaters and others; in fact, not one absentee was reported upon the entire roll. There were also many foreign amateurs present.

Dinner being over, and the cloth drawn, there was a general call made for the new glee of *Non est inventus*; but, as this would have interfered with the requisite gravity of the company during the earlier toasts, I overruled the call. After the national toasts had been given, the first official toast of the day was, *The Old Man of the Mountains*—drunk in solemn silence.

Toad-in-the-hole returned thanks in a neat speech. He likened himself to the Old Man of the Mountains, in a few brief allusions, that made the company yell with laughter; and he concluded with giving the health of

Mr. von Hammer, with many thanks to him for his learned History of the Old Man and his subjects the Assassins.

Upon this I rose and said, that doubtless most of the company were aware of the distinguished place assigned by Orientalists to the very learned Turkish scholar, Von Hammer the Austrian; that he had made the profoundest researches into our art, as connected with those early and eminent artists, the Syrian assassins in the period of the Crusaders; that his work had been for several years deposited, as a rare treasure of art, in the library of the club. Even the author's name, gentlemen, pointed him out as the historian of our art—Von Hammer——

'Yes, yes,' interrupted Toad-in-the-hole, 'Von Hammer—he's the man for a *malleus hæreticorum*. You all know what consideration Williams bestowed on the hammer, or the ship-carpenter's mallet, which is the same thing. Gentlemen, I give you another great hammer

—Charles the Hammer, the Marteau, or, in old French, the Martel—he hammered the Saracens till they were all as dead as door-nails.'

'*Charles the Hammer*, with all the honours.'

But the explosion of Toad-in-the-hole, together with the uproarious cheers for the grandpapa of Charlemagne, had now made the company unmanageable. The orchestra was again challenged with shouts the stormiest for the new glee. I foresaw a tempestuous evening ; and I ordered myself to be strengthened with three waiters on each side ; the vice-president with as many. Symptoms of unruly enthusiasm were beginning to show out ; and I own that I myself was considerably excited, as the orchestra opened with its storm of music, and the impassioned glee began— 'Et interrogatum est à Toad-in-the-hole—Ubi est ille Reporter ?' And the frenzy of the passion became absolutely convulsing, as the full chorus fell in—' Et iteratum est ab omnibus—Non est inventus.'

The next toast was—*The Jewish Sicarii.*

Upon which I made the following explanation to the company :—' Gentlemen, I am sure it will interest you all to hear that the assassins, ancient as they were, had a race of predecessors in the very same country. All over Syria, but particularly in Palestine, during the early years of the Emperor Nero, there was a band of murderers, who prosecuted their studies in a very novel manner. They did not practise in the night time, or in lonely places ; but, justly considering that great crowds are in themselves a sort of darkness by means of the dense pressure, and the impossibility of finding out who it was that gave the blow, they mingled with mobs everywhere ; particularly at the great paschal feast in Jerusalem ; where they actually had the audacity, as Josephus assures us, to press into the temple—and whom should they choose for operating upon but Jonathan himself, the Pontifex Maximus? They murdered him, gentlemen, as beautifully as if they had had him alone on a moonless night in a dark lane. And when it was asked, who was the murderer, and where he was—— '

'Why, then, it was answered,' interrupted Toad-in-the-hole, '" *Non est inventus.*"' And then, in spite of all I could do or say, the orchestra opened, and the whole company began—'Et interrogatum est à Toad-in-the-hole—Ubi est ille Sicarius? Et responsum est ab omnibus—*Non est inventus.*'

When the tempestuous chorus had subsided, I began again :—'Gentlemen, you will find a very circumstantial account of the Sicarii in at least three different parts of Josephus ; once in Book XX., sec. v., c. viii., of his *Antiquities ;* once in Book I. of his *Wars :* but in sec. **x.** of the chapter first cited you will find a particular description of their tooling. This is what he says :—"They tooled with small scimitars not much different from the Persian *acinacæ*, but more curved, and for all the world most like the Roman semi-lunar *sicæ*." It is perfectly magnificent, gentlemen, to hear the sequel of their history. Perhaps the only case on record where a regular army of murderers was assembled, a *justus exercitus*, was in the case of these *Sicarii*. They mustered in such strength in the wilderness, that Festus himself was obliged to march against them with the Roman legionary force. A pitched battle ensued ; and this army of amateurs was all cut to pieces in the desert. Heavens, gentlemen, what a sublime picture ! The Roman legions—the wilderness—Jerusalem in the distance—an army of murderers in the foreground !'

The next toast was—'To the further improvement of Tooling, and thanks to the Committee for their services.'

Mr. L., on behalf of the Committee who had reported on that subject, returned thanks. He made an interesting extract from the report, by which it appeared how very much stress had been laid formerly on the mode of tooling by the fathers, both Greek and Latin. In confirmation of this pleasing fact, he made a very striking statement in reference to the earliest work of antediluvian art. Father Mersenne, that learned French Roman Catholic, in page one thousand four hundred and thirty-one [1] of his operose

---

[1] 'Page one thousand four hundred and thirty-one'—*literally*, good reader, and no joke at all.

Commentary on Genesis, mentions, on the authority of
several rabbis, that the quarrel of Cain with Abel was
about a young woman ; that, according to various
accounts, Cain had tooled with his teeth (Abelem fuisse
morsibus dilaceratum a Cain) ; according to many others,
with the jaw-bone of an ass, which is the tooling adopted
by most painters. But it is pleasing to the mind of
sensibility to know that, as science expanded, sounder
views were adopted. One author contends for a pitch-
fork, St. Chrysostom for a sword, Irenæus for a scythe, and
Prudentius, the Christian poet of the fourth century, for a
hedging-bill. This last writer delivers his opinion thus :—

> Frater, probatæ sanctitatis æmulus,
> Germana curvo colla frangit sarculo :

i.e., his brother, jealous of his attested sanctity, fractures
his fraternal throat with a curved hedging-bill. 'All
which is respectfully submitted by your committee, not so
much as decisive of the question (for it is not), but in
order to impress upon the youthful mind the importance
which has ever been attached to the quality of the tooling
by such men as Chrysostom and Irenæus.'

   'Irenæus, be hanged!' said Toad-in-the-hole, who now
rose impatiently to give the next toast :—'Our Irish friends ;
wishing them a speedy revolution in their mode of tooling,
as well as in everything else connected with the art!'

   'Gentlemen, I'll tell you the plain truth. Every day
of the year we take up a paper, we read the opening of a
murder. We say, this is good, this is charming, this is
excellent! But, behold you! scarcely have we read a
little farther, before the word Tipperary or Ballina-some-
thing betrays the Irish manufacture. Instantly we loathe
it ; we call to the waiter ; we say, "Waiter, take away
this paper ; send it out of the house ; it is absolutely a
scandal in the nostrils of all just taste." I appeal to every
man, whether, on finding a murder (otherwise perhaps
promising enough) to be Irish, he does not feel himself as
much insulted as when, Madeira being ordered, he finds
it to be Cape ; or when, taking up what he takes to be a

mushroom, it turns out what children call a toad-stool?
Tithes, politics, something wrong in principle, vitiate
every Irish murder. Gentlemen, this must be reformed,
or Ireland will not be a land to live in ; at least, if we do
live there, we must import all our murders, that's clear.'
Toad-in-the-hole sat down, growling with suppressed
wrath ; and the uproarious 'Hear, hear!' clamorously
expressed the general concurrence.

The next toast was—'The sublime epoch of Burkism
and Harism!'

This was drunk with enthusiasm ; and one of the
members, who spoke to the question, made a very curious
communication to the company :—'Gentlemen, we fancy
Burkism to be a pure invention of our own times : and in
fact no Pancirollus has ever enumerated this branch of art
when writing *de rebus deperditis*. Still, I have ascertained
that the essential principle of this variety in the art *was*
known to the ancients ; although, like the art of painting
upon glass, of making the myrrhine cups, etc., it was lost
in the dark ages for want of encouragement. In the
famous collection of Greek epigrams made by Planudes, is
one upon a very fascinating case of Burkism : it is a
perfect little gem of art. The epigram itself I cannot lay
my hand upon at this moment ; but the following is an
abstract of it by Salmasius, as I find it in his notes on
Vopiscus : "Est et elegans epigramma Lucilii,[1] ubi
medicus et pollinctor de compacto sic egerunt, ut medicus
ægros omnes curæ suæ commissos occideret : this was the
basis of the contract, you see, that on the one part the
doctor, for himself and his assigns, doth undertake and
contract duly and truly to murder all the patients committed to his charge: but why? There lies the beauty
of the case — Et ut pollinctori amico suo traderet
pollingendos." The *pollinctor*, you are aware, was a

[1] The epigram, which had been preserved by Planudes in its
Greek form, is here attributed by Salmasius to the Latin satirical poet,
Caius Lucilius, who was born about B.C. 148, and died about B.C. 103.
It is not found, however, among the preserved fragments of Lucilius ;
and the Greek form of the epigram is anonymous.

person whose business it was to dress and prepare dead bodies for burial. The original ground of the transaction appears to have been sentimental : "He was my friend," says the murderous doctor ; "he was dear to me," in speaking of the pollinctor. But the law, gentlemen, is stern and harsh : the law will not hear of these tender motives : to sustain a contract of this nature in law, it is essential that a "consideration" should be given. Now what *was* the consideration ? For thus far all is on the side of the pollinctor : he will be well paid for his services ; but, meantime, the generous, the noble-minded doctor gets nothing. What *was* the equivalent, again I ask, which the law would insist on the doctor's taking, in order to establish that "consideration," without which the contract had no force ? You shall hear : "Et ut pollinctor vicissim τελαμῶνας quos furabatar de pollinctione mortuorum medico mitteret donis ad alliganda vulnera eorum quos curabat" ; *i.e.*, and that reciprocally the pollinctor should transmit to the physician, as free gifts for the binding up of wounds in those whom he treated medically, the belts or trusses (τελαμῶνας) which he had succeeded in purloining in the course of his functions about the corpses.

'Now, the case is clear : the whole went on a principle of reciprocity which would have kept up the trade for ever. The doctor was also a surgeon: he could not murder *all* his patients : some of the patients must be retained intact. For these he wanted linen bandages. But, unhappily, the Romans wore woollen, on which account it was that they bathed so often. Meantime, there *was* linen to be had in Rome ; but it was monstrously dear ; and the τελαμῶνες, or linen swathing bandages, in which superstition obliged them to bind up corpses, would answer capitally for the surgeon. The doctor, therefore, contracts to furnish his friend with a constant succession of corpses, provided, and be it understood always, that his said friend, in return, should supply him with one-half of the articles he would receive from the friends of the parties murdered or to be murdered. The doctor invariably recommended his invaluable friend the pollinctor (whom let us call the undertaker) ; the undertaker, with equal regard to the sacred rights of friendship, uniformly recommended the doctor.   Like Pylades and Orestes, they were models of a perfect friendship : in their lives they were lovely : and on the gallows, it is to be hoped, they were not divided.

'Gentlemen, it makes me laugh horribly, when I think of those two friends drawing and re-drawing on each other : "Pollinctor in account with Doctor, debtor by sixteen corpses : creditor by forty-five bandages, two of which damaged."   Their names unfortunately are lost ; but I conceive they must have been Quintus Burkius and Publius Harius.   By the way, gentlemen, has anybody heard lately of Hare ?   I understand he is comfortably settled in Ireland, considerably to the west, and does a little business now and then ; but, as he observes with a sigh, only as a retailer—nothing like the fine thriving wholesale concern so carelessly blown up at Edinburgh. "You see what comes of neglecting business"—is the chief moral, the ἐπιμύθιον, as Æsop would say, which Hare draws from his past experience.'

At length came the toast of the day—*Thugdom in all its branches.*

The speeches *attempted* at this crisis of the dinner were past all counting.   But the applause was so furious, the music so stormy, and the crashing of glasses so incessant, from the general resolution never again to drink an inferior toast from the same glass, that I am unequal to the task of reporting.   Besides which, Toad-in-the-hole now became ungovernable.   He kept firing pistols in every direction ; sent his servant for a blunderbuss, and talked of loading with ball-cartridge.   We conceived that his former madness had returned at the mention of Burke and Hare ; or that, being again weary of life, he had resolved to go off in a general massacre.   This we could not think of allowing ; it became indispensable, therefore, to kick him out ; which we did with universal consent, the whole company lending their toes *uno pede*, as I may say, though pitying

his gray hairs and his angelic smile.   During the operation,
the orchestra poured in their old chorus.   The universal
company sang, and (what surprised us most of all) Toad-
in-the-hole joined us furiously in singing—

Et interrogatum est ab omnibus—Ubi est ille Toad-in-the-hole?
Et responsum est ab omnibus—Non est inventus.

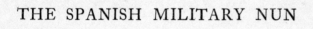

THE SPANISH MILITARY NUN

THE SPANISH MILITARY NUN

Section 1.—*An Extra Nuisance is introduced into Spain*

ON a night in the year 1592 (but which night is a secret liable to 365 answers), a Spanish 'son of somebody' (*i.e.*, hidalgo), in the fortified town of St. Sebastian, received the disagreeable intelligence from a nurse, that his wife had just presented him with a daughter. No present that the poor misjudging lady could possibly have made him was so entirely useless towards any purpose of his. He had three daughters already ; which happened to be more by 2 + 1, according to *his* reckoning, than any reasonable allowance of daughters. A supernumerary son might have been stowed away ; but supernumerary daughters were the very nuisance of Spain. He did, therefore, what in such cases every proud and lazy Spanish gentleman endeavoured to do. And surely I need not interrupt myself by any parenthesis to inform the base British reader, who makes it his glory to work hard, that the peculiar point of honour for the Spanish gentleman lay precisely in these two qualities of pride and laziness : for, if he were not proud, or had anything to do, what could you look for but ruin to the old Spanish aristocracy? some of whom boasted that no member of their house (unless illegitimate, and a mere *terræ filius*) had done a day's work since the Flood. In the ark they admitted that Noah kept them tightly to work ; because, in fact, there was work to do, that must be done by somebody. But once anchored upon Ararat, they insisted upon it most indignantly that no ancestor of the Spanish *noblesse* had ever worked, except through his slaves. And with a view to new leases of idleness, through new generations of slaves, it was (as many people think) that Spain went so heartily into the enterprises of Cortez and Pizarro. A sedentary body of Dons, without needing to uncross their thrice noble legs, would thus levy eternal tributes of gold and silver upon eternal mines, through eternal successions of nations that had been, and were to be, enslaved. Meantime, until these golden visions should be realised, aristocratic *daughters*, who constituted the hereditary torment of the true Castilian Don, were to be disposed of in the good old way ; viz., by quartering them for life upon nunneries : a plan which entailed no sacrifice whatever upon any of the parties concerned ; except, indeed, the little insignificant sacrifice of happiness and natural birthrights to the daughters. But this little inevitable wreck, when placed in the counter scale to the magnificent purchase of eternal idleness for an aristocracy so ancient, was surely entitled to little attention amongst philosophers. Daughters must perish by generations, and ought to be proud of perishing, in order that their papas, being hidalgos, might luxuriate in laziness. Accordingly, on this system, our hidalgo of St. Sebastian wrapped the new little daughter, odious to his paternal eyes, in a pocket-handkerchief, and then wrapping up his own throat with a great deal more care, off he bolted to the neighbouring convent of St. Sebastian, meaning by that term not merely a convent of that city, but also (amongst several convents) the one dedicated to that saint. It is well that in this quarrelsome world we quarrel furiously about tastes ; since, agreeing too closely about the objects to be liked, we should agree too closely about the objects to be appropriated ; which would breed much more fighting than is bred by disagreeing. That little human tadpole, which the old toad of a father would not suffer to stay ten minutes in his house, proved as welcome at the nunnery of St. Sebastian as she was odious at home. The lady superior of the convent was aunt, by the mother's side, to the new-born stranger. She therefore kissed and blessed the little lady. The poor nuns, who were never to have any babies of their own, and were languishing for some amusement, perfectly doated on this prospect of a wee pet. The superior thanked the hidalgo for his very splendid present. The nuns thanked him each and all; until the old crocodile actually began to whimper sentimentally at what he now perceived to be excess of munificence in himself. Munificence, indeed, he remarked, was his foible, next after parental tenderness.

2.—*Wait a little, Hidalgo!*

What a luxury it is, sometimes, to a cynic that there go two words to a bargain. In the convent of St. Sebastian all was gratitude; gratitude (as aforesaid) to the hidalgo from all the convent for his present, until at last the hidalgo began to express gratitude to *them* for their gratitude to *him*. Then came a rolling fire of thanks to St. Sebastian; from the superior, for sending a future saint; from the nuns, for sending such a love of a play-thing; and, finally, from papa, for sending such substantial board and well-bolted lodgings: 'From which,' said the malicious old fellow, 'my pussy will never find her way out to a thorny and dangerous world.' Won't she? I suspect, son of somebody, that the next time you see 'pussy,' which may happen to be also the last, will not be in a convent of any kind. At present, whilst this general rendering of thanks was going on, one person only took no part in them. That person was 'pussy,' whose little figure lay quietly stretched out in the arms of a smiling young nun, with eyes nearly shut, yet peering a little at the candles. Pussy said nothing. It's of no great use to say much, when all the world is against you. But if St. Sebastian had enabled her to speak out the whole truth, pussy *would* have said: 'So, Mr. Hidalgo, you have been engaging lodgings for me; lodgings for life. Wait a little. We'll try that question, when my claws are grown a little longer.'

3.—*Symptoms of Mutiny*

Disappointment, therefore, was gathering ahead. But for the present there was nothing of the kind. That noble old crocodile, papa, was not in the least disappointed as regarded *his* expectation of having no anxiety to waste, and no money to pay, on account of his youngest daughter. He insisted on his right to forget her ; and in a week *had* forgotten her, never to think of her again but once. The lady superior, as regarded *her* demands, was equally content, and through a course of several years ; for, as often as she asked pussy if she would be a saint, pussy replied that she would, if saints were allowed plenty of sweetmeats. But least of all were the nuns disappointed. Everything that they had fancied possible in a human plaything fell short of what pussy realised in racketing, racing, and eternal plots against the peace of the elder nuns. No fox ever kept a hen-roost in such alarm as pussy kept the dormitory of the senior sisters ; whilst the younger ladies were run off their legs by the eternal wiles, and had their gravity discomposed, even in chapel, by the eternal antics, of this privileged little kitten.

The kitten had long ago received a baptismal name, which was Kitty, or Kate ; and *that* in Spanish is Catalina. It was a good name, as it recalled her original name of ' pussy.' And, by the way, she had also an ancient and honourable surname—viz., *De Erauso*—which is to this day a name rooted in Biscay. Her father, the hidalgo, was a military officer in the Spanish service, and had little care whether his kitten should turn out a wolf or a lamb, having made over the fee simple of his own interest in the little Kate to St. Sebastian, ' to have and to hold,' so long as Kate should keep her hold of this present life. Kate had no apparent intention to let slip that hold ; for she was blooming as a rose-bush in June, tall and strong as a young cedar. Yet, notwithstanding this robust health, which forbade one to think of separation from St. Sebastian by death, and notwithstanding the strength of the convent walls, which forbade one to think of any other separation, the time was drawing near when St. Sebastian's lease in Kate must, in legal phrase, 'determine'; and any *chateaux en Espagne* that the saint might have built on the cloistral fidelity of his pet Catalina, must suddenly give way in one hour, like many other vanities in our own days of Spanish growth; such as Spanish constitutions and charters, Spanish financial reforms, Spanish bonds, and other little varieties of Spanish ostentatious mendacity.

4.—*The Symptoms Thicken*

After reaching her tenth year, Catalina became thoughtful and not very docile. At times she was even headstrong and turbulent, so that the gentle sisterhood of St. Sebastian, who had no other pet or plaything in the world, began to weep in secret, fearing that they might have been rearing by mistake some future tigress; for as to infancy, *that*, you know, is playful and innocent even in the cubs of a tigress. But *there* the ladies were going too far. Catalina was impetuous and aspiring, violent sometimes, headstrong and haughty towards those who presumed upon her youth, absolutely rebellious against all open harshness, but still generous and most forgiving, disdainful of petty arts, and emphatically a noble girl. She was gentle, if people would let her be so. But woe to those that took liberties with *her*! A female servant of the convent, in some authority, one day, in passing up the aisle to matins, *wilfully* gave Kate a push; and, in return, Kate, who never left her debts in arrear, gave the servant for a keepsake such a look, as that servant carried with her in fearful remembrance to her grave. It seemed as if Kate had tropic blood in her veins, that continually called her away to the tropics. It was all the fault of that 'blue rejoicing sky,' of those purple Biscayan mountains, of that glad tumultuous ocean, which she beheld daily from the nunnery gardens. Or, if only half of it was *their* fault, the other half lay in those golden tales, streaming upwards even into the sanctuaries of convents, like morning mists touched by earliest sunlight, of king-

doms overshadowing a new world, which had been founded
by her kinsmen with the simple aid of a horse and a lance.
The reader is to remember that this is no romance, or at
least no fiction, that he is reading ; and it is proper to
remind the reader of real romances in Ariosto or our own
Spenser, that such martial ladies as the *Marfisa* or *Brada-
mant* of the first, and *Britomart* of the other, were really
not the improbabilities that modern society imagines.
Many a stout man, as you will soon see, found that Kate,
with a sabre in hand, and well mounted, was no romance
at all, but far too serious a fact.

5.—*Good-night, St. Sebastian !*

The day is come—the evening is come—when our
poor Kate, that had for fifteen years been so tenderly
rocked in the arms of St. Sebastian and his daughters, and
that henceforth shall hardly find a breathing space between
eternal storms, must see her peaceful cell, must see the
holy chapel, for the last time. It was at vespers, it was
during the chanting of the vesper service, that she finally
read the secret signal for her departure, which long she
had been looking for. It happened that her aunt, the
Lady Principal, had forgotten her breviary. As this
was in a private 'scrutoire, the prudent lady did not
choose to send a servant for it, but gave the key to her
niece. The niece, on opening the 'scrutoire, saw, with
that rapidity of eye-glance for the one thing needed in
great emergencies which ever attended her through life,
that *now* was the moment, *now* had the clock struck, for
an opportunity which, if neglected, might never return.
There lay the total keys, in one massive *trousseau*, of that
monastic fortress, impregnable even to armies from without. St. Sebastian ! do you see what your pet is going
to do ? And do it she will, as sure as your name is St.
Sebastian. Kate went back to her aunt with the breviary
and the key ; but taking good care to leave that awful
door, on whose hinge revolved her whole future life,
unlocked. Delivering the two articles to the superior,

she complained of headache—(ah, Kate! what did *you* know of headaches?)—upon which her aunt, kissing her forehead, dismissed her to bed. Now, then, through three-fourths of an hour Kate will have free elbow-room for unanchoring her boat, for unshipping her oars, and for pulling ahead right out of St. Sebastian's cove into the main ocean of life.

Catalina, the reader is to understand, does not belong to the class of persons in whom pre-eminently I profess an interest. But everywhere one loves energy and indomitable courage. And always what is best in its kind one admires, even where the kind may happen to be not specially attractive. Kate's advantages for her *rôle* in this life lay in four things : viz., in a well-built person, and a particularly strong wrist ; 2nd, in a heart that nothing could appal ; 3rd, in a sagacious head, never drawn aside from the *hoc age* (from the instant question of the hour) by any weakness of imagination ; 4th, in a tolerably thick skin—not literally, for she was fair and blooming, and eminently handsome, having such a skin, in fact, as became a young woman of family in northernmost Spain ; but her sensibilities were obtuse as regarded *some* modes of delicacy, *some* modes of equity, *some* modes of the world's opinion, and *all* modes whatever of personal hardship. Lay a stress on that word *some*—for, as to delicacy, she never lost sight of that kind which peculiarly concerns her sex. Long afterwards she told the Pope himself, when confessing without disguise to the paternal old man her sad and infinite wanderings (and I feel convinced of her veracity), that in this respect—viz., all which concerned her sexual honour—even then she was as pure as a child. And, as to equity, it was only that she substituted the rude natural equity of camps for the specious and conventional equity of courts and towns. I must add, though at the cost of interrupting the story by two or three more sentences, that Catalina had also a fifth advantage, which sounds humbly, but is really of use in a world, where even to fold and seal a letter adroitly is not the lowest of accomplishments. She was a *handy* girl. She

could turn her hand to anything ; of which I will give
you two memorable instances.   Was there ever a girl in
this world but herself that cheated and snapped her fingers
at that awful Inquisition, which brooded over the convents
of Spain ? that did this without collusion from outside ;
trusting to nobody, but to herself, and what beside ? to
one needle, two skeins of thread, and a bad pair of
scissors !   For that the scissors were bad, though Kate
does not say so in her memoirs, I know by an *à priori*
argument ; viz., because *all* scissors were bad in the year
1607.   Now, say all decent logicians, from a universal to
a particular *valet consequentia*, the right of inference is
good.   *All* scissors were bad, *ergo some* scissors were bad.
The second instance of her handiness will surprise you
even more :—She once stood upon a scaffold, under
sentence of death (but, understand, on the evidence of
false witnesses).   Jack Ketch—or, as the present generation calls him, ' *Mr. Calcraft*,' or '——*Calcraft, Esq.*'—
was absolutely tying the knot under her ear, and the
shameful man of ropes fumbled so deplorably, that Kate
(who by much nautical experience had learned from
another sort of ' Jack ' how a knot *should* be tied in this
world) lost all patience with the contemptible artist, told
him she was ashamed of him, took the rope out of his
hand, and tied the knot irreproachably herself.   The
crowd saluted her with a festal roll, long and loud, of
vivas ; and this word *viva* being a word of good augury
—but stop ; let me not anticipate.

     From this sketch of Catalina's character, the reader is
prepared to understand the decision of her present proceeding.   She had no time to lose : the twilight, it is true,
favoured her ; but in any season twilight is as short-lived
as a farthing rushlight ; and she must get under hiding
before pursuit commenced.   Consequently she lost not
one of her forty-five minutes in picking and choosing.
No *shilly-shally* in Kate.   She saw with the eyeball of an
eagle what was indispensable.   Some little money perhaps,
in the first place, to pay the first toll-bar of life : so, out
of four shillings in Aunty's purse, or what amounted to

that English sum in various Spanish coins, she took one. You can't say *that* was exorbitant. Which of us wouldn't subscribe a shilling for poor Kate, to put into the first trouser-pockets that ever she will wear? I remember even yet, as a personal experience, that when first arrayed, at four years old, in nankeen trousers, though still so far retaining hermaphrodite relations of dress as to wear a petticoat above my trousers, all my female friends (because they pitied me, as one that had suffered from years of ague) filled my pockets with half-crowns, of which I can render no account at this day. But what were my poor pretensions by the side of Kate's? Kate was a fine blooming girl of fifteen, with no touch of ague; and, before the next sun rises, Kate shall draw on her first trousers, made by her own hand; and, that she may do so, of all the valuables in aunty's repository she takes nothing beside, first (for I detest your ridiculous and most pedantic neologism of *firstly*)—first, the shilling, for which I have already given a receipt; secondly, two skeins of suitable thread; thirdly, one stout needle, and (as I told you before, if you would please to remember things) one bad pair of scissors. Now she was ready; ready to cast off St. Sebastian's towing-rope; ready to cut and run for port anywhere, which port (according to a smart American adage) is to be looked for 'at the back of beyond.' The finishing touch of her preparations was to pick out the proper keys: even there she showed the same discretion. She did no gratuitous mischief. She did not take the wine-cellar key, which would have irritated the good father confessor; she did not take the key of the closet which held the peppermint-water and other cordials, for *that* would have distressed the elderly nuns. *She* took those keys only that belonged to *her*, if ever keys did; for they were the keys that locked her out from her natural birthright of liberty. Very different views are taken by different parties of this particular act now meditated by Kate. The Court of Rome treats it as the immediate suggestion of Hell, and open to no forgiveness. Another Court, far loftier, ampler, and of larger authority

—viz., the Court which holds its dreadful tribunal in the human heart and conscience—pronounces this act an inalienable privilege of man, and the mere reassertion of a birthright that can neither be bought nor sold.

6.—*Kate's First Bivouac and First March*

Right or wrong, however, in Romish casuistry, Kate was resolved to let herself out ; and *did ;* and for fear any man should creep in while vespers lasted, and steal the kitchen grate, she locked her old friends *in.* Then she sought a shelter. The air was moderately warm. She hurried into a chestnut wood, and upon withered leaves, which furnished to Kate her very first bivouac in a long succession of such experiences, she slept till earliest dawn. Spanish diet and youth leave the digestion undisordered, and the slumbers light. When the lark rose, up rose Catalina. No time to lose ; for she was still in the dress of a nun ; and therefore, by a law too flagrantly notorious, liable to the peremptory challenge and arrest of any man —the very meanest or poorest—in all Spain. With her *armed* finger (ay, by the way, I forgot the thimble ; but Kate did *not*), she set to work upon her amply-embroidered petticoat. She turned it wrong side out ; and with the magic that only female hands possess, she had soon sketched and finished a dashing pair of Wellington trousers. All other changes were made according to the materials she possessed, and quite sufficiently to disguise the two main perils—her sex, and her monastic dedication. What was she to do next ? Speaking of Wellington trousers anywhere in the north of Spain would remind *us,* but could hardly remind *her*, of Vittoria, where she dimly had heard of some maternal relative. To Vittoria, therefore, she bent her course ; and, like the Duke of Wellington, but arriving more than two centuries earlier, she gained a great victory at that place. She had made a two days' march, with no provisions but wild berries ; she depended, for anything better, as light-heartedly as the duke, upon attacking, sword in hand, storming her dear friend's

intrenchments, and effecting a lodgment in his breakfast-
room, should he happen to possess one.   This amiable
relative proved to be an elderly man, who had but one
foible, or perhaps it was a virtue, which had by continual
development overshadowed his whole nature—it was
pedantry.   On that hint Catalina spoke : she knew by
heart, from the services of the convent, a good number of
Latin phrases.   Latin !—Oh, but *that* was charming ; and
in one so young !   The grave Don owned the soft impeachment ; relented at once, and clasped the hopeful
young gentleman in the Wellington trousers to his *uncular*
and rather angular breast.   In this house the yarn of life
was of a mingled quality.   The table was good, but that
was exactly what Kate cared least about.   On the other
hand, the amusement was of the worst kind.   It consisted
chiefly in conjugating Latin verbs, especially such as were
obstinately irregular.   To show him a withered frost-bitten
verb, that wanted its preterite, wanted its gerunds, wanted
its supines, wanted, in fact, everything in this world, fruits
or blossoms, that make a verb desirable, was to earn the
Don's gratitude for life.   All day long he was, as you may
say, marching and counter-marching his favourite brigades
of verbs—verbs frequentative, verbs inceptive, verbs
desiderative—horse, foot, and artillery ; changing front,
advancing from the rear, throwing out skirmishing parties,
until Kate, not given to faint, must have thought of such
a resource, as once in her life she had thought so seasonably
of a vesper headache.   This was really worse than St.
Sebastian's.   It reminds one of a French gaiety in Thiebault,
who describes a rustic party, under equal despair, as em-
ploying themselves in conjugating the verb *s'ennuyer*—*Je
m'ennuie, tu t'ennuies, il s'ennuit ; nous nous ennuyons*, etc. ;
thence to the imperfect—*Je m'ennuyois, tu t'ennuyois*, etc. ;
thence to the imperative—*Qu'il s'ennuye*, etc. ; and so on,
through the whole dolorous conjugation.   Now, you know,
when the time comes that *nous nous ennuyons*, the best
course is, to part.   Kate saw *that ;* and she walked off
from the Don's (of whose amorous passion for defective
verbs one would have wished to know the catastrophe),

taking from his mantelpiece rather more silver than she
had levied on her aunt.   But then, observe, the Don also
was a relative ; and really he owed her a small cheque on
his banker for turning out on his field-days.   A man, if
he *is* a kinsman, has no unlimited privilege of boring one :
an uncle has a qualified right to bore his nephews, even
when they happen to be nieces ; but he has no right to
bore either nephew or niece *gratis*.

7.—*Kate at Court, where she Prescribes Phlebotomy, and is Promoted*

From Vittoria, Kate was guided by a carrier to Valladolid.   Luckily, as it seemed at first, but, in fact, it made
little difference in the end, here, at Valladolid, were
assembled the King and his Court.   Consequently, there
was plenty of regiments, and plenty of regimental bands.
Attracted by one of these, Catalina was quietly listening
to the music, when some street ruffians, in derision of the
gay colours and the particular form of her forest-made
costume (rascals ! what sort of trousers would *they* have
made with no better scissors ?), began to pelt her with
stones.   Ah, my friends of the genus *blackguard*, you
little know who it is that you are selecting for experiments.
This is the one creature of fifteen years old in all Spain,
be the other male or female, whom nature, and temper,
and provocation have qualified for taking the conceit out
of you.   This she very soon did, laying open with sharp
stones more heads than either one or two, and letting out
rather too little than too much of bad Valladolid blood.
But mark the constant villainy of this world.   Certain
Alguazils—very like some other Alguazils that I know
of nearer home—having stood by quietly to see the
friendless stranger insulted and assaulted, now felt it their
duty to apprehend the poor nun for her most natural
retaliation : and had there been such a thing as a tread-
mill in Valladolid, Kate was booked for a place on it
without further inquiry.   Luckily, injustice does not
always prosper.   A gallant young cavalier, who had wit-

nessed from his windows the whole affair, had seen the
provocation, and admired Catalina's behaviour—equally
patient at first, and bold at last—hastened into the street,
pursued the officers, forced them to release their prisoner,
upon stating the circumstances of the case, and instantly
offered to Catalina a situation amongst his retinue.   He
was a man of birth and fortune ; and the place offered,
that of an honorary page, not being at all degrading even
to a ' daughter of somebody,' was cheerfully accepted.

8.—*Too Good to Last !*

Here Catalina spent a happy quarter of a year !   She
was now splendidly dressed in dark blue velvet, by a tailor
that did not work within the gloom of a chestnut forest.
She and the young cavalier, Don Francisco de Cardenas,
were mutually pleased, and had mutual confidence.   All
went well—until one evening (but, luckily, not before the
sun had been set so long as to make all things indistinct),
who should march into the antechamber of the cavalier
but that sublime of crocodiles, *papa*, whom we lost sight
of fifteen years ago, and shall never see again after this
night.   He had his crocodile tears all ready for use, in
working order, like a good industrious fire-engine.   Whom
will he speak to first in this lordly mansion ?   It was
absolutely to Catalina herself that he advanced ; whom,
for many reasons, he could not be supposed to recognise
—lapse of years, male attire, twilight, were all against him.
Still, she might have the family countenance ; and Kate
fancied (but it must have been a fancy) that he looked
with a suspicious scrutiny into her face, as he inquired for
the young Don.   To avert her own face, to announce
him to Don Francisco, to wish papa on the shores of that
ancient river, the Nile, furnished but one moment's work
to the active Catalina.   She lingered, however, as her
place entitled her to do, at the door of the audience-
chamber.   She guessed already, but in a moment she
heard from papa's lips, what was the nature of his errand.
His daughter Catherine, he informed the Don, had eloped

from the convent of St. Sebastian, a place rich in delight, radiant with festal pleasure, overflowing with luxury. Then he laid open the unparalleled ingratitude of such a step. Oh, the unseen treasure that had been spent upon that girl! Oh, the untold sums of money, the unknown amounts of cash, that had been sunk in that unhappy speculation! The nights of sleeplessness suffered during her infancy! The fifteen years of solicitude thrown away in schemes for her improvement! It would have moved the heart of a stone. The *hidalgo* wept copiously at his own pathos. And to such a height of grandeur had he carried his Spanish sense of the sublime, that he disdained to mention —yes! positively not even in a parenthesis would he condescend to notice—that pocket-handkerchief which he had left at St. Sebastian's fifteen years ago, by way of envelope for 'pussy,' and which, to the best of pussy's knowledge, was the one sole memorandum of papa ever heard of at St. Sebastian's. Pussy, however, saw no use in revising and correcting the text of papa's remembrances. She showed her usual prudence, and her usual incomparable decision. It did not appear, as yet, that she would be reclaimed (or was at all suspected for the fugitive) by her father, or by Don Cardenas. For it is an instance of that singular fatality which pursued Catalina through life, that, to her own astonishment (as she now collected from her father's conference), nobody had traced her to Valladolid, nor had her father's visit any connection with any suspicious traveller in that direction. The case was quite different. Strangely enough, her street row had thrown her, by the purest of accidents, into the one sole household in all Spain that had an official connection with St. Sebastian's. That convent had been founded by the young cavalier's family; and, according to the usage of Spain, the young man (as present representative of his house) was the responsible protector and official visitor of the establishment. It was not to the Don as harbourer of his daughter, but to the Don as hereditary patron of the convent, that the hidalgo was appealing. This being so, Kate might have stayed safely some time longer. Yet,

again, that would but have multiplied the clues for tracing
her ; and, finally, she would too probably have been discovered ; after which, with all his youthful generosity,
the poor Don could not have protected her.   Too terrific
was the vengeance that awaited an abettor of any fugitive
nun ; but, above all, if such a crime were perpetrated by
an official mandatory of the church.   Yet, again, so far
it was the more hazardous course to abscond, that it
almost revealed her to the young Don as the missing
daughter.   Still, if it really *had* that effect, nothing at
present obliged him to pursue her, as might have been the
case a few weeks later.   Kate argued (I daresay) rightly,
as she always did.   Her prudence whispered eternally,
that safety there was none for her, until she had laid the
Atlantic between herself and St. Sebastian's.   Life was to
be for *her* a Bay of Biscay ; and it was odds but she had
first embarked upon this billowy life from the literal Bay
of Biscay.   Chance ordered otherwise.   Or, as a Frenchman says, with eloquent ingenuity, in connection with this
very story, ' Chance is but the *pseudonyme* of God for
those particular cases which he does not choose to subscribe openly with his own sign manual.'   She crept
upstairs to her bedroom.   Simple are the travelling
preparations of those that, possessing nothing, have no
imperials to pack.   She had Juvenal's qualification for
carolling gaily through a forest full of robbers ; for she
had nothing to lose but a change of linen, that rode
easily enough under her left arm, leaving the right free
for answering the questions of impertinent customers.
As she crept downstairs, she heard the crocodile still
weeping forth his sorrows to the pensive ear of twilight,
and to the sympathetic Don Francisco.   Ah ! what
a beautiful idea occurs to me at this point !   Once, on
the hustings at Liverpool, I saw a mob orator, whose
brawling mouth, open to its widest expansion, suddenly
some larking sailor, by the most dexterous of shots,
plugged up with a paving-stone.   Here, now, at Valladolid was another mouth that equally required plugging.
What a pity, then, that some gay brother page of Kate's

had not been there to turn aside into the room, armed with a roasted potato, and, taking a sportsman's aim, to have lodged it in the crocodile's abominable mouth! Yet, what an anachronism! There *were* no roasted potatoes in Spain at that date (1608), which can be apodeictically proved, because in Spain there were no potatoes at all, and very few in England. But anger drives a man to say anything.

9.—*How to Choose Lodgings*

Catalina had seen her last of friends and enemies in Valladolid. Short was her time there; but she had improved it so far as to make a few of both. There was an eye or two in Valladolid that would have glared with malice upon her, had she been seen by *all* eyes in that city, as she tripped through the streets in the dusk; and eyes there were that would have softened into tears, had they seen the desolate condition of the child, or in vision had seen the struggles that were before her. But what's the use of wasting tears upon our Kate? Wait till to-morrow morning at sunrise, and see if she is particularly in need of pity. What, now, should a young lady do—I propose it as a subject for a prize essay—that finds herself in Valladolid at nightfall, having no letters of introduction, and not aware of any reason, great or small, for preferring this or that street in general, except so far as she knows of some reason for avoiding one street in particular? The great problem I have stated, Kate investigated as she went along; and she solved it with the accuracy which she ever applied to *practical* exigencies. Her conclusion was —that the best door to knock at, in such a case, was the door where there was no need to knock at all, as being deliberately left open to all comers. For she argued, that within such a door there would be nothing to steal, so that, at least, you could not be mistaken in the dark for a thief. Then, as to stealing from *her*, they might do that if they could.

Upon these principles, which hostile critics will in vain endeavour to undermine, she laid her hand upon what

seemed a rude stable-door. Such it proved; and the
stable was not absolutely empty: for there was a cart
inside—a four-wheeled cart. True, there was so; but
you couldn't take *that* away in your pocket; and there
were also five loads of straw—but then of those a lady
could take no more than her *reticule* would carry, which
perhaps was allowed by the courtesy of Spain. So Kate
was right as to the difficulty of being challenged for a
thief. Closing the door as gently as she had opened it,
she dropped her person, handsomely dressed as she was,
upon the nearest heap of straw. Some ten feet further
were lying two muleteers, honest and happy enough, as
compared with the lords of the bedchamber then in
Valladolid: but still gross men, carnally deaf from eating
garlic and onions, and other horrible substances. Accordingly, they never heard her; nor were aware, until dawn,
that such a blooming person existed. But she was aware
of *them*, and of their conversation. In the intervals of
their sleep, they talked much of an expedition to America,
on the point of sailing under Don Ferdinand de Cordova.
It was to sail from some Andalusian port. That was the
thing for *her*. At daylight she woke, and jumped up,
needing little more toilet than the birds that already were
singing in the gardens, or than the two muleteers, who,
good, honest fellows, saluted the handsome boy kindly—
thinking no ill at his making free with *their* straw, though
no leave had been asked.

With these philo-garlic men Kate took her departure.
The morning was divine: and, leaving Valladolid with
the transports that befitted such a golden dawn, feeling
also already, in the very obscurity of her exit, the pledge
of her final escape, she cared no longer for the crocodile,
nor for St. Sebastian, nor (in the way of fear) for the protector of St. Sebastian, though of *him* she thought with
some tenderness; so deep is the remembrance of kindness
mixed with justice. Andalusia she reached rather slowly;
many weeks the journey cost her; but, after all, what are
weeks? She reached Seville many months before she was
sixteen years old, and quite in time for the expedition.

10.—*An Ugly Dilemma, where Right and Wrong is
reduced to a Question of Right or Left*

Ugly indeed is that dilemma where shipwreck and the
sea are on one side of you, and famine on the other ; or,
if a chance of escape is offered, apparently it depends upon
taking the right road where there is no guide-post.

St. Lucar being the port of rendezvous for the Peruvian
expedition, thither she went.   All comers were welcome
on board the fleet ; much more a fine young fellow like
Kate.   She was at once engaged as a mate ; and *her* ship, in
particular, after doubling Cape Horn without loss, made
the coast of Peru.   Paita was the port of her destination.
Very near to this port they were, when a storm threw them
upon a coral reef.   There was little hope of the ship from
the first, for she was unmanageable, and was not expected
to hold together for twenty-four hours.   In this condition,
with death before their faces, mark what Kate did ; and
please to remember it for her benefit, when she does any
other little thing that angers you.   The crew lowered the
long-boat.   Vainly the captain protested against this dis-
loyal desertion of a king's ship, which might yet, perhaps,
be run on shore, so as to save the stores.   All the crew, to
a man, deserted the captain.   You may say *that* literally ;
for the single exception was *not* a man, being our bold-
hearted Kate.   She was the only sailor that refused to
leave her captain, or the King of Spain's ship.   The rest
pulled away for the shore, and with fair hopes of reaching
it.   But one half-hour told another tale : just about that
time came a broad sheet of lightning, which, through the
darkness of evening, revealed the boat in the very act of
mounting like a horse upon an inner reef, instantly filling,
and throwing out the crew, every man of whom disappeared
amongst the breakers.   The night which succeeded was
gloomy for both the representatives of his Catholic Majesty.
It cannot be denied by the underwriters at Lloyd's, that
the muleteer's stable at Valladolid was worth twenty such
ships, though the stable was *not* insured against fire, and
the ship *was* insured against the sea and the wind by

some fellow that thought very little of his engagements.
But what's the use of sitting down to cry? That was
never any trick of Catalina's. By daybreak, she was at
work with an axe in her hand. I knew it, before ever I
came to this place in her memoirs. I felt, as sure as if I
had read it, that when day broke we should find Kate at
work. Thimble or axe, trousers or raft, all one to *her*.

The captain, though true to his duty, faithful to his
king, and on his king's account even hopeful, seems from
the first to have desponded on his own. He gave no help
towards the raft. Signs were speaking, however, pretty
loudly that he must do something; for notice to quit was
now served pretty liberally. Kate's raft was ready; and
she encouraged the captain to think that it would give
both of them something to hold by in swimming, if not even
carry double. At this moment, when all was waiting for
a start and the ship herself was waiting only for a final
lurch to say *Good-bye* to the King of Spain, Kate went and
did a thing which some erring people will misconstrue.
She knew of a box laden with gold coins, reputed to be
the King of Spain's, and meant for contingencies on the
voyage out. This she smashed open with her axe, and
took out a sum in ducats and pistoles equal to one hundred
guineas English; which, having well secured in a pillow-
case, she then lashed firmly to the raft. Now this, you
know, though not '*flotsom*,' because it would not float, was
certainly, by maritime law, '*jetsom*.' It would be the idlest
of scruples to fancy that the sea or a shark had a better
right to it than a philosopher, or a splendid girl who
showed herself capable of writing a very fair 8vo, to say
nothing of her decapitating in battle, as you will find, more
than one of the king's enemies, and recovering the king's
banner. No sane moralist would hesitate to do the same
thing under the same circumstances, even on board an
English vessel, and though the First Lord of the Admir-
alty, and the Secretary, that pokes his nose into everything nautical, should be looking on. The raft was now
thrown into the sea. Kate jumped after it, and then entreated the captain to follow her. He attempted it; but,

wanting her youthful agility, he struck his head against a spar, and sank like lead, giving notice below that his ship was coming after him as fast as she could make ready. Kate's luck was better : she mounted the raft, and by the rising tide was gradually washed ashore, but so exhausted, as to have lost all recollection. She lay for hours, until the warmth of the sun revived her. On sitting up, she saw a desolate shore stretching both ways—nothing to eat, nothing to drink, but fortunately the raft and the money had been thrown near her ; none of the lashings having given way—only what is the use of a gold ducat, though worth nine shillings in silver, or even of a hundred, amongst tangle and sea-gulls ? The money she distributed amongst her pockets, and soon found strength to rise and march forward. But which *was* forward ? and which backward ? She knew by the conversation of the sailors that Paita must be in the neighbourhood ; and Paita, being a port, could not be in the inside of Peru, but, of course, some-where on its outside—and the outside of a maritime land must be the shore ; so that, if she kept the shore, and went far enough, she could not fail of hitting her foot against Paita at last, in the very darkest of nights, provided only she could first find out which was *up* and which was *down ;* else she might walk her shoes off, and find herself, after all, a thousand miles in the wrong. Here was an awk-ward case, and all for want of a guide-post. Still, when one thinks of Kate's prosperous horoscope ; that, after so long a voyage, *she* only, out of the total crew, was thrown on the American shore, with one hundred and five pounds in her purse of clear gain on the voyage, a conviction arises that she *could* not guess wrongly. She might have tossed up, having coins in her pocket, *heads or tails !* but this kind of sortilege was then coming to be thought irreligious in Christendom, as a Jewish and a heathen mode of questioning the dark future. She simply guessed, therefore ; and very soon a thing happened which, though adding nothing to strengthen her guess as a true one, did much to sweeten it, if it should prove a false one. On turning a point of the shore, she came upon a barrel of

biscuit washed ashore from the ship. Biscuit is one of the
best things I know, even if not made by Mrs. Bobo[1]; but
it is the soonest spoiled; and one would like to hear
counsel on one puzzling point, why it is that a touch
of water utterly ruins it, taking its life, and leaving
behind a *caput mortuum*. Upon this *caput*, in default
of anything better, Kate breakfasted. And, breakfast
being over, she rang the bell for the waiter to take
away, and to ——— Stop! what nonsense! There could
be no bell; besides which, there could be no waiter.
Well, then, without asking the waiter's aid, she that
was always prudent packed up some of the Catholic
king's biscuit, as she had previously packed up far too
little of his gold. But in such cases a most delicate
question occurs, pressing equally on dietetics and algebra.
It is this: if you pack up too much, then, by this extra
burden of salt provisions, you may retard for days your
arrival at fresh provisions; on the other hand, if you pack
up too little, you may famish, and never arrive at all.
Catalina hit the *juste milieu*; and, about twilight on the
third day, she found herself entering Paita, without having
had to swim any *very* broad river in her walk.

11.—*From the Malice of the Sea, to the Malice of Man
and Woman*

The first thing, in such a case of distress, which a

[1] Who is Mrs. Bobo? The reader will say, 'I know not Bobo.'
Possibly; but, for all *that*, Bobo is known to senates. From the
American Senate (Friday March 10, 1854) Bobo received the amplest
testimonials of merits, that have not yet been matched. In the debate
on William Nevins' claim for the extension of his patent for a machine
that rolls and cuts crackers and biscuits, thus spoke Mr. Adams, a most
distinguished senator, against Mr. Badger—'It is said this is a discovery
of the patentee for making the best biscuits. Now, if it be so, he
must have got his invention from Mrs. Bobo of Alabama; for she certainly makes better biscuit than anybody in the world. I can prove
by my friend from Alabama (Mr. Clay), who sits beside me, and by
any man who ever stayed at Mrs. Bobo's house, that she makes better
biscuit than anybody else in the world; and if this man has the best
plan for making biscuit, he must have got it from *her*.' Henceforward
I hope we know where to apply for biscuit.

young lady does, even if she happens to be a young
gentleman, is to beautify her dress. Kate always attended
to *that*. The man she sent for was not properly a tailor,
but one who employed tailors, he himself furnishing the
materials. His name was Urquiza, a fact of very little
importance to us in 1854, if it had stood only at the head
and foot of Kate's little account. But, unhappily for
Kate's *début* on this vast American stage, the case was
otherwise. Mr. Urquiza had the misfortune (equally
common in the Old World and the New) of being a
knave; and also a showy, specious knave. Kate, who
had prospered under sea allowances of biscuit and hardship, was now expanding in proportions. With very little
vanity or consciousness on that head, she now displayed a
really magnificent person; and, when dressed anew in the
way that became a young officer in the Spanish service, she
looked [1] the representative picture of a Spanish *caballador*.
It is strange that such an appearance, and such a rank,
should have suggested to Urquiza the presumptuous idea
of wishing that Kate might become his clerk. He *did*,
however, wish it; for Kate wrote a beautiful hand; and a
stranger thing is, that Kate accepted his proposal. This
might arise from the difficulty of moving in those days to
any distance in Peru. The ship which threw Kate ashore
had been merely bringing stores to the station of Paita;
and no corps of the royal armies was readily to be reached,
whilst something must be done at once for a livelihood.
Urquiza had two mercantile establishments—one at Tru-

[1] '*She looked*,' etc. :—If ever the reader should visit Aix-la-Chapelle,
he will probably feel interest enough in the poor, wild, impassioned
girl to look out for a picture of her in that city, and the only one
known *certainly* to be authentic. It is in the collection of Mr.
Sempeller. For some time it was supposed that the best (if not the
only) portrait of her lurked somewhere in Italy. Since the discovery
of the picture at Aix-la-Chapelle, that notion has been abandoned.
But there is great reason to believe that, both in Madrid and Rome,
many portraits of her must have been painted to meet the intense
interest which arose in her history subsequently amongst all men of
rank, military or ecclesiastical, whether in Italy or Spain. The date
of these would range between sixteen and twenty-two years from the
period which we have now reached (1608).

jillo, to which he repaired in person, on Kate's agreeing to
undertake the management of the other in Paita. Like
the sensible girl that we have always found her, she
demanded specific instructions for her guidance in duties
so new. Certainly she was in a fair way for seeing life.
Telling her beads at St. Sebastian's, manœuvring irregular
verbs at Vittoria, acting as gentleman-usher at Valladolid,
serving his Spanish Majesty round Cape Horn, fighting
with storms and sharks off the coast of Peru, and now
commencing as book-keeper or *commis* to a draper at Paita
—does she not justify the character that I myself gave
her, just before dismissing her from St. Sebastian's, of
being a 'handy' girl? Mr. Urquiza's instructions were
short, easy to be understood, but rather comic; and yet
(which is odd) they led to tragic results. There were two
debtors of the shop (*many*, it is to be hoped, but two
meriting his affectionate notice), with respect to whom he
left the most opposite directions. The one was a very
handsome lady; and the rule as to *her* was, that she was
to have credit unlimited; strictly unlimited. That seemed
plain. The other customer, favoured by Mr. Urquiza's
valedictory thoughts, was a young man, cousin to the
handsome lady, and bearing the name of Reyes. This
youth occupied in Mr. Urquiza's estimate the same hyper-
bolical rank as the handsome lady, but on the opposite
side of the equation. The rule as to *him* was, that he was
to have *no* credit; strictly none. In this case, also, Kate
saw no difficulty; and when she came to know Mr. Reyes
a little, she found the path of pleasure coinciding with the
path of duty. Mr. Urquiza could not be more precise in
laying down the rule, than Kate was in enforcing it. But
in the other case a scruple arose. *Unlimited* might be a
word, not of Spanish law, but of Spanish rhetoric; such
as, '*Live a thousand years*,' which even annuity offices
utter without a pang. Kate therefore wrote to Trujillo,
expressing her honest fears, and desiring to have more
definite instructions. These were positive. If the lady
chose to send for the entire shop, her account was to be
debited instantly with *that*. She had, however, as yet

z

not sent for the shop, but she began to manifest strong signs of sending for the shop*man*.   Upon the blooming young Biscayan had her roving eye settled ; and she was in the course of making up her mind to take Kate for a sweetheart.   Poor Kate saw this with a heavy heart. And, at the same time that she had a prospect of a tender friend more than she wanted, she had become certain of an extra enemy that she wanted quite as little.   What she had done to offend Mr. Reyes, Kate could not guess, except as to the matter of the credit ; but then, in that she only followed her instructions.   Still, Mr. Reyes was of opinion that there were two ways of executing orders : but the main offence was unintentional on Kate's part. Reyes (though as yet she did not know it) had himself been a candidate for the situation of clerk ; and intended probably to keep the equation precisely as it was with respect to the allowance of credit, only to change places with the handsome lady—keeping *her* on the negative side, himself on the affirmative ; an arrangement, you know, that in the final result could have made no sort of pecuniary difference to Urquiza.

Thus stood matters, when a party of vagrant comedians strolled into Paita.   Kate, being a native Spaniard, ranked as one of the Paita aristocracy, and was expected to attend. She did so ; and there also was the malignant Reyes.   He came and seated himself purposely so as to shut out Kate from all view of the stage.   She, who had nothing of the bully in her nature, and was a gentle creature, when her wild Biscayan blood had not been kindled by insult, courteously requested him to move a little ; upon which Reyes replied, that it was not in his power to oblige the clerk as to that, but that he *could* oblige him by cutting his throat.   The tiger that slept in Catalina wakened at once.   She seized him, and would have executed vengeance on the spot, but that a party of young men interposed, for the present, to part them.   The next day, when Kate (always ready to forget and forgive) was thinking no more of the row, Reyes passed ; by spitting at the window, and other gestures insulting to Kate, again he roused her Spanish blood. Out she rushed, sword in hand ; a duel began in the street ; and very soon Kate's sword had passed into the heart of Reyes. Now that the mischief was done, the police were, as usual, all alive for the pleasure of avenging it. Kate found herself suddenly in a strong prison, and with small hopes of leaving it, except for execution.

12.—*From the Steps leading up to the Scaffold, to the Steps leading down to Assassination*

The relatives of the dead man were potent in Paita, and clamorous for justice ; so that the *corrégidor*, in a case where he saw a very poor chance of being corrupted by bribes, felt it his duty to be sublimely incorruptible. The reader knows, however, that amongst the connections of the deceased bully was that handsome lady, who differed as much from her cousin in her sentiments as to Kate, as she did in the extent of her credit with Mr. Urquiza. To *her* Kate wrote a note ; and, using one of the Spanish King's gold coins for bribing the jailer, got it safely delivered. That, perhaps, was unnecessary ; for the lady had been already on the alert, and had summoned Urquiza from Trujillo. By some means not very luminously stated, and by paying proper fees in proper quarters, Kate was smuggled out of the prison at nightfall, and smuggled into a pretty house in the suburbs. Had she known exactly the footing she stood on as to the law, she would have been decided. As it was, she was uneasy, and jealous of mischief abroad ; and, before supper, she understood it all. Urquiza briefly informed his clerk that it would be requisite for him (the clerk) to marry the handsome lady. But why? Because, said Urquiza, after talking for hours with the *corrégidor*, who was infamous for obstinacy, he had found it impossible to make him 'hear reason,' and release the prisoner, until this compromise of marriage was suggested. But how could public justice be pacified for the clerk's unfortunate homicide of Reyes, by a female cousin of the deceased man

engaging to love, honour, and obey the clerk for life?
Kate could not see her way through this logic. 'Nonsense, my friend,' said Urquiza, 'you don't comprehend.
As it stands, the affair is a murder, and hanging the
penalty. But, if you marry into the murdered man's
house, then it becomes a little family murder—all quiet
and comfortable amongst ourselves. What has the *corrégidor* to do with that? or the public either? Now, let
me introduce the bride.' Supper entered at that moment,
and the bride immediately after. The thoughtfulness of
Kate was narrowly observed, and even alluded to, but
politely ascribed to the natural anxieties of a prisoner, and
the very imperfect state of his liberation even yet from
prison *surveillance*. Kate had, indeed, never been in so
trying a situation before. The anxieties of the farewell
night at St. Sebastian were nothing to this; because, even
if she had failed *then*, a failure might not have been always
irreparable. It was but to watch and wait. But now, at
this supper table, she was not more alive to the nature of
the peril than she was to the fact, that if, before the night
closed, she did not by some means escape from it, she
never *would* escape with life. The deception as to her
sex, though resting on no motive that pointed to these
people, or at all concerned them, would be resented as if
it had. The lady would regard the case as a mockery;
and Urquiza would lose his opportunity of delivering
himself from an imperious mistress. According to the
usages of the times and country, Kate knew that within
twelve hours she would be assassinated.

People of infirmer resolution would have lingered at
the supper table, for the sake of putting off the evil
moment of final crisis. Not so Kate. She had revolved
the case on all its sides in a few minutes, and had formed
her resolution. This done, she was as ready for the trial
at one moment as another; and, when the lady suggested
that the hardships of a prison must have made repose
desirable, Kate assented, and instantly rose. A sort of
procession formed, for the purpose of doing honour to the
interesting guest, and escorting him in pomp to his bed-

room. Kate viewed it much in the same light as that
procession to which for some days she had been expecting
an invitation from the *corrégidor*. Far ahead ran the
servant-woman, as a sort of outrider ; then came Urquiza,
like a pacha of two tails, who granted two sorts of credit—
viz., unlimited and none at all—bearing two wax-lights,
one in each hand, and wanting only cymbals and kettle-
drums to express emphatically the pathos of his Castilian
strut ; next came the bride, a little in advance of the
clerk, but still turning obliquely towards him, and smiling
graciously into his face ; lastly, bringing up the rear, came
the prisoner—our poor ensnared Kate—the nun, the
page, the mate, the clerk, the homicide, the convict ; and
for this night only, by particular desire, the bridegroom
elect.

It was Kate's fixed opinion, that, if for a moment she
entered any bedroom having obviously no outlet, her fate
would be that of an ox once driven within the shambles.
Outside, the bullock might make some defence with his
horns ; but once in, with no space for turning, he is
muffled and gagged. She carried her eye, therefore, like
a hawk's, steady, though restless, for vigilant examination
of every angle she turned. Before she entered any bedroom, she was resolved to reconnoitre it from the doorway,
and, in case of necessity, show fight at once before entering, as the best chance in a crisis where all chances were
bad. Everything ends ; and at last the procession reached
the bedroom-door, the outrider having filed off to the
rear. One glance sufficed to satisfy Kate that windows
there were none, and therefore no outlet for escape.
Treachery appeared even in *that*; and Kate, though
unfortunately without arms, was now fixed for resistance.
Mr. Urquiza entered first, with a strut more than usually
grandiose, and inexpressibly sublime—'Sound the trumpets ! Beat the drums !' There were, as we know
already, no windows ; but a slight interruption to Mr.
Urquiza's pompous tread showed that there were steps
downwards into the room. Those, thought Kate, will
suit me even better. She had watched the unlocking of

the bedroom-door—she had lost nothing—she had marked that the key was left in the lock. At this moment, the beautiful lady, as one acquainted with the details of the house, turning with the air of a gracious monitress, held out her fair hand to guide Kate in careful descent of the steps. This had the air of taking out Kate to dance ; and Kate, at that same moment, answering to it by the gesture of a modern waltzer, threw her arm behind the lady's waist ; hurled her headlong down the steps right against Mr. Urquiza, draper and haberdasher ; and then, with the speed of lightning, throwing the door *home* within its architrave, doubly locked the creditor and unlimited debtor into the rat-trap which they had prepared for herself.

The affrighted outrider fled with horror ; she knew that the clerk had already committed one homicide ; a second would cost him still less thought ; and thus it happened that egress was left easy.

13.—*From Human Malice, back again to the Malice of Winds and Waves*

But, when abroad, and free once more in the bright starry night, which way should Kate turn ? The whole city would prove but one vast rat-trap for her, as bad as Mr. Urquiza's, if she was not off before morning. At a glance she comprehended that the sea was her only chance. To the port she fled. All was silent. Watchmen there were none ; and she jumped into a boat. To use the oars was dangerous, for she had no means of muffling them. But she contrived to hoist a sail, pushed off with a boat-hook, and was soon stretching across the water for the mouth of the harbour, before a breeze light but favourable. Having cleared the difficulties of exit, she lay down, and unintentionally fell asleep. When she awoke, the sun had been up three or four hours ; all was right otherwise ; but, had she not served as a sailor, Kate would have trembled upon finding that, during her long sleep of

perhaps seven or eight hours, she had lost sight of land;
by what distance she could only guess; and in what
direction, was to some degree doubtful.   All this, however, seemed a great advantage to the bold girl, throwing
her thoughts back on the enemies she had left behind.
The disadvantage was—having no breakfast, not even
damaged biscuit; and some anxiety naturally arose as to
ulterior prospects a little beyond the horizon of breakfast.
But who's afraid?   As sailors whistle for a wind, Catalina
really had but to whistle for anything with energy, and it
was sure to come.   Like Cæsar to the pilot of Dyrrhachium,
she might have said, for the comfort of her poor timorous
boat (though a boat that in fact was destined soon to
perish), ' *Catalinam vehis, et fortunas ejus.*'   Meantime,
being very doubtful as to the best course for sailing, and
content if her course did but lie off shore, she ' carried on,'
as sailors say, under easy sail, going, in fact, just whither
and just how the Pacific breezes suggested in the gentlest
of whispers.   *All right behind*, was Kate's opinion; and,
what was better, very soon she might say, *all right ahead;*
for, some hour or two before sunset, when dinner was for
once becoming, even to Kate, the most interesting of subjects
for meditation, suddenly a large ship began to swell upon
the brilliant atmosphere.   In those latitudes, and in those
years, any ship was pretty sure to be Spanish : sixty years
later, the odds were in favour of its being an English
buccaneer ; which would have given a new direction to
Kate's energy.   Kate continued to make signals with a
handkerchief whiter than the crocodile's of Ann. Dom.
1592, else it would hardly have been noticed.   Perhaps,
after all, it would not, but that the ship's course carried
her very nearly across Kate's.   The stranger lay to for
her.   It was dark by the time Kate steered herself under
the ship's quarter ; and *then* was seen an instance of this
girl's eternal wakefulness.   Something was painted on the
stern of her boat, she could not see *what ;* but she judged
that, whatever this might be, it would express some connection with the port that she had just quitted.   Now, it
was her wish to break the chain of traces connecting her

with such a scamp as Urquiza; since else, through his commercial correspondence, he might disperse over Peru a portrait of herself by no means flattering. How should she accomplish this? It was dark; and she stood, as you may see an Etonian do at times, rocking her little boat from side to side, until it had taken in water as much as might be agreeable. Too much it proved for the boat's constitution, and the boat perished of dropsy — Kate declining to tap it. She got a ducking herself; but what cared she? Up the ship's side she went, as gaily as ever, in those years when she was called pussy, she had raced after the nuns of St. Sebastian; jumped upon deck, and told the first lieutenant, when he questioned her about her adventures, quite as much truth as any man, under the rank of admiral, had a right to expect.

14.—*Bright Gleams of Sunshine*

This ship was full of recruits for the Spanish army, and bound to Conception. Even in that destiny was an iteration, or repeating memorial of the significance that ran through Catalina's most casual adventures. She had enlisted amongst the soldiers; and, on reaching port, the very first person who came off from shore was a dashing young military officer, whom at once, by his name and rank (though she had never consciously seen him), she identified as her own brother. He was splendidly situated in the service, being the Governor-General's secretary, besides his rank as a cavalry officer; and his errand on board being to inspect the recruits, naturally, on reading in the roll one of them described as a Biscayan, the ardent young man came up with high-bred courtesy to Catalina, took the young recruit's hand with kindness, feeling that to be a compatriot at so great a distance was to be a sort of relative, and asked with emotion after old boyish remembrances. There was a scriptural pathos in what followed, as if it were some scene of domestic re-union opening itself from patriarchal ages. The young officer was the eldest son of the house, and had left Spain when

Catalina was only three years old.   But, singularly enough,
Catalina it was, the little wild cat that he yet remembered
seeing at St. Sebastian's, upon whom his earliest inquiries
settled.   'Did the recruit know his family, the De
Erausos?' Oh yes; everybody knew *them*. 'Did the
recruit know little Catalina?' Catalina smiled, as she
replied that she did; and gave such an animated description of the little fiery wretch, as made the officer's eye
flash with gratified tenderness, and with certainty that the
recruit was no counterfeit Biscayan.   Indeed, you know,
if Kate couldn't give a good description of 'pussy,' who
could?   The issue of the interview was, that the officer
insisted on Kate's making a home of his quarters.   He
did other services for his unknown sister.   He placed her
as a trooper in his own regiment, and favoured her in
many a way that is open to one having authority.   But
the person, after all, that did most to serve our Kate, was
Kate.   War was then raging with Indians, both from
Chili and Peru.   Kate had always done her duty in action;
but at length, in the decisive battle of Puren, there was
an opening for doing something more.   Havoc had been
made of her own squadron; most of the officers were
killed, and the standard was carried off.   Kate gathered
around her a small party—galloped after the Indian
column that was carrying away the trophy—charged—
saw all her own party killed—but, in spite of wounds on
her face and shoulder, succeeded in bearing away the
recovered standard.   She rode up to the general and his
staff; she dismounted; she rendered up her prize; and
fainted away, much less from the blinding blood, than
from the tears of joy which dimmed her eyes, as the
general, waving his sword in admiration over her head, pronounced our Kate on the spot an *Alférez*,[1] or standard-
bearer, with a commission from the King of Spain and
the Indies.   Bonny Kate! noble Kate!   I would there
were not two centuries laid between us, so that I might
have the pleasure of kissing thy fair hand.

[1] '*Alférez*':—This rank in the Spanish army is, or was, on a level
with the modern *sous-lieutenant* of France.

15.—*The Sunshine is Overcast*

Kate had the good sense to see the danger of revealing her sex, or her relationship, even to her own brother. The grasp of the church never relaxed, never ' prescribed,' unless freely and by choice. The nun, if discovered, would have been taken out of the horse-barracks or the dragoon-saddle. She had the firmness, therefore, for many years, to resist the sisterly impulses that sometimes suggested such a confidence. For years, and those years the most important of her life—the years that developed her character—she lived undetected as a brilliant cavalry officer, under her brother's patronage. And the bitterest grief in poor Kate's whole life, was the tragical (and, were it not fully attested, one might say the ultra-scenical) event that dissolved their long connection. Let me spend a word of apology on poor Kate's errors. We all commit many; both you and I, reader. No, stop; that's not civil. You, reader, I know, are a saint; I am *not*, though very near it. I *do* err at long intervals; and then I think with indulgence of the many circumstances that plead for this poor girl. The Spanish armies of that day inherited, from the days of Cortez and Pizarro, shining remembrances of martial prowess, and the very worst of ethics. To think little of bloodshed, to quarrel, to fight, to gamble, to plunder, belonged to the very atmosphere of a camp, to its indolence, to its ancient traditions. In your own defence, you were obliged to do such things. Besides all these grounds of evil, the Spanish army had just then an extra demoralisation from a war with savages—faithless and bloody. Do not think too much, reader, of killing a man—do not, I beseech you! That word '*kill*' is sprinkled over every page of Kate's own autobiography. It ought not to be read by the light of these days. Yet, how if a man that she killed were—— ? Hush! It was sad; but is better hurried over in a few words. Years after this period, a young officer, one day dining with Kate, entreated her to become his second in a duel. Such things were every-day affairs. However, Kate had reasons for declining the service, and did so. But the officer, as he was sullenly departing, said, that if he were killed (as he thought he *should* be), his death would lie at Kate's door. I do not take *his* view of the case, and am not moved by his rhetoric or his logic. Kate *was*, and relented. The duel was fixed for eleven at night, under the walls of a monastery. Unhappily, the night proved unusually dark, so that the two principals had to tie white handkerchiefs round their elbows, in order to descry each other. In the confusion they wounded each other mortally. Upon that, according to a usage not peculiar to Spaniards, but extending (as doubtless the reader knows) for a century longer to our own countrymen, the two seconds were obliged in honour to do something towards avenging their principals. Kate had her usual fatal luck. Her sword passed sheer through the body of her opponent : this unknown opponent falling dead, had just breath left to cry out, ' Ah, villain ! you have killed me ! ' in a voice of horrific reproach ; and the voice was the voice of her brother !

The monks of the monastery under whose silent shadows this murderous duel had taken place, roused by the clashing of swords and the angry shouts of combatants, issued out with torches, to find one only of the four officers surviving. Every convent and altar had the right of asylum for a short period. According to the custom, the monks carried Kate, insensible with anguish of mind, to the sanctuary of their chapel. There for some days they detained her ; but then, having furnished her with a horse and some provisions, they turned her adrift. Which way should the unhappy fugitive turn ? In blindness of heart, she turned towards the sea. It was the sea that had brought her to Peru ; it was the sea that would perhaps carry her away. It was the sea that had first showed her this land and its golden hopes ; it was the sea that ought to hide from her its fearful remembrances. The sea it was that had twice spared her life in extremities ; the sea it was that might now, if it chose, take back the bauble that it had spared in vain.

16.—*Kate's Ascent of the Andes*

Three days our poor heroine followed the coast. Her horse was then almost unable to move ; and on *his* account she turned inland to a thicket, for grass and shelter. As she drew near to it, a voice challenged, '*Who goes there?*' —Kate answered, '*Spain.*'—'*What people?*'—'*A friend.*' It was two soldiers, deserters, and almost starving. Kate share her provisions with these men ; and, on hearing their plan, which was to go over the Cordilleras, she agreed to join the party. *Their* object was the wild one of seeking the river *Dorado*, whose waters rolled along golden sands, and whose pebbles were emeralds. *Hers* was to throw herself upon a line the least liable to pursuit, and the readiest for a new chapter of life, in which oblivion might be found for the past. After a few days of incessant climbing and fatigue, they found themselves in the regions of perpetual snow. Summer came even hither ; but came as vainly to this kingdom of frost as to the grave of her brother. No fire, but the fire of human blood in youthful veins, could ever be kept burning in these aerial solitudes. Fuel was rarely to be found, and kindling a fire by interfriction of dry sticks was a secret almost exclusively Indian. However, our Kate can do everything ; and she's the girl, if ever girl *did* such a thing, that I back at any odds for crossing the Cordilleras. I would bet you something now, reader, if I thought you would deposit your stakes by return of post (as they play at chess, through the post-office), that Kate does the trick ; that she gets down to the other side ; that the soldiers do *not* ; and that the horse, if preserved at all, is preserved in a way that will leave him very little to boast of.

The party had gathered wild berries and esculent roots at the foot of the mountains, and the horse was of very great use in carrying them. But this larder was soon emptied. There was nothing then to carry ; so that the horse's value, as a beast of burden, fell cent. per cent. In fact, very soon he could not carry himself, and it became easy to calculate when he would reach the bottom on the

wrong side the Cordilleras. He took three steps back for
one upwards. A council of war being held, the small
army resolved to slaughter their horse. He, though a
member of the expedition, had no vote; and, if he had,
the votes would have stood three to one—majority, two
against him. He was cut into quarters—a difficult fraction
to distribute amongst a triad of claimants. No saltpetre
or sugar could be had; but the frost was antiseptic. And
the horse was preserved in as useful a sense as ever apricots
were preserved or strawberries; and *that* was the kind of
preservation which one page ago I promised to the horse.

On a fire, painfully devised out of broom and withered
leaves, a horse-steak was dressed; for drink, snow was
allowed *à discretion*. This ought to have revived the
party: and Kate, perhaps, it *did*. But the poor deserters
were thinly clad, and they had not the boiling heart of
Catalina. More and more they drooped. Kate did her
best to cheer them. But the march was nearly at an end
for *them;* and they were going, in one half-hour, to receive
their last billet. Yet, before this consummation, they have
a strange spectacle to see—such as few places could show
but the upper chambers of the Cordilleras. They had
reached a billowy scene of rocky masses, large and small,
looking shockingly black on their perpendicular sides as
they rose out of the vast snowy expanse. Upon the
highest of these that was accessible, Kate mounted to look
around her, and she saw—oh, rapture at such an hour!—
a man sitting on a shelf of rock, with a gun by his side.
Joyously she shouted to her comrades, and ran down to
communicate the good news. Here was a sportsman, watching, perhaps, for an eagle; and now they would have
relief. One man's cheek kindled with the hectic of sudden
joy, and he rose eagerly to march. The other was fast
sinking under the fatal sleep that frost sends before herself as her merciful minister of death; but hearing in his
dream the tidings of relief, and assisted by his friends, he
also staggeringly arose. It could not be three minutes'
walk, Kate thought, to the station of the sportsman. That
thought supported them all. Under Kate's guidance, who

had taken a sailor's glance at the bearings, they soon un-
threaded the labyrinth of rocks so far as to bring the man
within view. He had not left his resting-place; their
steps on the soundless snow, naturally, he could not hear;
and, as their road brought them upon him from the rear,
still less could he see them. Kate hailed him; but so
keenly was he absorbed in some speculation, or in the
object of his watching, that he took no notice of them, not
even moving his head. Coming close behind him, Kate
touched his shoulder, and said, 'My friend, are you sleeping?' Yes, he *was* sleeping—sleeping the sleep from
which there is no awaking; and the slight touch of Kate
having disturbed the equilibrium of the corpse, down it
rolled on the snow: the frozen body rang like a hollow
iron cylinder; the face uppermost, and blue with mould,
mouth open, teeth ghastly and bleaching in the frost, and
a frightful grin upon the lips. This dreadful spectacle
finished the struggles of the weaker man, who sank and
died at once. The other made an effort with so much
spirit, that, in Kate's opinion, horror had acted upon him
beneficially as a stimulant. But it was not really so. It
was simply a spasm of morbid strength. A collapse succeeded; his blood began to freeze; he sat down in spite
of Kate, and *he* also died without further struggle. Yes,
gone are the poor suffering deserters; stretched out
and bleaching upon the snow; and insulted discipline
is avenged. Great kings have long arms; and sycophants
are ever at hand for the errand of the potent. What had
frost and snow to do with the quarrel? Yet *they* made
themselves sycophantic servants to the King of Spain; and
they it was that dogged his deserters up to the summit of
the Cordilleras, more surely than any Spanish bloodhound,
or any Spanish tirailleur's bullet.

17.—*Kate stands alone on the Summit of the Andes*

Now is our Kate standing alone on the summits of the
Andes; and in solitude that is frightful, for she is alone
with her own afflicted conscience. Twice before she had

stood in solitude as deep upon the wild, wild waters of the Pacific; but her conscience had been then untroubled. Now is there nobody left that can help; her horse is dead—the soldiers are dead. There is nobody that she can speak to, except God; and very soon you will find that she *does* speak to Him; for already on these vast aerial deserts He has been whispering to *her*. The condition of Kate in some respects resembled that of Coleridge's *Ancient Mariner*. But possibly, reader, you may be amongst the many careless readers that have never fully understood what that condition was. Suffer me to enlighten you; else you ruin the story of the mariner; and by losing all its pathos, lose half its beauty.

There are three readers of the *Ancient Mariner*. The first is gross enough to fancy all the imagery of the mariner's visions delivered by the poet for actual facts of experience; which being impossible, the whole pulverises, for that reader, into a baseless fairy tale. The second reader is wiser than *that*; he knows that the imagery is the imagery of febrile delirium; really seen, but not seen as an external reality. The mariner had caught the pestilential fever, which carried off all his mates; he only had survived—the delirium had vanished; but the visions that had haunted the delirium remained. 'Yes,' says the third reader, 'they remained; naturally they did, being scorched by fever into his brain; but how did they happen to remain on his belief as gospel truths? The delirium had vanished: why had not the painted scenery of the delirium vanished, except as visionary memorials of a sorrow that was cancelled? Why was it that craziness settled upon this mariner's brain, driving him, as if he were a Cain, or another Wandering Jew, to " pass like night from land to land"; and, at certain intervals, wrenching him until he made rehearsal of his errors, even at the difficult cost of " holding children from their play, and old men from the chimney corner"?'[1] That craziness, as the *third* reader deciphers, rose out of a deeper soil than any

[1] The beautiful words of Sir Philip Sidney in his *Defense of Poesie*.

bodily affection. It had its root in penitential sorrow. Oh, bitter is the sorrow to a conscientious heart, when, too late, it discovers the depth of a love that has been trampled under foot! This mariner had slain the creature that, on all the earth, loved him best. In the darkness of his cruel superstition he had done it, to save his human brothers from a fancied inconvenience; and yet, by that very act of cruelty, he had himself called destruction upon their heads. The Nemesis that followed punished *him* through *them*— him that wronged through those that wrongfully he sought to benefit. That spirit who watches over the sanctities of love is a strong angel—is a jealous angel; and this angel it was

> That loved the bird, that loved the man
> That shot him with his bow.

He it was that followed the cruel archer into silent and slumbering seas :—

> Nine fathom deep he had follow'd him,
> Through the realms of mist and snow.

This jealous angel it was that pursued the man into noon-day darkness, and the vision of dying oceans, into delirium, and finally (when recovered from disease), into an unsettled mind.

Not altogether unlike, though free from the criminal intention of the mariner, had been the offence of Kate; not unlike, also, was the punishment that now is dogging her steps. She, like the mariner, had slain the one sole creature that loved her upon the whole wide earth; she, like the mariner, for this offence, had been hunted into frost and snow—very soon will be hunted into delirium; and from *that* (if she escapes with life), will be hunted into the trouble of a heart that cannot rest. There was the excuse of one darkness, physical darkness, for *her;* there was the excuse of another darkness, the darkness of superstition, for the mariner. But, with all the excuses that earth, and the darkness of earth, can furnish, bitter it would be for any of us, reader, through every hour of life, waking or dreaming, to look back upon one fatal moment when we had pierced the heart that would have died for *us*. In this only the darkness had been merciful to Kate—that it had hidden for ever from her victim the hand that slew him. But now, in such utter solitude, her thoughts ran back to their earliest interview. She remembered with anguish, how, on touching the shores of America, almost the first word that met her ear had been from *him*, the brother whom she had killed, about the 'pussy' of times long past; how the gallant young man had hung upon her words, as in her native Basque she described her own mischievous little self, of twelve years back; how his colour went and came, whilst his loving memory of the little sister was revived by her own descriptive traits, giving back, as in a mirror, the fawn-like grace, the squirrel-like restlessness, that once had kindled his own delighted laughter; how he would take no denial, but showed on the spot, that simply to have touched—to have kissed—to have played with the little wild thing, that glorified, by her innocence, the gloom of St. Sebastian's cloisters, gave a *right* to his hospitality; how, through *him* only, she had found a welcome in camps; how, through *him*, she had found the avenue to honour and distinction. And yet this brother, so loving and generous, who, without knowing, had cherished and protected her, and all from pure holy love for herself as the innocent plaything of St. Sebastian's, *him* in a moment she had dismissed from life. She paused; she turned round, as if looking back for his grave; she saw the dreadful wildernesses of snow which already she had traversed. Silent they were at this season, even as in the panting heats of noon the Saharas of the torrid zone are oftentimes silent. Dreadful was the silence; it was the nearest thing to the silence of the grave. Graves were at the foot of the Andes, *that* she knew too well; graves were at the summit of the Andes, *that* she saw too well. And, as she gazed, a sudden thought flashed upon her, when her eyes settled upon the corpses of the poor deserters—Could she, like *them*, have been all this while unconsciously executing judgment upon herself? Running from a wrath that was doubtful, into the very jaws of

2 A

a wrath that was inexorable? Flying in panic—and
behold! there was no man that pursued? For the first
time in her life, Kate trembled. *Not* for the first time,
Kate wept. Far less for the first time was it, that Kate
bent her knee—that Kate clasped her hands—that Kate
prayed. But it *was* the first time that she prayed as *they*
pray, for whom no more hope is left but in prayer.

Here let me pause a moment, for the sake of making
somebody angry. A Frenchman, who sadly misjudges
Kate, looking at her through a Parisian opera-glass, gives
it as *his* opinion—that, because Kate first *records* her
prayer on this occasion, therefore, now first of all she
prayed. *I* think not so. *I* love this Kate, bloodstained
as she is; and I could not love a woman that never bent
her knee in thankfulness or in supplication. However,
we have all a right to our own little opinion; and it is
not *you* ' *mon cher*,' you Frenchman, that I am angry with,
but somebody else that stands behind you. You, Frenchman, and your compatriots, I love oftentimes for your
festal gaiety of heart; and I quarrel only with your levity,
and that eternal worldliness that freezes too fiercely—that
absolutely blisters with its frost, like the upper air of the
Andes. *You* speak of Kate only as too readily you speak
of all women; the instinct of a natural scepticism being to
scoff at all hidden depths of truth. Else you are civil
enough to Kate; and your ' *homage* ' (such as it may
happen to be) is always at the service of a woman on the
shortest notice. But behind *you* I see a worse fellow—a
gloomy fanatic, a religious sycophant, that seeks to pro-
pitiate his circle by bitterness against the offences that are
most unlike his own. And against him, I must say one
word for Kate to the too hasty reader. This villain opens
his fire on our Kate under shelter of a lie. For there is
a standing lie in the very constitution of civil society—a
necessity of error, misleading us as to the proportions of
crime. Mere necessity obliges man to create many acts
into felonies, and to punish them as the heaviest offences,
which his better sense teaches him secretly to regard as
perhaps among the lightest. Those poor mutineers or

deserters, for instance, were they necessarily without
excuse? They might have been oppressively used; but,
in critical times of war, no matter for the individual
palliations, the mutineer *must* be shot: there is no help for
it: as, in extremities of general famine, we shoot the man
(alas! we are *obliged* to shoot him) that is found robbing
the common stores, in order to feed his own perishing
children, though the offence is hardly visible in the sight
of God. Only blockheads adjust their scale of guilt to the
scale of human punishments. Now, our wicked friend the
fanatic, who calumniates Kate, abuses the advantage which,
for such a purpose, he derives from the exaggerated social
estimate of all violence. Personal security being so main
an object of social union, we are obliged to frown upon all
modes of violence, as hostile as the central principle of that
union. We are *obliged* to rate it, according to the
universal results towards which it tends, and scarcely at all
according to the special condition of circumstances in which
it may originate. Hence a horror arises for that class of
offences, which is (philosophically speaking) exaggerated;
and by daily use, the ethics of a police-office translate
themselves, insensibly, into the ethics even of religious
people. But I tell that sycophantish fanatic—not this
only, viz., that he abuses unfairly, against Kate, the
advantage which he has from the *inevitably* distorted bias
of society—but also I tell him this second little thing, that,
upon turning away the glass from that one obvious aspect
of Kate's character, her too fiery disposition to vindicate
all rights by violence, and viewing her in relation to
general religious capacities, she was a thousand times more
promisingly endowed than himself. It is impossible to be
noble in many things, without having many points of contact with true religion. If you deny *that*, you it is that
calumniate religion. Kate *was* noble in many things.
Her worst errors never took a shape of self-interest or
deceit. She was brave, she was generous, she was forgiving, she bore no malice, she was full of truth—qualities
that God loves either in man or woman. She hated
sycophants and dissemblers. *I* hate them; and more than

ever at this moment on her behalf. I wish she were but here, to give a punch on the head to that fellow who traduces her. And, coming round again to the occasion from which this short digression has started—viz., the question raised by the Frenchman, whether Kate were a person likely to *pray* under other circumstances than those of extreme danger—I offer it as *my* opinion, that she was. Violent people are not always such from choice, but perhaps from situation. And, though the circumstances of Kate's position allowed her little means for realising her own wishes, it is certain that those wishes pointed continually to peace and an unworldly happiness, if *that* were possible. The stormy clouds that enveloped her in camps, opened overhead at intervals, showing her a far-distant blue serene. She yearned, at many times, for the rest which is not in camps or armies ; and it is certain that she ever combined with any plans or day-dreams of tranquillity, as their most essential ally, some aid derived from that dove-like religion which, at St. Sebastian's, from her infant days she had been taught so profoundly to adore.

18.—*Kate begins to Descend the Mighty Staircase*

Now, let us rise from this discussion of Kate against libellers, as Kate herself is rising from prayer, and consider, in conjunction with *her*, the character and promise of that dreadful ground which lies immediately before her. What is to be thought of it? I could wish we had a theodolite here, and a spirit-level, and other instruments, for settling some important questions. Yet, no ; on consideration, if one *had* a wish allowed by that kind fairy, without whose assistance it would be quite impossible to send even for the spirit-level, nobody would throw away the wish upon things so paltry. I would not put the fairy upon such an errand : I would order the good creature to bring no spirit-level, but a stiff glass of spirits for Kate ; also, next after which, I would request a palanquin, and relays of fifty stout bearers—all drunk, in order that they might not feel the cold. The main interest at this moment, and the main difficulty—indeed, the 'open question' of the case—was, to ascertain whether the ascent were yet accomplished or not ; and when would the descent commence ? or had it, perhaps, long commenced ?   The character of the ground, in those immediate successions that could be connected by the eye, decided nothing ; for the undulations of the level had been so continual for miles, as to perplex any eye, even an engineer's, in attempting to judge whether, upon the whole, the tendency were upwards or downwards.   Possibly it was yet neither way ; it is indeed probable that Kate had been for some time travelling along a series of terraces that traversed the whole breadth of the topmost area at that point of crossing the Cordilleras ; and this area, perhaps, but not certainly, might compensate any casual tendencies downwards by corresponding reascents.   Then came the question, how long would these terraces yet continue ? and had the ascending parts *really* balanced the descending ?   Upon *that* seemed to rest the final chance for Kate.   Because, unless she very soon reached a lower level and a warmer atmosphere, mere weariness would oblige her to lie down, under a fierceness of cold that would not suffer her to rise after once losing the warmth of motion ; or, inversely, if she even continued in motion, continued extremity of cold would, of itself, speedily absorb the little surplus energy for moving which yet remained unexhausted by weariness — that is, in short, the excessive weariness would give a murderous advantage to the cold, or the excessive cold would give a corresponding advantage to the weariness.

At this stage of her progress, and whilst the agonising question seemed yet as indeterminate as ever, Kate's struggle with despair, which had been greatly soothed by the fervour of her prayer, revolved upon her in deadlier blackness.   All turned, she saw, upon a race against time, and the arrears of the road ; and she, poor thing ! how little qualified could *she* be, in such a condition, for a race of any kind—and against two such obstinate brutes as Time and Space !   This hour of the progress, this noontide of Kate's struggle, must have been the very crisis of the whole.   Despair was rapidly tending to ratify itself. Hope, in any degree, would be a cordial for sustaining her efforts.   But to flounder along a dreadful chaos of snow-drifts, or snow-chasms, towards a point of rock which, being turned, should expose only another interminable succession of the same character—might *that* be endured by ebbing spirits, by stiffening limbs, by the ghastly darkness that was now beginning to gather upon the inner eye?   And, if once despair became triumphant, all the little arrear of physical strength would collapse at once.

Oh! verdure of human fields, cottages of men and women (that now suddenly, in the eyes of Kate, seemed all brothers and sisters), cottages with children around them at play, that are so far below—oh! spring and summer, blossoms and flowers, to which, as to *his* symbols, God has given the gorgeous privilege of rehearsing for ever upon earth his most mysterious perfection—Life, and the resurrections of Life—is it indeed true that poor Kate must never see you more?   Mutteringly she put that question to herself.   But strange are the caprices of ebb and flow in the deep fountains of human sensibilities.   At this very moment, when the utter incapacitation of despair was gathering fast at Kate's heart, a sudden lightening, as it were, or flashing inspiration of hope, shot far into her spirit, a reflux almost supernatural, from the earliest effects of her prayer.   Dimmed and confused had been the accuracy of her sensations for hours ; but all at once a strong conviction came over her—that more and more was the sense of descent becoming steady and continuous. Turning round to measure backwards with her eye the ground traversed through the last half-hour, she identified, by a remarkable point of rock, the spot near which the three corpses were lying.   The silence seemed deeper than ever.   Neither was there any phantom memorial of life for the eye or for the ear, nor wing of bird, nor echo, nor green leaf, nor creeping thing that moved or stirred, upon the soundless waste.   Oh, what a relief to this burden of silence would be a human groan !   Here seemed a motive for still darker despair. And yet, at that very moment, a pulse of joy began to thaw the ice at her heart. It struck her, as she reviewed the ground, from that point where the corpses lay, that undoubtedly it had been for some time slowly descending. Her senses were much dulled by suffering; but this thought it was, suggested by a sudden apprehension of a continued descending movement, which had caused her to turn round. Sight had confirmed the suggestion first derived from her own steps. The distance attained was now sufficient to establish the tendency. Oh yes, yes; to a certainty she *was* descending—she *had* been descending for some time. Frightful was the spasm of joy which whispered that the worst was over. It was as when the shadow of midnight, that murderers had relied on, is passing away from your beleaguered shelter, and dawn will soon be manifest. It was as when a flood, that all day long has raved against the walls of your house, ceases (you suddenly think) to rise; yes! measured by a golden plummet, it *is* sinking beyond a doubt, and the darlings of your household are saved. Kate faced round in agitation to her proper direction. She saw, what previously, in her stunning confusion, she had *not* seen, that hardly two stone-throws in advance lay a mass of rock, split as into a gateway. Through that opening it now became certain that the road was lying. Hurrying forward, she passed within these natural gates. Gates of paradise they were. Ah, what a vista did that gateway expose before her dazzled eye! what a revelation of heavenly promise! Full two miles long, stretched a long narrow glen, everywhere descending, and in many parts rapidly. All was now placed beyond a doubt. She *was* descending; for hours, perhaps, *had* been descending insensibly, the mighty staircase. Yes, Kate is leaving behind her the kingdom of frost and the victories of death. Two miles farther, there may be rest, if there is not shelter. And very soon, as the crest of her new-born happiness, she distinguished at the other end of that rocky vista a pavilion-shaped mass of dark-green foliage—a belt of trees, such as we see in the lovely parks of England, but islanded by a screen of thick bushy undergrowth! Oh! verdure of dark olive foliage, offered suddenly to fainting eyes, as if by some winged patriarchal herald of wrath relenting—solitary Arab's tent, rising with saintly signals of peace in the dreadful desert— must Kate indeed die even yet, whilst she sees but cannot reach you? Outpost on the frontier of man's dominions, standing within life, but looking out upon everlasting death, wilt thou hold up the anguish of thy mocking invitation only to betray? Never, perhaps, in this world was the line so exquisitely grazed that parts salvation and ruin. As the dove to her dovecot from the swooping hawk—as the Christian pinnace to the shelter of Christian batteries, from the bloody Mahometan corsair—so flew, so tried to fly, towards the anchoring thickets, that, alas! could not weigh their anchors, and make sail to meet her, the poor exhausted Kate from the vengeance of pursuing frost.

And she reached them; staggering, fainting, reeling, she entered beneath the canopy of umbrageous trees. But as oftentimes the Hebrew fugitive to a city of refuge, flying for his life before the avenger of blood, was pressed so hotly, that on entering the archway of what seemed to *him* the heavenly city gate, as he kneeled in deep thankfulness to kiss its holy merciful shadow, he could not rise again, but sank instantly with infant weakness into sleep— sometimes to wake no more ; so sank, so collapsed upon the ground, without power to choose her couch, and with little prospect of ever rising again to her feet, the martial nun. She lay as luck had ordered it, with her head screened by the undergrowth of bushes from any gales that might arise ; she lay exactly as she sank, with her eyes up to heaven ; and thus it was that the nun saw, before falling asleep, the two sights that upon earth are fittest for the closing eyes of a nun, whether destined to open again, or to close for ever. She saw the interlacing of boughs overhead forming a dome, that seemed like the dome of a cathedral. She saw, through the fretwork of the foliage, another dome, far beyond the dome of an evening sky, the dome of some heavenly cathedral, not built with hands. She saw upon this upper dome the vesper lights, all alive with pathetic grandeur of colouring from a sunset that had just been rolling down like a chorus. She had not, till now, consciously observed the time of day; whether it were morning, or whether it were afternoon, in the confusion of her misery, she had not distinctly known. But now she whispered to herself, '*It is evening*': and what lurked half unconsciously in these words might be, 'The sun, that rejoices, has finished his daily toil; man, that labours, has finished *his*; I, that suffer, have finished mine.' That might be what she thought, but what she *said* was, 'It is evening; and the hour is come when the *Angelus* is sounding through St. Sebastian.' What made her think of St. Sebastian, so far away in depths of space and time? Her brain was wandering, now that her feet were *not*; and, because her eyes had descended from the heavenly to the earthly dome, *that* made her think of earthly cathedrals, and of cathedral choirs, and of St. Sebastian's chapel, with its silvery bells that carried the echoing *Angelus* far into mountain recesses. Perhaps, as her wanderings increased, she thought herself back into childhood; became 'pussy' once again; fancied that all since then was a frightful dream; that she was not upon the dreadful Andes, but still kneeling in the holy chapel at vespers; still innocent as then; loved as then she had been loved; and that all men were liars, who said her hand was ever stained with blood. Little is mentioned of the delusions which possessed her; but that little gives a key to the impulse which her palpitating heart obeyed, and which her rambling brain for ever reproduced in multiplying mirrors. Restlessness kept her in waking dreams for a brief half-hour. But then fever and delirium would wait no longer; the killing exhaustion would no longer be refused; the fever, the delirium, and the exhaustion, swept in together with power like an army with banners; and the nun ceased through the gathering twilight any more to watch the cathedrals of earth, or the more solemn cathedrals that rose in the heavens above.

19.—*Kate's Bedroom is Invaded by Horsemen*

All night long she slept in her verdurous St. Bernard's hospice without awaking ; and whether she would *ever* awake seemed to depend upon accident. The slumber that towered above her brain was like that fluctuating silvery column which stands in scientific tubes, sinking, rising, deepening, lightening, contracting, expanding ; or like the mist that sits, through sultry afternoons, upon the river of the American St. Peter, sometimes rarefying for minutes into sunny gauze, sometimes condensing for hours into palls of funeral darkness. You fancy that, after twelve hours of *any* sleep, she must have been refreshed ; better, at least, than she was last night. Ah ! but sleep is not always sent upon missions of refreshment. Sleep is sometimes the secret chamber in which death arranges his machinery, and stations his artillery. Sleep is sometimes that deep mysterious atmosphere, in which the human spirit is slowly unsettling its wings for flight from earthly tenements. It is now eight o'clock in the morning ; and, to all appearance, if Kate should receive no aid before noon, when next the sun is departing to his rest, then, alas ! Kate will be departing to hers : when next the sun is holding out his golden Christian signal to man, that the hour is come for letting his anger go down, Kate will be sleeping away for ever into the arms of brotherly forgiveness.

What is wanted just now for Kate, supposing Kate herself to be wanted by this world, is, that this world would be kind enough to send her a little brandy before it is too late. The simple truth was, and a truth which I have known to take place in more ladies than Kate, who died or did *not* die, accordingly as they had or had not an adviser like myself, capable of giving an opinion equal to Captain Bunsby's, on this point—viz., whether the jewelly star of life had descended too far down the arch towards setting, for any chance of reascending by *spontaneous* effort. The fire was still burning in secret, but needed, perhaps, to be rekindled by potent artificial breath. It lingered, and *might* linger, but apparently would never culminate again, without some stimulus from earthly vineyards.[1] Kate was ever lucky, though ever unfortunate ; and the world, being of my opinion that Kate was worth saving, made up its mind about half-past eight o'clock in the morning to save her. Just at that time, when the night was over, and its sufferings were hidden—in one of those intermitting gleams that for a moment or two lightened the clouds of her slumber—Kate's dull ear caught a sound that for years had spoken a familiar language to *her*.

---

[1] Though not exactly in the same circumstances as Kate, or sleeping, *à la belle étoile*, on a declivity of the Andes, I have known (or heard circumstantially reported) the cases of many ladies, besides Kate, who were in precisely the same critical danger of perishing for want of a little brandy. A dessert-spoonful or two would have saved them. Avaunt ! you wicked 'Temperance' medalist ! repent as fast as ever you can, or, perhaps, the next time we hear of you, *anasarca* and *hydrothorax* will be running after you, to punish your shocking excesses in water. Seriously, the case is one of constant recurrence, and constantly ending fatally from *unseasonable* and pedantic rigour of temperance. Dr. Darwin, the famous author of *Zoonomia, The Botanic Garden*, etc., sacrificed his life to the very pedantry and superstition of temperance, by refusing a glass of brandy in obedience to a system, at a moment when (according to the opinion of all around him) one single glass would have saved his life. The fact is, that the medical profession composes the most generous and liberal body of men amongst us ; taken generally, by much the most enlightened ; but, professionally, the most timid. Want of boldness in the administration of opium, etc., though they can be bold enough with mercury, is their besetting infirmity. And from this infirmity females suffer most. One instance I need hardly mention, the fatal case of an august lady, mourned by nations,[1] with respect to whom it was, and is, the belief of multitudes to this hour (well able to judge), that she would have been saved by a glass of brandy; and her chief medical attendant, Sir R. C.,[2] who shot himself, came to think so too late—too late for *her*, and too late for himself. Amongst many cases of the same nature, which personally I have been acquainted with, thirty years ago, a man illustrious for his intellectual accomplishments [3] mentioned to me that his own wife, during her first or second confinement, was suddenly reported to him, by one of her female attendants (who slipped away unobserved by the medical people), as undoubtedly sinking fast. He hurried to

---

[1] [The Princess Charlotte.]
[2] [Sir Richard Croft.]
[3] On second thoughts, I see no reason for scrupling to mention that this man was Robert Southey.

What was it? It was the sound, though muffled and deadened, like the ear that heard it, of horsemen advancing. Interpreted by the tumultuous dreams of Kate, was it the cavalry of Spain, at whose head so often she had charged the bloody Indian scalpers? Was it, according to the legend of ancient days, cavalry that had been sown by her brother's blood—cavalry that rose from the ground on an inquest of retribution, and were racing up the Andes to seize her? Her dreams, that had opened sullenly to the sound, waited for no answer, but closed again into pompous darkness. Happily, the horsemen had caught the glimpse of some bright ornament, clasp, or aiguillette, on Kate's dress. They were hunters and foresters from below — servants in the household of a beneficent lady ; and, in pursuit of some flying game, had wandered far beyond their ordinary limits. Struck by the sudden scintillation from Kate's dress played upon by the morning sun, they rode up to the thicket. Great was their surprise, great their pity, to see a young officer in

---

her chamber, and *saw* that it was so. On this, he suggested earnestly some stimulant—laudanum or alcohol. The presiding medical authority, however, was inexorable. 'Oh, by no means,' shaking his ambrosial wig ; 'any stimulant at this crisis would be fatal.' But no authority could overrule the concurrent testimony of all symptoms, and of all unprofessional opinions. By some pious falsehood, my friend smuggled the doctor out of the room, and immediately smuggled a glass of brandy into the poor lady's lips. She recovered as if under the immediate afflatus of magic ; so sudden was her recovery, and so complete. The doctor is now dead, and went to his grave under the delusive persuasion—that not any vile glass of brandy, but the stern refusal of all brandy, was the thing that saved his collapsing patient. The patient herself, who might naturally know something of the matter, was of a different opinion. She sided with the factious body around her bed (comprehending all, beside the doctor), who felt sure that death was rapidly approaching, *barring* that brandy. The same result, in the same appalling crisis, I have known repeatedly produced by twenty-five drops of laudanum. Many will say, 'Oh, never listen to a non-medical man like this writer. Consult in such a case your medical adviser.' You will, will you? Then let me tell you, that you are missing the very logic of all I have been saying for the improvement of blockheads, which is—that you should consult any man *but* a medical man, since no other man has any obstinate prejudice of professional timidity.

uniform stretched within the bushes upon the ground, and apparently dying. Borderers from childhood on this dreadful frontier, sacred to winter and death, they understood the case at once. They dismounted, and, with the tenderness of women, raising the poor frozen cornet in their arms, washed her temples with brandy, whilst one, at intervals, suffered a few drops to trickle within her lips. As the restoration of a warm bed was now most likely to be the one thing needed, they lifted the helpless stranger upon a horse, walking on each side with supporting arms. Once again our Kate is in the saddle, once again a Spanish caballero. But Kate's bridle-hand is deadly cold. And her spurs, that she had never unfastened since leaving the monastic asylum, hung as idle as the flapping sail that fills unsteadily with the breeze upon a stranded ship.

This procession had many miles to go, and over difficult ground ; but at length it reached the forest-like park and the chateau of the wealthy proprietress. Kate was still half-frozen and speechless, except at intervals. Heavens ! can this corpse-like, languishing young woman be the Kate that once, in her radiant girlhood, rode with a handful of comrades into a column of two thousand enemies, that saw her comrades die, that persisted when all were dead, that tore from the heart of all resistance the banner of her native Spain? Chance and change have 'written strange defeatures in her face.' Much is changed ; but some things are not changed, either in herself or in those about her : there is still kindness that overflows with pity : there is still helplessness that asks for this pity without a voice : she is now received by a senora, not less kind than that maternal aunt who, on the night of her birth, first welcomed her to a loving home ; and she, the heroine of Spain, is herself as helpless now as that little lady, who, then at ten minutes of age, was kissed and blessed by all the household of St. Sebastian.

20.—*A Second Lull in Kate's Stormy Life*

Let us suppose Kate placed in a warm bed. Let us suppose her in a few hours recovering steady consciousness; in a few days recovering some power of self-support; in a fortnight able to seek the gay saloon, where the senora was sitting alone, and able to render thanks, with that deep sincerity which ever characterised our wild-hearted Kate, for the critical services received from that lady and her establishment.

This lady, a widow, was what the French call a *métisse*, the Spaniards a *mestizza*—that is, the daughter of a genuine Spaniard and an Indian mother. I will call her simply a *Creole*,[1] which will indicate her want of pure Spanish blood sufficiently to explain her deference for those who had it. She was a kind, liberal woman; rich rather more than needed where there were no opera-boxes to rent; a widow about fifty years old in the wicked world's account, some forty-two in her own; and happy, above all, in the possession of a most lovely daughter, whom even the wicked world did not accuse of more than sixteen years. This daughter, Juana, was —— But stop—let her open the door of the saloon in which the senora and the cornet are conversing, and speak for herself. She did so, after an hour

---

[1] '*Creole*':—At that time the infusion of negro or African blood was small. Consequently, none of the negro hideousness was diffused. After those intercomplexities had arisen between all complications and interweavings of descent from three original strands—European, American, African—the distinctions of social consideration founded on them bred names so many, that a court calendar was necessary to keep you from blundering. As yet (*i.e.*, in Kate's time), the varieties were few. Meantime, the word *Creole* has always been misapplied in our English colonies to a person (though of strictly European blood), simply if *born* in the West Indies. In this English use, the word *Creole* expresses exactly the same difference as the Romans indicated by *Hispanus* and *Hispanicus*. The first meant a person of Spanish blood, a native of Spain; the second, a Roman born in Spain. So of *Germanus* and *Germanicus*, *Italus* and *Italicus*, *Anglus* and *Anglicus*, etc.; an important distinction, on which see Isaac Casaubon *apud Scriptores Hist. Augustan.*

had passed ; which length of time, to *her* that never had
any business whatever in her innocent life, seemed sufficient
to settle the business of the Old World and the New.   Had
Pietro Diaz (as Catalina now called herself) been really a
Peter, and not a sham Peter, what a vision of loveliness
would have rushed upon his sensibilities as the door opened.
Do not expect me to describe her, for which, however, there
are materials extant, sleeping in archives, where they have
slept for two hundred and twenty-eight years.   It is enough
that she is reported to have united the stately tread of Andalusian women with the innocent voluptuousness of Peruvian
eyes.   As to her complexion and figure, be it known that
Juana's father was a gentleman from Grenada, having in
his veins the grandest blood of all this earth—blood of
Goths and Vandals, tainted (for which Heaven be thanked!)
twice over with blood of Arabs—once through Moors, once
through Jews ; [1] whilst from her grandmother Juana drew
the deep subtle melancholy, and the beautiful contours of
limb, which belonged to the Indian race—a race destined
(ah, wherefore?) silently and slowly to fade away from the
earth.   No awkwardness was or could be in this antelope,
when gliding with forest grace into the room ; no town-
bred shame ; nothing but the unaffected pleasure of one
who wishes to speak a fervent welcome, but knows not if
she ought ; the astonishment of a Miranda, bred in utter
solitude, when first beholding a princely Ferdinand, and just
so much reserve as to remind you, that, if Catalina thought
fit to dissemble her sex, she did *not*.   And consider, reader,
if you look back, and are a great arithmetician, that whilst
the senora had only fifty per cent of Spanish blood, Juana

[1] It is well known, that the very reason why the Spanish beyond
all nations became so gloomily jealous of a Jewish cross in the pedigree,
was because, until the vigilance of the church rose into ferocity, in no
nation was such a cross so common.   The hatred of fear is ever the
deepest.   And men hated the Jewish taint, as once in Jerusalem they
hated the leprosy, because, even whilst they raved against it, the secret
proofs of it might be detected amongst their own kindred ; even as in
the Temple, whilst once a Hebrew king rose in mutiny against the
priesthood (2 Chron. xxvi. 16-20), suddenly the leprosy that dethroned
him, blazed out upon his forehead.

had seventy-five ; so that her Indian melancholy, after all, was swallowed up for the present by her Visigothic, by her Vandal, by her Arab, by her Spanish fire.

Catalina, seared as she was by the world, has left it evident in her memoirs that she was touched more than she wished to be by this innocent child. Juana formed a brief lull for Catalina in her too stormy existence. And if for *her* in this life the sweet reality of a sister had been possible, here was the sister she would have chosen. On the other hand, what might Juana think of the cornet ? To have been thrown upon the kind hospitalities of her native home, to have been rescued by her mother's servants from that fearful death which, lying but a few miles off, had filled her nursery with traditionary tragedies —*that* was sufficient to create an interest in the stranger. Such things it had been that wooed the heavenly Desdemona. But his bold martial demeanour, his yet youthful style of beauty, his frank manners, his animated conversation, that reported a hundred contests with suffering and peril, wakened for the first time her admiration. Men she had never seen before, except menial servants, or a casual priest. But here was a gentleman, young like herself, a splendid cavalier, that rode in the cavalry of Spain ; that carried the banner of the only potentate whom Peruvians knew of—the King of the Spains and the Indies ; that had doubled Cape Horn ; that had crossed the Andes ; that had suffered shipwreck ; that had rocked upon fifty storms ; and had wrestled for life through fifty battles.

The reader already guesses all that followed. The sisterly love which Catalina did really feel for this young mountaineer was inevitably misconstrued. Embarrassed, but not able, from sincere affection, or almost in bare propriety, to refuse such expressions of feeling as corresponded to the artless and involuntary kindnesses of the ingenuous Juana, one day the cornet was surprised by mamma in the act of encircling her daughter's waist with his martial arm, although waltzing was premature by at least two centuries in Peru. She taxed him instantly

THE SPANISH MILITARY NUN

with dishonourably abusing her confidence. The cornet
made but a bad defence. He muttered something about
'*fraternal affection*,' about 'esteem,' and a great deal of
metaphysical words that are destined to remain untrans-
lated in their original Spanish. The good senora, though
she could boast only of forty-two years' experience, or say
forty-four, was not altogether to be '*had*' in that fashion :
she was as learned as if she had been fifty, and she brought
matters to a speedy crisis. 'You are a Spaniard,' she said,
'a gentleman, therefore ; *remember* that you are a gentleman. This very night, if your intentions are not serious,
quit my house. Go to Tucuman ; you shall command
my horses and servants ; but stay no longer to increase
the sorrow that already you will have left behind you.
My daughter loves you. That is sorrow enough, if you
are trifling with us. But, if not, and you also love *her*,
and can be happy in our solitary mode of life, stay with
us—stay for ever. Marry Juana with my free consent.
I ask not for wealth. Mine is sufficient for you both.'
The cornet protested that the honour was one never
contemplated by *him*—that it was too great—that——
But, of course, reader, you know that 'gammon' flourishes
in Peru, amongst the silver mines, as well as in some
more boreal lands, that produce little better than copper
and tin. 'Tin,' however, has its uses. The delighted
senora overruled all objections, great and small ; and she
confirmed Juana's notion that the business of two worlds
could be transacted in an hour, by settling her daughter's
future happiness in exactly twenty minutes. The poor,
weak Catalina, not acting now in any spirit of recklessness,
grieving sincerely for the gulf that was opening before
her, and yet shrinking effeminately from the momentary
shock that would be inflicted by a firm adherence to her
duty, clinging to the anodyne of a short delay, allowed
herself to be installed as the lover of Juana. Considerations of convenience, however, postponed the marriage.
It was requisite to make various purchases ; and for this,
it was requisite to visit Tucuman, where also the marriage
ceremony could be performed with more circumstantial

2 B

splendour.   To Tucuman, therefore, after some weeks'
interval, the whole party repaired.   And at Tucuman it
was that the tragical events arose, which, whilst interrupting such a mockery for ever, left the poor Juana still
happily deceived, and never believing for a moment that
hers was a rejected or a deluded heart.

One reporter of Mr. De Ferrer's narrative forgets his
usual generosity when he says, that the senora's gift of
her daughter to the Alférez was not quite so disinterested
as it seemed to be.   Certainly it was not so disinterested
as European ignorance might fancy it: but it was quite
as much so as it ought to have been, in balancing the
interests of a child.   Very true it is, that, being a genuine
Spaniard, who was still a rare creature in so vast a world
as Peru—being a Spartan amongst Helots—a Spanish
Alférez would, in those days, and in that region, have
been a natural noble.   His alliance created honour for
his wife and for his descendants.   Something, therefore,
the cornet would add to the family consideration.   But,
instead of selfishness, it argued just regard for her
daughter's interest to build upon this, as some sort
of equipoise to the wealth which her daughter would
bring.

Spaniard, however, as she was, our Alférez, on reaching Tucuman, found no Spaniards to mix with, but instead, twelve Portuguese.

21.—*Kate once more in Storms*

Catalina remembered the Spanish proverb, ' Pump out
of a Spaniard all his good qualities, and the remainder
makes a pretty fair Portuguese ' ; but as there was nobody
else to gamble with, she entered freely into their society.
Soon she suspected that there was foul play : for all modes
of doctoring dice had been familiar to *her* by the experience
of camps.   She watched ; and, by the time she had lost
her final coin, she was satisfied that she had been plundered.
In her first anger, she would have been glad to switch the
whole dozen across the eyes ; but as twelve to one were

too great odds, she determined on limiting her vengeance
to the immediate culprit. Him she followed into the
street; and coming near enough to distinguish his profile
reflected on a wall, she continued to keep him in view
from a short distance. The light-hearted young cavalier
whistled, as he went, an old Portuguese ballad of romance,
and in a quarter-of-an-hour came up to a house, the front-
door of which he began to open with a pass-key. This
operation was the signal for Catalina that the hour of
vengeance had struck; and stepping up hastily, she tapped
the Portuguese on the shoulder, saying, 'Senor, you are a
robber!' The Portuguese turned coolly round, and seeing
his gaming antagonist, replied, 'Possibly, sir; but I have
no particular fancy for being told so,' at the same time
drawing his sword. Catalina had not designed to take
any advantage; and the touching him on the shoulder,
with the interchange of speeches, and the known character
of Kate, sufficiently imply it. But it is too probable, in
such cases, that the party whose intention had been
regularly settled from the first, will, and must, have an
advantage unconsciously over a man so abruptly thrown
on his defence. However this might be, they had not
fought a minute before Catalina passed her sword through
her opponent's body; and, without a groan or a sigh, the
Portuguese cavalier fell dead at his own door. Kate
searched the street with her ears, and (as far as the in-
distinctness of night allowed) with her eyes. All was
profoundly silent; and she was satisfied that no human
figure was in motion. What should be done with the
body? A glance at the door of the house settled *that*:
Fernando had himself opened it at the very moment when
he received the summons to turn round. She dragged the
corpse in, therefore, to the foot of the staircase, put the
key by the dead man's side, and then issuing softly into
the street, drew the door close with as little noise as
possible. Catalina again paused to listen and to watch,
went home to the hospitable senora's house, retired to
bed, fell asleep, and early the next morning was awakened
by the corrégidor and four alguazils.

The lawlessness of all that followed strikingly exposes the frightful state of criminal justice at that time, wherever Spanish law prevailed. No evidence appeared to connect Catalina in any way with the death of Fernando Acosta. The Portuguese gamblers, besides that perhaps they thought lightly of such an accident, might have reasons of their own for drawing off public attention from their pursuits in Tucuman. Not one of these men came forward openly, else the circumstances at the gaming-table, and the departure of Catalina so closely on the heels of her opponent, would have suggested reasonable grounds for detaining her until some further light should be obtained. As it was, her imprisonment rested upon no colourable ground whatever, unless the magistrate had received some anonymous information, which, however, he never alleged. One comfort there was, meantime, in Spanish injustice : it did not loiter. Full gallop it went over the ground : one week often sufficed for informations—for trial—for execution ; and the only bad consequence was, that a second or a third week sometimes exposed the disagreeable fact that everything had been 'premature' ; a solemn sacrifice had been made to offended justice, in which all was right except as to the victim ; it was the wrong man ; and *that* gave extra trouble ; for then all was to do over again—another man to be executed, and, possibly, still to be caught.

Justice moved at her usual Spanish rate in the present case. Kate was obliged to rise instantly ; not suffered to speak to anybody in the house, though, in going out, a door opened, and she saw the young Juana looking out with her saddest Indian expression. In one day the trial was finished. Catalina said (which was true) that she hardly knew Acosta ; and that people of her rank were used to attack their enemies face to face, not by murderous surprises. The magistrates were impressed with Catalina's answers (yet answers to *what*, or to *whom*, in a case where there was no distinct charge, and no avowed accuser?). Things were beginning to look well, when all

was suddenly upset by two witnesses, whom the reader
(who is a sort of accomplice after the fact, having been
privately let into the truths of the case, and having
concealed his knowledge) will know at once to be false
witnesses, but whom the old Spanish buzwigs doated on as
models of all that could be looked for in the best. Both
were ill-looking fellows, as it was their duty to be. And
the first deposed as follows :—That through *his* quarter of
Tucuman, the fact was notorious of Acosta's wife being
the object of a criminal pursuit on the part of the Alférez
(Catalina) ; that, doubtless, the injured husband had
surprised the prisoner, which, of course, had led to the
murder—to the staircase—to the key—to everything, in
short, that could be wished. No—stop ! what am I saying ?—to everything that ought to be abominated. Finally
—for he had now settled the main question—that he had a
friend who would take up the case where he himself, from
shortsightedness, was obliged to lay it down. This friend
—the Pythias of this shortsighted Damon—started up in
a frenzy of virtue at this summons, and, rushing to the
front of the alguazils, said, 'That since his friend had
proved sufficiently the fact of the Alférez having been
lurking in the house, and having murdered a man, all that
rested upon *him* to show was, how that murderer got out
of that house ; which he could do satisfactorily ; for there
was a balcony running along the windows on the second
floor, one of which windows he himself, lurking in a
corner of the street, saw the Alférez throw up, and from
the said balcony take a flying leap into the said street.'
Evidence like this was conclusive ; no defence was listened
to, nor indeed had the prisoner any to produce. The
Alférez could deny neither the staircase nor the balcony :
the street is there to this day, like the bricks in Jack
Cade's chimney, testifying all that may be required ; and
as to our friend who saw the leap, there he was—nobody
could deny *him*. The prisoner might indeed have
suggested that she never heard of Acosta's wife, nor had
the existence of such a wife been proved, or even ripened
into a suspicion. But the bench were satisfied ; chopping

logic in defence was henceforward impertinence ; and
sentence was pronounced—that, on the eighth day from
the day of arrest, the Alférez should be executed in the
public square.

It was not amongst the weaknesses of Catalina—who
had so often inflicted death, and, by her own journal,
thought so lightly of inflicting it (unless under cowardly
advantages)—to shrink from facing death in her own
person. Many incidents in her career show the coolness
and even gaiety with which, in any case where death was
apparently inevitable, she would have gone forward to
meet it. But in this case she *had* a temptation for
escaping it, which was certainly in her power. She had
only to reveal the secret of her sex, and the ridiculous
witnesses, beyond whose testimony there was nothing at
all against her, must at once be covered with derision.
Catalina had some liking for fun ; and a main inducement
to this course was, that it would enable her to say to the
judges, ‘ Now you see what old fools you’ve made of
yourselves ; every woman and child in Peru will soon be
laughing at you.’ I must acknowledge my own weakness ; this last temptation I could *not* have withstood ;
flesh is weak, and fun is strong. But Catalina *did*. On
consideration, she fancied that, although the particular
motive for murdering Acosta would be dismissed with
laughter, still this might not clear her of the murder,
which, on some *other* motive, she might be supposed to
have committed. But, allowing that she were cleared
altogether, what most of all she feared was, that the
publication of her sex would throw a reflex light upon
many past transactions in her life ; would instantly find its
way to Spain ; and would probably soon bring her within
the tender attentions of the Inquisition. She kept firm,
therefore, to the resolution of not saving her life by this
discovery. And so far as her fate lay in her own hands,
she would to a certainty have perished—which to me
seems a most fantastic caprice ; it was to court a certain
death and a present death, in order to evade a remote
contingency of death. But even at this point how strange

a case ! A woman *falsely* accused (because accused by lying witnesses) of an act which she really *did* commit ! And falsely accused of a true offence upon a motive that was impossible !

As the sun was setting upon the seventh day, when the hours were numbered for the prisoner, there filed into her cell four persons in religious habits. They came on the charitable mission of preparing the poor convict for death. Catalina, however, watching all things narrowly, remarked something earnest and significant in the eye of the leader, as of one who had some secret communication to make. She contrived, therefore, to clasp this man's hands, as if in the energy of internal struggles, and *he* contrived to slip into hers the very smallest of billets from poor Juana. It contained, for indeed it *could* contain, only these three words—'Do not confess.—J.' This one caution, so simple and so brief, proved a talisman. It did not refer to any confession of the crime ; *that* would have been assuming what Juana was neither entitled nor disposed to assume ; but it referred, in the technical sense of the church, to the act of devotional confession. Catalina found a single moment for a glance at it ; understood the whole ; resolutely refused to confess, as a person unsettled in her religious opinions, that needed spiritual instructions ; and the four monks withdrew to make their report. The principal judge, upon hearing of the prisoner's impenitence, granted another day. At the end of *that*, no change having occurred either in the prisoner's mind or in the circumstances, he issued his warrant for the execution. Accordingly, as the sun went down, the sad procession formed within the prison. Into the great square of Tucuman it moved, where the scaffold had been built, and the whole city had assembled for the spectacle. Catalina steadily ascended the ladder of the scaffold ; even then she resolved not to benefit by revealing her sex ; even then it was that she expressed her scorn for the lubberly executioner's mode of tying a knot ; did it herself in a 'ship-shape,' orthodox manner ; received in return the enthusiastic plaudits of the crowd, and so far ran the risk of precipitating her fate ; for the timid magistrates, fearing a rescue from the fiery clamours of the impetuous mob, angrily ordered the executioner to finish the scene. The clatter of a galloping horse, however, at this instant forced them to pause. The crowd opened a road for the agitated horseman, who was the bearer of an order from the President of La Plata to suspend the execution until two prisoners could be examined. The whole was the work of the senora and her daughter. The elder lady, having gathered informations against the witnesses, had pursued them to La Plata. There, by her influence with the governor, they were arrested, recognised as old malefactors, and in their terror had partly confessed their perjury. Catalina was removed to La Plata ; solemnly acquitted ; and, by the advice of the president, for the present the connection with the senora's family was indefinitely postponed.

22.—*Kate's Penultimate Adventure*

Now was the last-but-one adventure at hand that ever Catalina should see in the New World. Some fine sights she may yet see in Europe, but nothing after this (*which she has recorded*) in America. Europe, if it had ever heard of her name (as very shortly it *shall* hear), Kings, Pope, Cardinals, if they were but aware of her existence (which in six months they *shall* be), would thirst for an introduction to our Catalina. You hardly thought now, reader, that she was such a great person, or anybody's pet but yours and mine. Bless you, sir, she would scorn to look at *us*. I tell you, that Eminences, Excellencies, Highnesses— nay, even Royalties and Holinesses—are languishing to see her, or soon *will* be. But how can this come to pass, if she is to continue in her present obscurity ? Certainly it cannot without some great *peripeteia*, or vertiginous whirl of fortune ; which, therefore, you shall now behold taking place in one turn of her next adventure. *That* shall let in a light, *that* shall throw back a Claude Lorraine gleam

over all the past, able to make kings, that would have
cared not for her under Peruvian daylight, come to glorify
her setting beams.

The senora—and, observe, whatever kindness she does
to Catalina speaks secretly from two hearts, her own and
Juana's—had, by the advice of Mr. President Mendonia,
given sufficient money for Catalina's travelling expenses.
So far well. But Mr. M. chose to add a little codicil to
this bequest of the senora's, never suggested by her or by
her daughter. 'Pray,' said this inquisitive president, who
surely might have found business enough within his own
neighbourhood—'pray, Senor Pietro Diaz, did you ever
live at Conception? And were you ever acquainted there
with Signor Miguel de Erauso? That man, sir, was my
friend.' What a pity that on this occasion Catalina could
not venture to be candid! What a capital speech it would
have made to say, ' *Friend* were you? I think you could
hardly be *that*, with seven hundred miles between you.
But that man was *my* friend also ; and, secondly, my
brother. True it is I killed him. But if you happen to
know that this was by pure mistake in the dark, what an
old rogue you must be to throw *that* in my teeth, which
is the affliction of my life!' Again, however, as so often
in the same circumstances, Catalina thought that it would
cause more ruin than it could heal to be candid ; and,
indeed, if she were really *P. Diaz, Esq.*, how came she to
be brother to the late Mr. Erauso? On consideration,
also, if she could not tell *all*, merely to have professed a
fraternal connection which never was avowed by either
whilst living together, would not have brightened the
reputation of Catalina. Still, from a kindness for poor
Kate, I feel uncharitably towards the president for advising Senor Pietro 'to travel for his health.' What had *he*
to do with people's health? However, Mr. Peter, as he
had pocketed the senora's money, thought it right to
pocket also the advice that accompanied its payment.
That he might be in a condition to do so, he went off to
buy a horse. On that errand, in all lands, for some
reason only half explained, you must be in luck if you do

not fall in, and eventually fall out, with a knave.   But on
this particular day Kate *was* in luck.   For, beside money
and advice, she obtained at a low rate a horse both beautiful and serviceable for a journey.   To Paz it was, a city
of prosperous name, that the cornet first moved.   But
Paz did not fulfil the promise of its name.   For it laid
the grounds of a feud that drove our Kate out of
America.

Her first adventure was a bagatelle, and fitter for a
jest-book than for a serious history ; yet it proved no jest
either, since it led to the tragedy that followed.   Riding
into Paz, our gallant standard-bearer and her bonny black
horse drew all eyes, *comme de raison*, upon their separate
charms.   This was inevitable amongst the indolent population of a Spanish town ; and Kate was used to it.   But,
having recently had a little too much of the public attention, she felt nervous on remarking two soldiers eyeing
the handsome horse and the handsome rider, with an
attention that seemed too earnest for mere *æsthetics*.
However, Kate was not the kind of person to let anything dwell on her spirits, especially if it took the shape
of impudence ; and, whistling gaily, she was riding forward, when—who should cross her path but the Alcalde
of Paz !   Ah ! alcalde, you see a person now that has a
mission against you and all that you inherit ; though a
mission known to herself as little as to you.   Good were
it for you, had you never crossed the path of this Biscayan
Alférez.   The alcalde looked so sternly, that Kate asked
if his worship had any commands.   ‘Yes.   These men,’
said the alcalde, ‘these two soldiers, say that .this horse
is stolen.’   To one who had so narrowly and so lately
escaped the balcony witness and his friend, it was really
no laughing matter to hear of new affidavits in preparation.
Kate was nervous, but never disconcerted.   In a moment
she had twitched off a saddle-cloth on which she sat ; and
throwing it over the horse’s head, so as to cover up all
between the ears and the mouth, she replied, ‘ That she
had bought and paid for the horse at La Plata.   But now,
your worship, if this horse has really been stolen from

these men, they must know well of which eye it is blind;
for it *can* be only in the right eye or the left.' One of
the soldiers cried out instantly that it was the left eye;
but the other said, 'No, no; you forget, it's the right.'
Kate maliciously called attention to this little schism. But
the men said, 'Ah, *that* was nothing—they were hurried;
but now, on recollecting themselves, they were agreed that
it was the left eye.'—'Did they stand to that?'—'Oh yes,
positive they were—left eye—left.'

Upon which our Kate, twitching off the horse-cloth,
said gaily to the magistrate, 'Now, sir, please to observe
that this horse has nothing the matter with either eye.'
And, in fact, it *was* so. Upon *that*, his worship ordered
his alguazils to apprehend the two witnesses, who posted
off to bread and water, with other reversionary advantages;
whilst Kate rode in quest of the best dinner that Paz
could furnish.

23.—*Preparation for Kate's Final Adventure in Peru*

This alcalde's acquaintance, however, was not destined
to drop here. Something had appeared in the young
caballero's bearing which made it painful to have addressed
him with harshness, or for a moment to have entertained
such a charge against such a person. He despatched his
cousin, therefore, Don Antonio Calderon, to offer his
apologies; and at the same time to request that the
stranger, whose rank and quality he regretted not to have
known, would do him the honour to come and dine with
him. This explanation, and the fact that Don Antonio
had already proclaimed his own position as cousin to the
magistrate, and nephew to the Bishop of Cuzco, obliged
Catalina to say, after thanking the gentlemen for their
obliging attentions, 'I myself hold the rank of Alférez in
the service of his Catholic Majesty. I am a native of
Biscay, and I am now repairing to Cuzco on private
business.'—'To Cuzco!' exclaimed Antonio; 'and you
from dear lovely Biscay! How very fortunate! My
cousin is a Basque like you; and, like you, he starts for

Cuzco to-morrow morning ; so that, if it is agreeable to you, Senor Alférez, we will travel together.' It was settled that they should. To travel—amongst 'balcony witnesses,' and anglers for 'blind horses'—not merely with a just man, but with the very abstract idea and riding allegory of justice, was too delightful to the storm-wearied cornet ; and he cheerfully accompanied Don Antonio to the house of the magistrate, called Don Pedro de Chavarria. Distinguished was his reception ; the alcalde personally renewed his regrets for the ridiculous scene of the two scampish oculists, and presented Kate to his wife—a most splendid Andalusian beauty, to whom he had been married about a year.

This lady there is a reason for describing ; and the French reporter of Catalina's memoirs dwells upon the theme. She united, he says, the sweetness of the German lady with the energy of the Arabian—a combination hard to judge of. As to her feet, he adds, I say nothing, for she had scarcely any at all. ' *Je ne parle point de ses pieds, elle n'en avait presque pas.*' 'Poor lady !' says a compassionate rustic : ' no feet ! What a shocking thing that so fine a woman should have been so sadly mutilated !' Oh, my dear rustic, you're quite in the wrong box. The Frenchman means this as the very highest compliment. Beautiful, however, she must have been ; and a Cinderella, I hope, but still not a Cinderellula, considering that she had the inimitable walk and step of Andalusian women, which cannot be accomplished without something of a proportionate basis to stand upon.

The reason which there is (as I have said) for describing this lady, arises out of her relation to the tragic events which followed. She, by her criminal levity, was the cause of all. And I must here warn the moralising blunderer of two errors that he is likely to make : 1st, that he is invited to read some extract from a licentious amour, as if for its own interest ; 2ndly, or on account of Donna Catalina's memoirs, with a view to relieve their too martial character. I have the pleasure to assure him of his being so utterly in the darkness of error, that any possible

change he can make in his opinions, right or left, must be
for the better : he cannot stir, but he will mend, which is
a delightful thought for the moral and blundering mind.
As to the first point, what little glimpse he obtains of a
licentious amour is, as a court of justice will sometimes
show him such a glimpse, simply to make intelligible the
subsequent facts which depend upon it.   Secondly, as to
the conceit that Catalina wished to embellish her memoirs,
understand that no such practice then existed—certainly
not in Spanish literature.   Her memoirs are electrifying
by their facts ; else, in the manner of telling these facts,
they are systematically dry.

But let us resume.   Don Antonio Calderon was a
handsome, accomplished cavalier.   And in the course of
dinner Catalina was led to judge, from the behaviour to
each other of this gentleman and the lady, the alcalde's
beautiful wife, that they had an improper understanding.
This also she inferred from the furtive language of their
eyes.   Her wonder was, that the alcalde should be so
blind ; though upon that point she saw reason in a day or
two to change her opinion.   Some people see everything
by affecting to see nothing.   The whole affair, however,
was nothing at all to *her ;* and she would have dismissed
it altogether from her thoughts, but for the dreadful
events on the journey.

This went on but slowly, however steadily.   Owing
to the miserable roads, eight hours a day of travelling
was found quite enough for man and beast ; the product
of which eight hours was from ten to twelve leagues,
taking the league at $2\frac{1}{4}$ miles.   On the last day but one
of the journey, the travelling party, which was precisely
the original dinner party, reached a little town ten leagues
short of Cuzco.   The corrégidor of this place was a
friend of the alcalde; and through *his* influence the party
obtained better accommodations than those which they
had usually commanded in a hovel calling itself a *venta,*
or in a sheltered corner of a barn.   The alcalde was to
sleep at the corrégidor's house ; the two young cavaliers,
Calderon and our Kate, had sleeping-rooms at the public

locanda; but for the lady was reserved a little pleasure-house in an enclosed garden. This was a mere toy of a house; but the season being summer, and the house surrounded with tropical flowers, the lady preferred it (in spite of its loneliness) to the damp mansion of the official grandee, who, in her humble opinion, was quite as fusty as his mansion, and his mansion not much less so than himself.

After dining gaily together at the *locanda*, and possibly taking a 'rise' out of his worship the corrégidor, as a repeating echo of Don Quixote (then growing popular in Spanish America), the young man Don Antonio, who was no young officer, and the young officer Catalina, who was no young man, lounged down together to the little pavilion in the flower-garden, with the purpose of paying their respects to the presiding belle. They were graciously received, and had the honour of meeting there his musti-ness the alcalde, and his fustiness the corrégidor; whose conversation ought surely to have been edifying, since it was anything but brilliant. How they got on under the weight of two such muffs, has been a mystery for two centuries. But they *did* to a certainty, for the party did not break up till eleven. *Tea and turn out* you could not call it; for there was the *turn-out* in rigour, but not the *tea*. One thing, however, Catalina by mere accident had an opportunity of observing, and observed with pain. The two official gentlemen, on taking leave, had gone down the steps into the garden. Catalina, having forgot her hat, went back into the little vestibule to look for it There stood the lady and Don Antonio, exchanging a few final words (they *were* final) and a few final signs. Amongst the last Kate observed distinctly this, and dis-tinctly she understood it. First of all, by raising her forefinger, the lady drew Calderon's attention to the act which followed as one of significant pantomime; which done, she snuffed out one of the candles. The young man answered it by a look of intelligence; and then all three passed down the steps together. The lady was disposed to take the cool air, and accompanied them

to the garden-gate ; but, in passing down the walk, Catalina noticed a second ill-omened sign that all was not
right. Two glaring eyes she distinguished amongst the
shrubs for a moment, and a rustling immediately after.
'What's that?' said the lady; and Don Antonio answered, carelessly, 'A bird flying out of the bushes.'
But birds do not amuse themselves by staying up to midnight ; and birds do not wear rapiers.

Catalina, as usual, had read everything. Not a
wrinkle or a rustle was lost upon *her*. And, therefore,
when she reached the *locanda*, knowing to an iota all that
was coming, she did not retire to bed, but paced before
the house. She had not long to wait : in fifteen minutes
the door opened softly, and out stepped Calderon. Kate
walked forward, and faced him immediately ; telling him
laughingly that it was not good for his health to go
abroad on this night. The young man showed some
impatience ; upon which, very seriously, Kate acquainted
him with her suspicions, and with the certainty that the
alcalde was not so blind as he had seemed. Calderon
thanked her for the information ; would be upon his
guard, but, to prevent further expostulation, he wheeled
round instantly into the darkness. Catalina was too well
convinced, however, of the mischief on foot to leave him
thus. She followed rapidly, and passed silently into the
garden, almost at the same time with Calderon. Both
took their stations behind trees ; Calderon watching
nothing but the burning candles, Catalina watching circumstances to direct her movements. The candles burned
brightly in the little pavilion. Presently one was extinguished. Upon this, Calderon pressed forward to the
steps, hastily ascended them, and passed into the vestibule.
Catalina followed on his traces. What succeeded was all
one scene of continued, dreadful dumb show ; different
passions of panic, or deadly struggle, or hellish malice,
absolutely suffocated all articulate utterances.

In the first moments a gurgling sound was heard, as
of a wild beast attempting vainly to yell over some
creature that it was strangling. Next came a tumbling

out at the door of one black mass, which heaved and parted at intervals into two figures, which closed, which parted again, which at last fell down the steps together. Then appeared a figure in white. It was the unhappy Andalusian ; and she, seeing the outline of Catalina's person, ran up to her, unable to utter one syllable. Pitying the agony of her horror, Catalina took her within her own cloak, and carried her out at the garden gate. Calderon had by this time died ; and the maniacal alcalde had risen up to pursue his wife. But Kate, foreseeing what he would do, had stepped silently within the shadow of the garden wall. Looking down the road to the town, and seeing nobody moving, the maniac, for some purpose, went back to the house. This moment Kate used to recover the *locanda*, with the lady still panting in horror. What was to be done ? To think of concealment in this little place was out of the question. The alcalde was a man of local power, and it was certain that he would kill his wife on the spot. Kate's generosity would not allow her to have any collusion with this murderous purpose. At Cuzco, the principal convent was ruled by a near relative of the Andalusian ; and there she would find shelter. Kate therefore saddled her horse rapidly, placed the lady behind, and rode off in the darkness.

24.—*A Steeple Chase*

About five miles out of the town their road was crossed by a torrent, over which they could not hit the bridge. 'Forward!' cried the lady ; 'Oh, heavens ! forward!' and Kate repeating the word to the horse, the docile creature leaped down into the water. They were all sinking at first ; but, having its head free, the horse swam clear of all obstacles through the midnight darkness, and scrambled out on the opposite bank. The two riders were dripping from the shoulders downward. But, seeing a light twinkling from a cottage window, Kate rode up ; obtaining a little refreshment, and the benefit of a fire, from a poor labouring man. From this man

she also bought a warm mantle for the lady, who, besides
her torrent bath, was dressed in a light evening robe, so
that but for the horseman's cloak of Kate she would have
perished. But there was no time to lose. They had
already lost two hours from the consequences of their
cold bath. Cuzco was still eighteen miles distant; and
the alcalde's shrewdness would at once divine this to be
his wife's mark. They remounted: very soon the silent
night echoed the hoofs of a pursuing rider; and now
commenced the most frantic race, in which each party
rode as if the whole game of life were staked upon the
issue. The pace was killing: and Kate has delivered it
as her opinion, in the memoirs which she wrote, that the
alcalde was the better mounted. This may be doubted.
And certainly Kate had ridden too many years in the
Spanish cavalry, to have any fear of his worship's horsemanship; but it was a prodigious disadvantage that *her*
horse had to carry double; while the horse ridden by her
opponent was one of those belonging to the murdered
Don Antonio, and known to Kate as a powerful animal.
At length they had come within three miles of Cuzco.
The road after this descended the whole way to the city,
and in some places rapidly, so as to require a cool rider.
Suddenly a deep trench appeared traversing the whole
extent of a broad heath. It was useless to evade it. To
have hesitated, was to be lost. Kate saw the necessity of
clearing it; but she doubted much whether her poor
exhausted horse, after twenty-one miles of work so severe,
had strength for the effort. However, the race was
nearly finished; a score of dreadful miles had been
accomplished; and Kate's maxim, which never yet had
failed, both figuratively for life, and literally for the
saddle, was—to ride at everything that showed a front of
resistance. She did so now. Having come upon the
trench rather too suddenly, she wheeled round for the
advantage of coming down upon it with more impetus,
rode resolutely at it, cleared it, and gained the opposite
bank. The hind feet of her horse were sinking back
from the rottenness of the ground; but the strong

supporting bridle-hand of Kate carried him forward ; and
in ten minutes more they would be in Cuzco. This being
seen by the vengeful alcalde, who had built great hopes
on the trench, he unslung his carbine, pulled up, and
fired after the bonny black horse and its two bonny riders.
But this vicious manœuvre would have lost his worship
any bet that he might have had depending on this admirable steeple-chase.   For the bullets, says Kate in her
memoirs, whistled round the poor clinging lady *en croupe*
—luckily none struck *her*; but one wounded the horse.
And that settled the odds.   Kate now planted herself
well in her stirrups to enter Cuzco, almost dangerously a
winner ; for the horse was so maddened by the wound,
and the road so steep, that he went like blazes ; and it
really became difficult for Kate to guide him with any
precision through narrow episcopal [1] paths.   Henceforwards the wounded horse required unintermitting attention ; and yet, in the mere luxury of strife, it was
impossible for Kate to avoid turning a little in her saddle
to see the alcalde's performance on this tight-rope of the
trench.   His worship's horsemanship being, perhaps,
rather rusty, and he not perfectly acquainted with his
horse, it would have been agreeable for *him* to compromise the case by riding round, or dismounting. But
all *that* was impossible.   The job must be done.   And I
am happy to report, for the reader's satisfaction, the
sequel—so far as Kate could attend the performance.
Gathering himself up for mischief, the alcalde took a
mighty sweep, as if ploughing out the line of some vast
encampment, or tracing the *pomærium* for some future
Rome ; then, like thunder and lightning, with arms flying
aloft in the air, down he came upon the trembling trench.
But the horse refused the leap ; to take the leap was
impossible ; absolutely to refuse it, the horse felt, was
immoral ; and therefore, as the only compromise that *his*
unlearned brain could suggest, he threw his worship right
over his ears, lodging him safely in a sand-heap, that rose

----

[1] '*Episcopal*' :—The roads around Cuzco were made, and maintained, under the patronage and control of the bishop.

with clouds of dust and screams of birds into the morning
air. Kate had now no time to send back her compliments in a musical halloo. The alcalde missed breaking
his neck on this occasion very narrowly; but his neck
was of no use to him in twenty minutes more, as the
reader will find. Kate rode right onwards; and, coming
in with a lady behind her, horse bloody, and pace such as
no hounds could have lived with, she ought to have made
a great sensation in Cuzco. But, unhappily, the people
of Cuzco, the spectators that *should* have been, were fast
asleep in bed.

The steeple-chase into Cuzco had been a fine headlong
thing, considering the torrent, the trench, the wounded
horse, the lovely Andalusian lady, with her agonising fears,
mounted behind Kate, together with the meek dove-like
dawn: but the finale crowded together the quickest
succession of changes that out of a melodrama ever *can*
have been witnessed. Kate reached the convent in safety;
carried into the cloisters, and delivered like a parcel, the
fair Andalusian. But to rouse the servants and obtain
admission to the convent caused a long delay; and on
returning to the street through the broad gateway of the
convent, whom should she face but the alcalde! How he
had escaped the trench, who can tell? He had no time to
write memoirs; his horse was too illiterate. But he *had*
escaped; temper not at all improved by that adventure,
and now raised to a hell of malignity by seeing that he had
lost his prey. The morning light showed him how to use
his sword, and whom he had before him, and he attacked
Kate with fury. Both were exhausted; and Kate, besides
that she had no personal quarrel with the alcalde, having
now accomplished her sole object in saving the lady,
would have been glad of a truce. She could with difficulty wield her sword: and the alcalde had so far the
advantage, that he wounded Kate severely. That roused
her ancient Biscayan blood; and she turned on him now
with deadly determination. At that moment in rode two
servants of the alcalde, who took part with their master.
These odds strengthened Kate's resolution, but weakened

her chances. Just then, however, rode in and ranged himself on Kate's side, the servant of the murdered Don Calderon. In an instant Kate had pushed her sword through the alcalde, who died upon the spot. In an instant the servant of Calderon had fled. In an instant the alguazils had come up. They and the servants of the alcalde pressed furiously on Kate, who was again fighting for her life with persons not even known to her by sight. Against such odds, she was rapidly losing ground ; when, in an instant, on the opposite side of the street, the great gates of the Episcopal Palace rolled open. Thither it was that Calderon's servant had fled. The bishop and his attendants hurried across. 'Senor Caballero,' said the bishop, 'in the name of the Virgin, I enjoin you to surrender your sword.'—'My lord,' said Kate, 'I dare not do it with so many enemies about me.'—'But I,' replied the bishop, 'become answerable to the law for your safe keeping.' Upon which, with filial reverence, all parties dropped their swords. Kate being severely wounded, the bishop led her into his palace. In another instant came the catastrophe : Kate's discovery could no longer be delayed ; the blood flowed too rapidly ; and the wound was in her bosom. She requested a private interview with the bishop ; all was known in a moment ; surgeons and attendants were summoned hastily ; and Kate had fainted. The good bishop pitied her, and had her attended in his palace ; then removed to a convent ; then to a second convent at Lima ; and, after many months had passed, his report of the whole extraordinary case in all its details to the supreme government at Madrid, drew from the king, Philip IV., and from the papal legate, an order that the nun should be transferred to Spain.

25.—*St. Sebastian is finally Checkmated*

Yes, at length the warrior lady, the blooming cornet —this nun that is so martial, this dragoon that is so lovely —must visit again the home of her childhood, which now for seventeen years she has not seen. All Spain, Portugal,

Italy, rang with her adventures. Spain, from north to south, was frantic with desire to behold her fiery child, whose girlish romance, whose patriotic heroism, electrified the national imagination. The King of Spain must kiss his *faithful* daughter, that would not suffer his banner to see dishonour. The Pope must kiss his *wandering* daughter, that henceforwards will be a lamb travelling back into the Christian fold. Potentates so great as these, when *they* speak words of love, do not speak in vain. All was forgiven ; the sacrilege, the bloodshed, the flight, and the scorn of St. Sebastian's (consequently of St. Peter's) keys ; the pardons were made out, were signed, were sealed ; and the chanceries of earth were satisfied.

Ah! what a day of sorrow and of joy was *that* one day, in the first week of November 1624, when the returning Kate drew near to the shore of Andalusia ; when descending into the ship's barge, she was rowed to the piers of Cadiz by bargemen in the royal liveries ; when she saw every ship, street, house, convent, church, crowded, as if on some mighty day of judgment, with human faces, with men, with women, with children, all bending the lights of their flashing eyes upon herself! Forty myriads of people had gathered in Cadiz alone. All Andalusia had turned out to receive her. Ah! what joy for *her*, if she had not looked back to the Andes, to their dreadful summits, and their more dreadful feet. Ah! what sorrow, if she had not been forced by music, and endless banners, and the triumphant jubilations of her country-men, to turn away from the Andes, and to fix her thoughts for the moment upon that glad tumultuous shore which she approached.

Upon this shore stood, ready to receive her, in front of all this mighty crowd, the Prime Minister of Spain, that same Condé Olivarez, who but one year before had been so haughty and so defying to our haughty and defy-ing Duke of Buckingham. But a year ago the Prince of Wales had been in Spain, seeking a Spanish bride, and he also was welcomed with triumph and great joy ; but not with the hundredth part of that enthusiasm which now met the returning nun. And Olivarez, that had spoken so roughly to the English duke, to *her* 'was sweet as summer.'[1] Through endless crowds of welcoming compatriots he conducted her to the king. The king folded her in his arms, and could never be satisfied with listening to her. He sent for her continually to his presence ; he delighted in her conversation, so new, so natural, so spirited ; he settled a pension upon her (at that time of unprecedented amount) ; and by *his* desire, because the year 1625 was a year of jubilee, she departed in a few months from Madrid to Rome. She went through Barcelona ; there and everywhere welcomed as the lady whom the king delighted to honour. She travelled to Rome, and all doors flew open to receive her. She was presented to his Holiness, with letters from his most Catholic Majesty. But letters there needed none. The Pope admired her as much as all before had done. He caused her to recite all her adventures ; and what he loved most in her account was the sincere and sorrowing spirit in which she described herself as neither better nor worse than she had been. Neither proud was Kate, nor sycophantishly and falsely humble. Urban VIII. it was then that filled the chair of St. Peter. He did not neglect to raise his daughter's thoughts from earthly things : he pointed her eyes to the clouds that were floating in mighty volumes above the dome of St. Peter's Cathedral ; he told her what the cathedral had told her amongst the gorgeous clouds of the Andes and the solemn vesper lights—how sweet a thing, how divine a thing, it was for Christ's sake to forgive all injuries ; and how he trusted that no more she would think of bloodshed ; but that, if again she should suffer wrongs, she would resign all vindictive retaliation for them into the hands of God, the final Avenger. I must also find time to mention, although the press and the compositors are in a fury at my delays, that the Pope, in his farewell audience to his dear daughter, whom he was to see no more,

---

[1] Griffith in Shakspere, when vindicating, in that immortal scene with Queen Catherine, Cardinal Wolsey.

gave her a general license to wear henceforth in all countries—even in *partibus Infidelium*—a cavalry officer's dress — boots, spurs, sabre ; in fact, anything that she and the Horse Guards might agree upon. Consequently, reader, say not one word, nor suffer any tailor to say one word, or the ninth part of a word, against those Wellington trousers made in the chestnut forest ; for, understanding that the papal indulgence as to this point runs backwards as well as forwards, it sanctions equally those trousers in the forgotten rear, and all possible trousers yet to come.

From Rome, Kate returned to Spain. She even went to St. Sebastian's—to the city, but—whether it was that her heart failed her or not—never to the convent. She roamed up and down ; everywhere she was welcome— everywhere an honoured guest ; but everywhere restless. The poor and humble never ceased from their admiration of her ; and amongst the rich and aristocratic of Spain, with the king at their head, Kate found especial love from two classes of men. The cardinals and bishops all doated upon her—as their daughter that was returning. The military men all doated upon her—as their sister that was retiring.

26.—*Farewell to the Daughter of St. Sebastian !*

Now, at this moment, it has become necessary for me to close, but I allow to the reader one question before laying down my pen. Come now, reader, be quick ; 'look sharp' ; and ask what you *have* to ask ; for in one minute and a half I am going to write in capitals the word FINIS ; after which, you know, I am not at liberty to add a syllable. It would be shameful to do so ; since that word *Finis* enters into a secret covenant with the reader that he shall be molested no more with words, small or great. Twenty to one, I guess what your question will be. You desire to ask me, What became of Kate ? What was her end ?

Ah, reader ! but, if I answer that question, you will

say I have *not* answered it.   If I tell you that secret, you
will say that the secret is still hidden.   Yet, because I
have promised, and because you will be angry if I do not,
let me do my best.   After ten years of restlessness in
Spain, with thoughts always turning back to the dreadful
Andes, Kate heard of an expedition on the point of
sailing to Spanish America.   All soldiers knew *her*, so
that she had information of everything which stirred in
camps.   Men of the highest military rank were going
out with the expedition ; but Kate was a sister everywhere privileged ; she was as much cherished and as
sacred, in the eyes of every brigade or *tertia*, as their own
regimental colours ; and every member of the staff, from
the highest to the lowest, rejoiced to hear that she would
join their mess on board ship.   This ship, with others,
sailed ; whither finally bound, I really forget.   But, on
reaching America, all the expedition touched at *Vera Cruz*.
Thither a great crowd of the military went on shore.
The leading officers made a separate party for the same
purpose.   Their intention was, to have a gay, happy
dinner, after their long confinement to a ship, at the chief
hotel ; and happy in perfection the dinner could not be,
unless Kate would consent to join it.   She, that was ever
kind to brother soldiers, agreed to do so.   She descended
into the boat along with them, and in twenty minutes the
boat touched the shore.   All the bevy of gay laughing
officers, junior and senior, like so many schoolboys let
loose from school, jumped on shore, and walked hastily,
as their time was limited, up to the hotel.   Arriving
there, all turned round in eagerness, saying, ' Where is
our dear Kate ? '   Ah, yes, my dear Kate, at that solemn
moment, where, indeed, were *you ?*   She had, beyond all
doubt, taken her seat in the boat : that was certain,
though nobody, in the general confusion, was certain of
having seen her actually step ashore.   The sea was
searched for her—the forests were ransacked.   But the
sea did not give up its dead, if *there* indeed she lay ; and
the forests made no answer to the sorrowing hearts which
sought her amongst *them*.   Have I never formed a con-

jecture of my own upon the mysterious fate which thus suddenly enveloped her, and hid her in darkness for ever? Yes, I have. But it is a conjecture too dim and unsteady to be worth repeating. Her brother soldiers, that should naturally have had more materials for guessing than myself, were all lost in sorrowing perplexity, and could never arrive even at a plausible conjecture.

That happened two hundred and twenty-one years ago! And here is the brief upshot of all:—This nun sailed from Spain to Peru, and she found no rest for the sole of her foot. This nun sailed back from Peru to Spain, and she found no rest for the agitations of her heart. This nun sailed again from Spain to America, and she found—the rest which all of us find. But where it was, could never be made known to the father of Spanish camps, that sat in Madrid; nor to Kate's spiritual father, that sat in Rome. Known it is to the great Father of all, that once whispered to Kate on the Andes; but else it has been a secret for more than two centuries; and to man it remains a secret for ever and ever!

POSTSCRIPT

THERE are some narratives, which, though pure fictions from first to last, counterfeit so vividly the air of grave realities, that, if deliberately offered for such, they would for a time impose upon everybody. In the opposite scale there are other narratives, which, whilst rigorously true, move amongst characters and scenes so remote from our ordinary experience, and through a state of society so favourable to an adventurous cast of incidents, that they would everywhere pass for romances, if severed from the documents which attest their fidelity to facts. In the former class stand the admirable novels of Defoe; and, on a lower range within the same category, the inimitable *Vicar of Wakefield*; upon which last novel, without at all designing it, I once became the author of the following instructive experiment. I had given a copy of this little novel to a beautiful girl of seventeen, the daughter of a 'statesman in Westmoreland, not designing any deception (nor so much as any concealment) with respect to the fictitious character of the incidents and of the actors in that famous tale. Mere accident it was that had intercepted those explanations as to the extent of fiction in these points which in this case it would have been so natural to make. Indeed, considering the exquisite verisimilitude of the work, meeting with such absolute inexperience in the reader, it was almost a duty to have made them. This duty, however, something had caused me to forget; and when next I saw the young mountaineer, I forgot that I *had* forgotten it. Consequently,

at first I was perplexed by the unfaltering gravity with
which my fair young friend spoke of Dr. Primrose, of
Sophia and her sister, of Squire Thornhill, etc., as real
and probably living personages, who could sue and be
sued. It appeared that this artless young rustic, who had
never heard of novels and romances as a bare possibility
amongst all the shameless devices of London swindlers,
had read with religious fidelity every word of this tale, so
thoroughly life-like, surrendering her perfect faith and
loving sympathy to the different persons in the tale and
the natural distresses in which they are involved, without
suspecting for a moment that, by so much as a breathing
of exaggeration or of embellishment, the pure gospel
truth of the narrative could have been sullied. She
listened in a kind of breathless stupor to my frank
explanation—that not part only, but the whole, of this
natural tale was a pure invention. Scorn and indignation
flashed from her eyes. She regarded herself as one who
had been hoaxed and swindled ; begged me to take back
the book ; and never again, to the end of her life, could
endure to look into the book, or to be reminded of that
criminal imposture which Dr. Oliver Goldsmith had
practised upon her youthful credulity.

In that case, a book altogether fabulous, and not
meaning to offer itself for anything else, had been read
as genuine history. Here, on the other hand, the
adventures of the Spanish Nun, which, in every detail of
time and place have since been sifted and authenticated,
stood a good chance at one period of being classed as the
most lawless of romances. It is, indeed, undeniable—
and this arises as a natural result from the bold adventurous character of the heroine, and from the unsettled
state of society at that period in Spanish America—that
a reader, the most credulous, would at times be startled
with doubts upon what seems so unvarying a tenor of
danger and lawless violence. But, on the other hand, it
is also undeniable that a reader, the most obstinately
sceptical, would be equally startled in the very opposite
direction, on remarking that the incidents are far from

being such as a romance-writer would have been likely
to invent; since, if striking, tragic, and even appalling,
they are at times repulsive. And it seems evident, that,
once putting himself to the cost of a wholesale fiction,
the writer would have used his privilege more freely for
his own advantage. Whereas the author of these memoirs
clearly writes under the coercion and restraint of a
notorious reality, that would not suffer him to ignore or
to modify the leading facts. Then, as to the objection
that few people or none have an experience presenting
such uniformity of perilous adventure, a little closer attention shows that the experience in this case is *not* uniform;
and so far otherwise, that a period of several years in
Kate's South American life is confessedly suppressed; and
on no other ground whatever, than that this long parenthesis is *not* adventurous, not essentially differing from
the monotonous character of ordinary Spanish life.

Suppose the case, therefore, that Kate's memoirs had
been thrown upon the world with no vouchers for their
authenticity beyond such internal presumptions as would
have occurred to thoughtful readers, when reviewing the
entire succession of incidents, I am of opinion that the
person best qualified by legal experience to judge of
evidence would finally have pronounced a favourable
award; since it is easy to understand, that in a world
so vast as the Peru, the Mexico, the Chili, of Spaniards
during the first quarter of the seventeenth century, and
under the slender modification of Indian manners as yet
effected by the papal Christianisation of these countries,
and in the neighbourhood of a river-system so awful—
of a mountain-system so unheard-of in Europe,—there
would probably, by blind, unconscious sympathy, grow
up a tendency to lawless and gigantesque ideals of
adventurous life; under which, united with the duelling
code of Europe, many things would become trivial and
commonplace experiences that to us home-bred English
('*qui musas colimus severiores*') seem monstrous and
revolting.

Left, therefore, to itself, *my* belief is, that the story

of the Military Nun would have prevailed finally against the demurs of the sceptics.   However, in the meantime, all such demurs were suddenly and *officially* silenced for ever.   Soon after the publication of Kate's memoirs, in what you may call an early stage of her *literary* career, though two centuries after her *personal* career had closed, a regular controversy arose upon the degree of credit due to these extraordinary confessions (such they may be called) of the poor conscience-haunted nun.   Whether these in Kate's original MS. were entitled ' Autobiographic Sketches,' or 'Selections Grave and Gay,' from the military experiences of a Nun, or possibly ' The Confessions of a Biscayan Fire-Eater,' is more than I know. No matter : confessions they were ; and confessions that, when at length published, were absolutely mobbed and hustled by a gang of misbelieving (*i.e.*, *miscreant*) critics. And this fact is most remarkable, that the person who originally headed the incredulous party—viz., Senor De Ferrer, a learned Castilian—was the very same who finally authenticated, by *documentary* evidence, the extraordinary narrative in those parts which had most of all invited scepticism.   The progress of the dispute threw the decision at length upon the archives of the Spanish Marine.   Those for the southern ports of Spain had been transferred, I believe, from Cadiz and St. Lucar to Seville ; chiefly, perhaps, through the confusions incident to the two French invasions of Spain in our own day (1st, that under Napoleon ; 2ndly, that under the Duc d'Angoulême).   Amongst these archives, subsequently amongst those of Cuzco in South America ; 3rdly, amongst the records of some royal courts in Madrid ; 4thly, by collateral proof from the Papal Chancery ; 5thly, from Barcelona — have been drawn together ample attestations of all the incidents recorded by Kate.   The elopement from St. Sebastian's, the doubling of Cape Horn, the shipwreck on the coast of Peru, the rescue of the royal banner from the Indians of Chili, the fatal duel in the dark, the astonishing passage of the Andes, the tragical scenes at Tucuman and

Cuzco, the return to Spain in obedience to a royal and a papal summons, the visit to Rome and the interview with the pope; finally, the return to South America, and the mysterious disappearance at Vera Cruz, upon which no light was ever thrown—all these capital heads of the narrative have been established beyond the reach of scepticism : and, in consequence, the story was soon after adopted as historically established, and was reported at length by journals of the highest credit in Spain and Germany, and by a Parisian journal so cautious and so distinguished for its ability as the *Revue des Deux Mondes*. I must not leave the impression upon my readers, that this complex body of documentary evidences has been searched and appraised by myself. Frankly I acknowledge that, on the sole occasion when any opportunity offered itself for such a labour, I shrank from it as too fatiguing—and also as superfluous ; since, if the proofs had satisfied the compatriots of Catalina, who came to the investigation with hostile feelings of partisanship, and not dissembling their incredulity, armed also (and in Mr. De Ferrer's case conspicuously armed) with the appropriate learning for giving effect to this incredulity—it could not become a stranger to suppose himself qualified for disturbing a judgment that had been so deliberately delivered. Such a tribunal of native Spaniards being satisfied, there was no further opening for demur. The ratification of poor Kate's memoirs is now therefore to be understood as absolute, and without reserve.

This being stated—viz., such an attestation from competent authorities to the truth of Kate's narrative, as may save all readers from my fair Westmoreland friend's disaster—it remains to give such an answer, as without further research *can* be given, to a question pretty sure of arising in all reflective readers' thoughts— viz., Does there anywhere survive a portrait of Kate? I answer—and it would be both mortifying and per- plexing if I could *not*—*Yes*. One such portrait there is confessedly ; and seven years ago this was to be found

at Aix-la-Chapelle, in the collection of Herr Sempeller.
The name of the artist I am not able to report ; neither
can I say whether Herr Sempeller's collection still remains
intact, and remains at Aix-la-Chapelle.

But inevitably to most readers, who review the
circumstances of a case so extraordinary, it will occur,
that beyond a doubt *many* portraits of the adventurous
nun must have been executed. To have affronted the
wrath of the Inquisition, and to have survived such an
audacity, would of itself be enough to found a title for
the martial nun to a national interest. It is true that
Kate had not taken the veil ; she had stopped short of
the deadliest crime known to the Inquisition ; but still
her transgressions were such as to require a special
indulgence ; and this indulgence was granted by a pope
to the intercession of a king—the greatest then reigning.
It was a favour that could not have been asked by any
greater man in this world, nor granted by any less. Had
no other distinction settled upon Kate, this would have
been enough to fix the gaze of her own nation. But
her whole life constituted Kate's supreme distinction.
There can be no doubt, therefore, that, from the year
1624 (*i.e.*, the last year of our James I.), she became
the object of an admiration in her own country that was
almost idolatrous. And this admiration was not of a
kind that rested upon any partisan-schism amongst her
countrymen. So long as it was kept alive by her bodily
presence amongst them, it was an admiration equally
aristocratic and popular, shared alike by the rich and
the poor—by the lofty and the humble. Great, therefore, would be the demand for her portrait. There is
a tradition that Velasquez, who had in 1623 executed
a portrait of Charles I. (then Prince of Wales), was
amongst those who in the three or four following years
ministered to this demand. It is believed also, that in
travelling from Genoa and Florence to Rome, she sat to
various artists, in order to meet the interest about herself
already arising amongst the cardinals and other dignitaries
of the Romish Church. It is probable, therefore, that

numerous pictures of Kate are yet lurking both in Spain and Italy, but not known as such. For, as the public consideration granted to her had grown out of merits and qualities purely personal, and were kept alive by no local or family memorials rooted in the land, or surviving herself, it was inevitable that, as soon as she herself died, all identification of her portraits would perish : and the portraits would thenceforwards be confounded with the similar memorials, past all numbering, which every year accumulates as the wrecks from household remembrances of generations that are passing or passed, that are fading or faded, that are dying or buried. It is well, therefore, amongst so many irrecoverable ruins, that, in the portrait at Aix-la-Chapelle, we still possess one undoubted representation (and therefore in some degree a means for identifying *other* representations) of a female so memorably adorned by nature ; gifted with capacities so unparalleled both of doing and suffering ; who lived a life so stormy, and perished by a fate so unsearchably mysterious.

THE ENGLISH MAIL-COACH

THE ENGLISH MAIL-COACH

SECTION THE FIRST.—THE GLORY OF MOTION

SOME twenty or more years before I matriculated at Oxford, Mr. Palmer, at that time M.P. for Bath, had accomplished two things, very hard to do on our little planet, the Earth, however cheap they may be held by eccentric people in comets—he had invented mail-coaches, and he had married the daughter[1] of a duke. He was, therefore, just twice as great a man as Galileo, who did certainly invent (or, which is the same thing,[2] discover) the satellites of Jupiter, those very next things extant to mail-coaches in the two capital pretensions of speed and keeping time, but, on the other hand, who did *not* marry the daughter of a duke.

These mail-coaches, as organised by Mr. Palmer, are entitled to a circumstantial notice from myself, having had so large a share in developing the anarchies of my subsequent dreams; an agency which they accomplished, 1st, through velocity, at that time unprecedented—for they first revealed the glory of motion; 2ndly, through grand effects for the eye between lamp-light and the darkness upon solitary roads; 3rdly, through animal beauty and power so often displayed in the class of

---

[1] Lady Madeline Gordon.

[2] '*The same thing*' :—Thus, in the calendar of the Church Festivals, the discovery of the true cross (by Helen, the mother of Constantine) is recorded (and, one might think, with the express consciousness of sarcasm) as the *Invention* of the Cross.

horses selected for this mail service ; 4thly, through the conscious presence of a central intellect, that, in the midst of vast distances [1]—of storms, of darkness, of danger— overruled all obstacles into one steady co-operation to a national result.   For my own feeling, this post-office service spoke as by some mighty orchestra, where a thousand instruments, all disregarding each other, and so far in danger of discord, yet all obedient as slaves to the supreme *baton* of some great leader, terminate in a perfection of harmony like that of heart, brain, and lungs, in a healthy animal organisation.   But, finally, that particular element in this whole combination which most impressed myself, and through which it is that to this hour Mr. Palmer's mail-coach system tyrannises over my dreams by terror and terrific beauty, lay in the awful *political* mission which at that time it fulfilled.   The mail-coach it was that distributed over the face of the land, like the opening of apocalyptic vials, the heart- shaking news of Trafalgar, of Salamanca, of Vittoria, of Waterloo.   These were the harvests that, in the grandeur of their reaping, redeemed the tears and blood in which they had been sown.   Neither was the meanest peasant so much below the grandeur and the sorrow of the times as to confound battles such as these, which were gradually moulding the destinies of Christendom, with the vulgar conflicts of ordinary warfare, so often no more than gladiatorial trials of national prowess.   The victories of England in this stupendous contest rose of themselves as natural *Te Deums* to heaven ; and it was felt by the thoughtful that such victories, at such a crisis of general prostration, were not more beneficial to ourselves than finally to France, our enemy, and to the nations of all western or central Europe, through whose pusillanimity it was that the French domination had prospered.

The mail-coach, as the national organ for publishing

---

[1] '*Vast distances*' :—One case was familiar to mail-coach travellers, where two mails in opposite directions, north and south, starting at the same minute from points six hundred miles apart, met almost constantly at a particular bridge which bisected the total distance.

these mighty events thus diffusively influential, became itself a spiritualised and glorified object to an impassioned heart; and naturally, in the Oxford of that day, *all* hearts were impassioned, as being all (or nearly all) in *early* manhood. In most universities there is one single college; in Oxford there were five-and-twenty, all of which were peopled by young men, the *élite* of their own generation; not boys, but men; none under eighteen. In some of these many colleges, the custom permitted the student to keep what are called 'short terms'; that is, the four terms of Michaelmas, Lent, Easter, and Act, were kept by a residence, in the aggregate, of ninety-one days, or thirteen weeks. Under this interrupted residence, it was possible that a student might have a reason for going down to his home four times in the year. This made eight journeys to and fro. But, as these homes lay dispersed through all the shires of the island, and most of us disdained all coaches except his majesty's mail, no city out of London could pretend to so extensive a connection with Mr. Palmer's establishment as Oxford. Three mails, at the least, I remember as passing every day through Oxford, and benefiting by my personal patronage—viz., the Worcester, the Gloucester, and the Holyhead mail. Naturally, therefore, it became a point of some interest with us, whose journeys revolved every six weeks on an average, to look a little into the executive details of the system. With some of these Mr. Palmer had no concern; they rested upon bye-laws enacted by posting-houses for their own benefit, and upon other bye-laws, equally stern, enacted by the inside passengers for the illustration of their own haughty exclusiveness. These last were of a nature to rouse our scorn, from which the transition was not very long to systematic mutiny. Up to this time, say 1804, or 1805 (the year of Trafalgar), it had been the fixed assumption of the four inside people (as an old tradition of all public carriages derived from the reign of Charles II.), that they, the illustrious quaternion, constituted a porcelain variety of the human race, whose dignity would have been compromised by exchanging one

word of civility with the three miserable delf-ware outsides. Even to have kicked an outsider, might have been
held to attaint the foot concerned in that operation ; so
that, perhaps, it would have required an Act of Parliament
to restore its purity of blood. What words, then, could
express the horror, and the sense of treason, in that case,
which *had* happened, where all three outsides (the trinity
of Pariahs) made a vain attempt to sit down at the same
breakfast-table or dinner-table with the consecrated four?
I myself witnessed such an attempt ; and on that occasion
a benevolent old gentleman endeavoured to soothe his
three holy associates, by suggesting that, if the outsides
were indicted for this criminal attempt at the next assizes,
the court would regard it as a case of lunacy, or *delirium
tremens*, rather than of treason. England owes much of
her grandeur to the depth of the aristocratic element in
her social composition, when pulling against her strong
democracy. I am not the man to laugh at it. But sometimes, undoubtedly, it expressed itself in comic shapes.
The course taken with the infatuated outsiders, in the particular attempt which I have noticed, was, that the waiter,
beckoning them away from the privileged *salle-à-manger*,
sang out, 'This way, my good men,' and then enticed
these good men away to the kitchen. But that plan had
not always answered. Sometimes, though rarely, cases
occurred where the intruders, being stronger than usual,
or more vicious than usual, resolutely refused to budge,
and so far carried their point, as to have a separate table
arranged for themselves in a corner of the general room.
Yet, if an Indian screen could be found ample enough to
plant them out from the very eyes of the high table, or
dais, it then became possible to assume as a fiction of law
—that the three delf fellows, after all, were not present.
They could be ignored by the porcelain men, under the
maxim, that objects not appearing, and not existing, are
governed by the same logical construction.[1]
Such being, at that time, the usages of mail-coaches,

---

[1] *De non apparentibus et non existentibus eadem est lex.*

what was to be done by us of young Oxford? We, the
most aristocratic of people, who were addicted to the
practice of looking down superciliously even upon the
insides themselves as often very questionable characters
—were we, by voluntarily going outside, to court indig-
nities? If our dress and bearing sheltered us, generally,
from the suspicion of being 'raff' (the name at that period
for 'snobs'[1]) we really *were* such constructively, by the
place we assumed. If we did not submit to the deep
shadow of eclipse, we entered at least the skirts of its
penumbra. And the analogy of theatres was valid against
us, where no man can complain of the annoyances incident
to the pit or gallery, having his instant remedy in paying the
higher price of the boxes. But the soundness of this analogy
we disputed. In the case of the theatre, it cannot be pretended that the inferior situations have any separate attractions, unless the pit may be supposed to have an advantage
for the purposes of the critic or the dramatic reporter. But
the critic or reporter is a rarity. For most people, the
sole benefit is in the price. Now, on the contrary, the
outside of the mail had its own incommunicable advantages.
These we could not forego. The higher price we would
willingly have paid, but not the price connected with the
condition of riding inside ; which condition we pronounced
insufferable. The air, the freedom of prospect, the prox-
imity to the horses, the elevation of seat—these were what
we required ; but, above all, the certain anticipation of
purchasing occasional opportunities of driving.

Such was the difficulty which pressed us ; and under
the coercion of this difficulty, we instituted a searching
inquiry into the true quality and valuation of the different
apartments about the mail. We conducted this inquiry
on metaphysical principles ; and it was ascertained satisfactorily, that the roof of the coach, which by some weak

---

[1] '*Snobs*,' and its antithesis, '*nobs*,' arose among the internal factions
of shoemakers perhaps ten years later. Possibly enough, the terms may
have existed much earlier ; but they were then first made known,
picturesquely and effectively, by a trial at some assizes which happened
to fix the public attention.

men had been called the attics, and by some the garrets, was in reality the drawing-room ; in which drawing-room the box was the chief ottoman or sofa ; whilst it appeared that the *inside*, which had been traditionally regarded as the only room tenantable by gentlemen, was, in fact, the coal-cellar in disguise.

Great wits jump.   The very same idea had not long before struck the celestial intellect of China.   Amongst the presents carried out by our first embassy to that country was a state-coach.   It had been specially selected as a personal gift by George III. ; but the exact mode of using it was an intense mystery to Pekin.   The ambassador, indeed (Lord Macartney), had made some imperfect explanations upon this point ; but, as his excellency communicated these in a diplomatic whisper, at the very moment of his departure, the celestial intellect was very feebly illuminated, and it became necessary to call a cabinet council on the grand state question, 'Where was the Emperor to sit ?'   The hammer-cloth happened to be unusually gorgeous ; and partly on that consideration, but partly also because the box offered the most elevated seat, was nearest to the moon, and undeniably went foremost, it was resolved by acclamation that the box was the imperial throne, and for the scoundrel who drove, he might sit where he could find a perch.   The horses, therefore, being harnessed, solemnly his imperial majesty ascended his new English throne under a flourish of trumpets, having the first lord of the treasury on his right hand, and the chief jester on his left.   Pekin gloried in the spectacle ; and in the whole flowery people, constructively present by representation, there was but one discontented person, and *that* was the coachman.   This mutinous individual audaciously shouted, 'Where am *I* to sit ?'   But the privy council, incensed by his disloyalty, unanimously opened the door, and kicked him into the inside.   He had all the inside places to himself ; but such is the rapacity of ambition, that he was still dissatisfied.   'I say,' he cried out in an extempore petition, addressed to the emperor through the window—'I say, how am I to catch hold of the reins ?'—

'Anyhow,' was the imperial answer; 'don't trouble *me*, man, in my glory. How catch the reins? Why, through the windows, through the keyholes—*any*how.' Finally this contumacious coachman lengthened the check-strings into a sort of jury-reins, communicating with the horses; with these he drove as steadily as Pekin had any right to expect. The emperor returned after the briefest of circuits; he descended in great pomp from his throne, with the severest resolution never to remount it. A public thanksgiving was ordered for his majesty's happy escape from the disease of broken neck; and the state-coach was dedicated thenceforward as a votive offering to the god Fo, Fo—whom the learned more accurately called Fi, Fi.

A revolution of this same Chinese character did young Oxford of that era effect in the constitution of mail-coach society. It was a perfect French revolution; and we had good reason to say, *ça ira*. In fact, it soon became *too* popular. The 'public'—a well-known character, particularly disagreeable, though slightly respectable, and notorious for affecting the chief seats in synagogues—had at first loudly opposed this revolution; but when the opposition showed itself to be ineffectual, our disagreeable friend went into it with headlong zeal. At first it was a sort of race between us; and, as the public is usually from thirty to fifty years old, naturally we of young Oxford, that averaged about twenty, had the advantage. Then the public took to bribing, giving fees to horse-keepers, etc., who hired out their persons as warming-pans on the box-seat. *That*, you know, was shocking to all moral sensibilities. Come to bribery, said we, and there is an end to all morality, Aristotle's, Zeno's, Cicero's, or anybody's. And, besides, of what use was it? For *we* bribed also. And as our bribes, to those of the public, were as five shillings to sixpence, here again young Oxford had the advantage. But the contest was ruinous to the principles of the stables connected with the mails. This whole corporation was constantly bribed, rebribed, and often sur-rebribed; a mail-coach yard was like the hustings in a contested election ; and a horse-keeper, ostler, or helper, was held by the philosophical at that time to be the most corrupt character in the nation.

There was an impression upon the public mind, natural enough from the continually augmenting velocity of the mail, but quite erroneous, that an outside seat on this class of carriages was a post of danger. On the contrary, I maintained that, if a man had become nervous from some gipsy prediction in his childhood, allocating to a particular moon now approaching some unknown danger, and he should inquire earnestly, 'Whither can I fly for shelter? Is a prison the safest retreat? or a lunatic hospital? or the British Museum?' I should have replied, 'Oh, no; I'll tell you what to do. Take lodgings for the next forty days on the box of his majesty's mail. Nobody can touch you there. If it is by bills at ninety days after date that you are made unhappy—if noters and protesters are the sort of wretches whose astrological shadows darken the house of life—then note you what I vehemently protest— viz., that no matter though the sheriff and under-sheriff in every county should be running after you with his *posse*, touch a hair of your head he cannot whilst you keep house, and have your legal domicile on the box of the mail. It is felony to stop the mail; even the sheriff cannot do that. And an *extra* touch of the whip to the leaders (no great matter if it grazes the sheriff) at any time guarantees your safety.' In fact, a bedroom in a quiet house seems a safe enough retreat, yet it is liable to its own notorious nuisances —to robbers by night, to rats, to fire. But the mail laughs at these terrors. To robbers, the answer is packed up and ready for delivery in the barrel of the guard's blunderbuss. Rats again! there *are* none about mail- coaches, any more than snakes in Von Troil's Iceland;[1] except, indeed, now and then a parliamentary rat, who always hides his shame in what I have shown to be the 'coal cellar.' And as to fire, I never knew but one in a

[1] '*Von Troil's Iceland*':—The allusion is to a well-known chapter in Von Troil's work, entitled, "Concerning the Snakes of Iceland.' The entire chapter consists of these six words—'*There are no snakes in Iceland.*'

mail-coach, which was in the Exeter mail, and caused by
an obstinate sailor bound to Devonport. Jack, making
light of the law and the law-giver that had set their faces
against his offence, insisted on taking up a forbidden
seat [1] in the rear of the roof, from which he could exchange
his own yarns with those of the guard. No greater offence
was then known to mail-coaches ; it was treason, it was
læsa majestas, it was by tendency arson ; and the ashes of
Jack's pipe, falling amongst the straw of the hinder boot
containing the mail-bags, raised a flame which (aided by
the wind of our motion) threatened a revolution in the
republic of letters. Yet even this left the sanctity of the
box unviolated. In dignified repose, the coachman and
myself sat on, resting with benign composure upon our
knowledge that the fire would have to burn its way
through four inside passengers before it could reach ourselves. I remarked to the coachman, with a quotation
from Virgil's _Æneid_ really too hackneyed—

Jam proximus ardet
Ucalegon.

But, recollecting that the Virgilian part of the coachman's
education might have been neglected, I interpreted so far
as to say, that perhaps at that moment the flames were

---

1 '_Forbidden seat_' :—The very sternest code of rules was enforced
upon the mails by the Post-office. Throughout England, only three
outsides were allowed, of whom one was to sit on the box, and the
other two immediately behind the box ; none, under any pretext, to
come near the guard ; an indispensable caution ; since else, under the
guise of passenger, a robber might by any one of a thousand advantages
—which sometimes are created, but always are favoured, by the animation of frank social intercourse—have disarmed the guard. Beyond
the Scottish border, the regulation was so far relaxed as to allow of
four outsides, but not relaxed at all as to the mode of placing them.
One, as before, was seated on the box, and the other three on the front
of the roof, with a determinate and ample separation from the little
insulated chair of the guard. This relaxation was conceded by way of
compensating to Scotland her disadvantages in point of population.
England, by the superior density of her population, might always count
upon a large fund of profits in the fractional trips of chance passengers
riding for short distances of two or three stages. In Scotland, this chance
counted for much less. And therefore, to make good the deficiency,
Scotland was allowed a compensatory profit upon one _extra_ passenger.

catching hold of our worthy brother and inside passenger,
Ucalegon.   The coachman made no answer, which is my
own way when a stranger addresses me either in Syriac or
in Coptic, but by his faint sceptical smile he seemed to
insinuate that he knew better ; for that Ucalegon, as it
happened, was not in the way-bill, and therefore could not
have been booked.

No dignity is perfect which does not at some point
ally itself with the mysterious.   The connection of the
mail with the state and the executive government—a connection obvious, but yet not strictly defined—gave to the
whole mail establishment an official grandeur which did us
service on the roads, and invested us with seasonable
terrors.   Not the less impressive were those terrors,
because their legal limits were imperfectly ascertained.
Look at those turnpike gates ; with what deferential
hurry, with what an obedient start, they fly open at our
approach !   Look at that long line of carts and carters
ahead, audaciously usurping the very crest of the road.
Ah ! traitors, they do not hear us as yet ; but, as soon
as the dreadful blast of our horn reaches them with
proclamation of our approach, see with what frenzy of
trepidation they fly to their horses' heads, and deprecate
our wrath by the precipitation of their crane-neck quarter-
ings.   Treason they feel to be their crime ; each individual
carter feels himself under the ban of confiscation and
attainder ; his blood is attainted through six generations ;
and nothing is wanting but the headsman and his axe, the
block and the saw-dust, to close up the vista of his horrors.
What ! shall it be within benefit of clergy to delay the
king's message on the high road ?—to interrupt the great
respirations, ebb and flood, *systole* and *diastole*, of the
national intercourse ?—to endanger the safety of tidings,
running day and night between all nations and languages ?
Or can it be fancied, amongst the weakest of men, that
the bodies of the criminals will be given up to their widows
for Christian burial ?   Now the doubts which were raised
as to our powers did more to wrap them in terror, by
wrapping them in uncertainty, than could have been

effected by the sharpest definitions of the law from the
Quarter Sessions. We, on our parts (we, the collective
mail, I mean), did our utmost to exalt the idea of our
privileges by the insolence with which we wielded them.
Whether this insolence rested upon law that gave it a
sanction, or upon conscious power that haughtily dispensed
with that sanction, equally it spoke from a potential station,
and the agent, in each particular insolence of the moment,
was viewed reverentially, as one having authority.

Sometimes after breakfast his majesty's mail would
become frisky ; and in its difficult wheelings amongst the
intricacies of early markets, it would upset an apple-cart,
a cart loaded with eggs, etc. Huge was the affliction and
dismay, awful was the smash. I, as far as possible, endeavoured in such a case to represent the conscience and
moral sensibilities of the mail ; and, when wildernesses of
eggs were lying poached under our horses' hoofs, then
would I stretch forth my hands in sorrow, saying (in
words too celebrated at that time, from the false echoes[1]
of Marengo), 'Ah! wherefore have we not time to weep
over you?' which was evidently impossible, since, in fact,
we had not time to laugh over them. Tied to post-office
allowance, in some cases of fifty minutes for eleven miles,
could the royal mail pretend to undertake the offices of
sympathy and condolence? Could it be expected to provide tears for the accidents of the road? If even it
seemed to trample on humanity, it did so, I felt, in discharge of its own more peremptory duties.

Upholding the morality of the mail, *à fortiori* I upheld
its rights ; as a matter of duty, I stretched to the uttermost its privilege of imperial precedency, and astonished
weak minds by the feudal powers which I hinted to be
lurking constructively in the charters of this proud establishment. Once I remember being on the box of the

---

[1] '*False echoes*' :—Yes, false ! for the words ascribed to Napoleon,
as breathed to the memory of Desaix, never were uttered at all. They
stand in the same category of theatrical fictions as the cry of the
foundering line - of - battle ship *Vengeur*, as the vaunt of General
Cambronne at Waterloo, '*La Garde meurt, mais ne se rend pas,*' or as
the repartees of Talleyrand.

Holyhead mail, between Shrewsbury and Oswestry, when a tawdry thing from Birmingham, some 'Tallyho' or 'Highflyer,' all flaunting with green and gold, came up alongside of us. What a contrast to our royal simplicity of form and colour in this plebeian wretch! The single ornament on our dark ground of chocolate colour was the mighty shield of the imperial arms, but emblazoned in proportions as modest as a signet-ring bears to a seal of office. Even this was displayed only on a single panel, whispering, rather than proclaiming, our relations to the mighty state; whilst the beast from Birmingham, our green-and-gold friend from false, fleeting, perjured Brummagem, had as much writing and painting on its sprawling flanks as would have puzzled a decipherer from the tombs of Luxor. For some time this Birmingham machine ran along by our side—a piece of familiarity that already of itself seemed to me sufficiently jacobinical. But all at once a movement of the horses announced a desperate intention of leaving us behind. 'Do you see *that*?' I said to the coachman.—'I see,' was his short answer. He was wide awake, yet he waited longer than seemed prudent; for the horses of our audacious opponent had a disagreeable air of freshness and power. But his motive was loyal; his wish was, that the Birmingham conceit should be full-blown before he froze it. When *that* seemed right, he unloosed, or, to speak by a stronger word, he *sprang*, his known resources: he slipped our royal horses like cheetahs, or hunting-leopards, after the affrighted game. How they could retain such a reserve of fiery power after the work they had accomplished, seemed hard to explain. But on our side, besides the physical superiority, was a tower of moral strength, namely, the king's name, 'which they upon the adverse faction wanted.' Passing them without an effort, as it seemed, we threw them into the rear with so lengthening an interval between us, as proved in itself the bitterest mockery of their presumption; whilst our guard blew back a shattering blast of triumph, that was really too painfully full of derision.

I mention this little incident for its connection with
what followed.   A Welsh rustic, sitting behind me, asked
if I had not felt my heart burn within me during the
progress of the race ?   I said, with philosophic calmness,
No; because we were not racing with a mail, so that no
glory could be gained.   In fact, it was sufficiently mortifying that such a Birmingham thing should dare to
challenge us.   The Welshman replied, that he didn't see
that; for that a cat might look at a king, and a Brummagem coach might lawfully race the Holyhead mail.
'*Race* us, if you like,' I replied, 'though even *that* has an
air of sedition, but not *beat* us.   This would have been
treason ;   and for its own sake I am glad that the "Tallyho"
was disappointed.'   So dissatisfied did the Welshman seem
with this opinion, that at last I was obliged to tell him a
very fine story from one of our elder dramatists—viz.,
that once, in some far oriental kingdom, when the sultan
of all the land, with his princes, ladies, and chief omrahs,
were flying their falcons, a hawk suddenly flew at a
majestic eagle ;   and in defiance of the eagle's natural
advantages, in contempt also of the eagle's traditional
royalty, and before the whole assembled field of astonished
spectators from Agra and Lahore, killed the eagle on the
spot.   Amazement seized the sultan at the unequal contest, and burning admiration for its unparalleled result.
He commanded that the hawk should be brought before
him ;   he caressed the bird with enthusiasm ;   and he
ordered that, for the commemoration of his matchless
courage, a diadem of gold and rubies should be solemnly
placed on the hawk's head ;   but then that, immediately
after this solemn coronation, the bird should be led off to
execution, as the most valiant indeed of traitors, but not
the less a traitor, as having dared to rise rebelliously
against his liege lord and anointed sovereign, the eagle.
'Now,' said I to the Welshman, 'to you and me, as men
of refined sensibilities, how painful it would have been
that this poor Brummagem brute, the "Tallyho," in the
impossible case of a victory over us, should have been
crowned with Birmingham tinsel, with paste diamonds,

and Roman pearls, and then led off to instant execution.'
The Welshman doubted if that could be warranted by
law. And when I hinted at the 6th of Edward Long-
shanks, chap. 18, for regulating the precedency of coaches,
as being probably the statute relied on for the capital
punishment of such offences, he replied drily, that if the
attempt to pass a mail really were treasonable, it was a
pity that the 'Tallyho' appeared to have so imperfect an
acquaintance with law.

The modern modes of travelling cannot compare with
the old mail-coach system in grandeur and power. They
boast of more velocity, not, however, as a consciousness,
but as a fact of our lifeless knowledge, resting upon *alien*
evidence ; as, for instance, because somebody *says* that we
have gone fifty miles in the hour, though we are far from
feeling it as a personal experience, or upon the evidence
of a result, as that actually we find ourselves in York four
hours after leaving London. Apart from such an assertion,
or such a result, I myself am little aware of the pace.
But, seated on the old mail-coach, we needed no evidence
out of ourselves to indicate the velocity. On this system
the word was, *Non magna loquimur*, as upon railways, but
vivimus. Yes, 'magna *vivimus*'; we do not make verbal
ostentation of our grandeurs, we realise our grandeurs in
act, and in the very experience of life. The vital experience of the glad animal sensibilities made doubts impossible
on the question of our speed ; we heard our speed, we
saw it, we felt it as a thrilling; and this speed was not the
product of blind insensate agencies, that had no sympathy
to give, but was incarnated in the fiery eyeballs of the
noblest amongst brutes, in his dilated nostril, spasmodic
muscles, and thunder-beating hoofs. The sensibility of
the horse, uttering itself in the maniac light of his eye,
might be the last vibration of such a movement ; the
glory of Salamanca might be the first. But the intervening links that connected them, that spread the earthquake
of battle into the eyeball of the horse, were the heart of
man and its electric thrillings—kindling in the rapture of
the fiery strife, and then propagating its own tumults by

contagious shouts and gestures to the heart of his servant
the horse.

But now, on the new system of travelling, iron tubes
and boilers have disconnected man's heart from the
ministers of his locomotion. Nile nor Trafalgar has
power to raise an extra bubble in a steam-kettle. The
galvanic cycle is broken up for ever; man's imperial
nature no longer sends itself forward through the electric
sensibility of the horse; the inter-agencies are gone in the
mode of communication between the horse and his master,
out of which grew so many aspects of sublimity under
accidents of mists that hid, or sudden blazes that revealed,
of mobs that agitated, or midnight solitudes that awed.
Tidings, fitted to convulse all nations, must henceforwards
travel by culinary process; and the trumpet that once
announced from afar the laurelled mail, heart-shaking,
when heard screaming on the wind, and proclaiming
itself through the darkness to every village or solitary
house on its route, has now given way for ever to the
pot-wallopings of the boiler.

Thus have perished multiform openings for public
expressions of interest, scenical yet natural, in great
national tidings; for revelations of faces and groups that
could not offer themselves amongst the fluctuating mobs
of a railway station. The gatherings of gazers about a
laurelled mail had one centre, and acknowledged one sole
interest. But the crowds attending at a railway station
have as little unity as running water, and own as many
centres as there are separate carriages in the train.

How else, for example, than as a constant watcher for
the dawn, and for the London mail that in summer
months entered about daybreak amongst the lawny
thickets of Marlborough forest, couldst thou, sweet
Fanny of the Bath road, have become the glorified inmate
of my dreams? Yet Fanny, as the loveliest young
woman for face and person that perhaps in my whole life
I have beheld, merited the station which even now, from
a distance of forty years, she holds in my dreams; yes,
though by links of natural association she brings along

2 E

with her a troop of dreadful creatures, fabulous and not fabulous, that are more abominable to the heart, than Fanny and the dawn are delightful.

Miss Fanny of the Bath road, strictly speaking, lived at a mile's distance from that road ; but came so continually to meet the mail, that I on my frequent transits rarely missed her, and naturally connected her image with the great thoroughfare where only I had ever seen her. Why she came so punctually, I do not exactly know ; but I believe with some burden of commissions to be executed in Bath, which had gathered to her own residence as a central rendezvous for converging them. The mail-coachman who drove the Bath mail, and wore the royal livery,[1] happened to be Fanny's grandfather. A good man he was, that loved his beautiful granddaughter ; and, loving her wisely, was vigilant over her deportment in any case where young Oxford might happen to be concerned. Did my vanity then suggest that I myself, individually, could fall within the line of his terrors? Certainly not, as regarded any physical pretensions that I could plead ; for Fanny (as a chance passenger from her own neighbourhood once told me) counted in her train a hundred and ninety-nine professed admirers, if not open aspirants to her favour ; and probably not one of the whole brigade but excelled myself in personal advantages. Ulysses even, with the unfair advantage of his accursed bow, could hardly have undertaken that amount of suitors. So the danger might have seemed slight—only that woman is universally aristocratic ; it is amongst her nobilities of heart that she *is* so. Now, the aristocratic distinctions in my favour might easily with Miss Fanny

---

1 '*Wore the royal livery*' :—The general impression was, that the royal livery belonged of right to the mail-coachmen as their professional dress. But that was an error. To the guard it *did* belong, I believe, and was obviously essential as an official warrant, and as a means of instant identification for his person, in the discharge of his important public duties. But the coachman, and especially if his place in the series did not connect him immediately with London and the General Post-office, obtained the scarlet coat only as an honorary distinction after long (or, if not long, trying and special) service.

have compensated my physical deficiencies. Did I then make love to Fanny? Why, yes; about as much love as one *could* make whilst the mail was changing horses—a process which, ten years later, did not occupy above eighty seconds; but *then*—viz., about Waterloo—it occupied five times eighty. Now, four hundred seconds offer a field quite ample enough for whispering into a young woman's ear a great deal of truth, and (by way of parenthesis) some trifle of falsehood. Grandpapa did right, therefore, to watch me. And yet, as happens too often to the grandpapas of earth, in a contest with the admirers of granddaughters, how vainly would he have watched me had I meditated any evil whispers to Fanny! She, it is my belief, would have protected herself against any man's evil suggestions. But he, as the result showed, could not have intercepted the opportunities for such suggestions. Yet, why not? Was he not active? Was he not blooming? Blooming he was as Fanny herself.

> Say, all our praises why should lords——

Stop, that's not the line.

> Say, all our roses why should girls engross?

The coachman showed rosy blossoms on his face deeper even than his granddaughter's—*his* being drawn from the ale cask, Fanny's from the fountains of the dawn. But, in spite of his blooming face, some infirmities he had; and one particularly in which he too much resembled a crocodile. This lay in a monstrous inaptitude for turning round. The crocodile, I presume, owes that inaptitude to the absurd *length* of his back; but in our grandpapa it arose rather from the absurd *breadth* of his back, combined, possibly, with some growing stiffness in his legs. Now, upon this crocodile infirmity of his I planted a human advantage for tendering my homage to Miss Fanny. In defiance of all his honourable vigilance, no sooner had he presented to us his mighty Jovian back (what a field for displaying to mankind his royal scarlet!), whilst inspecting professionally the buckles, the straps,

and the silvery turrets[1] of his harness, than I raised
Miss Fanny's hand to my lips, and, by the mixed tenderness and respectfulness of my manner, caused her easily
to understand how happy it would make me to rank upon
her list as No. 10 or 12, in which case a few casualties
amongst her lovers (and observe, they *hanged* liberally
in those days) might have promoted me speedily to the
top of the tree ; as, on the other hand, with how much
loyalty of submission I acquiesced by anticipation in her
award, supposing that she should plant me in the very
rear-ward of her favour, as No. 199 + 1.   Most truly I
loved this beautiful and ingenuous girl ; and had it not
been for the Bath mail, timing all courtships by post-
office allowance, heaven only knows what might have
come of it.   People talk of being over head and ears in
love ; now, the mail was the cause that I sank only over
ears in love, which, you know, still left a trifle of brain
to overlook the whole conduct of the affair.

Ah, reader ! when I look back upon those days, it
seems to me that all things change—all things perish.
'Perish the roses and the palms of kings' : perish even
the crowns and trophies of Waterloo : thunder and
lightning are not the thunder and lightning which I
remember.   Roses are degenerating.   The Fannies of
our island—though this I say with reluctance—are not
visibly improving ; and the Bath road is notoriously
superannuated.   Crocodiles, you will say, are stationary.
Mr. Waterton tells me that the crocodile does *not* change ;
that a cayman, in fact, or an alligator, is just as good for
riding upon as he was in the time of the Pharaohs.   *That*
may be ; but the reason is, that the crocodile does not
live fast—he is a slow coach.   I believe it is generally

[1] '*Turrets*' :—As one who loves and venerates Chaucer for his
unrivalled merits of tenderness, of picturesque characterisation, and of
narrative skill, I noticed with great pleasure that the word *torrettes*
is used by him to designate the little devices through which the reins
are made to pass.   This same word, in the same exact sense, I heard
uniformly used by many scores of illustrious mail-coachmen, to whose
confidential friendship I had the honour of being admitted in my
younger days.

understood among naturalists, that the crocodile is a blockhead. It is my own impression that the Pharaohs were also blockheads. Now, as the Pharaohs and the crocodile domineered over Egyptian society, this accounts for a singular mistake that prevailed through innumerable generations on the Nile. The crocodile made the ridiculous blunder of supposing man to be meant chiefly for his own eating. Man, taking a different view of the subject, naturally met that mistake by another : he viewed the crocodile as a thing sometimes to worship, but always to run away from. And this continued until Mr. Waterton[1] changed the relations between the animals. The mode of escaping from the reptile he showed to be, not by running away, but by leaping on its back, booted and spurred. The two animals had misunderstood each other. The use of the crocodile has now been cleared up —viz., to be ridden ; and the final cause of man is, that he may improve the health of the crocodile by riding him a fox-hunting before breakfast. And it is pretty certain that any crocodile, who has been regularly hunted through the season, and is master of the weight he carries, will take a six-barred gate now as well as ever he would have done in the infancy of the pyramids.

If, therefore, the crocodile does *not* change, all things else undeniably *do :* even the shadow of the pyramids grows less. And often the restoration in vision of Fanny and the Bath road, makes me too pathetically sensible of that truth. Out of the darkness, if I happen to call back the image of Fanny, up rises suddenly from a gulf of forty years a rose in June ; or, if I think for an instant

---

[1] '*Mr. Waterton*':—Had the reader lived through the last generation, he would not need to be told that some thirty or thirty-five years back, Mr. Waterton, a distinguished country gentleman of ancient family in Northumberland, publicly mounted and rode in top-boots a savage old crocodile, that was restive and very impertinent, but all to no purpose. The crocodile jibbed and tried to kick, but vainly. He was no more able to throw the squire, than Sinbad was to throw the old scoundrel who used his back without paying for it, until he discovered a mode (slightly immoral, perhaps, though some think not) of murdering the old fraudulent jockey, and so circuitously of unhorsing him.

of the rose in June, up rises the heavenly face of Fanny. One after the other, like the antiphonies in the choral service, rise Fanny and the rose in June, then back again the rose in June and Fanny. Then come both together, as in a chorus—roses and Fannies, Fannies and roses, without end, thick as blossoms in paradise. Then comes a venerable crocodile, in a royal livery of scarlet and gold, with sixteen capes; and the crocodile is driving four-in-hand from the box of the Bath mail. And suddenly we upon the mail are pulled up by a mighty dial, sculptured with the hours, that mingle with the heavens and the heavenly host. Then all at once we are arrived at Marlborough forest, amongst the lovely house-holds[1] of the roe-deer; the deer and their fawns retire into the dewy thickets; the thickets are rich with roses; once again the roses call up the sweet countenance of Fanny; and she, being the granddaughter of a crocodile, awakens a dreadful host of semi-legendary animals—griffins, dragons, basilisks, sphinxes—till at length the whole vision of fighting images crowds into one towering armorial shield, a vast emblazonry of human charities and human loveliness that have perished, but quartered heraldically with unutterable and demoniac natures, whilst over all rises, as a surmounting crest, one fair female hand, with the forefinger pointing in sweet, sorrowful admonition, upwards to heaven, where is sculptured the eternal writing which proclaims the frailty of earth and her children.

GOING DOWN WITH VICTORY

But the grandest chapter of our experience, within the whole mail-coach service, was on those occasions when we went down from London with the news of victory. A

---

[1] '*Households*':—Roe-deer do not congregate in herds like the fallow or the red deer, but by separate families, parents and children; which feature of approximation to the sanctity of human hearths, added to their comparatively miniature and graceful proportions, conciliates to them an interest of peculiar tenderness, supposing even that this beautiful creature is less characteristically impressed with the grandeurs of savage and forest life.

period of about ten years stretched from Trafalgar to Waterloo; the second and third years of which period (1806 and 1807) were comparatively sterile; but the other nine (from 1805 to 1815 inclusively) furnished a long succession of victories; the least of which, in such a contest of Titans, had an inappreciable value of position— partly for its absolute interference with the plans of our enemy, but still more from its keeping alive through central Europe the sense of a deep-seated vulnerability in France. Even to tease the coasts of our enemy, to mortify them by continual blockades, to insult them by capturing if it were but a baubling schooner under the eyes of their arrogant armies, repeated from time to time a sullen proclamation of power lodged in one quarter to which the hopes of Christendom turned in secret. How much more loudly must this proclamation have spoken in the audacity [1] of having bearded the *élite* of their troops, and having beaten them in pitched battles! Five years of life it was worth paying down for the privilege of an outside place on a mail-coach, when carrying down the first tidings of any such event. And it is to be noted that, from our insular situation, and the multitude of our frigates disposable for the rapid transmission of intelligence, rarely did any unauthorised rumour steal away a prelibation from the first aroma of the regular despatches. The government news was generally the earliest news.

[1] '*Audacity*':—Such the French accounted it; and it has struck me that Soult would not have been so popular in London, at the period of her present Majesty's coronation, or in Manchester, on occasion of his visit to that town, if they had been aware of the insolence with which he spoke of us in notes written at intervals from the field of Waterloo. As though it had been mere felony in our army to look a French one in the face, he said in more notes than one, dated from two to four P.M. on the field of Waterloo, 'Here are the English—we have them; they are caught *en flagrant delit*.' Yet no man should have known us better; no man had drunk deeper from the cup of humiliation than Soult had in 1809, when ejected by us with headlong violence from Oporto, and pursued through a long line of wrecks to the frontier of Spain; subsequently at Albuera, in the bloodiest of recorded battles, to say nothing of Toulouse, he should have learned our pretensions.

From eight P.M., to fifteen or twenty minutes later, imagine the mails assembled on parade in Lombard Street, where, at that time,[1] and not in St. Martin's-le-Grand, was seated the General Post-office. In what exact strength we mustered I do not remember; but, from the length of each separate *attelage*, we filled the street, though a long one, and though we were drawn up in double file. On *any* night the spectacle was beautiful. The absolute perfection of all the appointments about the carriages and the harness, their strength, their brilliant cleanliness, their beautiful simplicity—but, more than all, the royal magnificence of the horses—were what might first have fixed the attention. Every carriage, on every morning in the year, was taken down to an official inspector for examination—wheels, axles, linchpins, pole, glasses, lamps, were all critically probed and tested. Every part of every carriage had been cleaned, every horse had been groomed, with as much rigour as if they belonged to a private gentleman; and that part of the spectacle offered itself always. But the night before us is a night of victory; and, behold! to the ordinary display, what a heart-shaking addition!—horses, men, carriages, all are dressed in laurels and flowers, oak-leaves and ribbons. The guards, as being officially his Majesty's servants, and of the coachmen such as are within the privilege of the post-office, wear the royal liveries of course; and as it is summer (for all the *land* victories were naturally won in summer), they wear, on this fine evening, these liveries exposed to view, without any covering of upper coats. Such a costume, and the elaborate arrangement of the laurels in their hats, dilate their hearts, by giving to them openly a personal connection with the great news, in which already they have the general interest of patriotism. That great national sentiment surmounts and quells all sense of ordinary distinctions. Those passengers who happen to be gentlemen are now hardly to be distinguished as such except by dress; for the usual reserve of their manner in speaking to the attendants has on this night melted away. One

---

[1] '*At that time*':—I speak of the era previous to Waterloo.

heart, one pride, one glory, connects every man by the transcendent bond of his national blood.   The spectators, who are numerous beyond precedent, express their sympathy with these fervent feelings by continual hurrahs.   Every moment are shouted aloud by the post-office servants, and summoned to draw up, the great ancestral names of cities known to history through a thousand years— Lincoln, Winchester, Portsmouth, Gloucester, Oxford, Bristol, Manchester, York, Newcastle, Edinburgh, Glasgow, Perth, Stirling, Aberdeen—expressing the grandeur of the empire by the antiquity of its towns, and the grandeur of the mail establishment by the diffusive radiation of its separate missions.   Every moment you hear the thunder of lids locked down upon the mail-bags.   That sound to each individual mail is the signal for drawing off, which process is the finest part of the entire spectacle.   Then come the horses into play.   Horses! can these be horses that bound off with the action and gestures of leopards?   What stir!—what sea-like ferment!—what a thundering of wheels!—what a trampling of hoofs!—what a sounding of trumpets!—what farewell cheers—what redoubling peals of brotherly congratulation, connecting the name of the particular mail —'Liverpool for ever!'—with the name of the particular victory—'Badajoz for ever!' or 'Salamanca for ever!'   The half-slumbering consciousness that, all night long, and all the next day—perhaps for even a longer period—many of these mails, like fire racing along a train of gunpowder, will be kindling at every instant new successions of burning joy, has an obscure effect of multiplying the victory itself, by multiplying to the imagination into infinity the stages of its progressive diffusion. A fiery arrow seems to be let loose, which from that moment is destined to travel, without intermission, westwards for three hundred[1] miles—northwards for six hundred ; and

---

[1] ' *Three hundred*' :—Of necessity, this scale of measurement, to an American, if he happens to be a thoughtless man, must sound ludicrous. Accordingly, I remember a case in which an American writer indulges himself in the luxury of a little fibbing, by ascribing to an Englishman

the sympathy of our Lombard Street friends at parting is exalted a hundredfold by a sort of visionary sympathy with the yet slumbering sympathies which in so vast a succession we are going to awake.

Liberated from the embarrassments of the city, and issuing into the broad uncrowded avenues of the northern suburbs, we soon begin to enter upon our natural pace of ten miles an hour. In the broad light of the summer evening, the sun, perhaps, only just at the point of setting, we are seen from every storey of every house. Heads of every age crowd to the windows—young and old understand the language of our victorious symbols—and rolling volleys of sympathising cheers run along us, behind us, and before us. The beggar, rearing himself against the wall, forgets his lameness—real or assumed—thinks not of his

---

a pompous account of the Thames, constructed entirely upon American ideas of grandeur, and concluding in something like these terms :— ' And, sir, arriving at London, this mighty father of rivers attains a breadth of at least two furlongs, having, in its winding course, traversed the astonishing distance of one hundred and seventy miles.' And this the candid American thinks it fair to contrast with the scale of the Mississippi. Now, it is hardly worth while to answer a pure fiction gravely, else one might say that no Englishman out of Bedlam ever thought of looking in an island for the rivers of a continent ; nor, consequently, could have thought of looking for the peculiar grandeur of the Thames in the length of its course, or in the extent of soil which it drains ; yet, if he *had* been so absurd, the American might have recollected that a river, not to be compared with the Thames even as to volume of water—viz., the Tiber—has contrived to make itself heard of in this world for twenty-five centuries to an extent not reached as yet by any river, however corpulent, of his own land. The glory of the Thames is measured by the destiny of the population to which it ministers, by the commerce which it supports, by the grandeur of the empire in which, though far from the largest, it is the most influential stream. Upon some such scale, and not by a transfer of Columbian standards, is the course of our English mails to be valued. The American may fancy the effect of his own valuations to our English ears, by supposing the case of a Siberian glorifying his country in these terms :—' These wretches, sir, in France and England, cannot march half a mile in any direction without finding a house where food can be had and lodging ; whereas, such is the noble desolation of our magnificent country, that in many a direction for a thousand miles, I will engage that a dog shall not find shelter from a snow-storm, nor a wren find an apology for breakfast.'

whining trade, but stands erect, with bold exulting smiles, as we pass him. The victory has healed him, and says, Be thou whole! Women and children, from garrets alike and cellars, through infinite London, look down or look up with loving eyes upon our gay ribbons and our martial laurels ; sometimes kiss their hands ; sometimes hang out, as signals of affection, pocket-handkerchiefs, aprons, dusters, anything that, by catching the summer breezes, will express an aerial jubilation. On the London side of Barnet, to which we draw near within a few minutes after nine, observe that private carriage which is approaching us. The weather being so warm, the glasses are all down ; and one may read, as on the stage of a theatre, everything that goes on within. It contains three ladies —one likely to be 'mamma,' and two of seventeen or eighteen, who are probably her daughters. What lovely animation, what beautiful unpremeditated pantomime, explaining to us every syllable that passes, in these ingenuous girls ! By the sudden start and raising of the hands, on first discovering our laurelled equipage !—by the sudden movement and appeal to the elder lady from both of them—and by the heightened colour on their animated countenances, we can almost hear them saying, 'See, see ! Look at their laurels ! Oh, mamma ! there has been a great battle in Spain ; and it has been a great victory.' In a moment we are on the point of passing them. We passengers—I on the box, and the two on the roof behind me—raise our hats to the ladies ; the coachman makes his professional salute with the whip ; the guard even, though punctilious on the matter of his dignity as an officer under the crown, touches his hat. The ladies move to us, in return, with a winning graciousness of gesture ; all smile on each side in a way that nobody could misunderstand, and that nothing short of a grand national sympathy could so instantaneously prompt. Will these ladies say that we are nothing to *them* ? Oh, no ; they will not say *that*. They cannot deny—they do not deny—that for this night they are our sisters ; gentle or simple, scholar or illiterate servant, for twelve hours to come, we on the outside have the honour to be their brothers. Those poor women, again, who stop to gaze upon us with delight at the entrance of Barnet, and seem, by their air of weariness, to be returning from labour—do you mean to say that they are washerwomen and charwomen?   Oh, my poor friend, you are quite mistaken.   I assure you they stand in a far higher rank ; for this one night they feel themselves by birth-right to be daughters of England, and answer to no humbler title.

Every joy, however, even rapturous joy—such is the sad law of earth—may carry with it grief, or fear of grief, to some.   Three miles beyond Barnet, we see approaching us another private carriage, nearly repeating the circumstances of the former case.   Here, also, the glasses are all down—here, also, is an elderly lady seated ; but the two daughters are missing ; for the single young person sitting by the lady's side, seems to be an attendant—so I judge from her dress, and her air of respectful reserve.   The lady is in mourning ; and her countenance expresses sorrow. At first she does not look up ; so that I believe she is not aware of our approach, until she hears the measured beating of our horses' hoofs.   Then she raises her eyes to settle them painfully on our triumphal equipage.   Our decorations explain the case to her at once ; but she beholds them with apparent anxiety, or even with terror. Some time before this, I, finding it difficult to hit a flying mark, when embarrassed by the coachman's person and reins intervening, had given to the guard a *Courier* evening paper, containing the gazette, for the next carriage that might pass.   Accordingly he tossed it in, so folded that the huge capitals expressing some such legend as— GLORIOUS VICTORY, might catch the eye at once.   To see the paper, however, at all, interpreted as it was by our ensigns of triumph, explained everything; and, if the guard were right in thinking the lady to have received it with a gesture of horror, it could not be doubtful that she had suffered some deep personal affliction in connection with this Spanish war.

Here, now, was the case of one who, having formerly suffered, might, erroneously perhaps, be distressing herself

with anticipations of another similar suffering.   That same
night, and hardly three hours later, occurred the reverse
case.   A poor woman, who too probably would find herself, in a day or two, to have suffered the heaviest of
afflictions by the battle, blindly allowed herself to express
an exultation so unmeasured in the news and its details, as
gave to her the appearance which amongst Celtic High-
landers is called *fey*.   This was at some little town where
we changed horses an hour or two after midnight.   Some
fair or wake had kept the people up out of their beds, and
had occasioned a partial illumination of the stalls and
booths, presenting an unusual but very impressive effect.
We saw many lights moving about as we drew near ;
and perhaps the most striking scene on the whole route
was our reception at this place.   The flashing of torches
and the beautiful radiance of blue lights (technically, Bengal lights) upon the heads of our horses ;   the fine effect of
such a showery and ghostly illumination falling upon our
flowers and glittering laurels ; [1] whilst all around ourselves,
that formed a centre of light, the darkness gathered on
the rear and flanks in massy blackness ;   these optical
splendours, together with the prodigious enthusiasm of the
people, composed a picture at once scenical and affecting,
theatrical and holy.   As we stayed for three or four minutes,
I alighted ;   and immediately from a dismantled stall in the
street, where no doubt she had been presiding through the
earlier part of the night, advanced eagerly a middle-aged
woman.   The sight of my newspaper it was that had
drawn her attention upon myself.   The victory which we
were carrying down to the provinces on *this* occasion, was
the imperfect one of Talavera—imperfect for its results,
such was the virtual treachery of the Spanish general,
Cuesta, but not imperfect in its ever-memorable heroism.
I told her the main outline of the battle.   The agitation of
her enthusiasm had been so conspicuous when listening, and
when first applying for information, that I could not but

[1] ' *Glittering laurels* ' :—I must observe, that the colour of *green*
suffers almost a spiritual change and exaltation under the effect of
Bengal lights.

ask her if she had not some relative in the Peninsular army. Oh, yes ; her only son was there. In what regiment ? He was a trooper in the 23rd Dragoons. My heart sank within me as she made that answer. This sublime regiment, which an Englishman should never mention without raising his hat to their memory, had made the most memorable and effective charge recorded in military annals. They leaped their horses—*over* a trench where they could, *into* it and with the result of death or mutilation when they could *not*. What proportion cleared the trench is nowhere stated. Those who *did*, closed up and went down upon the enemy with such divinity of fervour (I use the word *divinity* by design : the inspiration of God must have prompted this movement to those whom even then He was calling to His presence), that two results followed. As regarded the enemy, this 23rd Dragoons, not, I believe, originally three hundred and fifty strong, paralysed a French column, six thousand strong, then ascended the hill, and fixed the gaze of the whole French army. As regarded themselves, the 23rd were supposed at first to have been barely not annihilated ; but eventually, I believe, about one in four survived. And this, then, was the regiment—a regiment already for some hours glorified and hallowed to the ear of all London, as lying stretched, by a large majority, upon one bloody aceldama — in which the young trooper served whose mother was now talking in a spirit of such joyous enthusiasm. Did I tell her the truth ? Had I the heart to break up her dreams ? No. To-morrow, said I to myself—to-morrow, or the next day, will publish the worst. For one night more, wherefore should she not sleep in peace ? After to-morrow, the chances are too many that peace will forsake her pillow. This brief respite, then, let her owe to *my* gift and *my* forbearance. But, if I told her not of the bloody price that had been paid, not, therefore, was I silent on the contributions from her son's regiment to that day's service and glory. I showed her not the funeral banners under which the noble regiment was sleeping. I lifted not the overshadowing laurels from the bloody trench in which horse and rider lay mangled together. But I told her how these dear children of England, officers and privates, had leaped their horses over all obstacles as gaily as hunters to the morning's chase. I told her how they rode their horses into the mists of death (saying to myself, but not saying to *her*), and laid down their young lives for thee, O mother England! as willingly—poured out their noble blood as cheerfully—as ever, after a long day's sport, when infants, they had rested their wearied heads upon their mother's knees, or had sunk to sleep in her arms. Strange it is, yet true, that she seemed to have no fears for her son's safety, even after this knowledge that the 23rd Dragoons had been memorably engaged ; but so much was she enraptured by the knowledge that *his* regiment, and therefore that *he*, had rendered conspicuous service in the dreadful conflict—a service which had actually made them, within the last twelve hours, the foremost topic of conversation in London —so absolutely was fear swallowed up in joy—that, in the mere simplicity of her fervent nature, the poor woman threw her arms round my neck, as she thought of her son, and gave to *me* the kiss which secretly was meant for *him*.

THE ENGLISH MAIL-COACH

WHAT is to be taken as the predominant opinion of man, reflective and philosophic, upon SUDDEN DEATH? It is remarkable that, in different conditions of society, sudden death has been variously regarded as the consummation of an earthly career most fervently to be desired, or, again, as that consummation which is with most horror to be deprecated. Cæsar the Dictator, at his last dinner party (*cæna*), on the very evening before his assassination, when the minutes of his earthly career were numbered, being asked what death, in *his* judgment, might be pronounced the most eligible, replied, 'That which should be most sudden.' On the other hand, the divine Litany of our English Church, when breathing forth supplications, as if in some representative character for the whole human race prostrate before God, places such a death in the very van of horrors :—' From lightning and tempest ; from plague, pestilence, and famine ; from battle and murder, and from SUDDEN DEATH—*Good Lord, deliver us.*' Sudden death is here made to crown the climax in a grand ascent of calamities ; it is ranked among the last of curses ; and yet, by the noblest of Romans, it was ranked as the first of blessings. In that difference, most readers will see little more than the essential difference between Christianity and Paganism. But this, on consideration, I doubt. The Christian Church may be right in its estimate of sudden death ; and it is a natural feeling, though after all it may also be an infirm one, to wish for a quiet dismissal from life—as that which *seems* most reconcilable with meditation, with penitential retrospects, and with the humilities of farewell prayer. There does not, however, occur to me any direct scriptural warrant for this earnest petition of the English Litany, unless under a special construction of the word 'sudden.' It seems a petition—indulged rather and conceded to human infirmity, than exacted from human piety. It is not so much a doctrine built upon the eternities of the Christian system, as a plausible opinion built upon special varieties of physical temperament. Let that, however, be as it may, two remarks suggest themselves as prudent restraints upon a doctrine, which else *may* wander, and *has* wandered, into an uncharitable superstition. The first is this : that many people are likely to exaggerate the horror of a sudden death, from the disposition to lay a false stress upon words or acts, simply because by an accident they have become *final* words or acts. If a man dies, for instance, by some sudden death when he happens to be intoxicated, such a death is falsely regarded with peculiar horror ; as though the intoxication were suddenly exalted into a blasphemy. But *that* is unphilosophic. The man was, or he was not, *habitually* a drunkard. If not, if his intoxication were a solitary accident, there can be no reason for allowing special emphasis to this act, simply because through misfortune it became his final act. Nor, on the other hand, if it were no accident, but one of his *habitual* transgressions, will it be the more habitual or the more a transgression, because some sudden calamity, surprising him, has caused this habitual transgression to be also a final one. Could the man have had any reason even dimly to foresee his own sudden death, there would have been a new feature in his act of intemperance—a feature of presumption and irreverence, as in one that, having known himself drawing near to the presence of God, should have suited his demeanour to an expectation so awful. But this is no part of the case supposed. And the only new element in

2 F

the man's act is not any element of special immorality, but simply of special misfortune.

The other remark has reference to the meaning of the word *sudden*. Very possibly Cæsar and the Christian Church do not differ in the way supposed ; that is, do not differ by any difference of doctrine as between Pagan and Christian views of the moral temper appropriate to death, but perhaps they are contemplating different cases. Both contemplate a violent death, a βιαθανατος—death that is βιαιος, or, in other words, death that is brought about, not by internal and spontaneous change, but by active force having its origin from without. In this meaning the two authorities agree. Thus far they are in harmony. But the difference is, that the Roman by the word 'sudden' means *unlingering;* whereas the Christian Litany by 'sudden death' means a death *without warning*, consequently without any available summons to religious preparation. The poor mutineer, who kneels down to gather into his heart the bullets from twelve firelocks of his pitying comrades, dies by a most sudden death in Cæsar's sense ; one shock, one mighty spasm, one (possibly *not* one) groan, and all is over. But, in the sense of the Litany, the mutineer's death is far from sudden ; his offence originally, his imprisonment, his trial, the interval between his sentence and its execution, having all furnished him with separate warnings of his fate—having all summoned him to meet it with solemn preparation.

Here at once, in this sharp verbal distinction, we comprehend the faithful earnestness with which a holy Christian Church pleads on behalf of her poor departing children, that God would vouchsafe to them the last great privilege and distinction possible on a death-bed—viz., the opportunity of untroubled preparation for facing this mighty trial. Sudden death, as a mere variety in the modes of dying, where death in some shape is inevitable, proposes a question of choice which, equally in the Roman and the Christian sense, will be variously answered according to each man's variety of temperament. Meantime, one aspect of sudden death there is, one modification, upon which no doubt can arise, that of all martyrdoms it is the most agitating—viz., where it surprises a man under circumstances which offer (or which seem to offer) some hurrying, flying, inappreciably minute chance of evading it. Sudden as the danger which it affronts, must be any effort by which such an evasion can be accomplished. Even *that*, even the sickening necessity for hurrying in extremity where all hurry seems destined to be vain, even that anguish is liable to a hideous exasperation in one particular case — viz., where the appeal is made not exclusively to the instinct of self-preservation, but to the conscience, on behalf of some other life besides your own, accidentally thrown upon *your* protection. To fail, to collapse in a service merely your own, might seem comparatively venial ; though, in fact, it is far from venial. But to fail in a case where Providence has suddenly thrown into your hands the final interests of another—a fellow-creature shuddering between the gates of life and death ; this, to a man of apprehensive conscience, would mingle the misery of an atrocious criminality with the misery of a bloody calamity. You are called upon, by the case supposed, possibly to die ; but to die at the very moment when, by any even partial failure, or effeminate collapse of your energies, you will be self-denounced as a murderer. You had but the twinkling of an eye for your effort, and that effort might have been unavailing ; but to have risen to the level of such an effort, would have rescued you, though not from dying, yet from dying as a traitor to your final and farewell duty.

The situation here contemplated exposes a dreadful ulcer, lurking far down in the depths of human nature. It is not that men generally are summoned to face such awful trials. But potentially, and in shadowy outline, such a trial is moving subterraneously in perhaps all men's natures. Upon the secret mirror of our dreams such a trial is darkly projected, perhaps, to every one of us. That dream, so familiar to childhood, of meeting a lion, and, through languishing prostration in hope and the energies of hope, that constant sequel of lying down before

the lion, publishes the secret frailty of human nature—
reveals its deep-seated falsehood to itself—records its
abysmal treachery. Perhaps not one of us escapes that
dream ; perhaps, as by some sorrowful doom of man, that
dream repeats for every one of us, through every generation, the original temptation in Eden. Every one of us,
in this dream, has a bait offered to the infirm places of his
own individual will ; once again a snare is presented for
tempting him into captivity to a luxury of ruin ; once
again, as in aboriginal Paradise, the man falls by his own
choice ; again, by infinite iteration, the ancient earth
groans to Heaven, through her secret caves, over the
weakness of her child : 'Nature, from her seat, sighing
through all her works,' again 'gives signs of woe that all
is lost' ; and again the counter sigh is repeated to the
sorrowing heavens for the endless rebellion against God.
It is not without probability that in the world of dreams
every one of us ratifies for himself the original transgression. In dreams, perhaps under some secret conflict
of the midnight sleeper, lighted up to the consciousness at
the time, but darkened to the memory as soon as all is
finished, each several child of our mysterious race com-
pletes for himself the treason of the aboriginal fall.

.   .   .   .   .   .

The incident, so memorable in itself by its features of
horror, and so scenical by its grouping for the eye, which
furnished the text for this reverie upon *Sudden Death*,
occurred to myself in the dead of night, as a solitary
spectator, when seated on the box of the Manchester
and Glasgow mail, in the second or third summer after
Waterloo.   I find it necessary to relate the circumstances,
because they are such as could not have occurred unless
under a singular combination of accidents.   In those days,
the oblique and lateral communications with many rural
post-offices were so arranged, either through necessity or
through defect of system, as to make it requisite for the
main north-western mail (*i.e.*, the *down* mail), on reaching
Manchester, to halt for a number of hours ; how many,
I do not remember ; six or seven, I think ; but the result

was, that, in the ordinary course, the mail recommenced its journey northwards about midnight. Wearied with the long detention at a gloomy hotel, I walked out about eleven o'clock at night for the sake of fresh air ; meaning to fall in with the mail and resume my seat at the post-office. The night, however, being yet dark, as the moon had scarcely risen, and the streets being at that hour empty, so as to offer no opportunities for asking the road, I lost my way ; and did not reach the post-office until it was considerably past midnight ; but, to my great relief (as it was important for me to be in Westmoreland by the morning), I saw in the huge saucer eyes of the mail, blazing through the gloom, an evidence that my chance was not yet lost. Past the time it was ; but, by some rare accident, the mail was not even yet ready to start. I ascended to my seat on the box, where my cloak was still lying as it had lain at the Bridgewater Arms. I had left it there in imitation of a nautical discoverer, who leaves a bit of bunting on the shore of his discovery, by way of warning off the ground the whole human race, and notifying to the Christian and the heathen worlds, with his best compliments, that he has hoisted his pocket-handkerchief once and for ever upon that virgin soil ; thenceforward claiming the *jus dominii* to the top of the atmosphere above it, and also the right of driving shafts to the centre of the earth below it ; so that all people found after this warning, either aloft in upper chambers of the atmosphere, or groping in subterraneous shafts, or squatting audaciously on the surface of the soil, will be treated as trespassers— kicked, that is to say, or decapitated, as circumstances may suggest, by their very faithful servant, the owner of the said pocket-handkerchief. In the present case, it is probable that my cloak might not have been respected, and the *jus gentium* might have been cruelly violated in my person—for, in the dark, people commit deeds of darkness, gas being a great ally of morality—but it so happened that, on this night, there was no other outside passenger ; and thus the crime, which else was but too probable, missed fire for want of a criminal.

Having mounted the box, I took a small quantity of laudanum, having already travelled two hundred and fifty miles—viz., from a point seventy miles beyond London. In the taking of laudanum there was nothing extraordinary. But by accident it drew upon me the special attention of my assessor on the box, the coachman. And in *that* also there was nothing extraordinary. But by accident, and with great delight, it drew my own attention to the fact that this coachman was a monster in point of bulk, and that he had but one eye. In fact, he had been foretold by Virgil as

Monstrum horrendum, informe, ingens, cui lumen ademptum.

He answered to the conditions in every one of the items : —1. a monster he was ; 2. dreadful ; 3. shapeless ; 4. huge ; 5. who had lost an eye. But why should *that* delight me ? Had he been one of the Calendars in the *Arabian Nights,* and had paid down his eye as the price of his criminal curiosity, what right had *I* to exult in his misfortune ? I did *not* exult ; I delighted in no man's punishment, though it were even merited. But these personal distinctions (Nos. 1, 2, 3, 4, 5) identified in an instant an old friend of mine, whom I had known in the south for some years as the most masterly of mail-coachmen. He was the man in all Europe that could (if *any* could) have driven six-in-hand full gallop over *Al Sirat*— that dreadful bridge of Mahomet, with no side battlements, and of *extra* room not enough for a razor's edge—leading right across the bottomless gulf. Under this eminent man, whom in Greek I cognominated Cyclops *diphrélates* (Cyclops the charioteer), I, and others known to me, studied the diphrelatic art. Excuse, reader, a word too elegant to be pedantic. As a pupil, though I paid extra fees, it is to be lamented that I did not stand high in his esteem. It showed his dogged honesty (though, observe, not his discernment), that he could not see my merits. Let us excuse his absurdity in this particular, by remembering his want of an eye. Doubtless *that* made him blind to my merits. In the art of conversation, however, he admitted that I had the whip-hand of him. On this present occasion, great joy was at our meeting. But what was Cyclops doing here? Had the medical men recommended northern air, or how? I collected, from such explanations as he volunteered, that he had an interest at stake in some suit-at-law now pending at Lancaster; so that probably he had got himself transferred to this station, for the purpose of connecting with his professional pursuits an instant readiness for the calls of his lawsuit.

Meantime, what are we stopping for? Surely we have now waited long enough. Oh, this procrastinating mail, and this procrastinating post-office! Can't they take a lesson upon that subject from *me*? Some people have called *me* procrastinating. Yet you are witness, reader, that I was here kept waiting for the post-office. Will the post-office lay its hand on its heart, in its moments of sobriety, and assert that ever it waited for me? What are they about? The guard tells me that there is a large extra accumulation of foreign mails this night, owing to irregularities caused by war, by wind, by weather, in the packet service, which as yet does not benefit at all by steam. For an *extra* hour, it seems, the post-office has been engaged in threshing out the pure wheaten correspondence of Glasgow, and winnowing it from the chaff of all baser intermediate towns. But at last all is finished. Sound your horn, guard. Manchester, good-bye; we've lost an hour by your criminal conduct at the post-office: which, however, though I do not mean to part with a serviceable ground of complaint, and one which really *is* such for the horses, to me secretly is an advantage, since it compels us to look sharply for this lost hour amongst the next eight or nine, and to recover it (if we can) at the rate of one mile extra per hour. Off we are at last, and at eleven miles an hour; and for the moment I detect no changes in the energy or in the skill of Cyclops.

From Manchester to Kendal, which virtually (though not in law) is the capital of Westmoreland, there were at this time seven stages of eleven miles each. The first five of these, counting from Manchester, terminate in Lancaster, which is therefore fifty-five miles north of Manchester, and the same distance exactly from Liverpool. The first three stages terminate in Preston (called, by way of distinction from other towns of that name, *proud* Preston), at which place it is that the separate roads from Liverpool and from Manchester to the north become confluent.[1] Within these first three stages lay the foundation, the progress, and termination of our night's adventure. During the first stage, I found out that Cyclops was mortal : he was liable to the shocking affection of sleep— a thing which previously I had never suspected. If a man indulges in the vicious habit of sleeping, all the skill in aurigation of Apollo himself, with the horses of Aurora to execute his notions, avail him nothing. 'Oh, Cyclops ! ' I exclaimed, 'thou art mortal. My friend, thou snorest.' Through the first eleven miles, however, this infirmity— which I grieve to say that he shared with the whole Pagan Pantheon—betrayed itself only by brief snatches. On waking up, he made an apology for himself, which, instead of mending matters, laid open a gloomy vista of coming disasters. The summer assizes, he reminded me, were now going on at Lancaster : in consequence of which, for three nights and three days, he had not lain down in a bed. During the day, he was waiting for his own summons as a witness on the trial in which he was interested ; or else, lest he should be missing at the critical moment, was drinking with the other witnesses, under the pastoral surveillance of the attorneys. During the night, or that part of it which at sea would form the middle watch, he was driving. This explanation certainly accounted for his drowsiness, but in a way which made it much more alarming ; since now, after several days' resistance to this infirmity, at length he was steadily giving way.

[1] '*Confluent*' :—Suppose a capital Y (the Pythagorean letter) : Lancaster is at the foot of this letter ; Liverpool at the top of the *right* branch ; Manchester at the top of the *left ;* proud Preston at the centre, where the two branches unite. It is thirty-three miles along either of the two branches ; it is twenty-two miles along the stem— viz., from Preston in the middle, to Lancaster at the root. There's a lesson in geography for the reader.

Throughout the second stage he grew more and more drowsy. In the second mile of the third stage, he surrendered himself finally and without a struggle to his perilous temptation. All his past resistance had but deepened the weight of this final oppression. Seven atmospheres of sleep rested upon him ; and to consummate the case, our worthy guard, after singing 'Love amongst the Roses' for perhaps thirty times, without invitation, and without applause, had in revenge moodily resigned himself to slumber—not so deep, doubtless, as the coachman's, but deep enough for mischief. And thus at last, about ten miles from Preston, it came about that I found myself left in charge of his Majesty's London and Glasgow mail, then running at the least twelve miles an hour.

What made this negligence less criminal than else it must have been thought, was the condition of the roads at night during the assizes. At that time, all the law business of populous Liverpool, and also of populous Manchester, with its vast cincture of populous rural districts, was called up by ancient usage to the tribunal of Lilliputian Lancaster. To break up this old traditional usage required, 1. a conflict with powerful established interests ; 2. a large system of new arrangements ; and 3. a new parliamentary statute. But as yet this change was merely in contemplation. As things were at present, twice in the year [1] so vast a body of business rolled northwards, from the southern quarter of the county, that for a fortnight at least it occupied the severe exertions of two judges in its despatch. The consequence of this was, that every horse available for such a service, along the whole line of road, was exhausted in carrying down the multitudes of people who were parties to the different suits. By sunset, therefore, it usually happened that, through utter exhaustion amongst men and horses, the road sank into profound silence. Except the exhaustion in

---

[1] '*Twice in the year*' :—There were at that time only two assizes even in the most populous counties—viz., the Lent Assizes, and the Summer Assizes.

the vast adjacent county of York from a contested election, no such silence succeeding to no such fiery uproar was ever witnessed in England.

On this occasion, the usual silence and solitude prevailed along the road. Not a hoof nor a wheel was to be heard. And to strengthen this false luxurious confidence in the noiseless roads, it happened also that the night was one of peculiar solemnity and peace. For my own part, though slightly alive to the possibilities of peril, I had so far yielded to the influence of the mighty calm as to sink into a profound reverie. The month was August, in the middle of which lay my own birth-day—a festival to every thoughtful man suggesting solemn and often sigh-born[1] thoughts. The county was my own native county —upon which, in its southern section, more than upon any equal area known to man past or present, had descended the original curse of labour in its heaviest form, not mastering the bodies only of men, as of slaves, or criminals in mines, but working through the fiery will. Upon no equal space of earth was, or ever had been, the same energy of human power put forth daily. At this particular season also of the assizes, that dreadful hurricane of flight and pursuit, as it might have seemed to a stranger, which swept to and from Lancaster all day long, hunting the county up and down, and regularly subsiding back into silence about sunset, could not fail (when united with this permanent distinction of Lancashire as the very metropolis and citadel of labour) to point the thoughts pathetically upon that counter vision of rest, of saintly repose from strife and sorrow, towards which, as to their secret haven, the profounder aspirations of man's heart are in solitude continually travelling. Obliquely upon our left we were nearing the sea, which also must, under the present circumstances, be repeating the general state of halcyon repose. The sea, the atmosphere, the light, bore each an orchestral part in this universal lull. Moon-

---

[1] '*Sigh-born*':—I owe the suggestion of this word to an obscure remembrance of a beautiful phrase in "Giraldus Cambrensis"—viz., *suspiriosæ cogitationes*.

light, and the first timid tremblings of the dawn, were by this time blending ; and the blendings were brought into a still more exquisite state of unity by a slight silvery mist, motionless and dreamy, that covered the woods and fields, but with a veil of equable transparency.   Except the feet of our own horses, which, running on a sandy margin of the road, made but little disturbance, there was no sound abroad.   In the clouds, and on the earth, prevailed the same majestic peace ; and in spite of all that the villain of a schoolmaster has done for the ruin of our sublimer thoughts, which are the thoughts of our infancy, we still believe in no such nonsense as a limited atmosphere. Whatever we may swear with our false feigning lips, in our faithful hearts we still believe, and must for ever believe, in fields of air traversing the total gulf between earth and the central heavens.   Still, in the confidence of children that tread without fear *every* chamber in their father's house, and to whom no door is closed, we, in that Sabbatic vision which sometimes is revealed for an hour upon nights like this, ascend with easy steps from the sorrow-stricken fields of earth, upwards to the sandals of God.

Suddenly, from thoughts like these, I was awakened to a sullen sound, as of some motion on the distant road. It stole upon the air for a moment ; I listened in awe ; but then it died away.   Once roused, however, I could not but observe with alarm the quickened motion of our horses.   Ten years' experience had made my eye learned in the valuing of motion ; and I saw that we were now running thirteen miles an hour.   I pretend to no presence of mind.   On the contrary, my fear is, that I am miserably and shamefully deficient in that quality as regards action. The palsy of doubt and distraction hangs like some guilty weight of dark unfathomed remembrances upon my energies, when the signal is flying for *action*.   But, on the other hand, this accursed gift I have, as regards *thought*, that in the first step towards the possibility of a misfortune, I see its total evolution ; in the radix of the series I see too certainly and too instantly its entire expansion ; in the first syllable of the dreadful sentence, I read already the last. It was not that I feared for ourselves. *Us*, our bulk and impetus charmed against peril in any collision. And I had ridden through too many hundreds of perils that were frightful to approach, that were matter of laughter to look back upon, the first face of which was horror—the parting face a jest—for any anxiety to rest upon *our* interests. The mail was not built, I felt assured, nor bespoke, that could betray *me* who trusted to its protection. But any carriage that we could meet would be frail and light in comparison of ourselves. And I remarked this ominous accident of our situation. We were on the wrong side of the road. But then, it may be said, the other party, if other there was, might also be on the wrong side ; and two wrongs might make a right. *That* was not likely. The same motive which had drawn *us* to the right-hand side of the road—viz., the luxury of the soft beaten sand, as contrasted with the paved centre—would prove attractive to others. The two adverse carriages would therefore, to a certainty, be travelling on the same side ; and from this side, as not being ours in law, the crossing over to the other would, of course, be looked for from *us*.[1] Our lamps, still lighted, would give the impression of vigilance on our part. And every creature that met us would rely upon *us* for quartering.[2] All this, and if the separate links of the anticipation had been a thousand times more, I saw, not discursively, or by effort, or by succession, but by one flash of horrid simultaneous intuition.

Under this steady though rapid anticipation of the evil which *might* be gathering ahead, ah ! what a sullen mystery of fear, what a sigh of woe, was that which stole

[1] It is true that, according to the law of the case as established by legal precedents, all carriages were required to give way before Royal equipages, and therefore before the mail as one of them. But this only increased the danger, as being a regulation very imperfectly made known, very unequally enforced, and therefore often embarrassing the movements on both sides.

[2] '*Quartering*' :—This is the technical word, and, I presume, derived from the French *cartayer*, to evade a rut or any obstacle.

upon the air, as again the far-off sound of a wheel was
heard! A whisper it was—a whisper from, perhaps, four
miles off—secretly announcing a ruin that, being foreseen,
was not the less inevitable ; that, being known, was not,
therefore, healed. What could be done—who was it that
could do it—to check the storm-flight of these maniacal
horses? Could I not seize the reins from the grasp of
the slumbering coachman? You, reader, think that it
would have been in *your* power to do so. And I quarrel
not with your estimate of yourself. But, from the way
in which the coachman's hand was viced between his upper
and lower thigh, this was impossible. Easy, was it. See,
then, that bronze equestrian statue. The cruel rider has
kept the bit in his horse's mouth for two centuries. Un-
bridle him, for a minute, if you please, and wash his
mouth with water. Easy, was it? Unhorse me, then,
that imperial rider ; knock me those marble feet from
those marble stirrups of Charlemagne.

The sounds ahead strengthened, and were now too
clearly the sounds of wheels. Who and what could it be?
Was it industry in a taxed cart? Was it youthful gaiety
in a gig? Was it sorrow that loitered, or joy that raced?
For as yet the snatches of sound were too intermitting,
from distance, to decipher the character of the motion.
Whoever were the travellers, something must be done to
warn them. Upon the other party rests the active responsibility, but upon *us*—and, woe is me! that *us* was reduced
to my frail opium-shattered self—rests the responsibility
of warning. Yet, how should this be accomplished?
Might I not sound the guard's horn? Already, on the
first thought, I was making my way over the roof to the
guard's seat. But this, from the accident which I have
mentioned, of the foreign mails being piled upon the roof,
was a difficult and even dangerous attempt to one cramped
by nearly three hundred miles of outside travelling.
And, fortunately, before I had lost much time in the
attempt, our frantic horses swept round an angle of the
road, which opened upon us that final stage where the
collision must be accomplished, and the catastrophe sealed.

All was apparently finished. The court was sitting; the case was heard; the judge had finished; and only the verdict was yet in arrear.

Before us lay an avenue, straight as an arrow, six hundred yards, perhaps, in length; and the umbrageous trees, which rose in a regular line from either side, meeting high overhead, give to it the character of a cathedral aisle. These trees lent a deeper solemnity to the early light; but there was still light enough to perceive, at the further end of this Gothic aisle, a frail reedy gig, in which were seated a young man, and by his side a young lady. Ah, young sir! what are you about? If it is requisite that you should whisper your communications to this young lady—though really I see nobody, at an hour and on a road so solitary, likely to overhear you—is it therefore requisite that you should carry your lips forward to hers? The little carriage is creeping on at one mile an hour; and the parties within it being thus tenderly engaged, are naturally bending down their heads. Between them and eternity, to all human calculation, there is but a minute and a half. Oh heavens! what is it that I shall do? Speaking or acting, what help can I offer? Strange it is, and to a mere auditor of the tale might seem laughable, that I should need a suggestion from the *Iliad* to prompt the sole resource that remained. Yet so it was. Suddenly I remembered the shout of Achilles, and its effect. But could I pretend to shout like the son of Peleus, aided by Pallas? No: but then I needed not the shout that should alarm all Asia militant; such a shout would suffice as might carry terror into the hearts of two thoughtless young people, and one gighorse. I shouted—and the young man heard me not. A second time I shouted—and now he heard me, for now he raised his head.

Here, then, all had been done that, by me, *could* be done: more on *my* part was not possible. Mine had been the first step; the second was for the young man; the third was for God. If, said I, this stranger is a brave man, and if, indeed, he loves the young girl at his side—

or, loving her not, if he feels the obligation, pressing upon every man worthy to be called a man, of doing his utmost for a woman confided to his protection—he will, at least, make some effort to save her. If *that* fails, he will not perish the more, or by a death more cruel, for having made it ; and he will die as a brave man should, with his face to the danger, and with his arm about the woman that he sought in vain to save. But, if he makes no effort, shrinking, without a struggle, from his duty, he himself will not the less certainly perish for this baseness of poltroonery. He will die no less : and why not ? Wherefore should we grieve that there is one craven less in the world? No ; *let* him perish, without a pitying thought of ours wasted upon him ; and, in that case, all our grief will be reserved for the fate of the helpless girl who now, upon the least shadow of failure in *him*, must, by the fiercest of translations—must, without time for a prayer, must, within seventy seconds, stand before the judgment-seat of God.

But craven he was not : sudden had been the call upon him, and sudden was his answer to the call. He saw, he heard, he comprehended, the ruin that was coming down : already its gloomy shadow darkened above him ; and already he was measuring his strength to deal with it. Ah ! what a vulgar thing does courage seem, when we see nations buying it and selling it for a shilling a day : ah ! what a sublime thing does courage seem, when some fearful summons on the great deeps of life carries a man, as if running before a hurricane, up to the giddy crest of some tumultuous crisis, from which lie two courses, and a voice says to him audibly, 'One way lies hope ; take the other, and mourn for ever!' How grand a triumph, if, even then, amidst the raving of all around him, and the frenzy of the danger, the man is able to confront his situation—is able to retire for a moment into solitude with God, and to seek his counsel from *Him!*

For seven seconds, it might be, of his seventy, the stranger settled his countenance steadfastly upon us, as if to search and value every element in the conflict before him. For five seconds more of his seventy he sat immovably, like one that mused on some great purpose. For five more, perhaps, he sat with eyes upraised, like one that prayed in sorrow, under some extremity of doubt, for light that should guide him to the better choice. Then suddenly he rose; stood upright; and by a powerful strain upon the reins, raising his horse's fore-feet from the ground, he slewed him round on the pivot of his hind-legs, so as to plant the little equipage in a position nearly at right angles to ours. Thus far his condition was not improved; except as a first step had been taken towards the possibility of a second. If no more were done, nothing was done; for the little carriage still occupied the very centre of our path, though in an altered direction. Yet even now it may not be too late: fifteen of the seventy seconds may still be unexhausted; and one almighty bound may avail to clear the ground. Hurry, then, hurry! for the flying moments—*they* hurry. Oh, hurry, hurry, my brave young man! for the cruel hoofs of our horses—*they* also hurry! Fast are the flying moments, faster are the hoofs of our horses. But fear not for *him*, if human energy can suffice; faithful was he that drove to his terrific duty; faithful was the horse to *his* command. One blow, one impulse given with voice and hand, by the stranger, one rush from the horse, one bound as if in the act of rising to a fence, landed the docile creature's fore-feet upon the crown or arching centre of the road. The larger half of the little equipage had then cleared our over-towering shadow: *that* was evident even to my own agitated sight. But it mattered little that one wreck should float off in safety, if upon the wreck that perished were embarked the human freight-age. The rear part of the carriage—was *that* certainly beyond the line of absolute ruin? What power could answer the question? Glance of eye, thought of man, wing of angel, which of these had speed enough to sweep between the question and the answer, and divide the one from the other? Light does not tread upon the steps of light more indivisibly, than did our all-conquering

arrival upon the escaping efforts of the gig. *That* must
the young man have felt too plainly. His back was now
turned to us ; not by sight could he any longer communicate
with the peril ; but by the dreadful rattle of our harness,
too truly had his ear been instructed—that all was finished
as regarded any further effort of *his*.   Already in resignation he had rested from his struggle ; and perhaps in
his heart he was whispering, ' Father, which art in heaven,
do Thou finish above what I on earth have attempted.'
Faster than ever mill-race we ran past them in our inexorable flight.   Oh, raving of hurricanes that must have
sounded in their young ears at the moment of our transit !
Even in that moment the thunder of collision spoke
aloud.   Either with the swingle-bar, or with the haunch
of our near leader, we had struck the off-wheel of the
little gig, which stood rather obliquely, and not quite so
far advanced, as to be accurately parallel with the near-
wheel.   The blow, from the fury of our passage, resounded
terrifically.   I rose in horror, to gaze upon the ruins we
might have caused.   From my elevated station I looked
down, and looked back upon the scene, which in a
moment told its own tale, and wrote all its records on
my heart for ever.

Here was the map of the passion that now had finished.
The horse was planted immovably, with his fore-feet
upon the paved crest of the central road.   He of the
whole party might be supposed untouched by the passion
of death.   The little cany carriage—partly, perhaps, from
the violent torsion of the wheels in its recent movement,
partly from the thundering blow we had given to it—as
if it sympathised with human horror, was all alive with
tremblings and shiverings.   The young man trembled
not, nor shivered.   He sat like a rock.   But *his* was the
steadiness of agitation frozen into rest by horror.   As yet
he dared not to look round ; for he knew that, if anything
remained to do, by him it could no longer be done.   And
as yet he knew not for certain if their safety were accomplished.   But the lady——

But the lady——!   Oh, heavens ! will that spectacle

2 G

ever depart from my dreams, as she rose and sank upon her seat, sank and rose, threw up her arms wildly to heaven, clutched at some visionary object in the air, fainting, praying, raving, despairing? Figure to yourself, reader, the elements of the case ; suffer me to recall before your mind the circumstances of that unparalleled situation. From the silence and deep peace of this saintly summer night—from the pathetic blending of this sweet moonlight, dawnlight, dreamlight—from the manly tenderness of this flattering, whispering, murmuring love—suddenly as from the woods and fields—suddenly as from the chambers of the air opening in revelation—suddenly as from the ground yawning at her feet, leaped upon her, with the flashing of cataracts, Death the crownéd phantom, with all the equipage of his terrors, and the tiger roar of his voice.

The moments were numbered ; the strife was finished ; the vision was closed. In the twinkling of an eye, our flying horses had carried us to the termination of the umbrageous aisle ; at right angles we wheeled into our former direction, the turn of the road carried the scene out of my eyes in an instant, and swept it into my dreams for ever.

THE ENGLISH MAIL-COACH

SECTION THE THIRD.—DREAM-FUGUE

FOUNDED ON THE PRECEDING THEME OF SUDDEN DEATH

> Whence the sound
> Of instruments, that made melodious chime,
> Was heard, of harp and organ ; and who moved
> Their stops and chords, was seen ; his volant touch
> Instinct through all proportions, low and high,
> Fled and pursued transverse the resonant fugue.
> *Par. Lost,* Bk. XI.

Tumultuosissimamente

PASSION of sudden death ! that once in youth I read and interpreted by the shadows of thy averted signs ! [1]—rapture of panic taking the shape (which amongst tombs in churches I have seen) of woman bursting her sepulchral bonds—of woman's Ionic form bending forward from the ruins of her grave with arching foot, with eyes upraised, with clasped adoring hands—waiting, watching, trembling, praying for the trumpet's call to rise from dust for ever ! Ah, vision too fearful of shuddering humanity on the brink of almighty abysses !—vision that didst start back, that didst reel away, like a shrivelling scroll from before the wrath of fire racing on the wings of the wind !

---

[1] ' *Averted signs* ' :—I read the course and changes of the lady's agony in the succession of her involuntary gestures ; but it must be remembered that I read all this from the rear, never once catching the lady's full face, and even her profile imperfectly.

Epilepsy so brief of horror, wherefore is it that thou canst not die ? Passing so suddenly into darkness, wherefore is it that still thou sheddest thy sad funeral blights upon the gorgeous mosaics of dreams ? Fragment of music too passionate, heard once, and heard no more, what aileth thee, that thy deep rolling chords come up at intervals through all the worlds of sleep, and after forty years, have lost no element of horror ?

I

Lo, it is summer—almighty summer ! The everlasting gates of life and summer are thrown open wide ; and on the ocean, tranquil and verdant as a savannah, the unknown lady from the dreadful vision and I myself are floating—she upon a fairy pinnace, and I upon an English three-decker. Both of us are wooing gales of festal happiness within the domain of our common country, within that ancient watery park, within that pathless chase of ocean, where England takes her pleasure as a huntress through winter and summer, from the rising to the setting sun. Ah, what a wilderness of floral beauty was hidden, or was suddenly revealed, upon the tropic islands through which the pinnace moved ! And upon her deck what a bevy of human flowers—young women how lovely, young men how noble, that were dancing together, and slowly drifting towards *us* amidst music and incense, amidst blossoms from forests and gorgeous corymbi from vintages, amidst natural carolling, and the echoes of sweet girlish laughter. Slowly the pinnace nears us, gaily she hails us, and silently she disappears beneath the shadow of our mighty bows. But then, as at some signal from heaven, the music, and the carols, and the sweet echoing of girlish laughter—all are hushed. What evil has smitten the pinnace, meeting or overtaking her ? Did ruin to our friends couch within our own dreadful shadow ? Was our shadow the shadow of death ? I looked over the bow for an answer, and, behold ! the pinnace was dismantled ; the revel and the revellers were found no more ;

the glory of the vintage was dust; and the forests with their beauty were left without a witness upon the seas. 'But where,' and I turned to our crew—'where are the lovely women that danced beneath the awning of flowers and clustering corymbi? Whither have fled the noble young men that danced with *them*?' Answer there was none. But suddenly the man at the mast-head, whose countenance darkened with alarm, cried out, 'Sail on the weather beam! Down she comes upon us: in seventy seconds she also will founder.'

II

I looked to the weather side, and the summer had departed. The sea was rocking, and shaken with gathering wrath. Upon its surface sat mighty mists, which grouped themselves into arches and long cathedral aisles. Down one of these, with the fiery pace of a quarrel from a cross-bow, ran a frigate right athwart our course. 'Are they mad?' some voice exclaimed from our deck. 'Do they woo their ruin?' But in a moment, as she was close upon us, some impulse of a heady current or local vortex gave a wheeling bias to her course, and off she forged without a shock. As she ran past us, high aloft amongst the shrouds stood the lady of the pinnace. The deeps opened ahead in malice to receive her, towering surges of foam ran after her, the billows were fierce to catch her. But far away she was borne into desert spaces of the sea: whilst still by sight I followed her, as she ran before the howling gale, chased by angry sea-birds and by maddening billows; still I saw her, as at the moment when she ran past us, standing amongst the shrouds, with her white draperies streaming before the wind. There she stood, with hair dishevelled, one hand clutched amongst the tackling—rising, sinking, fluttering, trembling, praying—there for leagues I saw her as she stood, raising at intervals one hand to heaven, amidst the fiery crests of the pursuing waves and the raving of the storm; until at last, upon a sound from afar of malicious laughter and mockery, all was hidden for ever in driving showers; and afterwards, but when I know not, nor how.

III

Sweet funeral bells from some incalculable distance, wailing over the dead that die before the dawn, awakened me as I slept in a boat moored to some familiar shore. The morning twilight even then was breaking; and, by the dusky revelations which it spread, I saw a girl, adorned with a garland of white roses about her head for some great festival, running along the solitary strand in extremity of haste. Her running was the running of panic; and often she looked back as to some dreadful enemy in the rear. But when I leaped ashore, and followed on her steps to warn her of a peril in front, alas! from me she fled as from another peril, and vainly I shouted to her of quicksands that lay ahead. Faster and faster she ran; round a promontory of rocks she wheeled out of sight; in an instant I also wheeled round it, but only to see the treacherous sands gathering above her head. Already her person was buried; only the fair young head and the diadem of white roses around it were still visible to the pitying heavens; and, last of all, was visible one white marble arm. I saw by the early twilight this fair young head, as it was sinking down to darkness—saw this marble arm, as it rose above her head and her treacherous grave, tossing, faltering, rising, clutching, as at some false deceiving hand stretched out from the clouds—saw this marble arm uttering her dying hope, and then uttering her dying despair. The head, the diadem, the arm—these all had sunk; at last over these also the cruel quicksand had closed; and no memorial of the fair young girl remained on earth, except my own solitary tears, and the funeral bells from the desert seas, that, rising again more softly, sang a requiem over the grave of the buried child, and over her blighted dawn.

I sat, and wept in secret the tears that men have ever given to the memory of those that died before the dawn, and by the treachery of earth, our mother. But suddenly the tears and funeral bells were hushed by a shout as of many nations, and by a roar as from some great king's artillery, advancing rapidly along the valleys, and heard afar by echoes from the mountains. 'Hush!' I said, as I bent my ear earthwards to listen—'hush!— this either is the very anarchy of strife, or else'—and then I listened more profoundly, and whispered as I raised my head—'or else, oh heavens! it is *victory* that is final, victory that swallows up all strife.'

IV

Immediately, in trance, I was carried over land and sea to some distant kingdom, and placed upon a triumphal car, amongst companions crowned with laurel. The darkness of gathering midnight, brooding over all the land, hid from us the mighty crowds that were weaving restlessly about ourselves as a centre: we heard them, but saw them not. Tidings had arrived, within an hour, of a grandeur that measured itself against centuries ; too full of pathos they were, too full of joy, to utter them- selves by other language than by tears, by restless anthems, and *Te Deums* reverberated from the choirs and orchestras of earth. These tidings we that sat upon the laurelled car had it for our privilege to publish amongst all nations. And already, by signs audible through the darkness, by snortings and tramplings, our angry horses, that knew no fear of fleshly weariness, upbraided us with delay. Wherefore *was* it that we delayed? We waited for a secret word, that should bear witness to the hope of nations, as now accomplished for ever. At midnight the secret word arrived ; which word was—Waterloo and Recovered Christendom! The dreadful word shone by its own light ; before us it went ; high above our leaders' heads it rode, and spread a golden light over the paths which we traversed. Every city, at the presence of the secret word, threw open its gates. The rivers were con- scious as we crossed. All the forests, as we ran along their margins, shivered in homage to the secret word. And the darkness comprehended it.

Two hours after midnight we approached a mighty Minster. Its gates, which rose to the clouds, were closed. But when the dreadful word, that rode before us, reached them with its golden light, silently they moved back upon their hinges; and at a flying gallop our equipage entered the grand aisle of the cathedral. Headlong was our pace; and at every altar, in the little chapels and oratories to the right hand and left of our course, the lamps, dying or sickening, kindled anew in sympathy with the secret word that was flying past. Forty leagues we might have run in the cathedral, and as yet no strength of morning light had reached us, when before us we saw the aerial galleries of organ and choir. Every pinnacle of the fretwork, every station of advantage amongst the traceries, was crested by white-robed choristers, that sang deliverance; that wept no more tears, as once their fathers had wept; but at intervals that sang together to the generations, saying,

> Chant the deliverer's praise in every tongue,

and receiving answers from afar,

> Such as once in heaven and earth were sung.

And of their chanting was no end; of our headlong pace was neither pause nor slackening.

Thus, as we ran like torrents—thus, as we swept with bridal rapture over the Campo Santo[1] of the

---

[1] 'Campo Santo':—It is probable that most of my readers will be acquainted with the history of the Campo Santo (or cemetery) at Pisa, composed of earth brought from Jerusalem from a bed of sanctity, as the highest prize which the noble piety of crusaders could ask or imagine. To readers who are unacquainted with England, or who (being English) are yet unacquainted with the cathedral cities of England, it may be right to mention that the graves within-side the cathedrals often form a flat pavement over which carriages and horses *might* run; and perhaps a boyish remembrance of one particular cathedral, across which I had seen passengers walk and burdens carried, as about two centuries back they were through the middle of St. Paul's in London, may have assisted my dream.

cathedral graves—suddenly we became aware of a vast
necropolis rising upon the far-off horizon—a city of
sepulchres, built within the saintly cathedral for the
warrior dead that rested from their feuds on earth. Of
purple granite was the necropolis ; yet, in the first minute,
it lay like a purple stain upon the horizon, so mighty
was the distance.   In the second minute it trembled
through many changes, growing into terraces and towers
of wondrous altitude, so mighty was the pace.   In the
third minute already, with our dreadful gallop, we were
entering its suburbs.   Vast sarcophagi rose on every side,
having towers and turrets that, upon the limits of the
central aisle, strode forward with haughty intrusion, that
ran back with mighty shadows into answering recesses.
Every sarcophagus showed many bas-reliefs—bas-reliefs
of battles and of battle-fields ; battles from forgotten
ages—battles from yesterday—battle-fields that, long
since, nature had healed and reconciled to herself with the
sweet oblivion of flowers—battle-fields that were yet
angry and crimson with carnage.   Where the terraces
ran, there did *we* run ; where the towers curved, there
did *we* curve.   With the flight of swallows our horses
swept round every angle.   Like rivers in flood, wheeling
round headlands—like hurricanes that ride into the
secrets of forests—faster than ever light unwove the
mazes of darkness, our flying equipage carried earthly
passions, kindled warrior instincts, amongst the dust that
lay around us—dust oftentimes of our noble fathers that
had slept in God from Créci to Trafalgar.   And now
had we reached the last sarcophagus, now were we abreast
of the last bas-relief, already had we recovered the arrow-
like flight of the illimitable central aisle, when coming up
this aisle to meet us we beheld afar off a female child,
that rode in a carriage as frail as flowers.   The mists,
which went before her, hid the fawns that drew her, but
could not hide the shells and tropic flowers with which
she played—but could not hide the lovely smiles by
which she uttered her trust in the mighty cathedral, and
in the cherubim that looked down upon her from the

mighty shafts of its pillars. Face to face she was meeting us; face to face she rode, as if danger there were none. 'Oh, baby!' I exclaimed, 'shalt thou be the ransom for Waterloo? Must we, that carry tidings of great joy to every people, be messengers of ruin to thee!' In horror I rose at the thought; but then also, in horror at the thought, rose one that was sculptured on a bas-relief —a Dying Trumpeter. Solemnly from the field of battle he rose to his feet; and, unslinging his stony trumpet, carried it, in his dying anguish, to his stony lips—sounding once, and yet once again; proclamation that, in *thy* ears, oh baby! spoke from the battlements of death. Immediately deep shadows fell between us, and aboriginal silence. The choir had ceased to sing. The hoofs of our horses, the dreadful rattle of our harness, the groaning of our wheels, alarmed the graves no more. By horror the bas-relief had been unlocked unto life. By horror we, that were so full of life, we men and our horses, with their fiery fore-legs rising in mid air to their everlasting gallop, were frozen to a bas-relief. Then a third time the trumpet sounded; the seals were taken off all pulses; life, and the frenzy of life, tore into their channels again; again the choir burst forth in sunny grandeur, as from the muffling of storms and darkness; again the thunderings of our horses carried temptation into the graves. One cry burst from our lips, as the clouds, drawing off from the aisle, showed it empty before us—'Whither has the infant fled?—is the young child caught up to God?' Lo! afar off, in a vast recess, rose three mighty windows to the clouds; and on a level with their summits, at height insuperable to man, rose an altar of purest alabaster. On its eastern face was trembling a crimson glory. A glory was it from the reddening dawn that now streamed *through* the windows? Was it from the crimson robes of the martyrs painted *on* the windows? Was it from the bloody bas-reliefs of earth? There, suddenly, within that crimson radiance, rose the apparition of a woman's head, and then of a woman's figure. The child it was—grown up to woman's height.

Clinging to the horns of the altar, voiceless she stood—
sinking, rising, raving, despairing; and behind the volume
of incense, that, night and day, streamed upwards from
the altar, dimly was seen the fiery font, and the shadow
of that dreadful being who should have baptized her with
the baptism of death. But by her side was kneeling her
better angel, that hid his face with wings; that wept and
pleaded for *her;* that prayed when *she* could *not;* that
fought with Heaven by tears for *her* deliverance; which
also, as he raised his immortal countenance from his
wings, I saw, by the glory in his eye, that from Heaven
he had won at last.

V

Then was completed the passion of the mighty fugue.
The golden tubes of the organ, which as yet had but
muttered at intervals — gleaming amongst clouds and
surges of incense—threw up, as from fountains unfathom-
able, columns of heart-shattering music. Choir and anti-
choir were filling fast with unknown voices. Thou also,
Dying Trumpeter!—with thy love that was victorious,
and thy anguish that was finishing—didst enter the
tumult; trumpet and echo—farewell love, and farewell
anguish—rang through the dreadful *sanctus.* Oh, darkness of the grave! that from the crimson altar and from
the fiery font wert visited and searched by the effulgence
in the angel's eye — were these indeed thy children?
Pomps of life, that, from the burials of centuries, rose
again to the voice of perfect joy, did ye indeed mingle
with the festivals of Death? Lo! as I looked back for
seventy leagues through the mighty cathedral, I saw the
quick and the dead that sang together to God, together
that sang to the generations of man. All the hosts of
jubilation, like armies that ride in pursuit, moved with
one step. Us, that, with laurelled heads, were passing
from the cathedral, they overtook, and, as with a garment,
they wrapped us round with thunders greater than our
own. As brothers we moved together; to the dawn

that advanced—to the stars that fled ; rendering thanks
to God in the highest—that, having hid His face through
one generation behind thick clouds of War, once again
was ascending—from the Campo Santo of Waterloo was
ascending—in the visions of Peace ; rendering thanks for
thee, young girl ! whom, having overshadowed with His
ineffable passion of death, suddenly did God relent ;
suffered thy angel to turn aside His arm ; and even in
thee, sister unknown ! shown to me for a moment only to
be hidden for ever, found an occasion to glorify His
goodness.   A thousand times, amongst the phantoms of
sleep, have I seen thee entering the gates of the golden
dawn—with the secret word riding before thee—with
the armies of the grave behind thee ; seen thee sinking,
rising, raving, despairing ; a thousand times in the worlds
of sleep have seen thee followed by God's angel through
storms ; through desert seas ; through the darkness of
quicksands ; through dreams, and the dreadful revelations
that are in dreams—only that at the last, with one sling
of His victorious arm, He might snatch thee back from
ruin, and might emblazon in thy deliverance the endless
resurrections of His love !

THE END

Printed in Great Britain by R. & R. CLARK, LIMITED, *Edinburgh.*

MACMILLAN'S LIBRARY

OF

ENGLISH CLASSICS

EDITED BY A. W. POLLARD.

A Series of Reprints of Standard Works in Library form.

8*vo*.   *Price* 7*s*. 6*d*. *net per Volume*.

BACON'S ESSAYS; COLOURS OF GOOD AND EVIL and ADVANCE-
MENT OF LEARNING.   1 vol.

SHERIDAN'S PLAYS.   1 vol.

MALORY'S MORTE DARTHUR.   2 vols.

STERNE'S TRISTRAM SHANDY AND SENTIMENTAL
JOURNEY.   2 vols.

BOSWELL'S LIFE OF JOHNSON.   3 vols.

CARLYLE'S FRENCH REVOLUTION.   2 vols.

FIELDING'S TOM JONES.   2 vols.

WHITE'S NATURAL HISTORY OF SELBORNE.   1 vol.

TRAVELS OF SIR JOHN MANDEVILLE, with Illustrative Narratives from Hakluyt.   1 vol.

LOCKHART'S LIFE OF SCOTT.   5 vols.

DON QUIXOTE, Translated by SHELTON.   3 vols.

WALTON'S LIVES AND COMPLETE ANGLER.   1 vol.

DE QUINCEY'S CONFESSIONS OF AN ENGLISH OPIUM-
EATER; MURDER AS A FINE ART; THE ENGLISH MAIL
COACH, and other Essays.   1 vol.

CARLYLE'S SARTOR RESARTUS, AND ON HEROES, HERO-
WORSHIP, AND THE HEROIC IN HISTORY.   1 vol.

GOLDSMITH'S SELECT WORKS.   (VICAR OF WAKEFIELD,
PLAYS, and POEMS.)   1 vol.

HAZLITT'S CHARACTERS OF SHAKESPEAR'S PLAYS AND
LECTURES ON THE ENGLISH POETS.   1 vol.

MILTON'S POETICAL WORKS.   2 vols.

THE POLITICAL ECONOMY OF ART; UNTO THIS LAST;
SESAME AND LILIES; THE CROWN OF WILD OLIVE.   By JOHN
RUSKIN.   1 vol.

MACMILLAN AND CO., LTD., LONDON.